# CRIME, PRISONS, AND JAILS

ISSN 1938-890X

# CRIME, PRISONS, AND JAILS

INFORMATION PLUS® REFERENCE SERIES
Formerly Published by Information Plus, Wylie, Texas

Detroit • New York • San Francisco • New Haven, Conn. • Waterville, Maine • London

# Crime, Prisons, and Jails

Paula Kepos, Series Editor

**Project Editors**
Kathleen J. Edgar, John McCoy

**Permissions**
Aja Perales, Jhanay Williams

**Composition and Electronic Prepress**
Evi Seoud

**Manufacturing**
Cynde Bishop

ISBN-13: 978-0-7876-5103-9 (set)
ISBN-10: 0-7876-5103-6 (set)
ISBN-13: 978-1-4144-0767-8
ISBN-10: 1-4144-0767-X
ISSN 1938-890X

This title is also available as an e-book.
ISBN-13: 978-1-4144-2948-9 (set), ISBN-10: 1-4144-2948-7 (set)
Contact your Gale Group sales representative for ordering information.

Printed in the United States of America
10 9 8 7 6 5 4 3 2 1

# TABLE OF CONTENTS

**PREFACE** . . . . . . . . . . . . . . . . . . . . . . . . vii

**CHAPTER 1**
Crime in the United States. . . . . . . . . . . . . . . . . . 1
Crime rates have been falling since the early 1990s. This chapter examines the scope of crime in the United States by examining arrest trends according to geographic location, age, sex, and race and ethnicity. Crime rate statistics for murder, rape, robbery, assault, burglary, theft, and other offenses are also discussed. In addition, the government's role in law enforcement is explored.

**CHAPTER 2**
Victims of Crime . . . . . . . . . . . . . . . . . . . . . . 23
Criminals target all types of people, but some are more affected than others. What groups are most affected by various types of crimes? When and where do crimes occur? This chapter examines the trends and laws associated with crime victimization. Also discussed are such issues as the fear of being victimized and the reasons many crimes go unreported. Finally, this chapter examines the costs of victimization as well as victim assistance, victim compensation, and victims' rights.

**CHAPTER 3**
Hate Crimes and Terrorism in the United States . . . . 43
Some crimes are motivated by racial discrimination or by hatred based on religion, sexual orientation, or nationality. Federal and state governments have begun to create special laws to address these types of crimes. A section on terrorism provides the latest statistics on its victims and perpetrators.

**CHAPTER 4**
White-Collar Crime . . . . . . . . . . . . . . . . . . . . . 55
White-collar crimes include embezzlement, counterfeiting, and fraud. While not violent, these crimes have financial and emotional costs. This chapter explores crimes involving greed and dishonesty, including identity theft, insurance fraud, computer crimes, and money laundering.

**CHAPTER 5**
Controlling Crime . . . . . . . . . . . . . . . . . . . . . . 71
Law enforcement agencies take on the dangerous job of fighting crime. Other programs are designed to prevent crimes. In addition, this chapter reviews significant changes in recent decades relating to the sentencing of offenders. Also covered are alternative sentencing practices used by the courts and the results of public opinion polls on crime.

**CHAPTER 6**
Correctional Facilities: Prisons and Jails. . . . . . . . . 91
The rate of incarceration is increasing, resulting in overcrowded prisons, rapid construction of new prisons, and a reliance on private facilities and local jails to house prisoners. In addition to exploring these issues, this chapter offers reasons for the increase in the incarceration rate, the impact of the increase on costs and spending, the controversy surrounding the privatization of prisons, and details of prison work programs.

**CHAPTER 7**
Characteristics and Rights of Inmates . . . . . . . . . . 109
This chapter provides a statistical breakdown of the state and federal prison populations by race, ethnicity, age, sex, and type of crime for which inmates were imprisoned. Also discussed are inmates' educational attainment, history of mental and physical health problems and substance abuse, and children. In addition, this chapter describes key court decisions pertaining to prisoners' rights.

**CHAPTER 8**
Probation and Parole . . . . . . . . . . . . . . . . . . . . 127
The majority of the nation's offenders are not in prison; rather, they are on probation or parole. This chapter presents demographic information about probationers and parolees and compares these two populations. A recent alternative to probation and parole, supervised release, is also discussed.

**CHAPTER 9**
Juvenile Crime. . . . . . . . . . . . . . . . . . . . . . . . 141
Juveniles commit and are arrested for crimes ranging from murder to curfew violations. Changing approaches to juvenile delinquency are traced in this chapter. Also, trends in confining juveniles as adults are reported and the characteristics of juveniles in residential placement are explored.

**IMPORTANT NAMES AND ADDRESSES**. . . . . . 157
**RESOURCES**. . . . . . . . . . . . . . . . . . . . . . . . 159
**INDEX** . . . . . . . . . . . . . . . . . . . . . . . . . . . 161

# PREFACE

*Crime, Prisons, and Jails* is part of the *Information Plus Reference Series*. The purpose of each volume of the series is to present the latest facts on a topic of pressing concern in modern American life. These topics include today's most controversial and most studied social issues: abortion, capital punishment, care of senior citizens, crime, the environment, health care, immigration, minorities, national security, social welfare, women, youth, and many more. Although written especially for the high school and undergraduate student, this series is an excellent resource for anyone in need of factual information on current affairs.

By presenting the facts, it is the Gale Group's intention to provide its readers with everything they need to reach an informed opinion on current issues. To that end, there is a particular emphasis in this series on the presentation of scientific studies, surveys, and statistics. These data are generally presented in the form of tables, charts, and other graphics placed within the text of each book. Every graphic is directly referred to and carefully explained in the text. The source of each graphic is presented within the graphic itself. The data used in these graphics are drawn from the most reputable and reliable sources, in particular from the various branches of the U.S. government and from major independent polling organizations. Every effort has been made to secure the most recent information available. The reader should bear in mind that many major studies take years to conduct, and that additional years often pass before the data from these studies are made available to the public. Therefore, in many cases the most recent information available in 2007 dated from 2004 or 2005. Older statistics are sometimes presented as well if they are of particular interest and no more-recent information exists.

Although statistics are a major focus of the *Information Plus Reference Series*, they are by no means its only content. Each book also presents the widely held positions and important ideas that shape how the book's subject is discussed in the United States. These positions are explained in detail and, where possible, in the words of their proponents. Some of the other material to be found in these books includes: historical background; descriptions of major events related to the subject; relevant laws and court cases; and examples of how these issues play out in American life. Some books also feature primary documents, or have pro and con debate sections giving the words and opinions of prominent Americans on both sides of a controversial topic. All material is presented in an even-handed and unbiased manner; the reader will never be encouraged to accept one view of an issue over another.

## HOW TO USE THIS BOOK

In general, crime has been on the decline in recent years. Some crimes, however, are increasing in number among different segments of the population. For example, violent crime has decreased since the 1990s, while identity theft has increased. In addition to exploring crime in America, this volume examines the U.S. penal system as well as its inmates. Prisons and jails are an important and controversial part of the effort to control crime in the United States. Much public funding is spent on the construction of new prisons and jails and the maintenance of old facilities, but many people question the effectiveness of prisons and jails as a deterrent to crime. Who is locked up in U.S. prisons, what crimes have they committed, and how effective is the prison system? These and other basic questions are discussed in this volume.

*Crime, Prisons, and Jails* consists of nine chapters and three appendixes. Each of the chapters is devoted to a particular aspect of crime, prisons, and jails in the United States. For a summary of the information covered in each chapter, please see the synopses provided in the Table of Contents at the front of the book. Chapters generally begin with an overview of the basic facts and background information on the chapter's topic, then proceed to examine subtopics of particular interest. For example, Chapter 7, Characteristics and Rights of Inmates, begins with a discussion of the race, ethnicity, age, and gender of America's inmates. After reviewing the types of crimes committed by those in prison and jail, the chapter delves into the education attainment of those incarcerated before examining issues surrounding the health, both mental and physical, of inmates. The chapter concludes with a look at the rights of prisoners. Readers can find their way through a chapter by looking for the section and subsection headings, which are clearly set off from the text. Or, they can refer to the book's extensive Index, if they already know what they are looking for.

### Statistical Information

The tables and figures featured throughout *Crime, Prisons, and Jails* will be of particular use to the reader in learning about this topic. These tables and figures represent an extensive collection of the most recent and valuable statistics on prisons and jails, as well as related issues—for example, graphics in the book cover the number of people in jail or prison in the United States; characteristics of those incarcerated; and the amount of money spent on the prison system. The Gale Group believes that making this information available to the reader is the most important way in which we fulfill the goal of this book: to help readers understand the issues and controversies surrounding crime, prisons, and jails in the United States and to reach their own conclusions.

Each table or figure has a unique identifier appearing above it for ease of identification and reference. Titles for the tables and figures explain their purpose. At the end of each table or figure, the original source of the data is provided.

In order to help readers understand these often complicated statistics, all tables and figures are explained in the text. References in the text direct the reader to the relevant statistics. Furthermore, the contents of all tables and figures are fully indexed. Please see the opening section of the Index at the back of this volume for a description of how to find tables and figures within it.

### Appendixes

In addition to the main body text and images, *Crime, Prisons, and Jails* has three appendixes. The first is the Important Names and Addresses directory. Here the reader will find contact information for a number of government and private organizations that can provide further information on aspects of crime and the U.S. prison and jail system. The second appendix is the Resources section, which can also assist the reader in conducting his or her own research. In this section, the editors of *Crime, Prisons, and Jails* describe some of the sources that were most useful during the compilation of this book. The final appendix is the Index.

### ADVISORY BOARD CONTRIBUTIONS

The staff of Information Plus would like to extend its heartfelt appreciation to the Information Plus Advisory Board. This dedicated group of media professionals provides feedback on the series on an ongoing basis. Their comments allow the editorial staff who work on the project to make the series better and more user-friendly. Our top priorities are to produce the highest-quality and most useful books possible, and the Advisory Board's contributions to this process are invaluable.

The members of the Information Plus Advisory Board are:

- Kathleen R. Bonn, Librarian, Newbury Park High School, Newbury Park, California

- Madelyn Garner, Librarian, San Jacinto College–North Campus, Houston, Texas

- Anne Oxenrider, Media Specialist, Dundee High School, Dundee, Michigan

- Charles R. Rodgers, Director of Libraries, Pasco-Hernando Community College, Dade City, Florida

- James N. Zitzelsberger, Library Media Department Chairman, Oshkosh West High School, Oshkosh, Wisconsin

### COMMENTS AND SUGGESTIONS

The editors of the *Information Plus Reference Series* welcome your feedback on *Crime, Prisons, and Jails*. Please direct all correspondence to:

Editors
*Information Plus Reference Series*
27500 Drake Rd.
Farmington Hills, MI 48331-3535

CHAPTER 1

# CRIME IN THE UNITED STATES

A crime occurs whenever a person commits an act prohibited by law or fails to act where there is a legal responsibility to do so. State and federal laws both define criminal behavior and specify corresponding punishments. Such activities as murder, robbery, and burglary have been considered criminal since ancient civilizations first began to record legal codes. Other actions, such as domestic violence and driving under the influence of drugs or alcohol, were added to the list of criminal offenses during the twentieth century as public awareness grew concerning the devastating consequences of allowing such behaviors to go unchecked. Technology has also influenced crime. For example, the widespread use of computers has provided new opportunities for white-collar crime and added a new word—"cybercrime"—to our vocabulary.

Criminal behavior can range from activities as simple as taking chewing gum from a store without paying to those as tragic and violent as murder. Most people have broken the law, wittingly or unwittingly, at some time in their lives. Therefore, the true extent of criminality is impossible to measure. Researchers can compile and analyze records only of incidents reported by victims or known to the police.

The Federal Bureau of Investigation (FBI) and the Bureau of Justice Statistics (BJS) are the two main government sources that collect crime statistics. The FBI assembles the annual Uniform Crime Reports (UCR), which present data from about 17,000 city, county, and state law enforcement agencies. These jurisdictions contain approximately 94% of the total U.S. population. The National Crime Victimization Survey (NCVS), prepared by the Bureau of Justice Statistics, bases its findings on an annual survey of approximately 130,000 people.

## FACTORS IN THE RATE OF CRIME

The FBI lists many factors that can influence the rate of crime in a particular area, including:

- Population density and degree of urbanization
- Variations in the makeup of the population, particularly where youth is most concentrated
- Stability of the population—residents' mobility (tendency to move around), commuting patterns, and length of time residing in the area
- Types and condition of transportation and highway systems available
- Economic conditions, including average income, poverty, and job availability
- Cultural conditions, such as educational, recreational, and religious characteristics
- Family conditions with respect to divorce and family togetherness
- Climate and weather
- Effectiveness of law enforcement agencies
- Law enforcement agencies' administrative and investigative practices
- Policies of other parts of the criminal justice system, including prosecution, justice, corrections, and probation
- Attitudes of residents toward crime
- Crime-reporting practices of the citizens

## CRIME ON THE DECLINE

During the 1990s many people believed the crime rate was increasing. The randomness of crime and the sensational media reporting of such incidents as drive-by shootings and driveway robberies seemed to support this belief. Carol J. DeFrances and Steven K. Smith of the BJS reported in *Perceptions of Neighborhood Crime, 1995* (1998, http://www.ojp.usdoj.gov/bjs/pub/pdf/pnc95.pdf) that about 7.3% of U.S. households cited crime as a major problem in their neighborhoods. Not surprisingly, households in central cities were twice as likely (14.5%) to indicate that crime was a serious problem. In 1995, 19.6% of black central-city households identified crime as a neighborhood problem, compared with 13% of white central-city households.

However, the FBI, state agencies, and city governments have reported that the overall crime rate has been dropping steadily since 1991. According to the FBI in *Crime in the United States, 2005* (2006, http://www.fbi.gov/ucr/05cius/), violent crime declined 26%, from 1.9 million incidents in 1991 to 1.4 million in 2005, and property crime fell 22%, from 13 million incidents in 1991 to 10.2 million in 2005. (See Table 1.1.) Overall, the number of crimes in the United States declined from 14.9 million in 1991 to 11.6 million in 2005, a decrease of 22%.

The decrease in property crime rates continued through the first six months of 2006, according to preliminary UCR data released by the FBI. (In FBI reporting, property crime includes burglary, larceny-theft, motor vehicle theft, and arson.) Property crime rates were 2.6% lower during this period than during the same period in 2005. (See Table 1.2.) However, violent crime rates began increasing in 2005, and, as Table 1.2 also shows, 3.7% more violent crimes were reported during the first six months of 2006 than had been reported during the first six months of 2005. (The FBI defines violent crimes as those involving force or threat of force. These crimes include murder and nonnegligent manslaughter, forcible rape, robbery, and aggravated assault.)

## CHANGES IN 2006

According to preliminary data on violent crimes committed during 2006, the number of robberies increased by 9.7% compared with 2005, murders rose by 1.4%, aggravated assaults increased by 1.2%, and the number of forcible rapes was unchanged. Among property crimes, the FBI's 2006 preliminary data showed a decrease of 2.3% in motor vehicle thefts, a 1.2% increase in burglaries, a 6.8% increase in arsons, and a decrease of 3.8% in larceny-thefts from 2005. (See Table 1.2.)

By region, the preliminary data show that the number of violent crimes increased by 4.7% over 2005 figures in the nation's West, by 3.9% in the Midwest, by 3.3% in the South, and by 2.9% in the Northeast. Property crimes decreased by 5.7% in the West, 3% in the South, and 0.3% in the Northeast in 2006, according to the preliminary data, but they increased by 1.7% in the Midwest. Violent crime offenses increased in the nation's cities, with the largest increase of 6.8% recorded in cities with populations of 250,000 to 499,999. Cities with populations of 250,000 to 499,000 also experienced the greatest decrease—4.6%—in property crime rates. Cities of all sizes, from those with populations less than 10,000 to those with more than one

million residents, experienced an increase in violent crime and a decrease in property crime. (See Table 1.2.)

## THE UNIFORM CRIME REPORTS

The FBI compiles several sets of crime statistics, including the number and type of crimes reported by local police. The FBI also tracks cleared offenses, which are crimes for which at least one person has been arrested, charged, and turned over to the court for prosecution. This does not necessarily mean the person arrested was guilty or will be convicted of the crime. Cleared offenses also include those cleared by "extraordinary means," that is, offenses for which there can be no arrest. Such cases include, for example, a murder/suicide when the perpetrator is known to be deceased.

### Crime in Urban and Rural Areas

Although crime is certainly not limited to cities, it is far more likely to occur in urban areas than in rural areas. According to the FBI, the violent crime rate in metropolitan statistical areas during 2005 was 509.7 incidents per 100,000 inhabitants, almost two-and-a-half times the rate in rural areas (206.8 per 100,000 inhabitants). A "metropolitan statistical area," or MSA, as defined by the U.S. Census Bureau, is an urbanized area that includes a central city of 50,000 residents or more or an urbanized area with a total metropolitan population of 75,000 in New England and at least 100,000 elsewhere. In cities outside metropolitan areas, the violent crime rate was 373.5 per 100,000. (See Table 1.3.)

In all categories of violent crime except forcible rape, the rate was higher in metropolitan areas than smaller cities. In contrast, the rate of property crime was higher in cities outside metropolitan areas (3,998.1 per 100,000) than within metropolitan areas (3,598.8 per 100,000 inhabitants). The crime with the greatest disparity between MSAs and rural areas, robbery, occurred ten times more often in metropolitan areas than in rural areas. The incidence of motor vehicle theft was also significantly greater, about 3.3 times higher, in MSAs than in rural areas. Among property crimes, larceny-theft occurred at a significantly higher rate in smaller cities (3,001.8 per 100,000 residents) than in metropolitan areas (2,386.1 per 100,000). However, motor vehicle theft was much more common in MSAs (469.1 per 100,000) than in cities outside MSAs (141 per 100,000).

**VIOLENT CRIMES** According to the FBI in *Crime in the United States, Preliminary Semiannual Uniform Crime Report 2006* (2006, http://www.fbi.gov/ucr/prelim06/index.html), the nation's largest cities (those with more than one million in population) reported a 1.6% increase in violent crimes during the first six months of 2006 compared with the same period in 2005. (See Table 1.2.) With an increase of 6.8% between 2005 and 2006, cities with

**TABLE 1.1**

**Crime by volume and rate, 1986–2005, and percent change in crime volume and rate for selected periods, 1996–2005**

[Per 100,000 inhabitants]

| Year | Population[a] | Violent crime | Violent crime rate | Murder and nonnegligent manslaughter | Murder and nonnegligent manslaughter rate | Forcible rape | Forcible rape rate | Robbery | Robbery rate | Aggravated assault | Aggravated assault rate | Property crime | Property crime rate | Burglary | Burglary rate | Larceny-theft | Larceny-theft rate | Motor vehicle theft | Motor vehicle theft rate |
|---|---|---|---|---|---|---|---|---|---|---|---|---|---|---|---|---|---|---|---|
| 1986 | 240,132,887 | 1,489,169 | 620.1 | 20,613 | 8.6 | 91,459 | 38.1 | 542,775 | 226.0 | 834,322 | 347.4 | 11,722,700 | 4,881.8 | 3,241,410 | 1,349.8 | 7,257,153 | 3,022.1 | 1,224,137 | 509.8 |
| 1987 | 242,288,918 | 1,483,999 | 612.5 | 20,096 | 8.3 | 91,111 | 37.6 | 517,704 | 213.7 | 855,088 | 352.9 | 12,024,709 | 4,963.0 | 3,236,184 | 1,335.7 | 7,499,851 | 3,095.4 | 1,288,674 | 531.9 |
| 1988 | 244,498,982 | 1,566,221 | 640.6 | 20,675 | 8.5 | 92,486 | 37.8 | 542,968 | 222.1 | 910,092 | 372.2 | 12,356,865 | 5,054.0 | 3,218,077 | 1,316.2 | 7,705,872 | 3,151.7 | 1,432,916 | 586.1 |
| 1989 | 246,819,230 | 1,646,037 | 666.9 | 21,500 | 8.7 | 94,504 | 38.3 | 578,326 | 234.3 | 951,707 | 385.6 | 12,605,412 | 5,107.1 | 3,168,170 | 1,283.6 | 7,872,442 | 3,189.6 | 1,564,800 | 634.0 |
| 1990 | 249,464,396 | 1,820,127 | 729.6 | 23,438 | 9.4 | 102,555 | 41.1 | 639,271 | 256.3 | 1,054,863 | 422.9 | 12,655,486 | 5,073.1 | 3,073,909 | 1,232.2 | 7,945,670 | 3,185.1 | 1,635,907 | 655.8 |
| 1991 | 252,153,092 | 1,911,767 | 758.2 | 24,703 | 9.8 | 106,593 | 42.3 | 687,732 | 272.7 | 1,092,739 | 433.4 | 12,961,116 | 5,140.2 | 3,157,150 | 1,252.1 | 8,142,228 | 3,229.1 | 1,661,738 | 659.0 |
| 1992 | 255,029,699 | 1,932,274 | 757.7 | 23,760 | 9.3 | 109,062 | 42.8 | 672,478 | 263.7 | 1,126,974 | 441.9 | 12,505,917 | 4,903.7 | 2,979,884 | 1,168.4 | 7,915,199 | 3,103.6 | 1,610,834 | 631.6 |
| 1993 | 257,782,608 | 1,926,017 | 747.1 | 24,526 | 9.5 | 106,014 | 41.1 | 659,870 | 256.0 | 1,135,607 | 440.5 | 12,218,777 | 4,740.0 | 2,834,808 | 1,099.7 | 7,820,909 | 3,033.9 | 1,563,060 | 606.3 |
| 1994 | 260,327,021 | 1,857,670 | 713.6 | 23,326 | 9.0 | 102,216 | 39.3 | 618,949 | 237.8 | 1,113,179 | 427.6 | 12,131,873 | 4,660.2 | 2,712,774 | 1,042.1 | 7,879,812 | 3,026.9 | 1,539,287 | 591.3 |
| 1995 | 262,803,276 | 1,798,792 | 684.5 | 21,606 | 8.2 | 97,470 | 37.1 | 580,509 | 220.9 | 1,099,207 | 418.3 | 12,063,935 | 4,590.5 | 2,593,784 | 987.0 | 7,997,710 | 3,043.2 | 1,472,441 | 560.3 |
| 1996 | 265,228,572 | 1,688,540 | 636.6 | 19,645 | 7.4 | 96,252 | 36.3 | 535,594 | 201.9 | 1,037,049 | 391.0 | 11,805,323 | 4,451.0 | 2,506,400 | 945.0 | 7,904,685 | 2,980.3 | 1,394,238 | 525.7 |
| 1997 | 267,783,607 | 1,636,096 | 611.0 | 18,208 | 6.8 | 96,153 | 35.9 | 498,534 | 186.2 | 1,023,201 | 382.1 | 11,558,475 | 4,316.3 | 2,460,526 | 918.8 | 7,743,760 | 2,891.8 | 1,354,189 | 505.7 |
| 1998 | 270,248,003 | 1,533,887 | 567.6 | 16,974 | 6.3 | 93,144 | 34.5 | 447,186 | 165.5 | 976,583 | 361.4 | 10,951,827 | 4,052.5 | 2,332,735 | 863.2 | 7,376,311 | 2,729.5 | 1,242,781 | 459.9 |
| 1999 | 272,690,813 | 1,426,044 | 523.0 | 15,522 | 5.7 | 89,411 | 32.8 | 409,371 | 150.1 | 911,740 | 334.3 | 10,208,334 | 3,743.6 | 2,100,739 | 770.4 | 6,955,520 | 2,550.7 | 1,152,075 | 422.5 |
| 2000 | 281,421,906 | 1,425,486 | 506.5 | 15,586 | 5.5 | 90,178 | 32.0 | 408,016 | 145.0 | 911,706 | 324.0 | 10,182,584 | 3,618.3 | 2,050,992 | 728.8 | 6,971,590 | 2,477.3 | 1,160,002 | 412.2 |
| 2001[b] | 285,317,559 | 1,439,480 | 504.5 | 16,037 | 5.6 | 90,863 | 31.8 | 423,557 | 148.5 | 909,023 | 318.6 | 10,437,189 | 3,658.1 | 2,116,531 | 741.8 | 7,092,267 | 2,485.7 | 1,228,391 | 430.5 |
| 2002 | 287,973,924 | 1,423,677 | 494.4 | 16,229 | 5.6 | 95,235 | 33.1 | 420,806 | 146.1 | 891,407 | 309.5 | 10,455,277 | 3,630.6 | 2,151,252 | 747.0 | 7,057,379 | 2,450.7 | 1,246,646 | 432.9 |
| 2003 | 290,788,976 | 1,383,676 | 475.8 | 16,528 | 5.7 | 93,883 | 32.3 | 414,235 | 142.5 | 859,030 | 295.4 | 10,442,862 | 3,591.2 | 2,154,834 | 741.0 | 7,026,802 | 2,416.5 | 1,261,226 | 433.7 |
| 2004[c] | 293,656,842 | 1,360,088 | 463.2 | 16,148 | 5.5 | 95,089 | 32.4 | 401,470 | 136.7 | 847,381 | 288.6 | 10,319,386 | 3,514.1 | 2,144,446 | 730.3 | 6,937,089 | 2,362.3 | 1,237,851 | 421.5 |
| 2005 | 296,410,404 | 1,390,695 | 469.2 | 16,692 | 5.6 | 93,934 | 31.7 | 417,122 | 140.7 | 862,947 | 291.1 | 10,166,159 | 3,429.8 | 2,154,126 | 726.7 | 6,776,807 | 2,286.3 | 1,235,226 | 416.7 |
| **Percent change** | | | | | | | | | | | | | | | | | | | |
| 2005/2004 | | +2.3 | +1.3 | +3.4 | +2.4 | −1.2 | −2.1 | +3.9 | +2.9 | +1.8 | +0.9 | −1.5 | −2.4 | +0.5 | −0.5 | −2.3 | −3.2 | −0.2 | −1.1 |
| 2005/2001 | | −3.4 | −7.0 | +4.1 | +0.2 | +3.4 | −0.5 | −1.5 | −5.2 | −5.1 | −8.6 | −2.6 | −6.2 | +1.8 | −2.0 | −4.4 | −8.0 | +0.6 | −3.2 |
| 2005/1996 | | −17.6 | −26.3 | −15.0 | −24.0 | −2.4 | −12.7 | −22.1 | −30.3 | −16.8 | −25.5 | −13.9 | −22.9 | −14.1 | −23.1 | −14.3 | −23.3 | −11.4 | −20.7 |

[a]Populations are U.S. Census Bureau provisional estimates as of July 1 for each year except 1990 and 2000, which are decennial census counts.
[b]The murder and nonnegligent homicides that occurred as a result of the events of September 11, 2001, are not included in this table.
[c]The 2004 crime figures have been adjusted.
Note: Although arson data are included in the trend and clearance tables, sufficient data are not available to estimate totals for this offense.

SOURCE: Adapted from "Table 1. Crime in the United States, by Volume and Rate per 100,000 Inhabitants, 1986–2005," and "Table 1A. Crime in the United States, Percent Change in Volume and Rate per 100,000 Inhabitants for 2 Years, 5 Years, and 10 Years," in *Crime in the United States, 2005,* U.S. Department of Justice, Federal Bureau of Investigation, September 2006, http://www.fbi.gov/ucr/05cius/offenses/standard_links/national_estimates.html (accessed January 7, 2007)

# TABLE 1.2

## Percent change in crimes reported, by population group and region, January–June 2006, and by two-year trends, 2002–06

| Population group | Number of agencies | Population | Violent crime | Murder | Forcible rape | Robbery | Aggravated assault | Property crime | Burglary | Larceny-theft | Motor vehicle theft | Arson |
|---|---|---|---|---|---|---|---|---|---|---|---|---|
| **Total** | **11,535** | **235,905,717** | **+3.7** | **+1.4** | **\*** | **+9.7** | **+1.2** | **−2.6** | **+1.2** | **−3.8** | **−2.3** | **+6.8** |
| **Cities:** | | | | | | | | | | | | |
| 1,000,000 and over | 10 | 24,885,884 | +1.6 | +6.7 | +2.3 | +6.2 | −2.1 | −3.6 | −1.5 | −4.7 | −1.8 | +9.2 |
| 500,000 to 999,999 | 20 | 13,502,541 | +4.5 | +8.4 | +2.4 | +10.9 | +0.8 | −2.8 | +4.1 | −5.6 | −1.8 | +4.7 |
| 250,000 to 499,999 | 35 | 12,627,048 | +6.8 | +1.3 | +1.2 | +11.7 | +4.6 | −4.0 | +2.4 | −6.4 | −2.7 | −1.3 |
| 100,000 to 249,999 | 175 | 26,264,930 | +5.0 | +2.5 | +2.7 | +12.5 | +1.2 | −3.2 | +0.4 | −4.3 | −3.0 | +3.6 |
| 50,000 to 99,999 | 353 | 24,093,893 | +5.2 | −8.1 | −0.7 | +11.7 | +3.1 | −1.7 | +1.5 | −2.8 | −0.2 | +20.0 |
| 25,000 to 49,999 | 630 | 21,693,539 | +5.7 | −9.4 | +0.6 | +11.0 | +4.4 | −0.7 | +2.6 | −1.6 | −0.3 | +7.2 |
| 10,000 to 24,999 | 1,412 | 22,314,926 | +4.3 | +7.5 | 0.0 | +12.8 | +2.1 | −2.7 | +0.3 | −3.4 | −2.4 | +11.9 |
| Under 10,000 | 5,624 | 18,353,284 | +2.4 | −11.9 | −2.6 | +6.8 | +2.2 | −1.8 | +0.6 | −2.2 | −3.2 | +20.0 |
| **Counties:** | | | | | | | | | | | | |
| Metropolitan[a] | 1,332 | 50,760,060 | +3.0 | +3.1 | −0.8 | +8.4 | +1.8 | −1.8 | +3.1 | −3.2 | −4.0 | +3.1 |
| Nonmetropolitan[b] | 1,944 | 21,409,612 | −5.9 | −13.1 | −8.1 | −0.3 | −5.8 | −3.5 | −3.7 | −3.3 | −3.9 | −0.9 |
| **Region** | | | | | | | | | | | | |
| **Total** | | | **+3.7** | **+1.4** | **\*** | **+9.7** | **+1.2** | **−2.6** | **+1.2** | **−3.8** | **−2.3** | **+6.8** |
| Northeast | | | +2.9 | +0.5 | −2.5 | +5.8 | +1.7 | −0.3 | +4.1 | −0.6 | −5.6 | +4.3 |
| Midwest | | | +3.9 | −2.0 | +1.0 | +10.4 | +1.1 | +1.7 | +5.8 | +0.7 | +0.3 | +6.6 |
| South | | | +3.3 | +3.3 | +1.1 | +8.0 | +1.5 | −3.0 | +0.9 | −4.7 | −0.2 | +3.4 |
| West | | | +4.7 | +1.6 | −1.0 | +14.6 | +0.6 | −5.7 | −2.6 | −7.2 | −3.9 | +11.5 |
| **Years** | | | | | | | | | | | | |
| 2003/2002 | | | −3.1 | +1.1 | −4.0 | −0.5 | −4.4 | −0.8 | −1.0 | −1.1 | +0.9 | −10.0 |
| 2004/2003 | | | −2.0 | −5.7 | +1.4 | −5.0 | −0.9 | −1.9 | −2.2 | −1.9 | −1.6 | −6.8 |
| 2005/2004 | | | −0.5 | +2.1 | −4.7 | +0.6 | −0.7 | −2.8 | −1.1 | −3.5 | −2.1 | −5.6 |
| 2006/2005 | | | +3.7 | +1.4 | \* | +9.7 | +1.2 | −2.6 | +1.2 | −3.8 | −2.3 | +6.8 |

[a]Includes crimes reported to sheriffs' departments, county police departments, and state police within metropolitan statistical areas.
[b]Includes crimes reported to sheriffs' departments, county police departments, and state police outside metropolitan statistical areas.
\*Less than one-tenth of 1 percent.

SOURCE: Adapted from "Table 1. Percent Change by Population Group, January–June, 2006," "Table 2. Percent Change by Geographic Region, January–June 2006," and "Table 3. Percent Change for Consecutive Years, January–June, 2002–2006," in *Crime in the United States, Preliminary Semiannual Uniform Crime Report, January through June 2006,* U.S. Department of Justice, Federal Bureau of Investigation, December 18, 2006, http://www.fbi.gov/ucr/prelim06/index.html (accessed January 7, 2007)

**TABLE 1.3**

## Crime by community type, 2005

| Area | Population[a] | Violent crime | Murder and nonnegligent manslaughter | Forcible rape | Robbery | Aggravated assault | Property crime | Burglary | Larceny-theft | Motor vehicle theft |
|---|---|---|---|---|---|---|---|---|---|---|
| **United States total** | **296,410,404** | **1,390,695** | **16,692** | **93,934** | **417,122** | **862,947** | **10,166,159** | **2,154,126** | **6,776,807** | **1,235,226** |
| Rate per 100,000 inhabitants | | 469.2 | 5.6 | 31.7 | 140.7 | 291.1 | 3,429.8 | 726.7 | 2,286.3 | 416.7 |
| **Metropolitan statistical area** | **245,756,143** | | | | | | | | | |
| Area actually reporting[b] | 95.4% | 1,173,673 | 14,081 | 73,628 | 375,063 | 710,901 | 8,359,242 | 1,732,265 | 5,523,323 | 1,103,654 |
| Estimated total | 100.0% | 1,252,512 | 14,932 | 78,264 | 400,792 | 758,524 | 8,844,369 | 1,827,587 | 5,863,902 | 1,152,880 |
| Rate per 100,000 inhabitants | | 509.7 | 6.1 | 31.8 | 163.1 | 308.6 | 3,598.8 | 743.7 | 2,386.1 | 469.1 |
| **Cities outside metropolitan areas** | **20,044,706** | | | | | | | | | |
| Area actually reporting[b] | 86.8% | 66,509 | 609 | 6,901 | 10,122 | 48,877 | 703,885 | 141,386 | 527,186 | 35,313 |
| Estimated total | 100.0% | 74,868 | 691 | 7,893 | 11,516 | 54,768 | 801,411 | 160,537 | 601,701 | 39,173 |
| Rate per 100,000 inhabitants | | 373.5 | 3.4 | 39.4 | 57.5 | 273.2 | 3,998.1 | 800.9 | 3,001.8 | 195.4 |
| **Nonmetropolitan counties** | **30,609,555** | | | | | | | | | |
| Area actually reporting[b] | 88.1% | 57,685 | 943 | 6,812 | 4,253 | 45,677 | 461,562 | 147,548 | 275,389 | 38,625 |
| Estimated total | 100.0% | 63,315 | 1,069 | 7,777 | 4,814 | 49,655 | 520,379 | 166,002 | 311,204 | 43,173 |
| Rate per 100,000 inhabitants | | 206.8 | 3.5 | 25.4 | 15.7 | 162.2 | 1,700.1 | 542.3 | 1,016.7 | 141.0 |

[a]Populations are U.S. Census Bureau provisional estimates as of July 1, 2005.
[b]The percentage reported under "area actually reporting" is based on the population covered by agencies providing 3 months or more of crime reports to the FBI.
Note: Although arson data are included in the trend and clearance tables, sufficient data are not available to estimate totals for this offense. Therefore, no arson data are published in this table.

SOURCE: "Table 2. Crime in the United States, by Community Type, 2005," in *Crime in the United States, 2005,* U.S. Department of Justice, Federal Bureau of Investigation, September 2006, http://www.fbi.gov/ucr/05cius/data/table_02.html (accessed January 7, 2007) populations between 250,000 and 499,999 experienced even greater growth in the number of violent crimes.

During the first six months of 2006 murders were up by 6.7% in cities with over one million in population, compared with the same period in 2005. The largest increase in murders during this time was 8.4% in cities with populations between 500,000 and 999,999. In contrast, murders declined by 9.4% in cities with populations of between 25,000 and 49,999 and by 8.1% in cities with populations of 50,000 to 99,999. The percentage increase of forcible rapes during the first six months of 2006 was highest (2.7%) in cities with populations of 100,000 to 249,999, while forcible rapes were down by 2.6% in cities with fewer than 10,000 people.

**PROPERTY CRIMES.** In contrast to violent crimes, rates of some property crimes, such as larceny-theft and motor vehicle theft, declined in cities of all sizes between 2005 and 2006. Although burglary rates also declined by 1.5% in cities of one million or more people in 2006, they increased in smaller cities of all sizes, ranging from those with fewer than 10,000 people to those with 500,000 to 999,999 people. Furthermore, the number of arsons increased in cities of all sizes, except those with populations of 250,000 to 499,999, where they decreased by 1.3%. (See Table 1.2.)

### Regional Differences

Distinct crime patterns are commonly evident between different regions of the nation. In 2005 the South, the most populous region, had the highest crime rates for both violent crimes (542.6 per 100,000 residents) and property crimes (3,883.1 per 100,000). The least populous region, the nine states comprising the Northeast, had the lowest property crime rate (393.6 per 100,000) and the lowest violent crime rate (2,287.2 per 100,000). (See Figure 1.1.)

### ARRESTS

In *Crime in the United States, 2005*, the FBI reports that law enforcement agencies nationwide made 14.1 million arrests for all criminal infractions, excluding traffic violations, in 2005. This figure includes all offenses reported by local law enforcement agencies to the FBI, including crimes not counted in the FBI's tabulations on specific crimes. The FBI reports 603,503 arrests for violent crimes (murder, forcible rape, robbery, and aggravated assault) and 1.6 million arrests for property crimes (burglary, larceny-theft, motor vehicle theft, and arson) in 2005. Of the arrests for specific offenses on which the FBI collects statistics, drug abuse violations accounted for the greatest number (1.8 million), followed by driving under the influence (1.4 million), larceny-theft (1.1 million), and disorderly conduct (678,231). (See Table 1.4.)

### Age

In 2005, 44.3% of people arrested for all criminal offenses nationwide were under age twenty-five. (See Table 1.5.) Of those arrested, 15.3% were under the age of eighteen, and 4.6% were under age fifteen. More than three-quarters (76.5%) of those arrested for liquor law infractions were under twenty-five years old, and two-thirds of those arrested for vandalism (66.3%) and arson (66.3%) were also under age twenty-five. Those under age eighteen accounted for nearly half (48.6%) of all arson arrests in 2005.

Arrests of persons under eighteen years of age (considered juveniles by most states) fell 24.9% between 1996 and 2005; arrests of those aged eighteen and older increased by 0.7% during the same period, according to the FBI in *Crime in the United States, 2005*. Prostitution and commercialized vice violations saw the largest increase (20.3%) in arrests among persons under age eighteen between 1996 and 2005, followed by an increase of 3.7% for certain types of assault and an increase of 3.3% in arrests for disorderly conduct. Between 1996 and 2005, arrests of persons younger than eighteen years old declined for all other crimes on which the FBI collects data. Because curfew/loitering and running away are considered crimes for juveniles but not for adults, rates of these crimes are not measured for persons over eighteen years of age.

### Gender

In 2005, men were arrested 3.2 times more often than women, according to the FBI in *Crime in the United States, 2005*. Overall, males accounted for about 6.3 million arrests in 2005, compared with two million arrests of females. However, from 1996 to 2005, the number of males arrested for all offenses declined by 7.6%, while female arrests for all offenses increased by 7.4%. The number of arrests decreased for both males and females under age eighteen during this period, but the rate of decrease was twice as high for males (28.7%) as for females (14.3%). (See Table 1.6.)

### Race and Ethnicity

According to the U.S. Census Bureau, in 2005 whites comprised 80.2% of the population, while blacks accounted for 12.8%. During the same year Asians and Pacific Islanders totaled 4.5% of the population, and Native Americans/Alaska Natives accounted for 1% (http://quickfacts .census.gov/qfd/states/00000.html). In an analysis of 10.2 million arrests reported by nearly 11,000 law enforcement agencies nationwide in 2005, the FBI reports that 69.8% of those arrested were white, and 27.8% were black. (See Table 1.7.) Another 1.3% of those arrested were Native Americans or Alaska Natives, and 1% were Asians or Pacific Islanders. Whites were arrested in about half of the murder cases (49.1%), with black suspects arrested nearly as often (48.6%). White drivers accounted for nine

**FIGURE 1.1**

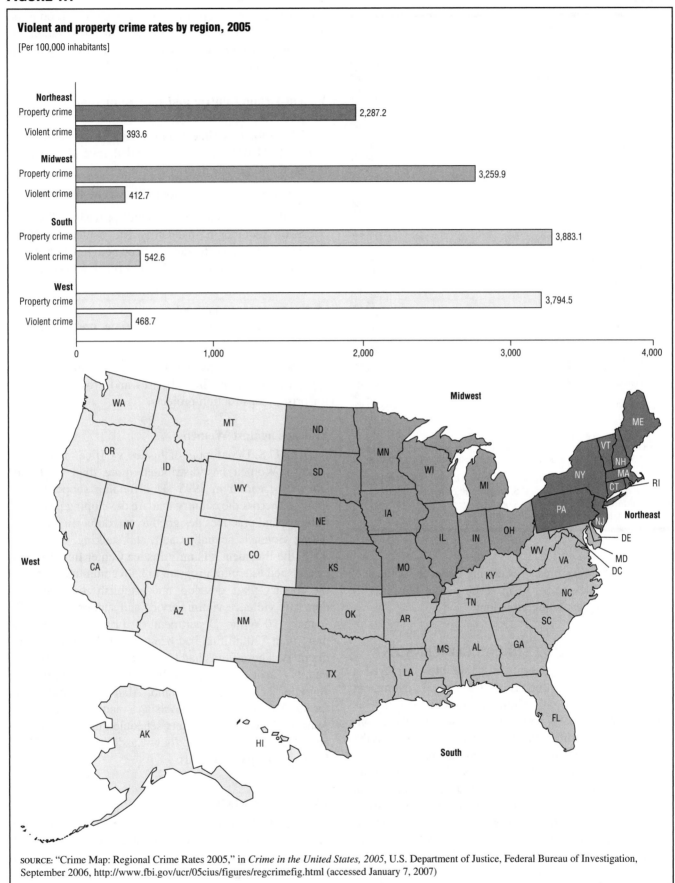

**Violent and property crime rates by region, 2005**

[Per 100,000 inhabitants]

**Northeast**
Property crime — 2,287.2
Violent crime — 393.6

**Midwest**
Property crime — 3,259.9
Violent crime — 412.7

**South**
Property crime — 3,883.1
Violent crime — 542.6

**West**
Property crime — 3,794.5
Violent crime — 468.7

SOURCE: "Crime Map: Regional Crime Rates 2005," in *Crime in the United States, 2005*, U.S. Department of Justice, Federal Bureau of Investigation, September 2006, http://www.fbi.gov/ucr/05cius/figures/regcrimefig.html (accessed January 7, 2007)

TABLE 1.4

**Estimated number of arrests, 2005**

| Total[a] | 14,094,186 |
|---|---|
| Murder and nonnegligent manslaughter | 14,062 |
| Forcible rape | 25,528 |
| Robbery | 114,616 |
| Aggravated assault | 449,297 |
| Burglary | 298,835 |
| Larceny-theft | 1,146,696 |
| Motor vehicle theft | 147,459 |
| Arson | 16,337 |
|     Violent crime[b] | 603,503 |
|     Property crime[b] | 1,609,327 |
| Other assaults | 1,301,392 |
| Forgery and counterfeiting | 118,455 |
| Fraud | 321,521 |
| Embezzlement | 18,970 |
| Stolen property; buying, receiving, possessing | 133,856 |
| Vandalism | 279,562 |
| Weapons; carrying, possessing, etc. | 193,469 |
| Prostitution and commercialized vice | 84,891 |
| Sex offenses (except forcible rape and prostitution) | 91,625 |
| Drug abuse violations | 1,846,351 |
| Gambling | 11,180 |
| Offenses against the family and children | 129,128 |
| Driving under the influence | 1,371,919 |
| Liquor laws | 597,838 |
| Drunkenness | 556,167 |
| Disorderly conduct | 678,231 |
| Vagrancy | 33,227 |
| All other offenses | 3,863,785 |
| Suspicion | 3,764 |
| Curfew and loitering law violations | 140,835 |
| Runaways | 108,954 |

[a]Does not include suspicion.
[b]Violent crimes are offenses of murder, forcible rape, robbery, and aggravated assault. Property crimes are offenses of burglary, larceny-theft, motor vehicle theft, and arson.

SOURCE: "Table 29. Estimated Number of Arrests, United States, 2005," in *Crime in the United States, 2005*, U.S. Department of Justice, Federal Bureau of Investigation, September 2006, http://www.fbi.gov/ucr/05cius/data/table_29.html (accessed January 7, 2007)

out of ten (88.4%) arrests for driving under the influence, while blacks were arrested in seven out of ten (71.1%) cases involving gambling violations.

## THE ROLE OF THE FEDERAL GOVERNMENT

State and local governments have always played a central role in controlling crime. The federal government enforces laws that fall within its jurisdiction, such as forgery and espionage, and operates prisons for those convicted of federal crimes. In addition, since the late 1960s the federal government has administered funding for several state and local crime control programs. (JoAnne O'Bryant, "Federal Crime Control Assistance to State and Local Governments," May 26, 2004, http://www.senate.gov/~hutchison/RS20539.pdf). Some of these funds are designated for programs that address juvenile justice, violence against women, drug courts, and community policing efforts.

### Federal Budget

Of the $39.7 billion in the federal budget proposed for administration of justice in fiscal year (FY) 2003, nearly

half was allocated for law enforcement. (See Table 1.8.) Some of the law enforcement and crime prevention priorities reflected in the FY 2003 budget included funding to investigate criminal activity and support for programs to tighten border and transportation security.

### Violent Crime Control and Law Enforcement Act of 1994

The Violent Crime Control and Law Enforcement Act of 1994 (P.L. 103-322) included several provisions intended to "get tough on crime":

- A ban on some semiautomatic assault-style rifles

- A "three strikes and you're out" provision. This provision requires a mandatory life sentence without parole when an offender has been convicted of at least three serious or violent felony crimes and/or serious or violent drug-related crimes

- Resources for more police and grants to help involve community organizations in crime prevention programs

The act also expanded the federal death penalty to apply to more than fifty offenses and provided funding for prison construction projects.

### Violence against Women

The U.S. Department of Justice's Office on Violence Against Women has distributed more than $2 billion since its creation in 1995. This funding supports communities across the country that are developing programs, policies, and practices designed to end domestic violence, dating violence, sexual assault, and stalking. In October 2003, the President's Family Justice Center Initiative was established as a pilot program to help communities across the country plan, develop, and establish comprehensive domestic violence victim service and support centers. By January 2006 the Department of Justice reported that more than $20 million had been awarded to fifteen communities. These funds had been used to open and operate Family Justice Centers in Brooklyn, New York, San Antonio, Texas, Nampa, Idaho, Alameda County, California, Monroe County, Louisiana, and St. Louis, Missouri, with additional centers scheduled to open throughout the country (http://www.usdoj.gov/opa/pr/2006/January/06_opa_014.html).

### TYPES OF CRIME

In 2005, the FBI's Uniform Crime Reports estimated that one violent crime was committed every 22.7 seconds and one property crime was committed every 3.1 seconds in the United States. (See Table 1.9.) The Crime Clock is not intended to imply that these crimes were committed at regular intervals; rather, it displays the relative frequency with which these crimes occur. Unlike the per

**TABLE 1.5**

## Arrests of persons under 15, 18, 21, and 25 years of age, 2005

[10,974 agencies; 2005 estimated population 217,722,329]

| Offense charged | Total all ages | Number of persons arrested | | | | Percent of total all ages | | | |
|---|---|---|---|---|---|---|---|---|---|
| | | Under 15 | Under 18 | Under 21 | Under 25 | Under 15 | Under 18 | Under 21 | Under 25 |
| Total | 10,369,819 | 479,926 | 1,582,068 | 3,020,386 | 4,588,884 | 4.6 | 15.3 | 29.1 | 44.3 |
| Murder and nonnegligent manslaughter | 10,335 | 97 | 929 | 2,864 | 5,129 | 0.9 | 9.0 | 27.7 | 49.6 |
| Forcible rape | 18,733 | 1,055 | 2,888 | 5,585 | 8,334 | 5.6 | 15.4 | 29.8 | 44.5 |
| Robbery | 85,309 | 4,986 | 21,515 | 39,470 | 52,915 | 5.8 | 25.2 | 46.3 | 62.0 |
| Aggravated assault | 331,469 | 15,468 | 45,150 | 82,245 | 132,179 | 4.7 | 13.6 | 24.8 | 39.9 |
| Burglary | 220,391 | 19,135 | 57,506 | 96,832 | 127,740 | 8.7 | 26.1 | 43.9 | 58.0 |
| Larceny-theft | 854,856 | 77,340 | 219,881 | 343,938 | 446,320 | 9.0 | 25.7 | 40.2 | 52.2 |
| Motor vehicle theft | 108,301 | 6,443 | 27,666 | 46,376 | 62,980 | 5.9 | 25.5 | 42.8 | 58.2 |
| Arson | 12,012 | 3,463 | 5,834 | 6,982 | 7,958 | 28.8 | 48.6 | 58.1 | 66.3 |
| Violent crime[a] | 445,846 | 21,606 | 70,482 | 130,164 | 198,557 | 4.8 | 15.8 | 29.2 | 44.5 |
| Property crime[a] | 1,195,560 | 106,381 | 310,887 | 494,128 | 644,998 | 8.9 | 26.0 | 41.3 | 53.9 |
| Other assaults | 958,477 | 74,377 | 182,578 | 275,372 | 405,867 | 7.8 | 19.0 | 28.7 | 42.3 |
| Forgery and counterfeiting | 87,346 | 370 | 3,096 | 14,245 | 29,171 | 0.4 | 3.5 | 16.3 | 33.4 |
| Fraud | 231,721 | 1,033 | 5,882 | 27,053 | 61,432 | 0.4 | 2.5 | 11.7 | 26.5 |
| Embezzlement | 14,097 | 49 | 856 | 3,681 | 6,220 | 0.3 | 6.1 | 26.1 | 44.1 |
| Stolen property; buying, receiving, possessing | 99,173 | 4,202 | 16,501 | 33,163 | 49,321 | 4.2 | 16.6 | 33.4 | 49.7 |
| Vandalism | 206,351 | 31,925 | 76,817 | 109,002 | 136,750 | 15.5 | 37.2 | 52.8 | 66.3 |
| Weapons; carrying, possessing, etc. | 142,878 | 11,246 | 33,069 | 58,278 | 83,649 | 7.9 | 23.1 | 40.8 | 58.5 |
| Prostitution and commercialized vice | 62,663 | 163 | 1,204 | 7,857 | 16,524 | 0.3 | 1.9 | 12.5 | 26.4 |
| Sex offenses (except forcible rape and prostitution) | 67,072 | 6,052 | 12,196 | 19,523 | 26,816 | 9.0 | 18.2 | 29.1 | 40.0 |
| Drug abuse violations | 1,357,841 | 22,596 | 141,035 | 376,106 | 621,104 | 1.7 | 10.4 | 27.7 | 45.7 |
| Gambling | 8,101 | 199 | 1,464 | 3,085 | 4,411 | 2.5 | 18.1 | 38.1 | 54.5 |
| Offenses against the family and children | 93,172 | 1,230 | 3,901 | 9,873 | 21,212 | 1.3 | 4.2 | 10.6 | 22.8 |
| Driving under the influence | 997,338 | 236 | 12,956 | 103,277 | 296,129 | * | 1.3 | 10.4 | 29.7 |
| Liquor laws | 437,923 | 8,706 | 92,556 | 302,455 | 334,862 | 2.0 | 21.1 | 69.1 | 76.5 |
| Drunkenness | 412,930 | 1,393 | 11,816 | 50,135 | 116,978 | 0.3 | 2.9 | 12.1 | 28.3 |
| Disorderly conduct | 501,129 | 59,395 | 148,795 | 210,857 | 284,993 | 11.9 | 29.7 | 42.1 | 56.9 |
| Vagrancy | 24,372 | 1,082 | 3,416 | 5,450 | 7,558 | 4.4 | 14.0 | 22.4 | 31.0 |
| All other offenses (except traffic) | 2,837,806 | 70,131 | 266,885 | 600,528 | 1,055,767 | 2.5 | 9.4 | 21.2 | 37.2 |
| Suspicion | 2,747 | 97 | 400 | 878 | 1,289 | 3.5 | 14.6 | 32.0 | 46.9 |
| Curfew and loitering law violations | 104,054 | 29,382 | 104,054 | 104,054 | 104,054 | 28.2 | 100.0 | 100.0 | 100.0 |
| Runaways | 81,222 | 28,075 | 81,222 | 81,222 | 81,222 | 34.6 | 100.0 | 100.0 | 100.0 |

[a]Violent crimes are offenses of murder, forcible rape, robbery, and aggravated assault. Property crimes are offenses of burglary, larceny-theft, motor vehicle theft, and arson.
*Less than one-tenth of 1 percent.

SOURCE: "Table 41. Arrests of Persons under 15, 18, 21, and 25 Years of Age, 2005," in *Crime in the United States, 2005*, U.S. Department of Justice, Federal Bureau of Investigation, September 2006, http://www.fbi.gov/ucr/05cius/data/table_41.html (accessed January 7, 2007)

capita crime rate, this frequency does not take into account population increases.

## Murder

The FBI defines murder and nonnegligent manslaughter as "the willful (non-negligent) killing of one human being by another." The figures for murder do not include suicides, accidents, or justifiable homicides by either citizens or law enforcement officers. In 2005 a murder was committed in the United States every 31.5 minutes according to the UCR Crime Clock; the murder rate was 5.6 murders for every 100,000 inhabitants. (See Table 1.1.)

MURDER RATE CHANGES. As reported by the FBI in *Crime in the United States, 2005*, the total number of homicides in 2005 was 16,692, compared with 21,606 in 1995. However, although the rates of murder and non-negligent manslaughter declined by 15% between 1996

and 2005, they increased by 4.1% between 2001 and 2005 and by 3.4% between 2004 and 2005. (See Table 1.1.)

MURDER RATE BY AREA. The South, the nation's most populous region, had the highest incidence of murder in 2005, accounting for 42.6% of all homicides in the United States, according to the FBI in *Crime in the United States, 2005*. Western states were next, at 23.6%, followed by the Midwest at 19.4%, and the Northeast at 14.4%. (See Table 1.10.) As seen in Table 1.3, metropolitan areas reported a murder rate in 2005 of 6.1 victims per 100,000 population. Rates for murder during 2005 were 3.4 per 100,000 population in cities outside metropolitan areas and 3.5 victims per 100,000 population in rural counties.

SEX, RACE, AND AGE. In 2005, about two-thirds of accused murder offenders were male (65.3%) and 7.3% were female; in 27.4% of cases, information about the sex of the offender was not provided. Of 17,029 murder offenders in 2005, 3,322 males and 284 females were

**TABLE 1.6**

**Arrest trends by sex in a ten-year period, 1996–2005**

[8,009 agencies; 2005 estimated population 178,017,991; 1996 estimated population 159,290,470]

| Offense charged | Male | | | | | | Female | | | | | |
|---|---|---|---|---|---|---|---|---|---|---|---|---|
| | Total | | | Under 18 | | | Total | | | Under 18 | | |
| | 1996 | 2005 | Percent change | 1996 | 2005 | Percent change | 1996 | 2005 | Percent change | 1996 | 2005 | Percent change |
| **Total**[a] | **6,773,900** | **6,261,672** | **−7.6** | **1,258,168** | **897,305** | **−28.7** | **1,845,799** | **1,982,649** | **+7.4** | **445,332** | **381,643** | **−14.3** |
| Murder and nonnegligent manslaughter | 8,572 | 7,114 | −17.0 | 1,290 | 664 | −48.5 | 992 | 875 | −11.8 | 98 | 75 | −23.5 |
| Forcible rape | 18,512 | 14,924 | −19.4 | 3,153 | 2,332 | −26.0 | 233 | 205 | −12.0 | 49 | 60 | +22.4 |
| Robbery | 73,192 | 60,096 | −17.9 | 22,962 | 15,118 | −34.2 | 7,788 | 7,745 | −0.6 | 2,356 | 1,673 | −29.0 |
| Aggravated assault | 260,469 | 224,080 | −14.0 | 36,972 | 28,312 | −23.4 | 54,936 | 57,923 | +5.4 | 9,152 | 8,655 | −5.4 |
| Burglary | 195,124 | 153,888 | −21.1 | 76,490 | 41,672 | −45.5 | 25,674 | 27,085 | +5.5 | 8,758 | 5,744 | −34.4 |
| Larceny-theft | 595,297 | 421,828 | −29.1 | 212,281 | 105,513 | −50.3 | 310,666 | 270,765 | −12.8 | 106,880 | 77,300 | −27.7 |
| Motor vehicle theft | 86,405 | 67,522 | −21.9 | 36,188 | 16,172 | −55.3 | 13,913 | 14,638 | +5.2 | 6,769 | 3,583 | −47.1 |
| Arson | 9,972 | 8,114 | −18.6 | 5,794 | 4,230 | −27.0 | 1,626 | 1,602 | −1.5 | 712 | 685 | −3.8 |
| Violent crime[b] | 360,745 | 306,214 | −15.1 | 64,377 | 46,426 | −27.9 | 63,949 | 66,748 | +4.4 | 11,655 | 10,463 | −10.2 |
| Property crime[b] | 886,798 | 651,352 | −26.6 | 330,753 | 167,587 | −49.3 | 351,879 | 314,090 | −10.7 | 123,119 | 87,312 | −29.1 |
| Other assaults | 597,763 | 554,044 | −7.3 | 99,610 | 95,555 | −4.1 | 158,366 | 183,431 | +15.8 | 38,240 | 47,402 | +24.0 |
| Forgery and counterfeiting | 45,250 | 43,068 | −4.8 | 3,388 | 1,768 | −47.8 | 26,853 | 27,670 | +3.0 | 2,045 | 832 | −59.3 |
| Fraud | 137,874 | 104,201 | −24.4 | 4,536 | 3,065 | −32.4 | 117,288 | 89,338 | −23.8 | 2,411 | 1,714 | −28.9 |
| Embezzlement | 5,545 | 5,979 | +7.8 | 486 | 419 | −13.8 | 4,607 | 6,108 | +32.6 | 394 | 332 | −15.7 |
| Stolen property; buying, receiving, possessing | 78,156 | 66,459 | −15.0 | 23,140 | 11,540 | −50.1 | 13,676 | 16,312 | +19.3 | 3,507 | 2,362 | −32.6 |
| Vandalism | 163,890 | 139,529 | −14.9 | 78,226 | 54,939 | −29.8 | 26,179 | 28,837 | +10.2 | 9,681 | 8,758 | −9.5 |
| Weapons; carrying, possessing, etc. | 113,685 | 103,184 | −9.2 | 28,657 | 24,052 | −16.1 | 9,331 | 8,870 | −4.9 | 2,410 | 2,782 | +15.4 |
| Prostitution and commercialized vice | 20,524 | 14,615 | −28.8 | 303 | 202 | −33.3 | 28,412 | 27,026 | −4.9 | 420 | 668 | +59.0 |
| Sex offenses (except forcible rape and prostitution) | 52,296 | 48,112 | −8.0 | 9,829 | 9,437 | −4.0 | 4,188 | 4,298 | +2.6 | 791 | 1,000 | +26.4 |
| Drug abuse violations | 688,006 | 832,707 | +21.0 | 100,568 | 86,895 | −13.6 | 142,678 | 202,137 | +41.7 | 16,832 | 19,255 | +14.4 |
| Gambling | 5,541 | 2,942 | −46.9 | 528 | 378 | −28.4 | 811 | 504 | −37.9 | 35 | 17 | −51.4 |
| Offenses against the family and children | 68,211 | 55,393 | −18.8 | 3,089 | 1,894 | −38.7 | 16,248 | 17,230 | +6.0 | 1,750 | 1,173 | −33.0 |
| Driving under the influence | 745,658 | 658,705 | −11.7 | 9,191 | 8,187 | −10.9 | 132,069 | 157,538 | +19.3 | 1,809 | 2,363 | +30.6 |
| Liquor laws | 286,425 | 255,746 | −10.7 | 66,537 | 49,116 | −26.2 | 78,367 | 93,228 | +19.0 | 29,149 | 27,640 | −5.2 |
| Drunkenness | 391,721 | 284,892 | −27.3 | 12,156 | 6,999 | −42.4 | 55,046 | 50,838 | −7.6 | 2,665 | 2,095 | −21.4 |
| Disorderly conduct | 324,503 | 279,714 | −13.8 | 83,418 | 78,552 | −5.8 | 95,729 | 99,725 | +4.2 | 29,279 | 37,870 | +29.3 |
| Vagrancy | 12,893 | 13,752 | +6.7 | 1,654 | 1,082 | −34.6 | 3,531 | 3,624 | +2.6 | 344 | 313 | −9.0 |
| All other offenses (except traffic) | 1,651,922 | 1,751,008 | +6.0 | 201,228 | 159,156 | −20.9 | 410,986 | 518,699 | +26.2 | 63,190 | 60,894 | −3.6 |
| Suspicion | 3,209 | 2,211 | −31.1 | 1,118 | 254 | −77.3 | 816 | 358 | −56.1 | 335 | 106 | −68.4 |
| Curfew and loitering law violations | 84,194 | 61,069 | −27.5 | 84,194 | 61,069 | −27.5 | 35,213 | 26,589 | −24.5 | 35,213 | 26,589 | −24.5 |
| Runaways | 52,300 | 28,987 | −44.6 | 52,300 | 28,987 | −44.6 | 70,393 | 39,809 | −43.4 | 70,393 | 39,809 | −43.4 |

[a]Does not include suspicion.
[b]Violent crimes are offenses of murder, forcible rape, robbery, and aggravated assault. Property crimes are offenses of burglary, larceny-theft, motor vehicle theft, and arson.

SOURCE: "Table 33. Ten-Year Arrest Trends, by Sex, 1996–2005," in *Crime in the United States, 2005*, U.S. Department of Justice, Federal Bureau of Investigation, September 2006, http://www.fbi.gov/ucr/05cius/data/table_33.html (accessed January 7, 2007)

**TABLE 1.7**

**Arrests by race, 2005**

[10,971 agencies; 2005 estimated population 217,692,433]

| Offense charged | Total arrests | | | | | Percent distribution[a] | | | | |
|---|---|---|---|---|---|---|---|---|---|---|
| | Total | White | Black | American Indian or Alaskan Native | Asian or Pacific Islander | Total | White | Black | American Indian or Alaskan Native | Asian or Pacific Islander |
| Total | 10,189,691 | 7,117,040 | 2,830,778 | 135,877 | 105,996 | 100.0 | 69.8 | 27.8 | 1.3 | 1.0 |
| Murder and nonnegligent manslaughter | 10,083 | 4,955 | 4,898 | 109 | 121 | 100.0 | 49.1 | 48.6 | 1.1 | 1.2 |
| Forcible rape | 18,405 | 11,980 | 6,015 | 222 | 188 | 100.0 | 65.1 | 32.7 | 1.2 | 1.0 |
| Robbery | 84,785 | 35,796 | 47,700 | 512 | 777 | 100.0 | 42.2 | 56.3 | 0.6 | 0.9 |
| Aggravated assault | 329,247 | 208,253 | 113,062 | 4,337 | 3,595 | 100.0 | 63.3 | 34.3 | 1.3 | 1.1 |
| Burglary | 217,894 | 151,757 | 62,045 | 2,196 | 1,896 | 100.0 | 69.6 | 28.5 | 1.0 | 0.9 |
| Larceny-theft | 846,213 | 586,393 | 236,608 | 11,332 | 11,880 | 100.0 | 69.3 | 28.0 | 1.3 | 1.4 |
| Motor vehicle theft | 107,604 | 67,578 | 37,489 | 1,103 | 1,434 | 100.0 | 62.8 | 34.8 | 1.0 | 1.3 |
| Arson | 11,780 | 9,026 | 2,493 | 124 | 137 | 100.0 | 76.6 | 21.2 | 1.1 | 1.2 |
| Violent crime[b] | 442,520 | 260,984 | 171,675 | 5,180 | 4,681 | 100.0 | 59.0 | 38.8 | 1.2 | 1.1 |
| Property crime[b] | 1,183,491 | 814,754 | 338,635 | 14,755 | 15,347 | 100.0 | 68.8 | 28.6 | 1.2 | 1.3 |
| Other assaults | 944,820 | 615,268 | 305,398 | 13,529 | 10,625 | 100.0 | 65.1 | 32.3 | 1.4 | 1.1 |
| Forgery and counterfeiting | 83,747 | 59,221 | 23,104 | 471 | 951 | 100.0 | 70.7 | 27.6 | 0.6 | 1.1 |
| Fraud | 217,650 | 149,618 | 65,424 | 1,243 | 1,365 | 100.0 | 68.7 | 30.1 | 0.6 | 0.6 |
| Embezzlement | 13,730 | 9,201 | 4,262 | 97 | 170 | 100.0 | 67.0 | 31.0 | 0.7 | 1.2 |
| Stolen property; buying, receiving, possessing | 97,075 | 62,215 | 33,184 | 748 | 928 | 100.0 | 64.1 | 34.2 | 0.8 | 1.0 |
| Vandalism | 203,578 | 152,621 | 45,807 | 3,095 | 2,055 | 100.0 | 75.0 | 22.5 | 1.5 | 1.0 |
| Weapons; carrying, possessing, etc. | 141,286 | 83,830 | 55,168 | 1,011 | 1,277 | 100.0 | 59.3 | 39.0 | 0.7 | 0.9 |
| Prostitution and commercialized vice | 62,501 | 34,436 | 26,104 | 612 | 1,349 | 100.0 | 55.1 | 41.8 | 1.0 | 2.2 |
| Sex offenses (except forcible rape and prostitution) | 64,395 | 47,392 | 15,647 | 687 | 669 | 100.0 | 73.6 | 24.3 | 1.1 | 1.0 |
| Drug abuse violations | 1,330,802 | 861,645 | 451,375 | 8,600 | 9,182 | 100.0 | 64.7 | 33.9 | 0.6 | 0.7 |
| Gambling | 8,064 | 2,087 | 5,731 | 24 | 222 | 100.0 | 25.9 | 71.1 | 0.3 | 2.8 |
| Offenses against the family and children | 89,170 | 61,122 | 25,834 | 1,683 | 531 | 100.0 | 68.5 | 29.0 | 1.9 | 0.6 |
| Driving under the influence | 976,797 | 863,955 | 88,656 | 13,682 | 10,504 | 100.0 | 88.4 | 9.1 | 1.4 | 1.1 |
| Liquor laws | 430,992 | 367,991 | 46,769 | 11,916 | 4,316 | 100.0 | 85.4 | 10.9 | 2.8 | 1.0 |
| Drunkenness | 399,059 | 334,158 | 53,709 | 8,976 | 2,216 | 100.0 | 83.7 | 13.5 | 2.2 | 0.6 |
| Disorderly conduct | 493,708 | 316,467 | 165,850 | 7,712 | 3,679 | 100.0 | 64.1 | 33.6 | 1.6 | 0.7 |
| Vagrancy | 24,359 | 14,452 | 9,364 | 412 | 131 | 100.0 | 59.3 | 38.4 | 1.7 | 0.5 |
| All other offenses (except traffic) | 2,794,372 | 1,881,076 | 842,609 | 39,022 | 31,665 | 100.0 | 67.3 | 30.2 | 1.4 | 1.1 |
| Suspicion | 2,744 | 1,840 | 885 | 12 | 7 | 100.0 | 67.1 | 32.3 | 0.4 | 0.3 |
| Curfew and loitering law violations | 103,886 | 64,881 | 36,928 | 876 | 1,201 | 100.0 | 62.5 | 35.5 | 0.8 | 1.2 |
| Runaways | 80,945 | 57,826 | 18,660 | 1,534 | 2,925 | 100.0 | 71.4 | 23.1 | 1.9 | 3.6 |

[a]Because of rounding, the percentages may not add to 100.0.
[b]Violent crimes are offenses of murder, forcible rape, robbery, and aggravated assault. Property crimes are offenses of burglary, larceny-theft, motor vehicle theft, and arson.

SOURCE: Adapted from "Table 43. Arrests, by Race, 2005," in *Crime in the United States, 2005*, U.S. Department of Justice, Federal Bureau of Investigation, September 2006, http://www.fbi.gov/ucr/05cius/data/table_43.html (accessed January 7, 2007)

under the age of 22, while 866 males and 76 females were under the age of 18. Of murder offenders in 2005 for whom race was known, 37.6% were black, 32% were white, and 2% were of other races. (See Table 1.11.)

Offenders and victims were usually of the same race, according to the FBI data reported in *Crime in the United States, 2005*. Of 3,785 white murder victims in 2005, 3,150 were killed by white offenders. Similarly, of 3,289 black victims of homicide, most (2,984) were killed by black offenders. Males and females were the victims of male offenders in most cases, although female murder offenders were more likely to kill males than females in 2005.

**MURDER CIRCUMSTANCES.** In 2005 relatives, acquaintances, or others with personal relationships to the victims committed three-quarters (74.6%) of all murders in which the relationship of the victim to the offender was known, according to the FBI in *Crime in the United States, 2005*.

(More than 45% of murder-victim relationships were unknown.) Of 14,860 murders in 2005, 594 wives were the victims of their husbands, and 461 girlfriends were the victims of their boyfriends. More sons (245) were murdered than daughters (190). Arguments resulted in 3,903 murders in 2005, up slightly from 3,816 in 2001. Robbery was the felony offense most likely to result in murder in 2005, as it has been since 2001. Juvenile gang killing accounted for 754 murders in 2005, down from 862 in 2001. (See Table 1.12.)

Sixty-eight percent of all murders were committed with firearms in 2005, according to the FBI in *Crime in the United States, 2005*. (See below for more information on firearms and crime.) Knives were used in 12.9% of murders; blunt instruments in 4%; personal weapons (fists, feet, and the like) in 6%; and other weapons, such as poisons and explosives, in the remaining 9.1%.

TABLE 1.8

**Federal criminal justice budget authorities, fiscal years 2003 (actual) and 2004–09 (estimated)[a]**

[In millions of dollars]

| Type of program | 2003 actual | Estimated | | | | | |
|---|---|---|---|---|---|---|---|
| | | 2004 | 2005 | 2006 | 2007 | 2008 | 2009 |
| Total | $39,689 | $42,719 | $41,958 | $42,202 | $43,573 | $44,904 | $47,189 |
| Discretionary, total | 35,741 | 36,993 | 38,146 | 39,304 | 40,602 | 41,918 | 44,188 |
| Federal law enforcement activities, total | 18,776 | 19,495 | 20,082 | 20,710 | 21,381 | 22,088 | 22,837 |
| Criminal investigations[b] | 6,213 | 6,253 | 6,433 | 6,632 | 6,844 | 7,070 | 7,309 |
| Bureau of Alcohol, Tobacco, Firearms and Explosives | 801 | 827 | 852 | 889 | 923 | 958 | 996 |
| Border and transportation security directorate activities[c] | 8,602 | 9,618 | 9,690 | 9,971 | 10,279 | 10,605 | 10,951 |
| Equal Employment Opportunity Commission | 322 | 325 | 337 | 351 | 363 | 377 | 392 |
| Tax law, criminal investigations[d] | 458 | 445 | 466 | 485 | 507 | 529 | 551 |
| U.S. Secret Service | 1,065 | 1,134 | 1,176 | 1,218 | 1,263 | 1,309 | 1,359 |
| Other law enforcement activities | 1,315 | 893 | 1,128 | 1,164 | 1,202 | 1,240 | 1,279 |
| Federal litigative and judicial activities, total | 7,978 | 8,208 | 8,544 | 8,836 | 9,199 | 9,526 | 10,747 |
| Civil and criminal prosecution and representation | 3,004 | 3,033 | 3,192 | 3,307 | 3,484 | 3,612 | 4,637 |
| Representation of indigents in civil cases | 337 | 335 | 339 | 344 | 350 | 357 | 364 |
| Federal judicial and other litigative activities | 4,637 | 4,840 | 5,013 | 5,185 | 5,365 | 5,557 | 5,746 |
| Correctional activities[e] | 5,259 | 5,564 | 5,743 | 5,923 | 6,116 | 6,322 | 6,540 |
| Criminal justice assistance, total | 3,728 | 3,726 | 3,777 | 3,835 | 3,906 | 3,982 | 4,064 |
| High-intensity drug trafficking areas program | 195 | 223 | 226 | 229 | 233 | 238 | 242 |
| Law enforcement assistance, community policing, and other justice programs | 3,533 | 3,503 | 3,551 | 3,606 | 3,673 | 3,744 | 3,822 |
| Mandatory, total | 3,948 | 5,726 | 3,812 | 2,898 | 2,971 | 2,986 | 3,001 |
| Federal law enforcement activities, total | −583 | −315 | 493 | 1,077 | 1,125 | 1,114 | 1,102 |
| Border and transportation security directorate activities[c] | 2,301 | 2,708 | 2,873 | 2,881 | 2,913 | 2,946 | 2,980 |
| Immigration fees | −1,981 | −2,079 | −2,240 | −2,265 | −2,293 | −2,341 | −2,391 |
| Customs fees | −1,326 | −1,396 | −591 | −6 | −6 | −7 | −7 |
| Treasury forfeiture fund | 253 | 251 | 251 | 251 | 251 | 251 | 251 |
| Other mandatory law enforcement programs | 170 | 201 | 200 | 216 | 260 | 265 | 269 |
| Federal litigative and judicial activities, total | 1,186 | 1,213 | 1,271 | 1,207 | 1,231 | 1,256 | 1,282 |
| Federal forfeiture fund | 530 | 489 | 500 | 448 | 458 | 468 | 478 |
| Federal judicial officers' salaries and expenses and other mandatory programs | 656 | 724 | 771 | 759 | 773 | 788 | 804 |
| Correctional activities | −3 | −3 | −3 | −3 | −3 | −3 | −3 |
| Criminal justice assistance, total | 3,348 | 4,831 | 2,051 | 617 | 618 | 619 | 620 |
| Crime victims' fund | 592 | 608 | 1,606 | 567 | 567 | 567 | 567 |
| September 11 victims' compensation | 2,700 | 4,174 | 396 | 0 | 0 | 0 | 0 |
| Public safety officers' benefits | 56 | 49 | 49 | 50 | 51 | 52 | 53 |

Note: These data are from the budget submitted by the President to Congress in 2004.
[a]Detail may not add to total because of rounding.
[b]Includes Drug Enforcement Administration, Federal Bureau of Investigation, Department of Homeland Security, Financial Crimes Enforcement Network, and interagency crime and drug enforcement programs.
[c]Department of Homeland Security.
[d]Internal Revenue Service.
[e]Federal prison system and detention trustee program.

SOURCE: Ann L. Pastore and Kathleen Maguire, editors, "Table 1.12. Federal Criminal Justice Budget Authorities, Fiscal Years 2003 (actual) and 2004–2009 (estimated)," in *Sourcebook of Criminal Justice Statistics 2003*, 31st ed., U.S. Department of Justice, Office of Justice Programs, Bureau of Justice Statistics, 2005, http://www.albany.edu/sourcebook/pdf/t112.pdf (accessed January 21, 2007).

TABLE 1.9

**Crime clock, 2005**

| **Every 22.7 seconds** | **One violent crime** |
|---|---|
| Every 31.5 minutes | One murder |
| Every 5.6 minutes | One forcible rape |
| Every 1.3 minutes | One robbery |
| Every 36.5 seconds | One aggravated assault |
| **Every 3.1 seconds** | **One property crime** |
| Every 14.6 seconds | One burglary |
| Every 4.7 seconds | One larceny-theft |
| Every 25.5 seconds | One motor vehicle theft |

SOURCE: "Crime Clock 2005," in *Crime in the United States, 2005*, U.S. Department of Justice, Federal Bureau of Investigation, September 2006, http://www.fbi.gov/ucr/05cius/about/crime_clock.html (accessed January 7, 2007)

**ARRESTS.** Because murder is considered the most serious crime, it receives the most police attention and, therefore, has the highest arrest rate of all felonies. According to the 2005 UCR on murder, about 62.1% of murders in 2005 were cleared by arrest. The rate was somewhat lower in large cities (populations of 250,000 or more), with 56.5% of murders and nonnegligent manslaughter offenses cleared by arrest in 2005. (See Table 1.13.) Making an arrest does not mean that the alleged offender is guilty or will be convicted in criminal or juvenile court.

## Rape

The FBI defines forcible rape as "the carnal knowledge of a female forcibly and against her will. Assaults

TABLE 1.10

## Violent and property crime rates by offense and region, 2005

| Region | Population | Violent crime | Murder and nonnegligent manslaughter | Forcible rape | Robbery | Aggravated assault | Property crime | Burglary | Larceny-theft | Motor vehicle theft |
|---|---|---|---|---|---|---|---|---|---|---|
| United States total* | 100.0 | 100.0 | 100.0 | 100.0 | 100.0 | 100.0 | 100.0 | 100.0 | 100.0 | 100.0 |
| Northeast | 18.4 | 15.5 | 14.4 | 12.8 | 19.4 | 13.9 | 12.3 | 10.8 | 13.1 | 10.5 |
| Midwest | 22.3 | 19.6 | 19.4 | 25.4 | 19.8 | 18.8 | 21.2 | 20.4 | 21.9 | 18.3 |
| South | 36.3 | 41.9 | 42.6 | 37.9 | 38.2 | 44.2 | 41.1 | 44.8 | 41.3 | 33.4 |
| West | 23.0 | 23.0 | 23.6 | 23.8 | 22.6 | 23.1 | 25.5 | 24.0 | 23.7 | 37.9 |

*Because of rounding, the percentages may not add to 100.0.
Note: Although arson data are included in the trend and clearance tables, sufficient data are not available to estimate totals for this offense. Therefore, no arson data are published in this table.
Note: The Northeast includes: Connecticut, Maine, Massachusetts, New Hampshire, New Jersey, New York, Pennsylvania, Rhode Island, and Vermont. The Midwest includes: Illinois, Indiana, Iowa, Kansas, Michigan, Minnesota, Missouri, Nebraska, North Dakota, Ohio, South Dakota, and Wisconsin. The South includes: Alabama, Arkansas, Delaware, District of Columbia, Florida, Georgia, Kentucky, Louisiana, Maryland, Mississippi, North Carolina, Oklahoma, South Carolina, Tennessee, Texas, Virginia, and West Virginia. The West includes: Alaska, Arizona, California, Colorado, Hawaii, Idaho, Montana, Nevada, New Mexico, Oregon, Utah, Washington, and Wyoming.

SOURCE: "Table 3. Crime in the United States: Offense and Population Percent Distribution within Region, 2005," in *Crime in the United States, 2005*, U.S. Department of Justice, Federal Bureau of Investigation, September 2006, http://www.fbi.gov/ucr/05cius/data/table_03.html (accessed January 23, 2007)

TABLE 1.11

## Murder offenders by age, sex, and race, 2005

| Age | Total | Sex | | | Race | | | |
|---|---|---|---|---|---|---|---|---|
| | | Male | Female | Unknown | White | Black | Other | Unknown |
| Total | 17,029 | 11,117 | 1,246 | 4,666 | 5,452 | 6,379 | 299 | 4,899 |
| Percent distribution[a] | 100.0 | 65.3 | 7.3 | 27.4 | 32.0 | 37.6 | 2.0 | 28.8 |
| Under 18[b] | 944 | 866 | 76 | 2 | 356 | 552 | 31 | 5 |
| Under 22[b] | 3,611 | 3,322 | 284 | 5 | 1,382 | 2,084 | 115 | 30 |
| 18 and over[b] | 10,354 | 9,195 | 1,141 | 18 | 4,911 | 5,046 | 258 | 139 |
| Infant (under 1) | 0 | 0 | 0 | 0 | 0 | 0 | 0 | 0 |
| 1 to 4 | 0 | 0 | 0 | 0 | 0 | 0 | 0 | 0 |
| 5 to 8 | 0 | 0 | 0 | 0 | 0 | 0 | 0 | 0 |
| 9 to 12 | 11 | 7 | 4 | 0 | 6 | 5 | 0 | 0 |
| 13 to 16 | 467 | 426 | 41 | 0 | 176 | 272 | 17 | 2 |
| 17 to 19 | 1,801 | 1,676 | 123 | 2 | 654 | 1,075 | 59 | 13 |
| 20 to 24 | 3,016 | 2,751 | 262 | 3 | 1,243 | 1,657 | 80 | 36 |
| 25 to 29 | 1,935 | 1,727 | 206 | 2 | 859 | 1,005 | 44 | 27 |
| 30 to 34 | 1,090 | 933 | 156 | 1 | 531 | 518 | 26 | 15 |
| 35 to 39 | 873 | 750 | 123 | 0 | 491 | 348 | 20 | 14 |
| 40 to 44 | 700 | 605 | 95 | 0 | 404 | 270 | 12 | 14 |
| 45 to 49 | 586 | 486 | 97 | 3 | 361 | 206 | 13 | 6 |
| 50 to 54 | 330 | 286 | 41 | 3 | 197 | 114 | 11 | 8 |
| 55 to 59 | 200 | 170 | 30 | 0 | 129 | 65 | 5 | 1 |
| 60 to 64 | 100 | 82 | 18 | 0 | 72 | 27 | 0 | 1 |
| 65 to 69 | 78 | 70 | 8 | 0 | 61 | 15 | 2 | 0 |
| 70 to 74 | 43 | 35 | 8 | 0 | 33 | 10 | 0 | 0 |
| 75 and over | 68 | 57 | 5 | 6 | 50 | 11 | 0 | 7 |
| Unknown | 5,731 | 1,056 | 29 | 4,646 | 185 | 781 | 10 | 4,755 |

[a]Because of rounding, the percentages may not add to 100.0.
[b]Does not include unknown ages.

SOURCE: "Expanded Homicide Data Table 3. Murder Offenders, by Age, Sex, and Race, 2005," in *Crime in the United States, 2005*, U.S. Department of Justice, Federal Bureau of Investigation, September 2006, http://www.fbi.gov/ucr/05cius/offenses/expanded_information/data/shrtable_03.html (accessed January 7, 2007)

and attempts to commit rape by force or threat of force are included; however, statutory rape (without force) [intercourse with a consenting minor] and other sex offenses are excluded." Rape is a crime of violence in which the victim may suffer serious physical injury and long-term psychological pain. In 2005, 93,934 forcible rapes were reported to law enforcement agencies, an increase of 3.4% from 2001. (See Table 1.1.) Forcible rape totals decreased by 2.4% between 1996 and 2005. The national rate of forcible rape in 2005 was 31.7 per 100,000 females; this represents a 12.7% rate decrease from 1996.

Rape is a very intimate crime, and many rape victims are unwilling, afraid, or ashamed to discuss it. As a result, it is relatively unlikely to be reported to law enforcement

**TABLE 1.12**

**Murder circumstances, 2001–05**

| Circumstances | 2001* | 2002 | 2003 | 2004 | 2005 |
|---|---|---|---|---|---|
| **Total** | **14,061** | **14,263** | **14,465** | **14,210** | **14,860** |
| **Felony type total:** | 2,364 | 2,340 | 2,385 | 2,099 | 2,161 |
| Rape | 61 | 44 | 43 | 37 | 44 |
| Robbery | 1,080 | 1,111 | 1,061 | 993 | 921 |
| Burglary | 80 | 97 | 94 | 78 | 88 |
| Larceny-theft | 17 | 16 | 21 | 17 | 12 |
| Motor vehicle theft | 22 | 15 | 32 | 36 | 31 |
| Arson | 71 | 59 | 77 | 28 | 37 |
| Prostitution and commercialized vice | 5 | 8 | 16 | 9 | 13 |
| Other sex offenses | 7 | 8 | 10 | 14 | 9 |
| Narcotic drug laws | 575 | 664 | 679 | 558 | 589 |
| Gambling | 3 | 5 | 6 | 7 | 2 |
| Other—not specified | 443 | 313 | 346 | 322 | 415 |
| **Suspected felony type** | 72 | 66 | 87 | 119 | 44 |
| **Other than felony type total:** | 7,073 | 7,185 | 7,130 | 7,008 | 7,044 |
| Romantic triangle | 118 | 129 | 98 | 97 | 117 |
| Child killed by babysitter | 37 | 39 | 27 | 17 | 26 |
| Brawl due to influence of alcohol | 152 | 149 | 128 | 140 | 120 |
| Brawl due to influence of narcotics | 118 | 85 | 53 | 99 | 97 |
| Argument over money or property | 198 | 203 | 220 | 221 | 211 |
| Other arguments | 3,618 | 3,577 | 3,850 | 3,772 | 3,692 |
| Gangland killings | 76 | 75 | 114 | 95 | 96 |
| Juvenile gang killings | 862 | 911 | 819 | 805 | 754 |
| Institutional killings | 8 | 12 | 13 | 17 | 12 |
| Sniper attack | 7 | 10 | 2 | 1 | 2 |
| Other—not specified | 1,879 | 1,995 | 1,806 | 1,744 | 1,917 |
| **Unknown** | 4,552 | 4,672 | 4,863 | 4,984 | 5,611 |

*The murder and nonnegligent homicides that occurred as a result of the events of September 11, 2001, are not included.

SOURCE: "Expanded Homicide Data Table 11. Murder Circumstances, 2001–2005," in *Crime in the United States, 2005*, U.S. Department of Justice, Federal Bureau of Investigation, September 2006, http://www.fbi.gov/ucr/05cius/offenses/expanded_information/data/shrtable_11.html (accessed January 7, 2007)

authorities. Callie Marie Rennison of the Bureau of Justice Statistics estimated that between 1992 and 2000, 63% of completed rapes, 65% of attempted rapes, and 74% of completed and attempted sexual assaults against women were not reported to a law enforcement agency (*Rape and Sexual Assault: Reporting to Police and Medical Attention, 1992–2000*, August 2002, http://www.ojp.usdoj.gov/bjs/pub/pdf/rsarp00.pdf).

From 1979 through 1992, the reported rape rate increased 23%. Most experts attributed at least part of the increase in reported rape cases to a more sympathetic attitude to rape victims by law enforcement authorities and a greater awareness of women's rights. After peaking in 1992, the rate has steadily declined. (See Table 1.1.)

WHEN AND WHERE. In keeping with a five-year trend, rapes in 2004 occurred most frequently during the summer months of July and August, according to FBI data. (See Table 1.14.) The rate of rape in metropolitan statistical areas in 2005 was 31.8 per 100,000 females. The rate of rape was highest in cities outside of metropolitan areas and lower in rural counties. (See Table 1.3.) Regionally, the highest total volume of rapes (37.9% of all rapes) occurred in the South, and 12.8% of all forcible rapes in 2005 occurred in the Northeast. (See Table 1.10.)

ARRESTS. Less than half (41.3%) of reported forcible rapes were cleared by arrest in 2005. (See Table 1.13.) Of persons arrested for forcible rape, 44.5% were under age twenty-five, and 15.4% were under age eighteen. (See Table 1.5.) Of those arrested for rape by agencies that reported race information in 2005, 65.1% were white and 32.7% were black. (See Table 1.7.)

**Robbery**

The FBI defines robbery as "the taking or attempting to take anything of value from the care, custody, or control of a person or persons by force or threat of force or violence and/or by putting the victim in fear." An estimated 417,122 robberies were reported during 2005, 3.9% more than in 2004. (See Table 1.1.) The number of robberies declined by 1.5% between 2001 and 2005 and by 22.1% between 1996 and 2005. Robbery represented 30% of the nation's violent crimes in 2005, according to the FBI.

RATE. The robbery rate in 2005 was 140.7 per 100,000 inhabitants, a 2.9% increase from 2004, as reported by the FBI in *Crime in the United States, 2005*. However, the rate represents a decrease of 5.2% compared with 2001 and of 30.3% compared with 1996. (See Table 1.1.)

**TABLE 1.13**

**Percent of offenses cleared by arrest, 2005**

| Population group | | Violent crime | Murder and nonnegligent manslaughter | Forcible rape | Robbery | Aggravated assault | Property crime | Burglary | Larceny-theft | Motor vehicle theft | Arson[a] | Number of agencies | 2005 estimated population |
|---|---|---|---|---|---|---|---|---|---|---|---|---|---|
| **Total all agencies:** | Offenses known | 1,197,089 | 14,430 | 82,118 | 353,050 | 747,491 | 8,935,714 | 1,906,980 | 5,915,843 | 1,112,891 | 64,231 | 13,441 | 255,115,278 |
| | Percent cleared by arrest | 45.5 | 62.1 | 41.3 | 25.4 | 55.2 | 16.3 | 12.7 | 18 | 13 | 17.9 | | |
| **Total cities** | Offenses known | 934,954 | 11,125 | 60,170 | 304,134 | 559,525 | 6,961,634 | 1,392,315 | 4,683,212 | 886,107 | 46,897 | 9,618 | 167,119,985 |
| | Percent cleared by arrest | 42.9 | 60.7 | 39.8 | 24.9 | 52.7 | 16.2 | 12.2 | 18.3 | 11.9 | 17.3 | | |
| Group I (all cities 250,000 and over) | Offenses known | 408,875 | 5,783 | 19,367 | 156,850 | 226,875 | 2,206,861 | 464,882 | 1,326,142 | 415,837 | 18,801 | 67 | 41,685,502 |
| | Percent cleared by arrest | 36.2 | 56.5 | 39 | 21.2 | 45.8 | 12.5 | 10.2 | 14.2 | 9.4 | 12.6 | | |
| 1,000,000 and over (Group 1 subset) | Offenses known | 127,623 | 1,904 | 5,681 | 53,623 | 66,415 | 669,625 | 135,906 | 394,296 | 139,423 | 6,045 | 8 | 13,896,753 |
| | Percent cleared by arrest | 34.9 | 61.1 | 43.5 | 21.7 | 44.1 | 12.2 | 10.4 | 14.2 | 8.2 | 8.9 | | |
| 500,000 to 999,999 (Group 1 subset) | Offenses known | 149,233 | 2,120 | 6,724 | 55,512 | 84,877 | 809,352 | 175,359 | 486,968 | 147,025 | 6,122 | 22 | 14,422,520 |
| | Percent cleared by arrest | 33.8 | 54.1 | 35.6 | 18.9 | 43 | 11.6 | 9.2 | 13.1 | 9.6 | 16.9 | | |
| 250,000 to 499,999 (Group 1 subset) | Offenses known | 132,019 | 1,759 | 6,962 | 47,715 | 75,583 | 727,884 | 153,617 | 444,878 | 129,389 | 6,634 | 37 | 13,366,229 |
| | Percent cleared by arrest | 40.2 | 54.5 | 38.7 | 23.4 | 50.6 | 13.6 | 11.2 | 15.4 | 10.4 | 11.8 | | |
| Group II (100,000 to 249,999) | Offenses known | 158,668 | 1,970 | 9,759 | 53,201 | 93,738 | 1,192,615 | 239,579 | 788,916 | 164,120 | 7,603 | 173 | 25,983,746 |
| | Percent cleared by arrest | 41.8 | 63.5 | 39.7 | 25 | 51.1 | 15 | 11 | 17.1 | 10.7 | 15.8 | | |
| Group III (50,000 to 99,999) | Offenses known | 133,966 | 1,362 | 9,855 | 40,637 | 82,112 | 1,107,071 | 226,543 | 758,923 | 121,605 | 6,596 | 416 | 28,490,290 |
| | Percent cleared by arrest | 46 | 58.1 | 38.3 | 28.3 | 55.5 | 17.3 | 12.2 | 19.7 | 11.8 | 18.3 | | |
| Group IV (25,000 to 49,999) | Offenses known | 90,994 | 835 | 7,926 | 25,096 | 57,137 | 886,669 | 169,837 | 637,075 | 79,757 | 5,348 | 714 | 24,684,401 |
| | Percent cleared by arrest | 49.7 | 69.2 | 38.9 | 31.2 | 59 | 18.7 | 12.7 | 20.6 | 15.5 | 20 | | |
| Group V (10,000 to 24,999) | Offenses known | 75,281 | 643 | 7,218 | 17,675 | 49,745 | 828,044 | 155,566 | 611,433 | 61,045 | 4,405 | 1,597 | 25,289,898 |
| | Percent cleared by arrest | 54 | 74.2 | 42 | 33.8 | 62.7 | 21 | 15.6 | 22.5 | 19.1 | 26.4 | | |
| Group VI (under 10,000) | Offenses known | 67,170 | 532 | 6,045 | 10,675 | 49,918 | 740,374 | 135,908 | 560,723 | 43,743 | 4,144 | 6,651 | 20,986,148 |
| | Percent cleared by arrest | 58.6 | 72.7 | 43.8 | 36 | 65.1 | 19.7 | 16.4 | 23.9 | 23.9 | 27 | | |
| Metropolitan counties | Offenses known | 208,839 | 2,422 | 15,576 | 45,051 | 145,790 | 1,551,069 | 378,400 | 981,519 | 191,150 | 13,365 | 1,598 | 63,038,742 |
| | Percent cleared by arrest | 53.1 | 63.2 | 45.1 | 27.1 | 61.8 | 16 | 13.5 | 17 | 15.5 | 18 | | |
| Nonmetropolitan counties | Offenses known | 53,296 | 883 | 6,372 | 3,865 | 42,176 | 423,011 | 136,265 | 251,112 | 35,634 | 3,969 | 2,225 | 24,956,551 |
| | Percent cleared by arrest | 61.6 | 76.7 | 46 | 41.7 | 65.5 | 18 | 16.3 | 17.8 | 26 | 24.7 | | |
| Suburban area[b] | Offenses known | 350,472 | 3,581 | 27,650 | 81,090 | 238,151 | 3,099,019 | 660,524 | 2,112,131 | 326,364 | 22,067 | 6,688 | 109,688,618 |
| | Percent cleared by arrest | 52.9 | 65 | 43.6 | 29 | 61.9 | 17.4 | 13.8 | 18.8 | 15.8 | 20 | | |

[a]Not all agencies submit reports for arson to the Federal Bureau of Investigation (FBI). As a result, the number of reports the FBI uses to compute the percent of offenses cleared for arson is less than the number it uses to compute the percent of offenses cleared for all other offenses.

[b]Suburban area includes law enforcement agencies in cities with less than 50,000 inhabitants and county law enforcement agencies that are within a metropolitan statistical area. Suburban area excludes all metropolitan agencies associated with a principal city. The agencies associated with suburban areas also appear in other groups within this table.

SOURCE: "Table 25. Percent of Offenses Cleared by Arrest or Exceptional Means, by Population Group, 2005," in Crime in the United States, 2005, U.S. Department of Justice, Federal Bureau of Investigation, September 2006, http://www.fbi.gov/ucr/05cius/data/table_25.html (accessed January 23, 2007)

**TABLE 1.14**

**Forcible rape, by month, 2000–04**

[Percent distribution]

| Month | 2000 | 2001 | 2002 | 2003 | 2004 |
|---|---|---|---|---|---|
| January | 8 | 7.7 | 7.6 | 7.9 | 8.1 |
| February | 7.5 | 7.1 | 7 | 6.8 | 7.7 |
| March | 8.5 | 8.4 | 7.8 | 8.3 | 8.7 |
| April | 8 | 8.3 | 8.6 | 8 | 8.4 |
| May | 9 | 8.8 | 9 | 9 | 9 |
| June | 9.1 | 8.7 | 9 | 8.8 | 8.5 |
| July | 9.5 | 9.7 | 9.6 | 9.5 | 9.2 |
| August | 9.3 | 9.4 | 9.5 | 9.6 | 9 |
| September | 8.4 | 8.6 | 9.1 | 8.9 | 8.4 |
| October | 8.3 | 8.5 | 8.4 | 8.4 | 8.5 |
| November | 7.5 | 7.6 | 7.4 | 7.8 | 7.6 |
| December | 6.9 | 7.2 | 6.9 | 7.1 | 7 |

SOURCE: Table 2.17. Forcible Rape by Month, Percent Distribution, 2000–2004, in *Crime in the United States, 2004*, U.S. Department of Justice, Federal Bureau of Investigation, February 17, 2006, http://www.fbi.gov/ucr/cius_04/offenses_reported/violent_crime/forcible_rape.html (accessed January 24, 2007)

Robbery is largely a big-city crime. Of 417,122 total robberies reported by law enforcement agencies nationwide in 2005, 400,792 occurred in metropolitan areas—a rate of 163.1 per 100,000 population. In contrast, the rate of robberies was 57.5 per 100,000 people in cities outside metropolitan areas and 15.7 per 100,000 people in rural counties. (See Table 1.3.)

**AVERAGE LOSSES.** The FBI estimates that in 2005, the average value of items stolen from robbery victims was $1,230 per incident. Average dollar losses in 2005 ranged from $4,169 for a bank robbery to $625 for a convenience-store robbery. Nearly half (44.1%) of robberies occurred on streets or highways. Similar percentages of robberies occurred in commercial establishments (14.3%) and residences (14.2%). (See Table 1.15.)

**ARRESTS.** In 2005 law authorities cleared about one-fourth (25.4%) of reported robbery offenses nationwide. (See Table 1.13.) Of 67,841 people arrested for robbery by 8,009 U.S. agencies in 2005, 60,096 (88.6%) of those arrested were male, and 7,745 (11.4%) were female.

**TABLE 1.15**

**Number and percent change of offenses by type, 2004–05**

| Classification | | Number of offenses 2005 | Percent change from 2004 | Percent distribution* | Average value |
|---|---|---|---|---|---|
| Murder | | 12,068 | +3.9 | — | |
| Forcible rape | | 70,472 | −1.7 | — | |
| Robbery: | Total | 298,403 | +4.6 | 100.0 | $1,230 |
| Robbery by location: | Street/highway | 131,666 | +5.8 | 44.1 | 1,005 |
| | Commercial house | 42,672 | +3.5 | 14.3 | 1,670 |
| | Gas or service station | 8,499 | +9.1 | 2.8 | 1,104 |
| | Convenience store | 17,029 | −0.3 | 5.7 | 625 |
| | Residence | 42,324 | +9.7 | 14.2 | 1,335 |
| | Bank | 6,266 | −8.9 | 2.1 | 4,169 |
| | Miscellaneous | 49,947 | +1.3 | 16.7 | 1,217 |
| Burglary: | Total | 1,612,683 | +0.8 | 100.0 | 1,725 |
| Burglary by location: | Residence (dwelling): | 1,060,513 | +1.1 | 65.8 | 1,745 |
| | Residence night | 301,431 | +1.2 | 18.7 | 1,331 |
| | Residence day | 500,972 | +2.6 | 31.1 | 1,877 |
| | Residence unknown | 258,110 | −1.9 | 16.0 | 1,971 |
| | Nonresidence (store, office, etc.): | 552,170 | +0.2 | 34.2 | 1,683 |
| | Nonresidence night | 228,743 | −0.1 | 14.2 | 1,485 |
| | Nonresidence day | 165,487 | +2.6 | 10.3 | 1,583 |
| | Nonresidence unknown | 157,940 | −1.6 | 9.8 | 2,076 |
| Larceny-theft (except motor vehicle theft): | Total | 5,036,548 | −2.1 | 100.0 | 764 |
| Larceny-theft by type: | Pocket-picking | 21,696 | −6.0 | 0.4 | 346 |
| | Purse-snatching | 31,214 | −5.2 | 0.6 | 377 |
| | Shoplifting | 698,233 | −5.3 | 13.9 | 163 |
| | From motor vehicles (except accessories) | 1,301,026 | −1.4 | 25.8 | 691 |
| | Motor vehicle accessories | 514,703 | −5.4 | 10.2 | 457 |
| | Bicycles | 184,722 | −2.3 | 3.7 | 268 |
| | From buildings | 632,933 | −0.7 | 12.6 | 1,155 |
| | From coin-operated machines | 30,356 | −10.5 | 0.6 | 233 |
| | All others | 1,621,665 | −0.4 | 32.2 | 1,106 |
| Larceny-theft by value: | Over $200 | 2,016,563 | +0.2 | 40.0 | 1,828 |
| | $50 to $200 | 1,130,650 | −2.6 | 22.4 | 111 |
| | Under $50 | 1,889,335 | −4.2 | 37.5 | 19 |
| Motor vehicle theft | | 973,451 | +0.2 | — | 6,173 |

*Because of rounding, the percentages may not add to 100.0.

SOURCE: Table 23. Offense Analysis, Number and Percent Change, 2004–2005, in *Crime in the United States, 2005*, U.S. Department of Justice, Federal Bureau of Investigation, September 2006, http://www.fbi.gov/ucr/05cius/data/table_23.html (accessed January 7, 2007)

**TABLE 1.16**

**Weapons used in aggravated assaults by region, 2005**

| Region | Total all weapons* | Firearms | Knives or cutting instruments | Other weapons (clubs, blunt objects, etc.) | Personal weapons (hands, fists, feet, etc.) |
|---|---|---|---|---|---|
| Total | 100.0 | 21.0 | 18.9 | 35.1 | 25.0 |
| Northeast | 100.0 | 15.6 | 20.4 | 33.3 | 30.7 |
| Midwest | 100.0 | 21.3 | 17.0 | 33.1 | 28.6 |
| South | 100.0 | 22.7 | 19.9 | 36.1 | 21.3 |
| West | 100.0 | 20.0 | 17.6 | 35.1 | 27.3 |

*Because of rounding, the percentages may not add to 100.0.

SOURCE: "Aggravated Assault Table: Aggravated Assault, Types of Weapons Used, Percent Distribution within Region, 2005," in *Crime in the United States, 2005*, U.S. Department of Justice, Federal Bureau of Investigation, September 2006, http://www.fbi.gov/ucr/05cius/offenses/expanded_information/data/agassaulttable.html (accessed January 8, 2007)

(See Table 1.6.) An analysis by race conducted with data from 10,971 reporting agencies in 2005 indicated that blacks represented 56.3% of those arrested for robbery, compared with 42.2% who were white. (See Table 1.7.)

**Aggravated Assault**

The FBI defines aggravated assault as "an unlawful attack by one person upon another for the purpose of inflicting severe or aggravated bodily injury.... This type of assault is usually accompanied by the use of a weapon or by other means likely to produce death or great bodily harm." In 2005, 862,947 offenses of aggravated assault were reported to law enforcement agencies nationwide. The 2005 aggravated assault rate, 291.1 per 100,000 inhabitants, showed an increase of 1.8% over 2004. In contrast, the rate of aggravated assault declined by 5.1% between 2001 and 2005 and by 16.8% between 1996 and 2005. (See Table 1.1.)

Metropolitan statistical areas reported a rate of aggravated assault of 308.6 per 100,000 people in 2005, compared with 273.2 per 100,000 in cities outside metropolitan areas and 162.2 per 100,000 in rural counties. (See Table 1.3.) Aggravated assault was more likely to occur in the South (44.2% of all cases), followed by the West (23.1%), the Midwest (18.8%), and the Northeast (13.9%). (See Table 1.10.)

WEAPONS USED. More than one-third (35.1%) of all aggravated assaults in 2005 were committed with such weapons as clubs or other blunt objects. Personal weapons—hands, fists, and feet—were used in 25% of the offenses, firearms in 21%, and knives or cutting instruments in 18.9%. By region, 22.7% of assaults were committed with firearms in Southern states, 21.3% in Midwestern states, 20% in Western states, and 15.6% in Northeastern states. (See Table 1.16.)

ARRESTS. According to FBI data, law enforcement agencies cleared an average of 55.2% of the reported cases of aggravated assault in 2005 (http://www.fbi.gov/ucr/05cius/offenses/clearances/index.html). Almost three-quarters (74.4%) of violent crime arrests (449,297 of 603,503) were for aggravated assault. (See Table 1.4.) Offenders under the age of eighteen made up 13.6% of all those arrested for aggravated assault. (See Table 1.5.) In an analysis of data from 8,009 reporting agencies, males comprised 79.5% of aggravated assault offenders (224,080 of 282,003; see Table 1.6.) Among those arrested for aggravated assault in 2005 by agencies that provided race information to the FBI, 63.3% were white, and 34.3% were black. (See Table 1.7.)

**Burglary**

The FBI defines burglary as "the unlawful entry of a structure to commit a felony or theft. To classify an offense as a burglary, the use of force to gain entry need not have occurred." An estimated 2.2 million burglaries were reported in 2005, up 0.5% from 2004. Burglaries in 2005 increased by 1.8% over 2001 but declined by 14.1% compared with 1996. (See Table 1.1.)

In 2005 the burglary rate was 726.7 per 100,000 persons, a 0.5% decrease from 2004. Burglary rates declined by 2% compared with the 2001 rate, and by 23.1% compared with the 1996 rate. (See Table 1.1.) The burglary rate in 2005 was highest in cities outside metropolitan areas (800.9 per 100,000 inhabitants), followed by metropolitan areas (743.7 per 100,000). Rural counties reported the lowest rate, at 542.3 per 100,000 population. (See Table 1.3.) The highest burglary volume was in the most populous region, the South, with 44.8% of total burglaries. Total burglary volume was lower in the West (24% of all burglaries) and Midwest (20.4%), and lowest in the Northeast (10.8%). (See Table 1.10.)

LOSSES. Of the 1.6 million burglaries reported in 2005, 65.8% were residential, and 34.2% involved other properties, such as stores and offices. The average value of items taken in burglaries was $1,725 per incident. Nonresidential losses from burglary averaged $1,683, compared with $1,745 for residential burglaries. (See Table 1.15.)

**ARRESTS.** Law officers cleared 12.7% of reported burglaries in 2005 through arrest. (See Table 1.13.) In 2005 juveniles under age eighteen accounted for 26.1% of all burglary arrests. (See Table 1.5.) Of those arrested for burglary by 10,971 agencies that reported race information, 69.6% were white, and 28.5% were black. (See Table 1.7.) In cases reported by agencies that provided information about the sex of offenders, about 85% (153,888 of 180,973) of those arrested for burglary in 2005 were males. (See Table 1.6.)

## Larceny-Theft

The FBI defines larceny-theft as "the unlawful taking, carrying, leading, or riding away of property from the possession . . . of another" in which no use of force or fraud occurs. This crime category includes offenses such as shoplifting, pocket-picking, purse-snatching, thefts from motor vehicles, bicycle thefts, and so on. It does not include embezzlement, con games, forgery, and passing bad checks. (See Figure 1.2.)

In 2005 law enforcement agencies reported 6.8 million larceny-theft offenses for a rate of 2,286.3 per 100,000 people. The rate of larceny-theft per 100,000 population declined by 3.2% between 2004 and 2005, by 8% between 2001 and 2005, and by 23.3% between 1996 and 2005. (See Table 1.1.)

The larceny-theft rate in 2005 was 3,001.8 per 100,000 inhabitants in cities outside metropolitan areas and 2,386.1 per 100,000 in metropolitan areas. Rural counties reported an average rate of 1,016.7 larceny-thefts per 100,000 residents. (See Table 1.3.) The South accounted for 41.3% of all larceny-theft offenses, followed by the West (23.7%), Midwest (21.9%), and Northeast (13.1%). (See Table 1.10.)

**LOSSES.** The average value of property stolen (excluding motor vehicles) in 2005 was $764. The average value of items stolen by pocket-picking was $346, while the average amount stolen by purse-snatching was $377. Shoplifting resulted in an average loss of $163. (See Table 1.15.)

**ARRESTS.** About 18% of larceny-thefts reported in 2005 were cleared by arrests (See Table 1.13.) Of those arrested for larceny-theft by 10,974 agencies nationwide, 25.7% were under eighteen years of age. (See Table 1.5.) Females were arrested more often for larceny-theft than for any other offense in 2005. In a ten-year analysis of arrest trends covering 8,009 agencies, females represented 39% of those arrested for larceny-theft (270,765 of 692,593). (See Table 1.6.) About two-thirds (69.3%) of those arrested for larceny-theft in 2005 were white, compared with 28% who were black, among those arrested by agencies that reported race information. (See Table 1.7.)

## Motor Vehicle Theft

The FBI defines motor vehicle theft as "the theft or attempted theft of a motor vehicle." In 2005 just over 1.2

FIGURE 1.2

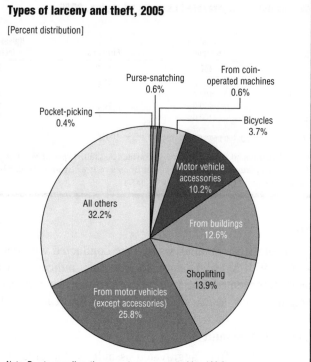

**Types of larceny and theft, 2005**

[Percent distribution]

Note: Due to rounding, the percentages may not add to 100.0.

SOURCE: "Larceny-Theft Figure, Percent Distribution, 2005," in *Crime in the United States, 2005*, U.S. Department of Justice, Federal Bureau of Investigation, September 2006, http://www.fbi.gov/ucr/05cius/offenses/property_crime/larceny-theft.html (accessed January 8, 2007)

million cases of auto theft were reported in the United States. The number of motor vehicle thefts in 2005 decreased by 0.2% from 2004. The rate of motor vehicle thefts was 416.7 per 100,000 inhabitants, down by 1.1% from 2004, 3.2% from 2001, and 20.7% from 1996. (See Table 1.1.)

In 2005 the highest rate of motor vehicle theft occurred in metropolitan areas (469.1 per 100,000 population). In cities outside metropolitan areas, the motor vehicle theft rate was 195.4 per 100,000 inhabitants, while rural counties had a rate of 141 per 100,000 population. (See Table 1.3.) The West accounted for 37.9% of vehicle thefts, followed by the South (33.4%), the Midwest (18.3%), and the Northeast (10.5%). (See Table 1.10.)

**LOSSES.** Total property losses due to motor vehicle theft in 2005 were $7.6 billion, or an average of $6,173 per stolen vehicle (http://www.fbi.gov/ucr/05cius/offenses/property_crime/motor_vehicle_theft.html).

**TYPES OF VEHICLES STOLEN.** Automobiles were the most frequently stolen vehicle in 2005, representing 73.4% of motor vehicle thefts, as reported by the FBI in *Crime in the United States, 2005*. The Highway Loss Data Institute lists the make and series of cars for which the most theft claims are made. In mid-2006, the most frequent passenger vehicle theft claims among 2003–05 models were for the Cadillac Escalade, Mitsubishi Lancer Evolution, and Dodge Ram 1500 quad cab pickup (http://www.iihs.org/news/rss/pr060706.html).

ARRESTS. In 2005 law enforcement agencies reported that 13% of motor vehicle thefts were cleared by arrest. (See Table 1.13.) Of those arrested by 8,009 agencies nationwide, 82.2% (67,522 of 82,160) were male. (See Table 1.6.) In an analysis of data from 10,974 agencies, some 58.2% of persons arrested for motor vehicle theft in 2005 were under twenty-five years of age, and 25.5% were under age eighteen. (See Table 1.5.) Of those arrested by agencies that reported race information, 62.8% were white, and 34.8% were black. (See Table 1.7.)

## Arson

The FBI defines arson as "any willful or malicious burning or attempt to burn, with or without intent to defraud, a dwelling house, public building, motor vehicle or aircraft, personal property of another, etc." Arson statistics do not include fires of suspicious or unknown origins that are not known for certain to be arson. In 2005, 67,504 arson offenses were reported by 13,868 law enforcement agencies nationwide that provided arson data to the FBI (http://www.fbi.gov/ucr/05cius/offenses/property_crime/arson.html).

RATE. The FBI reported that the rate of arson in the United States in 2005 was 26.9 offenses per 100,000 people nationwide. The arson rate was highest in cities with a population of 250,000 to 499,999, at 50.7 per 100,000 inhabitants, while cities with 10,000 to 24,999 inhabitants had the lowest rate (18.3 per 100,000 population). Overall, cities reported an arson rate of 29.7 per 100,000 inhabitants in 2005, while metropolitan counties reported a rate of 22.8, suburban counties reported an arson rate of 20.9, and rural counties reported 17.2 arsons per 100,000 people. (See Table 1.17.)

WHAT IS BEING BURNED? In *Crime in the United States, 2005* the FBI reports that structural arson accounted for 43.6% of all arson offenses, or 25,952 reported incidents that year. Residential property was involved in 26.9% of arsons in 2005, including 19.3% single occupancy residential and 7.6% other residential. Mobile property (including motor vehicles) was involved in 29% of all arson incidents in 2005.

ARRESTS. About 17.9% of all reported arsons were cleared by arrest in 2005. The highest clearance rate for arson, 27%, occurred in cities with less than 10,000 inhabitants, while the lowest clearance rate, 8.9%, was in cities of one million or more inhabitants. Metropolitan counties overall had a clearance rate of 18%, while rural counties reported a 24.7% clearance by arrest. (See Table 1.13.) In 2005 juveniles under the age of eighteen accounted for almost half (48.6%) of all arson arrests reported by nearly

**TABLE 1.17**

**Arson rate by population group, 2005**

| Population group | Rate |
|---|---|
| **Total** | **26.9** |
| **Total cities** | 29.7 |
| Group I (cities 250,000 and over) | 46.3 |
| (Cities 1,000,000 and over) | 44.0 |
| (Cities 500,000 to 999,999) | 45.1 |
| (Cities 250,000 to 499,999) | 50.7 |
| Group II (cities 100,000 to 249,999) | 30.2 |
| Group III (cities 50,000 to 99,999) | 24.0 |
| Group IV (cities 25,000 to 49,999) | 22.6 |
| Group V (cities 10,000 to 24,999) | 18.3 |
| Group VI (cities under 10,000) | 21.4 |
| Metropolitan counties | 22.8 |
| Nonmetropolitan counties | 17.2 |
| Suburban area* | 20.9 |

*Suburban area includes law enforcement agencies in cities with less than 50,000 inhabitants and county law enforcement agencies that are within a metropolitan statistical area. Suburban area excludes all metropolitan agencies associated with a principal city. The agencies associated with suburban areas also appear in other groups within this table.

SOURCE: "Arson Table 1. Arson Rate, by Population Group, 2005," in *Crime in the United States, 2005*, U.S. Department of Justice, Federal Bureau of Investigation, September 2006, http://www.fbi.gov/ucr/05cius/offenses/expanded_information/data/arsontable_01.html (accessed January 24, 2007)

11,000 U.S. law enforcement agencies; almost two-thirds of those arrested (66.3%) were under age twenty-five. (See Table 1.5.) Most people arrested for arson in 2005 were male (83.5%; 8,114 of 9,716), according to data gathered from 8,009 agencies, and more than seven out of ten (76.6%) were white, based on data from agencies that reported on race. (See Table 1.6 and Table 1.7.)

## GUNS AND CRIME

In an analysis of data from the 1994 Injury Control and Risk Survey, R. M. Ikeda and colleagues found that 27.9% of respondents reported that they had a firearm in the household and had ready access to it. An additional 8.1% had a firearm but could not access it. Although 7.2% did not have a firearm in or around their home, they were able to retrieve and fire one within ten minutes ("Studying 'Exposure' to Firearms: Household Ownership *v* Access," *Injury Prevention*, March 2003, http://ip.bmj.com/cgi/content/full/9/1/53).

In 2005, of the 14,860 weapons used to commit murder, 10,100 were firearms, according to FBI data reported in *Crime in the United States, 2005*. Of those firearms, 7,543 were handguns. Among murders in which firearms were used, 74.7% of the firearms were handguns, 5.1% were shotguns, and 4.8% were rifles.

### Crimes Committed with Firearms

From 1973 to 1993 the number of violent offenses (murders, robberies, and aggravated assaults) committed with firearms increased 61%, from 361,141 to 581,697.

TABLE 1.18

**Crimes committed with firearms, 1973–2005**

| Year | Total firearm crimes | | Murders with firearms | | Robberies with firearms | | Aggravated assaults firearms | |
|------|--------|------|--------|------|--------|------|--------|------|
| | Number | Rate | Number | Rate | Number | Rate | Number | Rate |
| 1973 | 361,141 | 172.1 | 13,072 | 6.2 | 241,088 | 114.9 | 106,981 | 51.0 |
| 1974 | 326,235 | 154.3 | 13,987 | 6.6 | 197,257 | 93.3 | 114,991 | 54.4 |
| 1975 | 342,495 | 160.7 | 13,496 | 6.3 | 208,307 | 97.7 | 120,693 | 56.6 |
| 1976 | 307,252 | 143.1 | 11,982 | 5.6 | 179,430 | 83.6 | 115,841 | 54.0 |
| 1977 | 301,590 | 139.4 | 11,950 | 5.5 | 168,418 | 77.9 | 121,222 | 56.0 |
| 1978 | 307,603 | 141.1 | 12,437 | 5.7 | 170,152 | 78.0 | 125,015 | 57.3 |
| 1979 | 340,202 | 154.6 | 13,582 | 6.2 | 185,352 | 84.2 | 141,269 | 64.2 |
| 1980 | 392,083 | 174.0 | 14,377 | 6.4 | 221,170 | 98.1 | 156,535 | 69.5 |
| 1981 | 396,197 | 172.9 | 14,052 | 6.1 | 230,226 | 100.5 | 151,918 | 66.3 |
| 1982 | 372,477 | 160.9 | 12,648 | 5.5 | 214,219 | 92.5 | 145,609 | 62.9 |
| 1983 | 330,419 | 141.2 | 11,258 | 4.8 | 183,581 | 78.5 | 135,580 | 57.9 |
| 1984 | 329,232 | 139.4 | 10,990 | 4.7 | 173,634 | 73.5 | 144,609 | 61.2 |
| 1985 | 340,942 | 142.8 | 11,141 | 4.7 | 175,748 | 73.6 | 154,052 | 64.5 |
| 1986 | 376,064 | 156.0 | 12,181 | 5.1 | 186,174 | 77.2 | 177,710 | 73.7 |
| 1987 | 365,709 | 150.3 | 11,879 | 4.9 | 170,841 | 70.2 | 182,989 | 75.2 |
| 1988 | 385,934 | 157.0 | 12,553 | 5.1 | 181,352 | 73.8 | 192,029 | 78.1 |
| 1989 | 410,039 | 165.2 | 13,416 | 5.4 | 192,006 | 77.3 | 204,618 | 82.4 |
| 1990 | 492,671 | 198.1 | 15,025 | 6.0 | 233,973 | 94.1 | 243,673 | 98.0 |
| 1991 | 548,667 | 217.6 | 16,376 | 6.5 | 274,404 | 108.8 | 257,887 | 102.3 |
| 1992 | 565,575 | 221.7 | 16,204 | 6.4 | 271,009 | 106.2 | 278,362 | 109.1 |
| 1993 | 581,697 | 225.5 | 17,048 | 6.6 | 279,738 | 108.5 | 284,910 | 110.5 |
| 1994 | 542,529 | 208.4 | 16,314 | 6.3 | 257,428 | 98.9 | 268,788 | 103.2 |
| 1995 | 504,421 | 192.0 | 14,686 | 5.6 | 238,023 | 90.6 | 251,712 | 95.8 |
| 1996 | 458,458 | 172.8 | 13,319 | 5.0 | 218,579 | 82.4 | 226,559 | 85.4 |
| 1997 | 414,530 | 154.9 | 12,346 | 4.6 | 197,686 | 73.9 | 204,498 | 76.4 |
| 1998 | 364,776 | 135.0 | 10,977 | 4.1 | 170,611 | 63.1 | 183,188 | 67.8 |
| 1999 | 338,535 | 124.1 | 10,128 | 3.7 | 163,458 | 59.9 | 164,949 | 60.5 |
| 2000 | 341,831 | 121.5 | 10,179 | 3.6 | 166,807 | 59.3 | 164,845 | 58.6 |
| 2001 | 354,754 | 124.3 | 11,106 | 3.9 | 177,627 | 62.3 | 166,021 | 58.2 |
| 2002 | 357,822 | 124.3 | 10,808 | 3.8 | 177,088 | 61.5 | 169,926 | 59.0 |
| 2003 | 347,705 | 119.6 | 11,041 | 3.8 | 172,802 | 59.4 | 163,863 | 56.3 |
| 2004 | 338,587 | 115.3 | 10,650 | 3.6 | 162,938 | 55.5 | 164,998 | 56.2 |
| 2005 | 368,178 | 124.2 | 11,351 | 3.8 | 175,608 | 59.2 | 181,219 | 61.1 |

SOURCE: "Crimes Committed with Firearms, 1973–2005," in *Key Facts at a Glance*, U.S. Department of Justice, Office of Justice Programs, Bureau of Justice Statistics, 2006, http://www.ojp.usdoj.gov/bjs/glance/tables/guncrimetab.htm (accessed January 24, 2007)

However, from 1993 to 2005, the total number of violent crimes committed with firearms decreased by 36.7%, from 581,697 to 368,178. (See Table 1.18.)

According to Caroline Wolf Harlow in *Firearm Use by Offenders* (Bureau of Justice Statistics, November 2001, http://www.ojp.usdoj.gov/bjs/pub/pdf/fuo.pdf), some 18% of state prisoners and 15% of federal prisoners in 1997 reported that they carried a firearm at the time of their offenses. Of those, 9% of state prisoners and 2% of federal prisoners in 1997 said that they fired a gun during the commission of the offense for which they were incarcerated. Most (83% of state prisoners and 87% of federal prisoners) reported carrying a handgun.

Harlow reports that crimes committed with firearms often carry a higher penalty. About 40% of all state prisoners and 56% of all federal prisoners in the study who used firearms were given more severe sentences than prisoners who committed similar crimes without using a firearm. On average, state inmates who used a firearm received a sentence of eighteen years in prison, while those who committed similar crimes without firearms received twelve years.

### Firearm-Related Deaths

The rate per 100,000 people of crimes involving firearms in the United States increased from 172.1 in 1973 to 225.5 in 1993. (See Table 1.18.) In 1994, the overall firearm crime rate began dropping and was 124.2 per 100,000 in 2005. The national rate of homicides with firearms remained relatively stable from 1973 to 1994, increasing from 6.2 to 6.3 per 100,000. However, starting in 1995 the rate of homicides with firearms began dropping; in 2005, the national rate was 3.8 per 100,000 people. The FBI reported that 9% of the 4.7 million violent crimes committed in 2005 involved a firearm.

According to the Johns Hopkins University Center for Gun Policy and Research, there were 29,573 gun-related deaths in the United States in 2001, or about eighty deaths a day ("Factsheet: Firearm Injury and Death in the United States," 2004, http://www.jhsph.edu/gunpolicy/US_factsheet_2004.pdf). Of these deaths, 57% (16,869) were suicides, 38% (11,348) were homicides, and about 3% (802) were unintentional. Between 1993 and 2001, the number of gun-related deaths decreased by 25%.

## Background Checks for Firearms

According to the Brady Handgun Violence Prevention Act (P.L. 103–159, 1993), criminal history background checks must be conducted on anyone who applies to purchase a firearm from a licensed firearm dealer. The Bureau of Justice Statistics reports that background checks were conducted on 8.3 million applications for firearm transfers or permits in 2005 under the Brady Act and similar state laws. This represents a 2.4% increase from 8.1 million applications in 2004. Of the 2005 applications, 60% (five million) were processed by the FBI and 40% (3.3 million) were processed by state and local agencies. Of the 8.3 million applications, 1.6% were rejected by the FBI or state and local agencies; 46% of these rejections were due to a felony conviction or indictment, and 15% were due to a domestic violence misdemeanor conviction or restraining order (Michael Bowling et al., *Background Checks for Firearm Transfers, 2005*, November 2006, http://www.ojp.usdoj.gov/bjs/pub/pdf/bcft05.pdf).

# CHAPTER 2
# VICTIMS OF CRIME

## THE TRAUMA OF BEING VICTIMIZED

Becoming a crime victim can have serious consequences—outcomes the victim neither asks for nor deserves. Victims rarely expect to be victimized and seldom know where to turn for help. Victims may end up in the hospital to be treated and released, or they may be confined to bed for days, weeks, or longer. Injuries may be temporary, or they may be permanent and change forever the way the victims live. Victims may lose money or property, or they may even lose their lives—the ultimate cost for which victims and their families can never be repaid.

The effects of crime are not limited to the victims. Relatives of victims may also experience feelings of fear, anger, shame, self-blame, helplessness, and depression—emotions that can taint life and health for years after the event. Those who have been attacked in their homes or whose homes have been entered may no longer feel secure anywhere. They often blame themselves, feeling that they could have handled themselves better or done something differently to prevent being victimized.

In the aftermath of crime, when victims most need support and comfort, no one may be available who understands what victims have been through. Parents or spouses may be dealing with their own feelings of anger or guilt for not being able to protect their loved ones. Friends may withdraw, not knowing what to say or do. As a result, victims may experience a loss of self-esteem or may find it difficult to trust other people.

## FEAR OF BECOMING A VICTIM

The fear of becoming a victim is often much greater than the likelihood of being one. Fear of crime has permeated American society so completely that it plays a role in many people's daily lives. In 2006 despite a steadily declining crime trend, 51% of respondents to a Gallup Poll thought there was more crime in their area than

the year before, and 68% thought there was more crime in the United States as a whole (http://www.galluppoll.com/content/default.aspx?ci=1603). More than half of those surveyed thought that crime was either a very serious or extremely serious problem.

The crime that Americans were most frequently worried about was having their home burglarized when they are not there; 50% of respondents in 2006 said that they worried about this either frequently or occasionally. Those who were polled also expressed concerns about having their car stolen or broken into (47%), being a victim of terrorism (44%), and having their school-aged children physically harmed at school (40%). A higher percentage of the public expressed concern in 2006 than in previous years about the possibility that their children would be harmed at school. The percentages of those worried about burglary while people were home and about terrorism also increased substantially in 2006 over previous years.

## THE NATIONAL CRIME VICTIMIZATION SURVEY

In 1972 the Law Enforcement Assistance Administration established the National Crime Victimization Survey (NCVS). This annual federal statistical study measures the levels of victimization resulting from criminal activity in the United States. The survey was previously known as the National Crime Survey, but it was renamed in 1991 to emphasize the measurement of victimization experienced by citizens. Each year the NCVS collects data from a nationally representative sample of 77,200 households representing nearly 134,000 people on the frequency, characteristics, and consequences of criminal victimization in the United States.

The survey was created because of a concern that the Uniform Crime Reports (UCR) issued by the Federal Bureau of Investigation (FBI) did not fully portray the true volume of crime. The UCR provides data on crimes reported to law enforcement authorities, but it does not estimate how many crimes go unreported.

The National Crime Victimization Survey is sponsored by the Bureau of Justice Statistics (BJS) and is designed to complement the Uniform Crime Reports. It measures the levels of criminal victimization of persons and households for the crimes of rape, robbery, assault, burglary, motor vehicle theft, and larceny. Murder is not included because NCVS data are gathered through interviews with victims. Definitions for these crimes are the same as those established by the FBI in the Uniform Crime Reports.

Many observers believe that the National Crime Victimization Survey is a better indicator of the volume of crime in the United States than the FBI statistics. Nonetheless, like all surveys, it is subject to error. The survey depends on people's memories of incidents that happened up to six months earlier. Many times, a victim is not sure what happened, even moments after the crime occurred.

Errors can come from other factors as well. Individuals who have been repeatedly victimized—by spousal or parental abuse, for example—may not remember individual incidents or may remember only the most recent event. In addition, the NCVS data show that a disproportionately large number of incidents occurred at the end of the time period covered by the survey when the victim's memory was perhaps fresher. Furthermore, the NCVS only collects data from victims aged twelve and older—an admittedly arbitrary age selection. Despite these factors, however, the Bureau of Justice Statistics claims a 90% to 95% confidence level in the data reported in the NCVS.

The National Crime Victimization Survey and the FBI's Uniform Crime Reports are generally considered the primary sources of statistical information on crime in the United States. Like all reporting systems, both have their shortcomings, but each provides valuable insights into crime in the United States. Over the years, some significant differences have occurred in their findings. For example, the UCR documented a 15% increase in crime from 1982 to 1991, while the NCVS reported a leveling off and, in 1990, a decrease in crime. These differences require the reader to evaluate both sets of statistics carefully, not relying solely on one or the other.

### Redesigned Survey

Beginning in 1979 the NCVS underwent a thorough, decade-long redesign. The new design was intended to improve the survey's ability to measure victimization in general and particularly difficult-to-measure crimes, such as rape, sexual assault, and domestic violence. Improvements included the introduction of "short cues" or techniques to jog respondents' memories of events. In general, as

anticipated, the redesign resulted in an increased number of crimes counted by the survey. Therefore, pre-1992 data cannot be directly compared with the later data.

### A GENERAL DOWNTURN IN CRIME

From 1993 to 2005 the NCVS found that the rate of violent crime fell 57.6%. During this period, the violent victimization rate dropped 57.6%, the personal theft rate fell by 59.6%, and the rate of rape and sexual assault plummeted by 68.6%. Property crime rates also fell, by 51.7%, between 1993 and 2005. Specifically, household burglary rates fell by 49.3%, motor vehicle thefts dropped by 56%, and there were 51.9% fewer thefts. (See Table 2.1.)

### HOW MANY VICTIMIZATIONS IN 2005?

The National Crime Victimization Survey shows that in 2005 U.S. residents aged twelve and older were the victims of approximately 23.4 million crimes. About eighteen million were property crimes, and 5.4 million were personal crimes. The 5.4 million personal crimes in 2005 included 1.7 million completed acts of violence and 3.5 million acts of attempted violence. (See Table 2.2.)

#### Victims of Violent Crimes

Victimization rates in 2005 were 22.1 per 1,000 population for personal crime and 154 per 1,000 households for property crime. Among violent crimes, the victimization rate was highest (17.8 per 1,000 population) for assault, followed by attempted or threatened violence (14.4 per 1,000) and simple assault without injury (10.3 per 1,000). (See Table 2.2.)

According to the Bureau of Justice Statistics in *Criminal Victimization in the United States, 2005 Statistical Tables* (http://www.ojp.usdoj.gov/bjs/abstract/cvusst.htm) violent crime rates for all age groups fell between 1973 and 2005. Rates rose from 1986 to 1991 for people under age twenty-five but have decreased steadily and significantly since the early 1990s. In contrast, violent crime victimization rates have dropped only slightly for those aged fifty and older. For people aged twenty-five to forty-nine, rates of violent crime remained relatively stable from 1973 to the mid-1990s and have declined steadily since then (See Figure 2.1.)

#### Victims of Property Crimes

In 2005 property crimes accounted for about 77% of all victimizations. Respondents to the NCVS reported eighteen million property crimes, including 13.6 million thefts, 3.5 million household burglaries, and 978,120 motor vehicle thefts. Among property crimes, the highest victimization rate was for theft (116.2 per 1,000 households), followed by household burglary (29.5 per 1,000

TABLE 2.1

## Rates of criminal victimization and percent change, 1993 and 2005

[Per 1,000 persons age 12 or older per 1,000 households]

| Type of crime | Victimization rates | | Percent change[a] 1993–2005 |
|---|---|---|---|
| | 1993 | 2005 | |
| **Personal crimes[b]** | 52.2 | 22.1 | −57.7% |
| Crimes of violence | 49.9 | 21.2 | −57.6 |
|   Completed violence[c] | 15.0 | 6.8 | −54.8 |
|   Attempted/threatened violence | 34.9 | 14.4 | −58.8 |
|   Rape/sexual assault | 2.5 | 0.8 | −68.6 |
|     Rape/attempted rape | 1.6 | 0.5 | −66.7 |
|       Rape | 1.0 | 0.3 | −71.6 |
|       Attempted rape | 0.7 | 0.2 | −64.5 |
|     Sexual assault | 0.8 | 0.3 | −68.5 |
|   Robbery | 6.0 | 2.6 | −57.4 |
|     Completed/property taken | 3.8 | 1.7 | −55.3 |
|       With injury | 1.3 | 0.6 | −55.1 |
|       Without injury | 2.5 | 1.1 | −55.4 |
|     Attempted to take property | 2.2 | 0.9 | −61.0 |
|       With injury | 0.4 | 0.3 | −34.1 |
|       Without injury | 1.8 | 0.6 | −67.0 |
|   Assault | 41.4 | 17.8 | −57.0 |
|     Aggravated | 12.0 | 4.3 | −64.1 |
|       With injury | 3.4 | 1.4 | −60.3 |
|       Threatened with weapon | 8.6 | 3.0 | −65.7 |
|     Simple | 29.4 | 13.5 | −54.0 |
|       With minor injury | 6.1 | 3.3 | −46.7 |
|       Without injury | 23.3 | 10.3 | −55.9 |
| Personal theft[d] | 2.3 | 0.9 | −59.6 |
| **Property crimes** | 318.9 | 154.0 | −51.7% |
| Household burglary | 58.2 | 29.5 | −49.3 |
|   Completed | 47.2 | 24.8 | −47.5 |
|     Forcible entry | 18.1 | 9.1 | −49.6 |
|     Unlawful entry without force | 29.1 | 15.6 | −46.2 |
|   Attempted forcible entry | 10.9 | 4.7 | −56.5 |
| Motor vehicle theft | 19.0 | 8.4 | −56.0 |
|   Completed | 12.4 | 6.6 | −46.7 |
|   Attempted | 6.6 | 1.7 | −73.7 |
| Theft | 241.7 | 116.2 | −51.9 |
|   Completed[e] | 230.1 | 112.0 | −51.3 |
|     Less than $50 | 98.7 | 34.8 | −64.7 |
|     $50–$249 | 76.1 | 39.8 | −47.8 |
|     $250 or more | 41.6 | 27.6 | −33.7 |
|   Attempted | 11.6 | 4.2 | −64.0 |

Note: In 1993 the total population age 12 or older was 211,524,770; and 244,493,430 in 2005. The total number of households in 1993 was 99,927,410; and 117,110,800 in 2005.

[a]Differences between the annual rates shown do not take into account changes that may have occurred during interim years.

[b]The National Crime Victimization Survey is based on interviews with victims and therefore cannot measure murder.

[c]Completed violent crimes include rape, sexual assault, robbery with or without injury, aggravated assault with injury, and simple assault with minor injury.

[d]Includes pocket picking, completed purse snatching, and attempted purse snatching.

[e]Includes theft with unknown losses.

SOURCE: Shannan M. Catalano, "Table 3. Rates of Criminal Victimization and Percent Change, 1993 and 2005," in *Criminal Victimization, 2005*, U.S. Department of Justice, Office of Justice Programs, Bureau of Justice Statistics, September 2006, http://www.ojp.usdoj.gov/bjs/pub/pdf/cv05.pdf (accessed January 9, 2007)

households) and motor vehicle theft (8.4 per 1,000 households). (See Table 2.2.)

In 2005 about 58% of all reported crimes were thefts. Of the 13.1 million completed thefts, 4 million involved property worth less than $50. Another 4.7 million involved items valued between $50 and $249, and 3.2 million thefts were of property worth $250 or more. The value of the losses from the remaining thefts was unknown. (See Table 2.2.)

## REPORTING CRIME TO POLICE

According to the Bureau of Justice Statistics in *Criminal Victimization in the United States, 2005 Statistical Tables*, less than half of all violent crimes (47.4%) committed in 2005 were reported to the police. Black, Hispanic, and white women were more likely than men to report crimes of violence. White female victims reported 53.9% of the violent crimes that they experienced, but white male victims reported only 42.8%. The difference in reporting rates was even greater for African-Americans; African-American female victims reported 58.3% of the violent crimes they experienced, compared with 41.5% of violent crimes reported by African-American males. Similarly, Hispanic females reported 60.3% of the violent crimes against them, compared with 43.5% reported by Hispanic males. (See Table 2.3.)

Victims in 2005 reported 39.6% of the property crimes they experienced to the police. Similar rates of males and females reported these crimes. For example, 38.8% of white females reported property crimes, compared with 39.6% of crimes reported by white males. The rates for African-Americans were 44.7% for females and 44% for males, and 36.8% for Hispanic females compared with 37.8% for Hispanic males.

### Reasons for Reporting and Not Reporting Crimes

In *Reporting Crime to the Police, 1992–2000* (Bureau of Justice Statistics, March 2003, http://www.ojp.usdoj.gov/bjs/pub/pdf/rcp00.pdf) Timothy C. Hart and Callie Rennison indicate that a higher percentage of violent crimes were reported to the police than property crimes in 2000. Violence against females was more likely to be reported than violence against males. Similarly, violence against older persons was more likely to be reported than violence against younger persons. Victims were more likely to report a violent crime to the police if the offender had a weapon or was under the influence of drugs or alcohol.

In 2000 victims reported violent crimes more often than property crimes to prevent future violence, stop the offender from hurting others, or protect other people. The main reasons why some violent crimes were not reported were that victims perceived the crimes as a private or personal matter, the crime did not seem important enough to report, or the victims had reported the crime to an official other than the police.

## CHARACTERISTICS OF VICTIMS
### Gender

White males are more likely than white females to be victims of every category of violent crime, except rape/

**TABLE 2.2**

**Number of personal and property crimes, 2005**

| Type of crime | Number of victimizations | Percent of all victimizations | Rate per 1,000 persons or households |
|---|---|---|---|
| **All crimes** | **23,440,720** | **100.0%** | — |
| **Personal crimes** | 5,400,790 | 23.0% | 22.1 |
| Crimes of violence | 5,173,720 | 22.1 | 21.2 |
|   Completed violence | 1,658,660 | 7.1 | 6.8 |
|   Attempted/threatened violence | 3,515,060 | 15.0 | 14.4 |
|   Rape/sexual assault | 191,670 | 0.8 | 0.8 |
|     Rape/attempted rape | 130,140 | 0.6 | 0.5 |
|       Rape | 69,370 | 0.3 | 0.3 |
|       Attempted rape[a] | 60,770 | 0.3 | 0.2 |
|     Sexual assault[b] | 61,530 | 0.3 | 0.3 |
|   Robbery | 624,850 | 2.7 | 2.6 |
|     Completed/property taken | 415,320 | 1.8 | 1.7 |
|       With injury | 142,830 | 0.6 | 0.6 |
|       Without injury | 272,490 | 1.2 | 1.1 |
|     Attempted to take property | 209,530 | 0.9 | 0.9 |
|       With injury | 64,450 | 0.3 | 0.3 |
|       Without injury | 145,090 | 0.6 | 0.6 |
|   Assault | 4,357,190 | 18.6 | 17.8 |
|     Aggravated | 1,052,260 | 4.5 | 4.3 |
|       With injury | 330,730 | 1.4 | 1.4 |
|       Threatened with weapon | 721,530 | 3.1 | 3.0 |
|     Simple | 3,304,930 | 14.1 | 13.5 |
|       With minor injury | 795,240 | 3.4 | 3.3 |
|       Without injury | 2,509,690 | 10.7 | 10.3 |
| Purse snatching/pocket picking | 227,070 | 1.0 | 0.9 |
|   Completed purse snatching | 43,550 | 0.2 | 0.2 |
|   Attempted purse snatching | 3,260* | 0.0* | 0.0* |
|   Pocket picking | 180,260 | 0.8 | 0.7 |
| Total population age 12 and over | 244,493,430 | — | — |
| **Property crimes** | 18,039,930 | 77.0% | 154.0 |
| Household burglary | 3,456,220 | 14.7 | 29.5 |
|   Completed | 2,900,460 | 12.4 | 24.8 |
|     Forcible entry | 1,068,430 | 4.6 | 9.1 |
|     Unlawful entry without force | 1,832,030 | 7.8 | 15.6 |
|   Attempted forcible entry | 555,760 | 2.4 | 4.7 |
| Motor vehicle theft | 978,120 | 4.2 | 8.4 |
|   Completed | 774,650 | 3.3 | 6.6 |
|   Attempted | 203,470 | 0.9 | 1.7 |
| Theft | 13,605,590 | 58.0 | 116.2 |
|   Completed | 13,116,270 | 56.0 | 112.0 |
|     Less than $50 | 4,079,120 | 17.4 | 34.8 |
|     $50–$249 | 4,656,120 | 19.9 | 39.8 |
|     $250 or more | 3,231,440 | 13.8 | 27.6 |
|     Amount not available | 1,149,590 | 4.9 | 9.8 |
|   Attempted | 489,320 | 2.1 | 4.2 |
| **Total number of households** | **117,110,800** | — | — |

Note: Detail may not add to total shown because of rounding.
*Estimate is based on about 10 or fewer sample cases.
Percent distribution is based on unrounded figures.
—Not applicable.
[a]Includes verbal threats of rape.
[b]Includes threats.

SOURCE: "Table 1. Personal and Property Crimes, 2005: Number, Percent Distribution, and Rate of Victimizations, by Type of Crime," in *Criminal Victimization in the United States, 2005 Statistical Tables*, U.S. Department of Justice, Office of Justice Programs, Bureau of Justice Statistics, December 2006, http://www.ojp.usdoj.gov/bjs/pub/pdf/cvus05.pdf (accessed January 9, 2007)

sexual assault, according to the Bureau of Justice Statistics in *Criminal Victimization in the United States, 2005 Statistical Tables*. African-American males are also more likely to be victims of violent crime than African-American females. In 2005, 24.6 of every 1,000 white males were victimized by violent crime, compared with 15.6 per 1,000 white females. For African-American males the rate was 31.6 per 1,000, compared with 23.2 per 1,000 African-American females. (See Table 2.4.)

## Age

Although teenagers and young adults are more likely than older persons to be victims of violent crime, the rates for all age groups have been falling over the last

FIGURE 2.1

**Violent crime rates by age of victim, 1973–2005**

[Per 1,000 persons in age group]

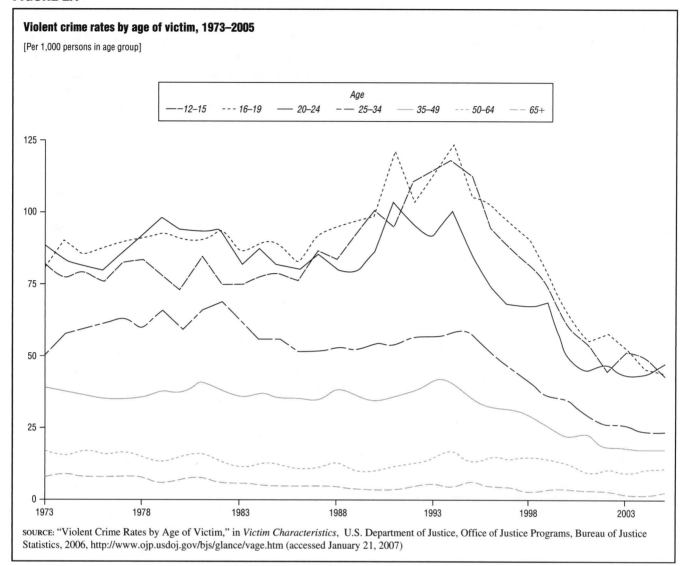

SOURCE: "Violent Crime Rates by Age of Victim," in *Victim Characteristics*, U.S. Department of Justice, Office of Justice Programs, Bureau of Justice Statistics, 2006, http://www.ojp.usdoj.gov/bjs/glance/vage.htm (accessed January 21, 2007)

three decades. In 2005 the victimization rate among 12- to 15-year-olds was 44 victims per 1,000 teens; the rate for 16- to 19-year-olds was 44.2 per 1,000 in that age group, and the rate for 20- to 24-year-olds was 46.9 per 1,000 (http://www.ojp.usdoj.gov/bjs/pub/pdf/cvus/current /cv0503.pdf). The rates for victims aged 12 to 15 and 16 to 19 in 2005 were the lowest recorded since 1973; the rate for young adults aged 20 to 24 increased slightly between 2003 and 2005. By contrast, only 2.4 of 1,000 people 65 or older were victims of violent crime in 2005; this rate has increased slightly since its lowest point of 2 per 1,000 in 2003.

According the Office of Juvenile Justice and Delinquency Prevention, youth in single-parent families experience more violence than those in two-parent families (*Juvenile Offenders and Victims: 2006 National Report*, March 2006). They are also more likely to be victims of violent crime if they live in a disadvantaged community (with many people living in poverty, many single-parent families, high unemployment, and many households receiving public assistance).

**Race and Ethnicity**

The Bureau of Justice Statistics reports in *Criminal Victimization in the United States, 2005 Statistical Tables* that in 2005 African-Americans were more likely than whites or persons of other races to be victims of most types of violent crime. (See Table 2.4.) For example, 31.6 of every 1,000 African-American males were victims of violent crimes, compared with 24.6 of every 1,000 white males. Similarly, 23.2 per 1,000 African-American females were victimized by violent crime, compared with 15.6 per 1,000 white women.

Further, Table 2.4 also shows that African-American males were more than twice as likely to be victims of completed violence (15.8 per 1,000 African-American males compared with 7.1 per 1,000 white males), robbery (7.3 per 1,000 African-American males compared with

TABLE 2.3

**Percent of victimizations reported to police, by type of crime, gender, and race or ethnicity of victims, 2005**

| Characteristic | Percent of all victimizations reported to the police | |
| --- | --- | --- |
| | Crimes of violence[a] | Property crimes |
| **Total** | **47.4%** | **39.6%** |
| **Male** | | |
| White only | 42.8 | 39.6 |
| Black only | 41.5 | 44.0 |
| Other race only[b] | 49.0 | 37.2 |
| Two or more races[c] | 25.9* | 42.1 |
| **Female** | | |
| White only | 53.9 | 38.8 |
| Black only | 58.3 | 44.7 |
| Other race only[b] | 58.1 | 30.2 |
| Two or more races[c] | 49.3 | 31.6 |
| **Male** | | |
| Hispanic | 43.5 | 37.8 |
| Non-Hispanic | 42.3 | 40.3 |
| **Female** | | |
| Hispanic | 60.3 | 36.8 |
| Non-Hispanic | 53.5 | 39.6 |

*Estimate is based on about 10 or fewer sample cases. Excludes data on persons whose ethnicity was not ascertained.
[a]Includes data on rape and sexual assault, not shown separately.
[b]Includes American Indian, Eskimo, Asian Pacific Islander if only one of these races is given.
[c]Includes all persons of any race, indicating two or more races.

SOURCE: "Table 91b. Violent Crimes, 2005: Percent of Victimizations Reported to the Police, by Type of Crime and Gender and Race or Ethnicity of Victims," in *Criminal Victimization in the United States, 2005 Statistical Tables*, U.S. Department of Justice, Office of Justice Programs, Bureau of Justice Statistics, December 2006, http://www.ojp.usdoj.gov/bjs/pub/pdf/cvus05.pdf (accessed January 9, 2007)

3.3 per 1,000 white males), and aggravated assault (9.1 per 1,000 African-American males compared with 5.3 per 1,000 white males). However, they were less likely than white males to be victims of attempts to take property (0.4 per 1,000 African-American males compared with 1.7 per 1,000 white males), attempted or threatened violence (15.7 per 1,000 African-American males compared with 17.5 per 1,000 white males), or simple assault (14.9 per 1,000 African-American males compared with 15.9 per 1,000 white males).

Similarly, African-American women were more than twice as likely as white women to be victims of completed violence (9.5 per 1,000 African-American females compared with 4.7 per 1,000 white females), rape and sexual assault (3.1 per 1,000 African-American females compared with 1.1 per 1,000 white females), and robbery (2.4 per 1,000 African-American females compared with 1.2 per 1,000 white females). They were less likely than white women to be victims of attempts to take property without injury (0.0 per 1,000 African-American females compared with 0.3 per 1,000 white females) and simple assault with minor injury (2.2 per 1,000 African-American

females compared with 2.4 per 1,000 white females). (See Table 2.4.)

In 2005, 155.7 per 1,000 white households and 144.6 per 1,000 African-American households were victims of property crime. Whites were more likely than African-Americans to be victims of theft (119.6 per 1,000 households compared with 96.9 of every 1,000 African-American households) and attempted robbery (4 per 1,000 households for whites compared with 3.6 per 1,000 households for African-Americans). African-Americans were more likely than whites to be victims of household burglary (35 per 1,000 African-Americans compared with 28.6 per 1,000 whites) and motor vehicle theft (12.7 per 1,000 African-Americans compared with 7.6 per 1,000 whites). (See Table 2.5.)

## Income, Marital Status, and Area

**INCOME.** In general, the less money that households earn, the more likely they are to become victims of violent crime. In 2005 those earning less than $7,500 annually were victims of violent crime at a higher rate (37.7 per 1,000 persons) than any other income group, and this rate was more than twice as high as the rate for those earning $75,000 or more (16.4 per 1,000). (See Table 2.6.)

**MARITAL STATUS.** In 2005 the violent crime victimization rate for males who never married (44.5 per 1,000 population) was nearly four times higher than the rate for married men (12.7 per 1,000). Rates for never-married women (29.3 per 1,000) were also about four times higher than for married women (7.8 per 1,000). Victimization rates for divorced or separated men (29.2 per 1,000) and women (33.4 per 1,000) were significantly higher than for married men and women, respectively. (See Table 2.7.) The rate for divorced or separated persons (30.7 per 1,000) was almost three times higher than the rate for married people.

**REGIONS AND TYPES OF RESIDENCE.** Those living in the West and in urban areas are more likely to be victimized by property crimes than those living in other parts of the country and in rural or suburban areas. In 2005, 206.5 per 1,000 households in the West and 200 per 1,000 urban households nationally were victims of property crimes. Rates in all categories of property crime in the West and in urban locations were higher than rates in other regions and locations, respectively. The lowest rates of property crime victimization were in rural and suburban areas of the Northeast. (See Table 2.8.)

## Victim/Offender Relationship

Table 2.9 from *Criminal Victimization in the United States, 2005* displays victimization rates per 1,000 persons age twelve and over in several demographic categories. According to data on crimes for which the

TABLE 2.4

**Number of victimizations and victimization rates for people age 12 and over by crime type, gender, and race of victims, 2005**

| | Rate per 1,000 people age 12 and over | | | | | | | |
|---|---|---|---|---|---|---|---|---|
| | Male | | | | Female | | | |
| | White only | | Black only | | White only | | Black only | |
| Type of crime | Number | Rate | Number | Rate | Number | Rate | Number | Rate |
| All personal crimes | 2,504,510 | 25.5 | 437,900 | 32.6 | 1,686,100 | 16.5 | 408,830 | 25.5 |
| Crimes of violence | 2,419,750 | 24.6 | 423,560 | 31.6 | 1,596,160 | 15.6 | 373,240 | 23.2 |
| Completed violence | 698,330 | 7.1 | 212,720 | 15.8 | 479,810 | 4.7 | 151,930 | 9.5 |
| Attempted/threatened violence | 1,721,430 | 17.5 | 210,840 | 15.7 | 1,116,350 | 10.9 | 221,310 | 13.8 |
| Rape/sexual assault[a] | 12,430* | 0.1* | 2,700* | 0.2* | 112,500 | 1.1 | 49,280 | 3.1 |
| Robbery | 320,590 | 3.3 | 98,330 | 7.3 | 126,430 | 1.2 | 37,990 | 2.4 |
| Completed/property taken | 157,480 | 1.6 | 92,490 | 6.9 | 95,800 | 0.9 | 35,310* | 2.2* |
| With injury | 74,300 | 0.8 | 13,730* | 1.0* | 31,950* | 0.3* | 14,960* | 0.9* |
| Without injury | 83,170 | 0.8 | 78,750 | 5.9 | 63,850 | 0.6 | 20,360* | 1.3* |
| Attempted to take property | 163,120 | 1.7 | 5,840* | 0.4* | 30,640* | 0.3* | 2,670* | 0.2* |
| With injury | 58,100 | 0.6 | 0* | 0.0* | 0* | 0.0* | 2,670* | 0.2* |
| Without injury | 105,020 | 1.1 | 5,840* | 0.4* | 30,640* | 0.3* | 0* | 0.0* |
| Assault | 2,086,730 | 21.2 | 322,540 | 24.0 | 1,357,230 | 13.3 | 285,970 | 17.8 |
| Aggravated | 520,370 | 5.3 | 122,210 | 9.1 | 237,570 | 2.3 | 103,270 | 6.4 |
| With injury | 151,150 | 1.5 | 46,380 | 3.5 | 68,770 | 0.7 | 38,710 | 2.4 |
| Threatened with weapon | 369,230 | 3.8 | 75,830 | 5.6 | 168,800 | 1.7 | 64,550 | 4.0 |
| Simple | 1,566,350 | 15.9 | 200,330 | 14.9 | 1,119,650 | 11.0 | 182,710 | 11.4 |
| With minor injury | 389,700 | 4.0 | 71,150 | 5.3 | 246,200 | 2.4 | 35,120* | 2.2* |
| Without injury | 1,176,650 | 12.0 | 129,170 | 9.6 | 873,450 | 8.6 | 147,580 | 9.2 |
| Purse snatching/pocket picking | 84,760 | 0.9 | 14,340* | 1.1* | 89,940 | 0.9 | 35,590* | 2.2* |
| Population age 12 and over | 98,238,010 | — | 13,422,840 | — | 102,025,400 | — | 16,055,050 | — |

Note: Detail may not add to total shown because of rounding.
Excludes data on persons of "other" races and persons indicating two or more races.
*Estimate is based on about 10 or fewer sample cases.
—Not applicable.
[a]Includes verbal threats of rape and threats of sexual assault

SOURCE: "Table 6. Personal Crimes, 2005: Number of Victimizations and Victimization Rates for Persons Age 12 and Over, by Type of Crime and Gender and Race of Victims," in *Criminal Victimization in the United States, 2005 Statistical Tables*, U.S. Department of Justice, Office of Justice Programs, Bureau of Justice Statistics, December 2006, http://www.ojp.usdoj.gov/bjs/pub/pdf/cvus05.pdf (accessed January 9, 2007)

TABLE 2.5

**Number of victimizations and victimization rates by type of crime and race of head of household, 2005**

| | Rate per 1,000 households | | | | | | | | | |
|---|---|---|---|---|---|---|---|---|---|---|
| | All races | | White only | | Black only | | Other race only[a] | | Two or more races[b] | |
| Type of crime | Number | Rate | Number | Rate | Number | Rate | Number | Rate | Number | Rate |
| **Property crimes** | 18,039,930 | 154.0 | 15,025,220 | 155.7 | 2,106,020 | 144.6 | 635,210 | 122.8 | 273,480 | 308.9 |
| Household burglary | 3,456,220 | 29.5 | 2,757,440 | 28.6 | 510,080 | 35.0 | 120,800 | 23.3 | 67,900 | 76.7 |
| Completed | 2,900,460 | 24.8 | 2,314,160 | 24.0 | 441,970 | 30.3 | 85,730 | 16.6 | 58,610 | 66.2 |
| Forcible entry | 1,068,430 | 9.1 | 794,180 | 8.2 | 235,210 | 16.1 | 21,650* | 4.2* | 17,390* | 19.6* |
| Unlawful entry without force | 1,832,030 | 15.6 | 1,519,980 | 15.8 | 206,760 | 14.2 | 64,080 | 12.4 | 41,210 | 46.5 |
| Attempted forcible entry | 555,760 | 4.7 | 443,280 | 4.6 | 68,110 | 4.7 | 35,070* | 6.8* | 9,290* | 10.5* |
| Motor vehicle theft | 978,120 | 8.4 | 731,160 | 7.6 | 184,490 | 12.7 | 51,450 | 9.9 | 11,020* | 12.4* |
| Completed | 774,650 | 6.6 | 556,970 | 5.8 | 169,820 | 11.7 | 36,840 | 7.1 | 11,020* | 12.4* |
| Attempted | 203,470 | 1.7 | 174,190 | 1.8 | 14,660* | 1.0* | 14,610* | 2.8* | 0* | 0.0* |
| Theft | 13,605,590 | 116.2 | 11,536,620 | 119.6 | 1,411,450 | 96.9 | 462,950 | 89.5 | 194,560 | 219.7 |
| Completed | 13,116,270 | 112.0 | 11,151,040 | 115.6 | 1,358,870 | 93.3 | 428,210 | 82.8 | 178,150 | 201.2 |
| Less than $50 | 4,079,120 | 34.8 | 3,537,120 | 36.7 | 357,740 | 24.6 | 127,800 | 24.7 | 56,460 | 63.8 |
| $50–$249 | 4,656,120 | 39.8 | 3,917,150 | 40.6 | 532,380 | 36.5 | 146,770 | 28.4 | 59,810 | 67.6 |
| $250 or more | 3,231,440 | 27.6 | 2,703,640 | 28.0 | 339,830 | 23.3 | 130,900 | 25.3 | 57,080 | 64.5 |
| Amount not available | 1,149,590 | 9.8 | 993,140 | 10.3 | 128,910 | 8.8 | 22,740* | 4.4* | 4,800* | 5.4* |
| Attempted | 489,320 | 4.2 | 385,580 | 4.0 | 52,580 | 3.6 | 34,740* | 6.7* | 16,410* | 18.5* |
| **Total number of households** | 117,110,800 | — | 96,483,760 | — | 14,567,210 | — | 5,174,380 | — | 885,450 | — |

Note: Detail may not add to total shown because of rounding.
*Estimate is based on about 10 or fewer sample cases.
—Not applicable.
[a]Includes American Indian, Eskimo, Asian Pacific Islander if only one of these races is given.
[b]Includes all persons of any race, indicating two or more races.

SOURCE: "Table 16. Property Crimes, 2005: Number of Victimizations and Victimization Rates by Type of Crime and Race of Head of Household," in *Criminal Victimization in the United States, 2005 Statistical Tables*, U.S. Department of Justice, Office of Justice Programs, Bureau of Justice Statistics, December 2006, http://www.ojp.usdoj.gov/bjs/pub/pdf/cvus05.pdf (accessed January 9, 2007)

TABLE 2.6

**Victimization rates for people age 12 and over, by type of crime and annual family income of victims, 2005**

| Type of crime | Rate per 1,000 people age 12 and over | | | | | | |
|---|---|---|---|---|---|---|---|
| | Less than $7,500 | $7,500– $14,999 | $15,000– $24,999 | $25,000– $34,999 | $35,000– $49,999 | $50,000– $74,999 | $75,000 or more |
| **All personal crimes** | **40.9** | **28.1** | **31.2** | **27.1** | **23.6** | **21.7** | **17.4** |
| Crimes of violence | 37.7 | 26.5 | 30.1 | 26.1 | 22.4 | 21.1 | 16.4 |
| Completed violence | 14.4 | 10.5 | 9.7 | 9.5 | 6.8 | 6.0 | 4.9 |
| Attempted/threatened violence | 23.3 | 16.0 | 20.4 | 16.6 | 15.7 | 15.1 | 11.4 |
| Rape/sexual assault | 2.2* | 0.6* | 1.4* | 1.7 | 0.9* | 0.5* | 0.6* |
| Rape/attempted rape | 1.9* | 0.6* | 0.7* | 0.9* | 0.7* | 0.5* | 0.4* |
| Rape | 1.9* | 0.4* | 0.4* | 0.9* | 0.3* | 0.1* | 0.0* |
| Attempted rape[a] | 0.0* | 0.2* | 0.3* | 0.0* | 0.3* | 0.4* | 0.4* |
| Sexual assault[b] | 0.3* | 0.0* | 0.7* | 0.8* | 0.2* | 0.0* | 0.2* |
| Robbery | 5.6 | 4.9 | 3.5 | 2.8 | 2.5 | 1.8 | 2.1 |
| Completed/property taken | 3.7* | 4.1 | 2.2 | 2.0 | 1.4 | 1.2 | 1.6 |
| With injury | 1.8* | 1.5* | 1.5* | 0.6* | 0.6* | 0.2* | 0.4* |
| Without injury | 1.9* | 2.6 | 0.7* | 1.5* | 0.8* | 1.0* | 1.2 |
| Attempted to take property | 2.0* | 0.8* | 1.3* | 0.8* | 1.2* | 0.6* | 0.5* |
| With injury | 0.7* | 0.0* | 0.7* | 0.3* | 0.4* | 0.2* | 0.1* |
| Without injury | 1.3* | 0.8* | 0.6* | 0.5* | 0.7* | 0.4* | 0.4* |
| Assault | 29.9 | 21.0 | 25.2 | 21.6 | 19.0 | 18.8 | 13.7 |
| Aggravated | 9.7 | 6.8 | 6.4 | 5.2 | 4.3 | 4.3 | 2.6 |
| With injury | 2.9* | 2.5 | 1.8 | 2.0 | 1.5 | 1.3 | 0.8 |
| Threatened with weapon | 6.8 | 4.3 | 4.6 | 3.3 | 2.8 | 2.9 | 1.8 |
| Simple | 20.1 | 14.2 | 18.8 | 16.4 | 14.7 | 14.5 | 11.1 |
| With minor injury | 6.0 | 3.4 | 4.8 | 3.9 | 3.4 | 3.3 | 2.4 |
| Without injury | 14.2 | 10.8 | 14.0 | 12.5 | 11.4 | 11.2 | 8.7 |
| Purse snatching/pocket picking | 3.2* | 1.6* | 1.1* | 1.0* | 1.1* | 0.6* | 1.0 |
| Population age 12 and over | 8,367,490 | 14,798,200 | 22,414,530 | 22,504,200 | 30,575,740 | 35,692,930 | 52,979,190 |

Note: Detail may not add to total shown because of rounding.
Excludes data on persons whose family income level was not ascertained.
*Estimate is based on about 10 or fewer sample cases.
[a]Includes verbal threats of rape.
[b]Includes threats.

SOURCE: "Table 14. Personal Crimes, 2005: Victimization Rates for Persons Age 12 and Over, by Type of Crime and Annual Family Income of Victims," in *Criminal Victimization in the United States, 2005 Statistical Tables*, U.S. Department of Justice, Office of Justice Programs, Bureau of Justice Statistics, December 2006, http://www.ojp.usdoj.gov/bjs/pub/pdf/cvus05.pdf (accessed January 9, 2007)

perpetrator is known, males were the victims of violent crimes committed by strangers at a rate of 13.8 per 1,000 population in 2005. This is a higher rate than victimizations among males by acquaintances (3.6 per 1,000 population), relatives (1.2 per 1,000 population), or others whom the victims knew well (4.6 per 1,000 population). Victimization rates among females in 2005 were also highest for crimes involving strangers. For every 1,000 females over age twelve, 5.8 were victims of violent crimes committed by strangers, 2.4 were victims of violent acts committed by casual acquaintances or relatives, and 5.3 were victimized by others they knew well. Firearms were used by strangers in 12.6% of violent crimes and by nonstrangers in 4.8% of violent crimes. (See Table 2.10.)

## WHEN AND WHERE DOES VIOLENT CRIME HAPPEN?

According to the National Crime Victimization Survey, certain crimes are more likely to occur at certain times of the day (http://www.ojp.usdoj.gov/bjs/pub/pdf/cvus0504.pdf). In 2005 violent crimes (52.6% of cases), attempted or threatened violence (58% of cases), and assaults (55.4% of cases) occurred most frequently between 6 a.m. and 6 p.m. In contrast, almost two-thirds (61.8%) of rapes/sexual assaults occurred at night. Property crimes occurred more frequently (43.8% of cases) at night than during the day (36%), except for household burglaries: 34% of cases were committed at night compared with 37.7% cases during the day.

NCVS respondents reported in addition that in 2005, 14.8% of violent crimes occurred at or near the victim's residence. Other common sites for violent crimes were on a street not near the victim's home (18.6% of cases), inside a school building or on school property (12.3%), and near the victim's home (10.4%).

### Victims' Activities

According to the National Crime Victimization Survey, 22.3% of violent crimes in 2005 occurred while victims were engaged in leisure activity away from home and 16.3% while victims were working or on duty. Another 10.3% of victims were on the way to or from some place other than work or school, and 8.1% were attending school. Rapes occurred most frequently at

**TABLE 2.7**

**Victimization rates for people age 12 and over, by gender and marital status of victims and type of crime, 2005**

| | | | | | | Robbery | | | Assault | | | Purse snatching/ Pocket picking |
| Gender and marital status | Total population | Crimes of violence | Completed violence | Attempted/ threatened violence | Rape/ sexual assault[a] | Total | With injury | Without injury | Total | Aggravated | Simple | |
|---|---|---|---|---|---|---|---|---|---|---|---|---|
| **Male** | | | | | | | | | | | | |
| Never married | 42,578,470 | 44.5 | 16.0 | 28.6 | 0.2* | 7.0 | 2.2 | 4.8 | 37.3 | 9.7 | 27.6 | 1.5 |
| Married | 61,416,700 | 12.7 | 3.0 | 9.7 | 0.1* | 1.6 | 0.6* | 1.0 | 11.1 | 2.7 | 8.3 | 0.4* |
| Widowed | 2,872,990 | 5.6* | 3.2* | 2.4* | 0.0* | 2.2* | 1.2* | 1.1* | 3.4* | 2.3* | 1.1* | 0.0* |
| Divorced or separated | 10,989,230 | 29.2 | 7.9 | 21.3 | 0.0* | 4.8 | 2.0 | 2.8 | 24.4 | 6.7 | 17.7 | 1.0 |
| **Female** | | | | | | | | | | | | |
| Never married | 37,085,750 | 29.3 | 9.2 | 20.0 | 2.8 | 2.3 | 0.6* | 1.6 | 24.2 | 5.4 | 18.8 | 1.5 |
| Married | 60,781,390 | 7.8 | 1.9 | 5.9 | 0.4* | 0.5* | 0.1* | 0.4* | 7.0 | 2.1 | 4.9 | 0.7 |
| Widowed | 11,439,370 | 6.3 | 2.9* | 3.4 | 0.9* | 1.1* | 1.1* | 0.0* | 4.2 | 0.0* | 4.2 | 0.9* |
| Divorced or separated | 15,090,680 | 33.4 | 13.0 | 20.4 | 2.5 | 3.0 | 0.9* | 2.2* | 27.9 | 4.1 | 23.8 | 1.2* |

Rate per 1,000 people age 12 and over

Note: Detail may not add to total shown because of rounding.
Excludes data on persons whose marital status was not ascertained.
*Estimate is based on about 10 or fewer sample cases.
[a]Includes verbal threats of rape and threats of sexual assault

SOURCE: "Table 12. Personal Crimes, 2005: Victimization Rates for Persons Age 12 and Over, by Gender and Marital Status of Victims and Type of Crime," in *Criminal Victimization in the United States, 2005 Statistical Tables*, U.S. Department of Justice, Office of Justice Programs, Bureau of Justice Statistics, December 2006, http://www.ojp.usdoj.gov/bjs/pub/pdf/cvus05.pdf (accessed January 9, 2007)

## TABLE 2.8

### Property crime victimization rates, by type of crime, region, and residence locality, 2005

**Rate per 1,000 households**

| Type of crime | All regions | | | | Northeast | | | | Midwest | | | |
|---|---|---|---|---|---|---|---|---|---|---|---|---|
| | All areas | Urban | Suburban | Rural | All areas | Urban | Suburban | Rural | All areas | Urban | Suburban | Rural |
| **Property crimes** | **154.0** | **200.0** | **141.4** | **125.1** | **103.9** | **130.9** | **96.2** | **81.1** | **155.8** | **203.9** | **140.7** | **138.8** |
| Household burglary | 29.5 | 37.7 | 24.7 | 29.4 | 18.1 | 24.8 | 14.9 | 16.6 | 34.8 | 49.2 | 25.4 | 36.9 |
| Completed | 24.8 | 31.1 | 20.8 | 25.2 | 14.9 | 19.9 | 12.4 | 13.9 | 29.0 | 38.1 | 22.4 | 31.1 |
| Forcible entry | 9.1 | 13.0 | 7.0 | 8.8 | 6.5 | 8.6 | 5.7 | 5.3* | 10.1 | 17.5 | 7.0 | 8.4 |
| Unlawful entry without force | 15.6 | 18.0 | 13.8 | 16.5 | 8.4 | 11.3 | 6.6 | 8.6* | 18.9 | 20.5 | 15.4 | 22.7 |
| Attempted forcible entry | 4.7 | 6.7 | 3.9 | 4.2 | 3.3 | 4.9* | 2.5* | 2.7* | 5.8 | 11.1 | 3.0 | 5.8 |
| Motor vehicle theft | 8.4 | 12.7 | 7.7 | 4.6 | 5.9 | 11.0 | 4.5 | 1.4* | 6.8 | 11.3 | 5.2 | 5.6 |
| Completed | 6.6 | 10.0 | 6.3 | 3.2 | 4.2 | 8.2 | 3.4 | 0.0* | 5.3 | 8.2 | 4.1 | 4.6 |
| Attempted | 1.7 | 2.8 | 1.4 | 1.3 | 1.7* | 2.9* | 1.2* | 1.4* | 1.5 | 3.0* | 1.0* | 1.1* |
| Theft | 116.2 | 149.6 | 109.0 | 91.1 | 79.9 | 95.1 | 76.8 | 63.1 | 114.1 | 143.4 | 110.1 | 96.2 |
| Completed | 112.0 | 142.9 | 105.0 | 89.6 | 78.1 | 92.1 | 75.3 | 62.5 | 109.2 | 134.5 | 104.9 | 94.9 |
| Less than $50 | 34.8 | 41.9 | 32.9 | 30.3 | 25.9 | 28.1 | 25.3 | 24.2 | 36.9 | 44.4 | 35.9 | 32.2 |
| $50–$249 | 39.8 | 53.7 | 34.8 | 33.1 | 27.5 | 33.0 | 25.8 | 23.4 | 40.8 | 53.2 | 36.7 | 36.7 |
| $250 or more | 27.6 | 35.5 | 27.4 | 18.7 | 14.2 | 17.6 | 14.1 | 8.3* | 21.9 | 29.0 | 21.5 | 16.7 |
| Amount not available | 9.8 | 11.8 | 9.9 | 7.4 | 10.5 | 13.4 | 10.2 | 6.5* | 9.7 | 7.9 | 10.8 | 9.3 |
| Attempted | 4.2 | 6.7 | 4.0 | 1.5 | 1.8 | 2.9* | 1.5* | 0.6* | 5.0 | 8.8 | 5.2 | 1.4* |
| **Total number of households** | 117,110,800 | 33,045,250 | 56,101,350 | 27,964,200 | 21,191,890 | 6,350,350 | 11,101,200 | 3,740,340 | 27,836,820 | 6,891,510 | 12,511,970 | 8,433,340 |

**Rate per 1,000 households**

| Type of crime | South | | | | West | | | |
|---|---|---|---|---|---|---|---|---|
| | All areas | Urban | Suburban | Rural | All areas | Urban | Suburban | Rural |
| **Property crimes** | **146.8** | **214.5** | **136.1** | **105.6** | **206.5** | **228.5** | **189.5** | **211.7** |
| Household burglary | 31.3 | 45.1 | 25.2 | 28.9 | 30.3 | 29.4 | 31.8 | 26.9 |
| Completed | 26.6 | 37.7 | 21.7 | 24.8 | 25.3 | 25.7 | 25.3 | 24.5 |
| Forcible entry | 10.9 | 17.9 | 8.0 | 9.4 | 7.2 | 6.9 | 6.5 | 10.8* |
| Unlawful entry without force | 15.7 | 19.8 | 13.7 | 15.3 | 18.1 | 18.8 | 18.7 | 13.7 |
| Attempted forcible entry | 4.7 | 7.4 | 3.5 | 4.2 | 4.9 | 3.7* | 6.5 | 2.4* |
| Motor vehicle theft | 7.2 | 11.5 | 7.5 | 2.8* | 14.1 | 16.5 | 13.0 | 11.9 |
| Completed | 5.8 | 9.5 | 6.3 | 1.9* | 11.5 | 13.2 | 11.0 | 8.5* |
| Attempted | 1.4 | 2.0* | 1.3* | 0.9* | 2.6 | 3.3* | 2.0* | 3.3 |
| Theft | 108.4 | 157.9 | 103.3 | 73.8 | 162.2 | 182.6 | 144.7 | 172.9 |
| Completed | 105.0 | 151.3 | 100.2 | 72.8 | 155.5 | 174.8 | 138.2 | 168.5 |
| Less than $50 | 31.8 | 45.0 | 30.4 | 22.6 | 45.2 | 46.1 | 40.4 | 60.9 |
| $50–$249 | 37.5 | 56.4 | 34.6 | 25.7 | 52.8 | 65.3 | 41.3 | 62.4 |
| $250 or more | 27.6 | 38.8 | 27.0 | 18.9 | 45.2 | 49.0 | 45.1 | 34.7 |
| Amount not available | 8.1 | 11.1 | 8.1 | 5.5 | 12.3 | 14.4 | 11.3 | 10.4* |
| Attempted | 3.4 | 6.6 | 3.1 | 1.0* | 6.7 | 7.8 | 6.5 | 4.4* |
| **Total number of households** | 42,851,180 | 10,698,980 | 19,723,360 | 12,428,840 | 25,230,910 | 9,104,400 | 12,764,830 | 3,361,680 |

Note: Detail may not add to total shown because of rounding.
The term "urban" is used to denote "central cities."
The term "suburban" is used to denote "outside central cities."
The term "rural" is used to denote "nonmetropolitan areas."
*Estimate is based on about 10 or fewer sample cases.

SOURCE: "Table 58. Property Crimes, 2005: Victimization Rates by Type of Crime, Region, and Locality of Residence," in *Criminal Victimization in the United States, 2005 Statistical Tables*, U.S. Department of Justice, Office of Justice Programs, Bureau of Justice Statistics, December 2006, http://www.ojp.usdoj.gov/bjs/pub/pdf/cvus05.pdf (accessed January 9, 2007)

TABLE 2.9

**Family violence victimization rates, by victim-offender relationship, type of crime, and selected victim characteristics, 2005**

| | | Rate per 1,000 persons age 12 and over | | | | | | | |
| | | Crimes of violence[a] | | | | Assault | | | |
| Characteristic | Total population | Relatives | Well-known | Casual acquaintances | Strangers | Relatives | Well-known | Casual acquaintances | Strangers |
|---|---|---|---|---|---|---|---|---|---|
| **Gender** | | | | | | | | | |
| Male | 118,937,730 | 1.2 | 4.6 | 3.6 | 13.8 | 1.2 | 4.4 | 3.4 | 10.8 |
| Female | 125,555,710 | 2.4 | 5.3 | 2.4 | 5.8 | 2.3 | 4.5 | 1.8 | 4.8 |
| **Race** | | | | | | | | | |
| White only | 200,263,410 | 1.7 | 4.6 | 2.9 | 9.5 | 1.6 | 4.2 | 2.6 | 7.7 |
| Black only | 29,477,880 | 2.1 | 7.6 | 3.4 | 10.4 | 1.8 | 6.4 | 2.5 | 7.0 |
| Other race only[b] | 12,522,090 | 0.4* | 2.2* | 1.8* | 7.7 | 0.4* | 1.7* | 1.8* | 5.7 |
| Two or more races[c] | 2,230,050 | 18.8 | 21.2 | 8.4* | 30.8 | 18.8 | 18.1 | 7.1* | 29.6 |
| **Age** | | | | | | | | | |
| 12–15 | 17,061,940 | 1.5* | 14.1 | 8.8 | 15.7 | 1.1* | 13.3 | 8.4 | 13.1 |
| 16–19 | 16,524,940 | 1.9* | 10.7 | 5.6 | 21.3 | 1.9* | 7.9 | 4.6 | 15.0 |
| 20–24 | 20,363,570 | 1.2* | 12.7 | 5.5 | 23.5 | 1.2* | 11.9 | 4.7 | 19.8 |
| 25–34 | 39,607,310 | 3.0 | 5.3 | 2.1 | 12.1 | 3.0 | 4.6 | 1.8 | 9.6 |
| 35–49 | 65,707,720 | 2.7 | 3.3 | 2.4 | 7.6 | 2.5 | 2.9 | 2.3 | 6.3 |
| 50–64 | 50,164,650 | 1.1 | 1.8 | 2.4 | 5.0 | 1.1 | 1.8 | 1.8 | 4.1 |
| 65 and over | 35,063,310 | 0.4* | 0.6* | 0.2* | 1.1 | 0.4* | 0.5* | 0.2* | 0.6* |
| **Marital status[d]** | | | | | | | | | |
| Married | 122,198,090 | 1.0 | 2.0 | 1.4 | 5.2 | 0.9 | 1.9 | 1.2 | 4.5 |
| Widowed | 14,312,360 | 0.4* | 0.2* | 1.5* | 3.5 | 0.2* | 0.2* | 1.5* | 2.0* |
| Divorced or separated | 26,079,910 | 7.4 | 7.1 | 4.7 | 11.0 | 7.1 | 5.8 | 4.2 | 8.3 |
| Never married | 79,664,210 | 1.6 | 9.8 | 5.2 | 17.3 | 1.5 | 8.7 | 4.6 | 13.6 |
| **Family income[e]** | | | | | | | | | |
| Less than $7,500 | 8,367,490 | 3.0* | 8.9 | 3.6* | 16.6 | 3.0* | 6.8 | 3.1* | 12.1 |
| $7,500–$14,999 | 14,798,200 | 1.4* | 7.7 | 4.2 | 10.6 | 1.4* | 7.4 | 4.0 | 6.2 |
| $15,000–$24,999 | 22,414,530 | 2.3 | 7.9 | 3.7 | 13.5 | 2.1 | 7.2 | 3.2 | 11.0 |
| $25,000–$34,999 | 22,504,200 | 2.7 | 5.8 | 3.6 | 12.1 | 2.3 | 4.9 | 3.3 | 9.7 |
| $35,000–$49,999 | 30,575,740 | 2.5 | 5.4 | 4.2 | 9.1 | 2.5 | 5.0 | 3.2 | 7.1 |
| $50,000–$74,999 | 35,692,930 | 1.4 | 5.5 | 3.4 | 10.0 | 1.3 | 5.0 | 3.1 | 8.7 |
| $75,000 or more | 52,979,190 | 1.1 | 3.0 | 2.2 | 8.9 | 1.0 | 2.6 | 2.0 | 7.2 |

| | Rate per 1,000 persons age 12 and over | | | | | | | |
| | Aggravated assault | | | | Simple assault | | | |
| Characteristic | Relatives | Well-known | Casual acquaintances | Strangers | Relatives | Well-known | Casual acquaintances | Strangers |
|---|---|---|---|---|---|---|---|---|
| **Gender** | | | | | | | | |
| Male | 0.4 | 1.1 | 0.6 | 3.0 | 0.8 | 3.3 | 2.8 | 7.8 |
| Female | 0.4 | 1.0 | 0.2* | 1.1 | 1.9 | 3.4 | 1.7 | 3.7 |
| **Race** | | | | | | | | |
| White only | 0.3 | 0.9 | 0.3 | 2.0 | 1.3 | 3.3 | 2.3 | 5.8 |
| Black only | 0.4* | 2.4 | 0.7* | 2.6 | 1.4 | 4.0 | 1.9 | 4.4 |
| Other race only | 0.4* | 0.3* | 0.0* | 1.8* | 0.0* | 1.4* | 1.8* | 3.8 |
| Two or more races | 3.7* | 4.8* | 3.9* | 2.8* | 15.1* | 13.4* | 3.2* | 26.8 |
| **Age** | | | | | | | | |
| 12–15 | 0.2* | 3.1 | 1.7* | 3.2 | 0.9* | 10.2 | 6.7 | 9.9 |
| 16–19 | 0.8* | 2.4 | 0.9* | 4.6 | 1.1* | 5.5 | 3.7 | 10.4 |
| 20–24 | 0.0* | 2.8 | 0.4* | 5.5 | 1.2* | 9.1 | 4.3 | 14.3 |
| 25–34 | 0.5* | 0.9* | 0.4* | 2.6 | 2.5 | 3.7 | 1.4 | 7.0 |
| 35–49 | 0.5* | 0.6 | 0.3* | 1.3 | 2.0 | 2.3 | 2.0 | 5.0 |
| 50–64 | 0.4* | 0.4* | 0.1* | 1.1 | 0.6* | 1.4 | 1.6 | 3.0 |
| 65 and over | 0.1* | 0.3* | 0.1* | 0.3* | 0.3* | 0.2* | 0.1* | 0.3* |
| **Marital status[d]** | | | | | | | | |
| Married | 0.2* | 0.5 | 0.1* | 1.2 | 0.7 | 1.4 | 1.1 | 3.3 |
| Widowed | 0.0* | 0.0* | 0.0* | 0.3* | 0.2* | 0.2* | 1.5* | 1.7* |
| Divorced or separated | 1.2* | 0.9* | 0.6* | 2.1 | 5.9 | 4.9 | 3.6 | 6.1 |
| Never married | 0.4* | 2.1 | 0.9 | 3.6 | 1.1 | 6.5 | 3.7 | 10.0 |

home while victims were either sleeping (20.3% of cases) or engaged in other activities (24.7%). Robberies were more likely to occur while victims were involved in leisure activities away from home (21.7%) or on their way to or from some place other than school or work (20%). (See Table 2.11.)

TABLE 2.9

Family violence victimization rates, by victim-offender relationship, type of crime, and selected victim characteristics, 2005 [CONTINUED]

| | Rate per 1,000 persons age 12 and over | | | | | | | |
|---|---|---|---|---|---|---|---|---|
| | Aggravated assault | | | | Simple assault | | | |
| Characteristic | Relatives | Well-known | Casual acquaintances | Strangers | Relatives | Well-known | Casual acquaintances | Strangers |
| Family income[e] | | | | | | | | |
| Less than $7,500 | 0.7* | 2.3* | 0.0* | 4.6 | 2.2* | 4.5 | 3.1* | 7.6 |
| $7,500–$14,999 | 0.8* | 2.2* | 1.2* | 1.6* | 0.6* | 5.1 | 2.8 | 4.6 |
| $15,000–$24,999 | 0.8* | 1.9 | 0.0* | 2.7 | 1.3* | 5.3 | 3.2 | 8.3 |
| $25,000–$34,999 | 0.6* | 0.4* | 0.5* | 3.3 | 1.7 | 4.5 | 2.8 | 6.4 |
| $35,000–$49,999 | 0.3* | 0.7* | 0.7* | 1.9 | 2.3 | 4.2 | 2.5 | 5.2 |
| $50,000–$74,999 | 0.4* | 1.3 | 0.3* | 2.2 | 0.9* | 3.7 | 2.8 | 6.5 |
| $75,000 or more | 0.1* | 0.4* | 0.1* | 2.0 | 1.0 | 2.2 | 1.9 | 5.2 |

*Estimate is based on about 10 or fewer sample cases.
[a]Crimes of violence includes data on rape, sexual assault, and robbery, not shown separately.
[b]Includes American Indian, Eskimo, Asian Pacific Islander if only one of these races is given.
[c]Includes all persons of any race indicating two or more races.
[d]Excludes data on persons whose marital status was not ascertained.
[e]Excludes data on persons whose family income was not ascertained.

SOURCE: "Table 35. Family Violence, 2005: Victimization Rate, by Victim-Offender Relationship, by Type of Crime, and Selected Victim Characteristics," in *Criminal Victimization in the United States, 2005 Statistical Tables*, U.S. Department of Justice, Office of Justice Programs, Bureau of Justice Statistics, December 2006, http://www.ojp.usdoj.gov/bjs/pub/pdf/cvus05.pdf (accessed January 9, 2007)

Property crimes, as shown in Table 2.11, were most likely to occur while victims were either sleeping (27% of cases) or involved in other activities at home (11.5%). Another 14.5% of property crime victims were engaged in leisure activities away from home or working or on duty (13.8%). Some household burglaries occurred while the victim was at home sleeping (16.8% of cases) or involved in other home-based activities (8.8%). About half of all motor vehicle thefts (49.9%) took place while victims were sleeping. A significant proportion of thefts (28%) also occurred while victims were sleeping.

## TRENDS IN VICTIMIZATION
### Trends, 1973–2005

The National Crime Victimization Survey, like the Uniform Crime Reports issued by the FBI, found that the overall levels of both violent crime and property crime decreased between 1973 and 2005. According to the NCVS, the violent crime victimization rate increased between 1973 and 1981 and then declined until 1986. From 1986 to 1994 the violent crime victimization rate increased, reaching 51.2 per 1,000 in 1994. From 1994 to 2005, however, violent crime victimization rates fell by 59% to 21 per 1,000 (http://www.ojp.usdoj.gov/bjs/glance/tables/viortrdtab.htm). The victimization rates of most violent crimes dropped significantly between 1973 and 2005. The exception is murder, which has remained at a steady rate of 0.1 per 1,000 population every year between 1973 and 2005. In contrast, the rate of robbery reported in the NCVS has declined from 6.7 per 1,000 in 1973 to 2.6 per 1,000 in 2005, aggravated assault from 12.5 per 1,000 to 4.3 per 1,000, and simple assault from 25.9 per 1,000 to 13.5 per 1,000.

Property crime victimization rates fell dramatically between 1973 and 1995. After a slight increase from 1973 (519.9 per 1,000 households) to 1975 (553.6 per 1,000), the rates have dropped more or less consistently through 2005, when the total property crime rate was 154 per 1,000 (http://www.ojp.usdoj.gov/bjs/glance/tables/proptrdtab.htm). The rates of all property crime types on which the NCVS collects data fell significantly from 1973 to 2005. The burglary rate fell from 110 per 1,000 households in 1973 to just 29.5 per 1,000 in 2005, the theft rate from 390.8 per 1,000 households to 116.2 per 1,000, and the motor vehicle theft rate from 19.1 per 1,000 households to 8.4 per 1,000.

## COST OF VICTIMIZATION

The costs borne by crime victims include direct costs, such as the value of items that have been stolen, and indirect costs, such as the expenses of the criminal justice system, which must be shared by the entire society. The Bureau of Justice Statistics reports in the NCVS that in 2005, victims suffered a total economic loss of some $17 billion due to crime. This is the cost of property losses and does not include such additional expenses as medical or insurance costs. Although material losses are very important, emotional costs can also be significant, affecting victims for the rest of their lives, sometimes leading to radical and permanent lifestyle changes.

### Violent Crime

The direct economic cost to victims of violent crimes was $1.4 billion in 2005, according to the Bureau of

**TABLE 2.10**

## Violent crimes by victim-offender relationship, type of crime, and weapon used, 2005

| | Percent of incidents | | | | | | |
| | Total accidents | | | Weapon used | | | |
| All incidents | Number | Percent | No weapon used | Total | Total firearm | Hand gun | Other gun |
|---|---|---|---|---|---|---|---|
| **Crimes of violence** | 4,718,330 | 100.0% | 67.4% | 24.3% | 8.9% | 7.8% | 0.8% |
| Completed violence | 1,536,990 | 100.0 | 63.1 | 28.5 | 11.2 | 10.9 | 0.2 * |
| Attempted/threatened violence | 3,181,340 | 100.0 | 69.5 | 22.3 | 7.8 | 6.3 | 1.1 * |
| Rape/sexual assault | 188,960 | 100.0 | 84.6 | 6.5* | 3.1* | 1.8* | 1.4* |
| Robbery | 569,470 | 100.0 | 38.5 | 48.3 | 26.3 | 26.3 | 0.0* |
| Completed/property taken | 381,070 | 100.0 | 36.5 | 51.3 | 32.8 | 32.8 | 0.0* |
| With injury | 126,440 | 100.0 | 41.7 | 39.7 | 21.7* | 21.7* | 0.0* |
| Without injury | 254,640 | 100.0 | 33.9 | 57.1 | 38.3 | 38.3 | 0.0* |
| Attempted to take property | 188,400 | 100.0 | 42.5 | 42.2 | 13.1* | 13.1* | 0.0* |
| With injury | 62,230 | 100.0 | 61.9 | 18.8* | 7.2* | 7.2* | 0.0* |
| Without injury | 126,170 | 100.0 | 33.0 | 53.8 | 16.0* | 16.0* | 0.0* |
| Assault | 3,959,900 | 100.0 | 70.8 | 21.7 | 6.7 | 5.4 | 0.9* |
| Aggravated | 926,060 | 100.0 | 7.2 | 92.8 | 28.5 | 23.3 | 3.9* |
| With injury | 306,480 | 100.0 | 21.8 | 78.2 | 14.4 | 12.5 | 1.0* |
| Threatened with weapon | 619,580 | 100.0 | 0.0* | 100.0 | 35.5 | 28.6 | 5.3* |
| Simple[b] | 3,033,840 | 100.0 | 90.2 | — | — | — | — |
| With minor injury | 732,080 | 100.0 | 89.5 | — | — | — | — |
| Without injury | 2,301,770 | 100.0 | 90.4 | — | — | — | — |
| **Involving strangers** | | | | | | | |
| Crimes of violence | 2,465,360 | 100.0 | 56.7 | 30.4 | 12.6 | 11.2 | 1.0* |
| Rape/sexual assault[a] | 65,960 | 100.0 | 65.5 | 13.1* | 9.0* | 5.1* | 3.9* |
| Robbery | 454,990 | 100.0 | 32.3 | 51.2 | 28.1 | 28.1 | 0.0* |
| Aggravated assault | 524,430 | 100.0 | 3.3* | 96.7 | 33.8 | 27.5 | 4.4* |
| Simple assault[b] | 1,419,990 | 100.0 | 83.8 | — | — | — | — |
| **Involving nonstrangers** | | | | | | | |
| Crimes of violence | 2,252,970 | 100.0 | 79.2 | 17.7 | 4.8 | 4.2 | 0.6* |
| Rape/Sexual assault[a] | 123,010 | 100.0 | 94.9 | 3.0* | 0.0* | 0.0* | 0.0* |
| Robbery | 114,490 | 100.0 | 63.0 | 37.0 | 19.3* | 19.3* | 0.0* |
| Aggravated assault | 401,620 | 100.0 | 12.3 | 87.7 | 21.5 | 17.8 | 3.2* |
| Simple assault[b] | 1,613,860 | 100.0 | 95.8 | — | — | — | — |

| | Percent of incidents | | | | | |
| | Weapon used | | | | | Don't know if weapon present |
| | Gun type unknown | Knife | Sharp object | Blunt object | Other weapon | Weapon type unknown | |
|---|---|---|---|---|---|---|---|
| **Crimes of violence** | 0.3%* | 5.4% | 0.6%* | 3.9% | 4.2% | 1.1% | 8.3% |
| Completed violence | 0.2* | 7.2 | 0.4* | 4.7 | 3.6 | 1.5* | 8.4 |
| Attempted/threatened violence | 0.3* | 4.6 | 0.8* | 3.6 | 4.6 | 1.0* | 8.2 |
| Rape/sexual assault[a] | 0.0* | 3.4* | 0.0* | 0.0* | 0.0* | 0.0* | 8.9* |
| Robbery | 0.0* | 9.2 | 2.2* | 4.2* | 5.2* | 1.1* | 13.2 |
| Completed/property taken | 0.0* | 10.6 | 0.8* | 4.5* | 1.9* | 0.8* | 12.2 |
| With injury | 0.0* | 0.0* | 0.0* | 12.4* | 5.6* | 0.0* | 18.6* |
| Without injury | 0.0* | 15.8 | 1.1* | 0.6* | 0.0* | 1.2* | 9.0* |
| Attempted to take property | 0.0* | 6.5* | 5.2* | 3.7* | 11.9* | 1.8* | 15.3* |
| With injury | 0.0* | 0.0* | 0.0* | 0.0* | 6.3* | 5.3* | 19.3* |
| Without injury | 0.0* | 9.7* | 7.8* | 5.5* | 14.7* | 0.0* | 13.2* |
| Assault | 0.3* | 5.0 | 0.5* | 4.1 | 4.3 | 1.2 | 7.5 |
| Aggravated | 1.3* | 21.3 | 1.9* | 17.5 | 18.4 | 5.1 | 0.0* |
| With injury | 0.9* | 23.0 | 1.0* | 17.8 | 15.7 | 6.3* | 0.0* |
| Threatened with weapon | 1.6* | 20.5 | 2.4* | 17.3 | 19.8 | 4.5* | 0.0* |
| Simple[b] | — | — | — | — | — | — | 9.8 |
| With minor injury | — | — | — | — | — | — | 10.5 |
| Without injury | — | — | — | — | — | — | 9.6 |
| **Involving strangers** | | | | | | | |
| Crimes of violence | 0.4* | 5.3 | 1.1* | 5.4 | 4.8 | 1.2* | 12.9 |
| Rape/sexual assault[a] | 0.0* | 4.1* | 0.0* | 0.0* | 0.0* | 0.0* | 21.4* |
| Robbery | 0.0* | 9.6 | 2.8* | 3.9* | 5.4* | 1.4* | 16.5 |
| Aggravated assault | 2.0* | 16.0 | 2.6* | 22.1 | 17.8 | 4.4* | 0.0* |
| Simple assault[b] | — | — | — | — | — | — | 16.2 |

**TABLE 2.10**

**Violent crimes by victim-offender relationship, type of crime, and weapon used, 2005** [CONTINUED]

| | Percent of incidents | | | | | | |
|---|---|---|---|---|---|---|---|
| | Weapon used | | | | | | Don't know if weapon present |
| | Gun type unknown | Knife | Sharp object | Blunt object | Other weapon | Weapon type unknown | |
| **Involving nonstrangers** | | | | | | | |
| Crimes of violence | 0.1 | 5.6 | 0.2* | 2.3 | 3.7 | 1.1 | 3.2 |
| Rape/sexual assault[a] | 0.0* | 3.0* | 0.0* | 0.0* | 0.0* | 0.0* | 2.2* |
| Robbery | 0.0* | 7.7* | 0.0* | 5.7* | 4.2* | 0.0* | 0.0* |
| Aggravated assault | 0.5* | 28.2 | 1.0* | 11.5 | 19.3 | 6.1* | 0.0* |
| Simple assault[b] | — | — | — | — | — | — | 4.2 |

Note: Responses for weapons use are tallied once, based upon a hierarchy.
—Not applicable
*Estimate is based on about 10 or fewer sample cases.
[a]Includes verbal threats of rape and threats of sexual assault.
[b]Simple assault, by definition, does not involve the use of a weapon.

SOURCE: "Table 66. Personal Crimes of Violence, 2005: Percent of Incidents, by Victim-Offender Relationship, Type of Crime and Weapons Used," in *Criminal Victimization in the United States, 2005 Statistical Tables*, U.S. Department of Justice, Office of Justice Programs, Bureau of Justice Statistics, December 2006, http://www.ojp.usdoj.gov/bjs/pub/pdf/cvus05.pdf (accessed January 9, 2007)

**TABLE 2.11**

**Crimes by victim's activity at time of incident and type of crime, 2005**

| | | | Percent of incidents | | | | |
|---|---|---|---|---|---|---|---|
| Type of crime | Number of incidents | Total | Working or on duty | On the way to or from work | On the way to or from school | On the way to or from some other place | Shopping or running errands |
| **Crimes of violence** | 4,718,330 | 100.0% | 16.3% | 3.8% | 4.2% | 10.3% | 4.2% |
| Rape/sexual assault[a] | 188,960 | 100.0% | 11.0* | 1.3* | 3.2* | 4.3* | 0.0* |
| Robbery | 569,470 | 100.0% | 4.9* | 10.0 | 7.4 | 20.0 | 10.7 |
| Aggravated assault | 926,060 | 100.0% | 15.4 | 2.3* | 4.1 | 11.9 | 3.6* |
| Simple assault | 3,033,840 | 100.0% | 19.0 | 3.3 | 3.7 | 8.4 | 3.5 |
| Purse snatching/pocket picking | 227,070 | 100.0% | 1.7* | 3.6* | 0.0* | 3.0* | 34.6 |
| **Property crimes** | 18,039,930 | 100.0% | 13.8% | 0.6% | 0.4% | 1.2% | 5.6% |
| Household burglary | 3,456,220 | 100.0% | 21.5 | 1.4 | 0.3* | 1.5 | 5.1 |
| Motor vehicle theft | 978,120 | 100.0% | 12.2 | 0.3* | 0.0* | 1.1* | 1.6* |
| Theft | 13,605,590 | 100.0% | 12.0 | 0.5 | 0.4 | 1.2 | 6.0 |

| | | Percent of incidents | | | | | |
|---|---|---|---|---|---|---|---|
| Type of crime | Attending school | Leisure activity away from home | Sleeping | Other activities at home | Other | Don't know | Not available |
| **Crimes of violence** | 8.1% | 22.3% | 2.1% | 21.5% | 6.6% | 0.5%* | 0.0%* |
| Rape/sexual assault[a] | 4.6* | 29.1 | 20.3 | 24.7 | 1.7* | 0.0* | 0.0* |
| Robbery | 3.2* | 21.7 | 3.1* | 13.3 | 4.8* | 1.0* | 0.0* |
| Aggravated assault | 3.3* | 31.2 | 1.8* | 21.4 | 4.9 | 0.0* | 0.0* |
| Simple assault | 10.7 | 19.3 | 0.8* | 22.9 | 7.7 | 0.6* | 0.0* |
| **Property crimes** | 5.5% | 14.5% | 27.0% | 11.5% | 4.5% | 15.4% | 0.0%* |
| Household burglary | 1.5 | 18.4 | 16.8 | 8.8 | 4.9 | 19.8 | 0.0* |
| Motor vehicle theft | 0.4* | 11.0 | 49.9 | 12.4 | 3.7* | 7.4 | 0.0* |
| Theft | 6.9 | 13.7 | 28.0 | 12.1 | 4.4 | 14.9 | 0.0* |

Note: Detail may not add to total shown because of rounding.
*Estimate is based on about 10 or fewer sample cases.
[a]Includes verbal threats of rape and threats of sexual assault.

SOURCE: "Table 64. Personal and Property Crimes, 2005: Percent Distribution of Incidents, by Victim's Activity at Time of Incident and Type of Crime," in *Criminal Victimization in the United States, 2005 Statistical Tables*, U.S. Department of Justice, Office of Justice Programs, Bureau of Justice Statistics, December 2006, http://www.ojp.usdoj.gov/bjs/pub/pdf/cvus05.pdf (accessed January 26, 2007)

Justice Statistics (http://www.ojp.usdoj.gov/bjs/pub/pdf/cvus/current/cv0582.pdf). This included $836 million for assaults, $494 million for robberies, and $26 million for rape and sexual assaults. The average amount lost in violent crimes was highest ($791) for robbery, followed by $205 for attempted rape or assault and $194 for rape or sexual assault.

**INTIMATE PARTNER VIOLENCE.** The National Center for Injury Prevention and Control reported in 2003 that the annual health-related costs of rape, physical assault, stalking, and homicide by intimate partners was more than $5.8 billion per year (*Costs of Intimate Partner Violence against Women in the United States*, http://www.cdc.gov/ncipc/pub-res/ipv_cost/IPVBook-Final-Feb18.pdf). As a result of intimate partner violence, almost $4.1 billion is spent each year on medical and mental health care services. The total annual costs of non-fatal intimate partner violence include $0.9 billion in lost productivity from paid work and household chores and $0.9 billion in lifetime earnings lost by victims of intimate partner homicide.

## Property Crime

According to the Bureau of Justice Statistics, the total economic cost of property crime was $15.6 billion in 2005 (http://www.ojp.usdoj.gov/bjs/pub/pdf/cvus/current/cv0582.pdf). This total includes losses of $5.1 billion for household burglary, $5.2 billion for motor vehicle theft, and $5.3 billion for theft. Mean dollar losses were highest ($5,354) for motor vehicle theft, followed by household burglary ($1,471) and theft ($390).

The FBI estimates the value of property stolen in 2005 at more than $13 billion and of property recovered at nearly $4.4 billion. About one-third of all property that is stolen is recovered, according to the FBI statistics. Stolen motor vehicles had the highest dollar value in 2005 with an estimated value of nearly $6.2 billion; however, motor vehicles were more likely to be returned to their owners than any other type of stolen property, with a recovery rate of 62.1%. Jewelry and precious metals accounted for $1 billion in stolen property but proved more difficult to recover, with just 4.5% returned to victims. (See Table 2.12.)

## Justice System Expenditures

In *Justice Expenditures and Employment in the United States, 2003* (Bureau of Justice Statistics, 2006, http://www.ojp.usdoj.gov/bjs/pub/pdf/jeeus03.pdf), the BJS reports that the United States spent $185 billion on police protection, corrections, and judicial and legal activities in 2003. This represented an increase of more than 400% since 1982, when justice expenditures approached $36 billion. This increase is particularly striking when it is compared with the inflation rate, estimated by the Bureau of Labor Statistics to have been 184% between the period

**TABLE 2.12**

**Property stolen and recovered, by type and value, 2005**

[11,686 agencies; 2005 estimated population 222,568,838]

| Type of property | Value of property | | Percent recovered |
|---|---|---|---|
| | Stolen | Recovered | |
| **Total** | **$13,075,382,963** | **$4,359,583,231** | **33.3** |
| Currency, notes, etc. | 979,345,861 | 32,177,230 | 3.3 |
| Jewelry and precious metals | 1,030,082,045 | 46,562,582 | 4.5 |
| Clothing and furs | 215,948,745 | 28,866,408 | 13.4 |
| Locally stolen motor vehicles | 6,186,522,823 | 3,839,499,496 | 62.1 |
| Office equipment | 530,721,906 | 20,331,812 | 3.8 |
| Televisions, radios, stereos, etc. | 792,464,592 | 30,390,889 | 3.8 |
| Firearms | 93,487,243 | 8,107,822 | 8.7 |
| Household goods | 219,147,349 | 10,741,009 | 4.9 |
| Consumable goods | 95,776,212 | 12,408,529 | 13.0 |
| Livestock | 18,726,081 | 2,209,729 | 11.8 |
| Miscellaneous | 2,913,160,106 | 328,287,725 | 11.3 |

SOURCE: "Table 24. Property Stolen and Recovered, by Type and Value, 2005," in *Crime in the United States, 2005*, U.S. Department of Justice Federal Bureau of Investigation, September 2006, http://www.fbi.gov/ucr/05cius/data/table_24.html (accessed January 21, 2007)

1982–84 and 2003. This means that the cost of the justice system increased by more than twice the inflation rate. About half of all justice system expenses are funded by local governments, and states fund another third of these expenses.

Almost half (45%) of all justice spending nationwide in 2003 funded local police departments, according to the BJS. Local governments covered more than two-thirds (69%) of the costs of police protection. State governments paid the largest share of the corrections expenditures (61%). Local (42%) and state (36%) governments funded most of the costs of judicial and legal services.

## VICTIM SERVICES AND ASSISTANCE

Programs and policies that offer assistance to crime victims have received widespread public and legislative support in the United States. Restitution (monetary compensation) paid victims is the most fundamental type of victim assistance because it represents an attempt to repay the victim for what was lost during the commission of a crime. Restitution for criminal acts has a long history that dates back to biblical times. The Bible often cites money payments for injuries, and this practice continued well into the Middle Ages. In about 1100, England's King Henry I began to take a portion of each restitution payment as compensation for holding a trial and for injury inflicted on the state because the criminal act had disturbed the peace within his kingdom. Eventually, assault on an individual began to be considered an assault on society, and the king took the entire payment.

For many years victims received little consideration in justice proceedings; to some it seemed that victims were victimized again by the very system to which they had turned for help. In 1982 Lois Haight Herrington observed in the *Final Report of the President's Task Force on Victims of Crime* (http://www.ojp.usdoj.gov/ovc/publications/presdntstskforcrprt/front.pdf), "Somewhere along the way the system began to serve lawyers and judges and defendants, treating the victim with institutionalized disinterest."

"Revictimization" may take several forms. For example, police questioning might seem to accuse a rape victim of enticing her attacker or participating willingly in the act. An assault victim might find that the hospital is more concerned with whether he or she can pay for treatment than with helping the victim recover from the incident. In their efforts to make sure each defendant receives a fair trial, judges and lawyers might seem to be more concerned about the accused than the victim. Crime victims might not be informed of court dates, sentencing hearings, or probation or parole hearings concerning their cases. They might not be informed when their attacker escapes or is released from prison. Victims who do participate in a trial might be kept outside the courtroom without ever being called to the witness stand. Situations such as these led many to advocate for victims' rights, including the right to be protected from harassment and the right to communicate to the court the impact a crime has had on their lives.

## Changing Attitudes toward Victims

Attempts to improve the situation for victims gained momentum during the 1980s and 1990s. State and federal governments, the judicial system, and private groups all reflected an increased awareness of victims' concerns. By 1996 thousands of organizations offered services to victims of crime. These organizations included domestic violence shelters, rape crisis centers, and child abuse programs. Law enforcement agencies, hospitals, and social services agencies also provided victims' services. The types of services provided include:

• Crisis intervention

• Counseling

• Emergency shelter and transportation

• Legal services

## Victim Compensation

Victim compensation programs pay money from a public fund to help victims with expenses incurred because of a violent crime. Margery Fry, a British magistrate and legal reformer, began advocating for a victim compensation program during the 1950s. In her book *Arms of the Law* (1951), Fry suggested that society had neglected the restitution customs of earlier generations. She noted that making up for a wrongful act held wide

currency in earlier societies, and recommended revisiting this form of punishment. Her book and articles advocating compensation programs aroused considerable discussion in the United Kingdom and New Zealand. As a result, New Zealand's legislature passed a law permitting the government to award compensation to victims. After several years of debate, the British Parliament created an experimental program in 1964.

**VICTIM COMPENSATION PROGRAMS IN THE UNITED STATES.** In the United States interest in victim compensation grew rapidly in the mid-1960s. In 1965 California became the first state to develop a victim compensation program. The idea spread across the country, with New York (1966), Hawaii (1967), Maryland (1968), Massachusetts (1968), and New Jersey (1971) soon adopting compensation programs.

By the year 2002 all fifty states, the District of Columbia, Puerto Rico, Guam, and the Virgin Islands had victim compensation programs. Most state laws include reimbursement for medical treatment and physical therapy costs, counseling fees, lost wages, funeral and burial expenses, and loss of support to dependents of homicide victims. The Department of Justice's Office for Victims of Crimes reported in 2006 (*Victims' Rights, Strength in Unity*, http://www.ojp.usdoj.gov/ovc/ncvrw/2006/pdf/resource_guide.pdf) that state compensation programs had paid crime victims and their families $426 million in benefits in fiscal year 2004. In that year, 51% of all compensation payments were for medical expenses, 19% were for lost wages and lost support in homicides, 11% for funeral bills, and 9% for mental health costs. Maximum awards generally ranged from $10,000 to $25,000, although a few state maximums are higher or lower.

Victim compensation normally does not cover the costs of pain and suffering, future income loss, or property loss and damage (except the loss of eyeglasses, dentures, etc., by the elderly). Compensation is paid only when other resources—private insurance or offender restitution, for example—do not cover the loss.

The federal government maintains the Crime Victims Fund, which is administered by the Office for Victims of Crime of the U.S. Department of Justice. The Federal Victims of Crime Act of 1984 (VOCA, PL 98-473) established the fund, which supports the Victim Compensation and Victim Assistance grant programs. Like the state funds, victim compensation grants cover medical treatment and physical therapy costs, counseling fees, lost wages, funeral and burial expenses, and loss of support to dependents of homicide victims. Victim assistance funds cover the costs of crisis intervention, counseling, emergency shelter, and criminal justice advocacy. Deposits to the fund come from fines, penalty assessments, and bond forfeitures collected from convicted federal criminal offenders. In 2001 legislation was passed allowing the fund to receive gifts, donations, and bequests from private entities.

Previously, VOCA provided each state with a grant worth 40% of the amount that the state had spent the previous year on victim compensation. However, in 2003 VOCA began providing 60% of the amount that states spent. This means that for every $160 awarded to a victim, $100 comes from the state and $60 comes from VOCA. Between 1985 and 2004 the fund distributed over $5.5 billion to support victim assistance and services. During this period more than $5.5 billion was deposited into the VOCA Fund.

## Offender Restitution Programs

Restitution programs require those who have harmed an individual to repay the victim. In the past, the criminal justice system focused primarily on punishing the criminal, leaving victims to rely on civil court cases for damage repayment. By 2000 most states permitted criminal courts to allow restitution payments as a condition of probation and/or parole. According to the Office for Victims of Crime, every state gives courts the statutory authority to order restitution, and most state crime victims' rights constitutional amendments give victims a right to restitution (*Ordering Restitution to the Crime Victim, Legal Series Bulletin #6*, 2002, http://www.ojp.usdoj.gov/ovc/publications/bulletins/legalseries/bulletin6/welcome.html).

Most restitution laws provide for restitution to the direct victim(s) of a crime, including surviving family members of homicide victims. In most cases, restitution is only provided to victims of crimes for which a defendant was convicted.

Most states allow victims to claim medical expenses and property damage or loss, and most permit families of homicide victims to claim costs for loss of support. The state of Washington allows courts to determine damages for pain and suffering as well as "punitive damages" valued at twice the victim's actual loss. In assessing damages, the courts must take into consideration the offender's ability to pay.

Restitution can be ordered for several types of crime-related expenses that a victim experiences. The restitution amount is typically based on:

- Medical care costs
- Lost wages
- Counseling
- Lost or damaged property
- Funeral expenses
- Other direct out-of-pocket expenses

An offender may lose parole privileges and be imprisoned for nonpayment of restitution fees (http://www.ojp.usdoj.gov/ovc/publications/bulletins/legalseries/bulletin5/4.html). The courts have upheld the constitutionality of incarcerating offenders for nonpayment, but the Supreme Court, in *Beardon v. Georgia* (461 US 660, 1983), ruled that an offender could not be sent to prison for nonpayment if he or she had made a good-faith effort to pay and could not do so. In most cases offenders must prove their inability to make the payments. When offenders prove that they cannot pay, the courts can reduce the amount, change the schedule of payments, or suspend payment.

Besides threatening offenders with imprisonment, some jurisdictions have other methods of collection. These include garnishment of wages (taking the payment amount from wages before the employee receives his or her salary) or attaching the offender's assets (not allowing the offender to use bank accounts, stocks, or bonds) until he or she pays the restitution. Some jurisdictions can even sell the offender's home.

## Civil Suits

A victim can sue in civil court for damages even if the offender has not been found guilty of a criminal offense. Victims often follow this route because it is easier to win civil cases than criminal cases. In a criminal case, a jury or judge can find an alleged offender guilty only if the proof is "beyond a reasonable doubt." In a civil case, the burden of proof requires merely a "preponderance of the evidence" against the accused. Proof is still needed that a crime was committed, that there were damages, and that the accused is liable to pay for those damages. Even when victims win a civil suit, they often have trouble collecting damage payment.

## VICTIMS' RIGHTS
### State Laws

Victims' rights guaranteed by state laws include the right to attend criminal proceedings, to be notified of proceedings such as parole hearings, and to be free from harassment. As of 2007, thirty-four states included crime victims' rights in their state constitutions.

### Federal Action

The U.S. government has passed several laws intended to strengthen the legal rights of victims and make social services more widely accessible to crime victims. The Keeping Children and Families Safe Act of 2003 (P.L. 108-36) was signed into law on June 25, 2003. The act supports state efforts toward preventing and treating child abuse and neglect, including a basic grant program for improving state child protective services. The Justice for All Act of 2004 (P.L. 108-405), which was signed into law on October 30, 2004, contains four major sections related to crime victims and the criminal justice process. The act contains provisions intended to protect crime victims' rights, eliminate the substantial backlog of DNA samples collected from crime scenes and convicted offenders, and improve and expand the DNA testing capacity of federal, state, and local crime laboratories. The Crime Victims' Rights Act (CVRA) is a key component of the Justice for All Act. It guarantees crime victims the following rights:

1. The right to be reasonably protected from the accused.

2. The right to reasonable, accurate, and timely notice of any public court proceeding, or any parole proceeding, involving the crime or of any release or escape of the accused.

3. The right not to be excluded from any such public court proceeding, unless the court, after receiving clear and convincing evidence, determines that testimony by the victim would be materially altered if the victim heard other testimony at that proceeding.

4. The right to be reasonably heard at any public proceeding in the district court involving release, plea, sentencing, or any parole proceeding.

5. The reasonable right to confer with the attorney for the Government in the case.

6. The right to full and timely restitution as provided in law.

7. The right to proceedings free from unreasonable delay.

8. The right to be treated with fairness and with respect for the victim's dignity and privacy.

On January 5, 2006, President George W. Bush signed into law a reauthorization of the Violence Against Women Act (P.L. 109-162). The Violence Against Women Act funds programs and services for victims of domestic violence, sexual assault, dating violence, and stalking.

### Victims' Participation at Sentencing

Every state allows courts to consider or ask for information from victims concerning the impact of the offense on their lives. The National Center for Victims of Crime reported in 2007 that virtually all states permit victim input at sentencing and most allow written victim-impact statements (detailing the effect the crime has on the victim or, in the case of murder, on the victim's family). The Child Protection Restoration and Penalties Enhancement Act of 1990 (P.L. 101-647) permits child victims of federal crimes to present statements commensurate with their age, including drawings. Although most impact statements are used at sentencing and parole hearings, victims often have input at bail hearings, pretrial release hearings, and plea-bargaining hearings.

Many state legislatures have developed strong victims' rights legislation. For example, California's Proposition Eight, the state's "Victims' Bill of Rights," includes Penal Code Section 1191.1, which states:

> The victim or next of kin has the right to appear, personally or by counsel, at the sentencing proceeding and to reasonably express his or her views concerning the crime, the person responsible, and the need for restitution. The court, in imposing sentence, shall consider the statements of victims and next of kin ... and shall state on the record its conclusion concerning whether the person would pose a threat to public safety if granted probation....

### Witnessing Executions

According to the National Center for Victims of Crime, several states have statutes allowing victims' family members to be present at executions. Other states have informal policies permitting victims' families to view executions. Most states limit the viewing to immediate family members and sometimes limit the total number of viewers.

## FEDERAL ACTIONS

### The Federal Victim and Witness Protection Act of 1982

In 1982 Congress enacted the Federal Victim and Witness Protection Act, a bill designed to protect and assist victims and witnesses of federal crimes. The law permits victim-impact statements in sentencing hearings to provide judges with information concerning financial, psychological, or physical harm suffered by victims. The law also provides for restitution to victims and prevents victims and/or witnesses from being intimidated by threatening verbal harassment. The law establishes penalties for acts of retaliation by defendants against those who testify against them.

Victims who provide addresses and telephone numbers are to be notified of major events in the criminal proceedings, including the arrest of the accused, the times of any court appearances at which the victim may appear, the release or detention of the accused, and the victim's opportunities to address the sentencing court. The guidelines also recommend that federal officials consult victims and witnesses to obtain their views on such procedures as proposed dismissals and plea negotiations. Officials must not disclose the names and addresses of victims and witnesses.

### The Comprehensive Crime Control Act of 1990

In 1990 President George H.W. Bush signed the Comprehensive Crime Control Act (P.L. 101-647), which addressed many aspects of crime control, including protection for victims of child abuse, penalties for savings and loan fraud, and mandatory death penalties. The law includes the Victims' Rights and Restitution Act of 1990, which provides victims of federal crimes with the right to be treated with fairness and respect, reasonably protected from the accused, notified of court proceedings, afforded an opportunity to meet with a federal prosecutor, and provided with restitution. The act also bars criminals and convicted drunken drivers from declaring bankruptcy to avoid paying restitution.

## Compensation and Assistance to Victims of Terrorism or Mass Violence

In spring of 1996 Congress authorized compensation for citizens victimized by terrorist acts, both at home and abroad. The Justice for Victims of Terrorism Act of 1996 allows the director of the Victims Crime Fund (see above) to make supplemental grants to states to assist residents who are victims of terrorism. After the terrorist attacks on the United States on September 11, 2001, the October 2001 USA Patriot Act (P.L. 107-56) authorized the transfer of emergency supplemental appropriation funding into the Emergency Reserve account to assist victims of the attacks.

## The Air Transportation Safety and System Stabilization Act

On September 22, 2001, the 107th Congress enacted The Air Transportation Safety and System Stabilization Act (P.L. 107-42). In addition to requiring the federal government to compensate the air carriers for losses incurred as a result of the September 11th attacks, the act established the September 11th Victim Compensation Fund of 2001. The fund provided compensation to victims of the attacks who chose not to join in litigation (lawsuits) seeking additional money. The fund compensated any individual who was physically injured, and the families and beneficiaries of victims killed, as a result of the terrorist-related aircraft crashes of September 11, 2001.

# CHAPTER 3
# HATE CRIMES AND TERRORISM IN THE UNITED STATES

Hate crimes and terrorist incidents often have similar methods and effects. For example, a person committing a hate crime from a motive of religious bias might use an incendiary device (one that causes fire, such as a Molotov cocktail) to burn down a mosque, church, or synagogue. A terrorist group might use the same type of device to burn down a government building. In both cases the results are property damage, intimidation, and possibly even the deaths of or injuries to innocent people.

The primary difference between these types of crime is the motive behind the act. While no single, comprehensive definitions are available for hate crimes and terrorism, the Federal Bureau of Investigation (FBI) uses these working definitions:

- Hate crime (also known as bias crime) is a criminal offense committed against a person, property, or society that is motivated, in whole or in part, by the offender's bias against a race, religion, ethnic or national origin, sexual orientation, or disability.

- Terrorism is the unlawful use of force or violence against persons or property to intimidate or coerce a government, the civilian population, or any segment thereof, to further political or social objectives.

## HATE AND TERRORIST GROUPS

The Southern Poverty Law Center (SPLC), a civil-rights advocacy group based in Montgomery, Alabama, reports that 803 hate groups were active in the United States during 2005. This represented a 5% increase from 2004 and a 33% increase from 2000 (*The Year in Hate, 2005*, spring 2006, http://www.splcenter.org/). The SPLC categorizes these groups as Ku Klux Klan, Neo-Nazi, Racist Skinhead, and Neo-Confederate. Klan groups include those that advocate white supremacy and are related to the Ku Klux Klan in ideology if not in organization; their number increased from 158 active groups in 2003 to 179 in 2005. Neo-Nazi groups, which numbered 157 in 2005, combine white-supremacist doctrines with anti-Semitism and militarism. Skinhead groups that espouse racial hatred are included in the SPLC list, and these numbered 56 in 2005; however, skinhead fashion and music encompass a wide range of political opinions, including anti-racists. Targets of hate groups in 2005 included African-Americans, Jews, Muslims, homosexuals, and others.

One reason hate groups are gaining momentum, according to the SPLC, is that these groups have benefited from media coverage of hate rallies. Among the most widely reported of these events was the riot sparked by a National Socialist Movement demonstration in Toledo, Ohio, in October 2005. In the aftermath of the march, police clashed with groups that had gathered to express their disapproval of the neo-Nazi organization, and more than 100 counter-protestors were arrested for looting, arson, and assaulting police officers. Hate groups also use radio, literature, music, and the Internet to publicize their point of view; the SPLC counted 524 hate Web sites in 2005, up 18% from 443 in 2002.

## HATE CRIME LEGISLATION
### Federal Laws

In 1990 Congress passed the Hate Crime Statistics Act (P.L. 101-275), which required the attorney general to "acquire data...about crimes that manifest evidence of prejudice based on race, religion, sexual orientation or ethnicity" and to publish a summary of the data. The Hate Crimes Statistics Act was amended by the Violent Crime and Law Enforcement Act of 1994 (P.L. 103-322) to include bias-motivated acts against disabled persons. Further amendments in the Church Arsons Prevention Act of 1996 (P.L. 104-155) directed the FBI to track bias-related church arsons as a permanent part of its duties. In 1990 only 11 states reported information on hate crimes. By 2005, 12,417 law enforcement agencies reported their data.

## State Laws

According to the Anti-Defamation League (ADL), an organization that fights anti-Semitism and bigotry, forty-five states and the District of Columbia had adopted some form of penalty-enhancement hate crime statute as of January 2007; states that had not criminalized bias-motivated violence and intimidation included Arkansas, Georgia, Indiana, South Carolina, and Wyoming. As of June 2006 race, religion, and ethnicity were included in the hate crime laws of all forty-five states; thirty-two state statutes included sexual orientation, twenty-eight states included gender, and thirty-two states included disability (http://www.adl.org/99hatecrime/state_hate_crime_laws.pdf).

The constitutionality of these laws has been challenged on the grounds that they punish free thought. In 1992 the U.S. Supreme Court, in *R.A.V. v. City of St. Paul* (112 S.Ct. 2538), found a Minnesota law outlawing certain "fighting words" to be unconstitutional. In this case, the defendant had burned a cross "inside the fenced yard of a African-American family." The Court ruled that

> Although there is an important governmental interest in protecting the exercise of the African-American resident's right to occupy a dwelling free from intimidation, we cannot say that, under the circumstances before us, the government interest is unrelated to the suppression of free expression.

A law limiting pure speech or symbolic speech can only be upheld if it meets the "clear and present danger" standard of *Brandenburg v. Ohio* (395 U.S. 444, 1969). This standard means that speech may be outlawed if it incites or produces "imminent lawless action."

In June 1993, however, the Supreme Court, in *Mitchell v. Wisconsin* (113 S.Ct. 2194), upheld laws that impose harsher prison sentences and greater fines for criminals who are motivated by bigotry. The Court found that such statutes as the Wisconsin law do not illegally restrict free speech and are not so general as to restrict constitutional behavior.

## HATE CRIME OFFENSES

Hate crimes are criminal offenses motivated by the offender's personal prejudice or bias. The FBI includes hate crimes in its Uniform Crime Reporting (UCR) program. The UCR Program's first publication on hate crimes was *Hate Crime Statistics, 1990: A Resource Book*, which compiled hate crime data from eleven states that had collected the information under state authority in 1990. The UCR Program continued to work with agencies that were already investigating hate crimes and collecting related information to develop a more uniform method of nationwide data collection. *Hate Crime Statistics, 1992*, offered the first data reported by law enforcement agencies across the country

that participated in UCR hate crime data collection. In the 1994 Violent Crime and Law Enforcement Act, Congress added hate-motivated crimes against disabled persons to the list of bias crimes; the FBI began gathering data on hate crimes against this population on January 1, 1997.

Data on hate crimes are incomplete because many incidents are not reported or cannot be verified as hate crimes. Some victims do not report hate crimes due to fear that the criminal justice system is biased against the group to which the victim belongs and that law enforcement authorities will not be responsive. Many attacks against homosexuals are not reported because the victims do not want to reveal their sexual orientation to others. In addition, proving that an offender acted from bias can be a long, tedious process, requiring much investigation. Until a law enforcement investigator can find enough evidence in a particular case to be sure the offender's actions came, at least in part, from bias, the crime is not counted as a hate crime.

## Hate Crime Statistics

Although the number of hate crimes reported to the authorities has fluctuated somewhat between 1993 and 2005, the overall trend has been a downward one. According to the FBI's UCR, 7,684 hate crimes were reported in 1993; this number fell to 7,163 in 2005. A majority of hate crimes (55.4%) that were reported in 2005 were motivated by racial bias. Other common reasons for hate crimes were association with people who have certain characteristics (30.7% of incidents), ethnicity (28.7%), and sexual orientation (18%). (See Table 3.1.) Among the specific bias types tracked in 2005, anti–African-American incidents accounted for the largest number of single-bias incidents (2,630), followed by anti-homosexual incidents (971 combined) and anti-Jewish incidents (848). (See Table 3.2.)

A hate crime incident can have more than one victim and several offenders. To tabulate hate-crime data the FBI counts one offense for each victim of a crime against persons and one offense for each distinct act of crime against property and crime against society. Therefore more offenses (8,380) and victims (8,804) were reported than incidents (7,163) in 2005. (See Table 3.2.)

In 2005, 7,160 incidents of single-bias hate crime were reported. A single-bias incident is a hate crime in which one type of offense (such as assault) is committed as a result of one bias-motivation (such as anti–African-American sentiment). The FBI reported 3,919 incidents due to racial bias, 1,227 incidents due to bias against a religion, and 1,017 incidents due to sexual-orientation bias. (See Table 3.3.)

**TABLE 3.1**

**Hate crime motivation as perceived by victims, 2000–03**

| | Percent of hate crime | |
| --- | --- | --- |
| | Incidents | Victimizations |
| **Motivation** | | |
| Race | 55.4% | 56.0% |
| Association | 30.7 | 30.6 |
| Ethnicity | 28.7 | 27.9 |
| Sexual orientation | 18.0 | 17.9 |
| Perceived characteristic | 13.7 | 13.2 |
| Religion | 12.9 | 12.4 |
| Disability | 11.2 | 10.5 |
| **Evidence of motivation** | | |
| Negative comments, hurtful words, abusive language | 98.5% | 98.5% |
| Confirmation by police investigation | 7.9 | 8.4 |
| Hate symbols | 7.6 | 7.8 |

Note: Detail adds to more than 100% because some respondents included more than one motivation or evidence of motivation.

SOURCE: Caroline Wolf Harlow, "Table 2. Motivation and Evidence in Hate Crime," in *Hate Crime Reported by Victims and Police*, U.S. Department of Justice, Office of Justice Programs, Bureau of Justice Statistics, November 2005, http://www.ojp.usdoj.gov/bjs/pub/pdf/hcrvp.pdf (accessed January 15, 2007)

## Kinds of Crime Motivated by Hate

The FBI categorizes hate crimes as crimes against persons, crimes against property, and crimes against society. In 2005 about 4,208 (58.7%) of hate offenses were crimes against persons. Of these crimes, almost half (2,044) were acts of intimidation and approximately one-quarter (1,324) were simple assaults. (See Table 3.4.) Property crimes, which are also represented in Table 3.4, accounted for 3,109 (43.4%) of all hate crime incidents in 2005. Most property crimes were acts of destruction (2,528 incidents), larceny-theft (221), or robbery (127).

In the wake of the events of September 11, 2001, a surge in attacks against people of Arab descent and Muslims in general was reported, including fire bombings, shootings, and other acts of violence. The Civil Rights Division, the FBI, and United States Attorneys offices (all of the U.S. Department of Justice) have investigated more than 750 incidents since 9/11 involving violence, threats, vandalism, and arson against Arab-Americans, Muslims, Sikhs, South-Asian Americans, and other individuals thought to be of Middle Eastern

**TABLE 3.2**

**Hate crime incidents, offenses, victims, and known offenders, by bias motivation, 2005**

| Bias motivation | Incidents | Offenses | Victims[a] | Known offenders[b] |
| --- | --- | --- | --- | --- |
| **Total** | **7,163** | **8,380** | **8,804** | **6,804** |
| **Single-bias incidents** | 7,160 | 8,373 | 8,795 | 6,800 |
| Race: | 3,919 | 4,691 | 4,895 | 3,913 |
| Anti-white | 828 | 935 | 975 | 963 |
| Anti-black | 2,630 | 3,200 | 3,322 | 2,581 |
| Anti-American Indian/Alaskan Native | 79 | 95 | 97 | 73 |
| Anti-Asian/Pacific Islander | 199 | 231 | 240 | 163 |
| Anti-multiple races, group | 183 | 230 | 261 | 133 |
| Religion: | 1,227 | 1,314 | 1,405 | 580 |
| Anti-Jewish | 848 | 900 | 977 | 364 |
| Anti-Catholic | 58 | 61 | 61 | 22 |
| Anti-Protestant | 57 | 58 | 58 | 32 |
| Anti-Islamic | 128 | 146 | 151 | 89 |
| Anti-other religion | 93 | 102 | 106 | 54 |
| Anti-multiple religions, group | 39 | 42 | 47 | 18 |
| Anti-atheism/agnosticism/etc. | 4 | 5 | 5 | 1 |
| Sexual orientation: | 1,017 | 1,171 | 1,213 | 1,138 |
| Anti-male homosexual | 621 | 713 | 743 | 715 |
| Anti-female homosexual | 155 | 180 | 186 | 146 |
| Anti-homosexual | 195 | 228 | 233 | 237 |
| Anti-heterosexual | 21 | 23 | 23 | 18 |
| Anti-bisexual | 25 | 27 | 28 | 22 |
| Ethnicity/national origin: | 944 | 1,144 | 1,228 | 1,115 |
| Anti-Hispanic | 522 | 660 | 722 | 691 |
| Anti-other ethnicity/national origin | 422 | 484 | 506 | 424 |
| Disability: | 53 | 53 | 54 | 54 |
| Anti-physical | 21 | 21 | 21 | 21 |
| Anti-mental | 32 | 32 | 33 | 33 |
| **Multiple-bias incidents[c]** | 3 | 7 | 9 | 4 |

[a]The term *victim* may refer to a person, business, institution, or society as a whole.
[b]The term *known offender* does not imply that the identity of the suspect is known, but only that an attribute of the suspect has been identified, which distinguishes him/her from an unknown offender.
[c]In a *multiple-bias incident* two conditions must be met: 1) more than one offense type must occur in the incident and 2) at least two offense types must be motivated by different biases.

SOURCE: "Table 1. Incidents, Offenses, Victims, and Known Offenders, by Bias Motivation, 2005," in *Hate Crime Statistics 2005*, U.S. Department of Justice, Federal Bureau of Investigation, October 2006, http://www.fbi.gov/ucr/hc2005/table1.htm (accessed January 10, 2007)

TABLE 3.3

**Hate crime incidents by victim type and bias motivation, 2005**

| Bias motivation | Total incidents | Victim type | | | | | |
| | | Individual | Business/ financial institution | Government | Religious organization | Society/ public[a] | Other/ unknown/ multiple |
|---|---|---|---|---|---|---|---|
| Total | 7,163 | 5,662 | 295 | 270 | 202 | 67 | 667 |
| Single-bias incidents | 7,160 | 5,661 | 295 | 269 | 202 | 67 | 666 |
| Race | 3,919 | 3,199 | 180 | 168 | 19 | 51 | 302 |
| Religion | 1,227 | 639 | 74 | 63 | 174 | 5 | 272 |
| Sexual orientation | 1,017 | 935 | 16 | 19 | 5 | 4 | 38 |
| Ethnicity/national origin | 944 | 839 | 22 | 19 | 4 | 6 | 54 |
| Disability | 53 | 49 | 3 | 0 | 0 | 1 | 0 |
| Multiple-bias incidents[b] | 3 | 1 | 0 | 1 | 0 | 0 | 1 |

[a]The victim type *society/public* is collected only in the national incident-based reporting system.
[b]In a *multiple-bias incident* two conditions must be met: 1) more than one offense type must occur in the incident and 2) at least two offense types must be motivated by different biases.

SOURCE: "Table 8. Incidents: Victim Type, by Bias Motivation, 2005," in *Hate Crime Statistics 2005*, U.S. Department of Justice, Federal Bureau of Investigation, October 2006, http://www.fbi.gov/ucr/hc2005/table8.htm (accessed January 10, 2007)

TABLE 3.4

**Hate crime incidents, offenses, and known offenders, by type of offense, 2005**

| Offense type | Incidents[a] | Offenses | Victims[b] | Known offenders[c] |
|---|---|---|---|---|
| Total | 7,163 | 8,380 | 8,804 | 6,804 |
| **Crimes against persons:** | 4,208 | 5,190 | 5,190 | 5,357 |
| Murder and nonnegligent manslaughter | 6 | 6 | 6 | 17 |
| Forcible rape | 3 | 3 | 3 | 3 |
| Aggravated assault | 817 | 1,062 | 1,062 | 1,381 |
| Simple assault | 1,324 | 1,566 | 1,566 | 1,957 |
| Intimidation | 2,044 | 2,539 | 2,539 | 1,974 |
| Other[d] | 14 | 14 | 14 | 25 |
| **Crimes against property:** | 3,109 | 3,109 | 3,530 | 1,680 |
| Robbery | 127 | 127 | 154 | 289 |
| Burglary | 136 | 136 | 165 | 88 |
| Larceny-theft | 221 | 221 | 232 | 146 |
| Motor vehicle theft | 18 | 18 | 19 | 14 |
| Arson | 39 | 39 | 48 | 32 |
| Destruction/damage/vandalism | 2,528 | 2,528 | 2,869 | 1,072 |
| Other[d] | 40 | 40 | 43 | 39 |
| **Crimes against society[d]** | 81 | 81 | 84 | 114 |

[a]The actual number of incidents is 7,163. However, the column figures will not add to the total because incidents may include more than one offense type, and these are counted in each appropriate offense type category.
[b]The term *victim* may refer to a person, business, institution, or society as a whole.
[c]The term *known offender* does not imply that the identity of the suspect is known, but only that an attribute of the suspect has been identified, which distinguishes him/her from an unknown offender. The actual number of known offenders is 6,804. However, the column figures will not add to the total because some offenders are responsible for more than one offense type, and they are, therefore, counted more than once in this table.
[d]Includes additional offenses collected in the national incident-based reporting system.

SOURCE: "Table 2. Incidents, Offenses, Victims, and Known Offenders, by Offense Type, 2005," in *Hate Crime Statistics 2005*, U.S. Department of Justice, Federal Bureau of Investigation, October 2006, http://www.fbi.gov/ucr/hc2005/table2.htm (accessed January 10, 2007)

origin (U.S. Department of Justice, *FY 2008 Performance Budget*, http://www.usdoj.gov/jmd/2008justification/pdf/18_crt.pdf). Federal charges had been brought against 35 defendants as of fiscal year (FY) 2006, with 32 convictions to date. State and local charges were pursued against more than 150 defendants.

One of the people convicted for an anti-Muslim hate crime was Erik K. Nix. Nix was convicted on March 6, 2006, of planting an explosive device in a van owned by a Muslim family of Palestinian descent. The van was parked outside the family's home in Burbank, Illinois, at the time of the explosion in 2003. Although Nix had been tried by the state and sentenced to two years' probation and anger management classes in the same incident, the subsequent federal charges resulted in a sentence of fifteen months in prison for Nix.

## Hate-Motivated Murders

The most extreme hate-motivated crime against a person is murder. In 2005, six bias-motivated murders were reported to the FBI, less than 1% of all hate offenses. By their very nature, however, murders motivated by hate or bias are the most horrible and unforgettable to society.

The nation was shocked and outraged by the brutal killing of an African-American man, James Byrd, Jr., near the small town of Jasper, Texas, in June 1998. Two white men convicted of the murder, John William King and Lawrence Russell Brewer, were suspected of ties to white supremacy organizations. A third man, Shawn Allen Berry, was also convicted. These men beat and kicked Byrd and then chained him to the back of a pickup truck and dragged him until his body was torn apart.

In the aftermath of the murder, members of the Ku Klux Klan gathered in Jasper, saying that they were there to protect whites from African-Americans. In response, Black activist groups, including the Black Muslims and the New Black Panthers, assembled in Jasper to protect African-Americans from whites. Fortunately law enforcement officers and the townspeople of Jasper were able to prevent further violence. Jasper residents repeatedly expressed their sorrow for the murder and begged outsiders to go away and let them try to cope with the crime and its consequences. The Byrd family issued a written statement asking the public not to use the murder as an excuse for further hatred and retribution. They asked that Americans view the incident as a wake-up call and expressed the hope that it would lead to self-examination and reflection. Eventually, the murder led to state legislation that intensifies penalties for crimes motivated by the victim's race, religion, sex, disability, sexual orientation, age, or national origin. The James Byrd Jr. Hate Crimes Act was signed into law by Texas governor Rick Perry on May 11, 2001.

Despite the publicity the Byrd case received, the pleas of his family seem to have had little effect on national hate crime murder statistics. Each year, equally shocking cases of hate-motivated murders occur. In March 2000 in Wilkinsburg, Pennsylvania, Ronald Taylor, an African-American, shot five white men, killing three of them. One month later, five people, including a Jewish woman, an Indian, two Asians, and one African-American, were killed in Pittsburgh, Pennsylvania, when Richard Scott Baumhammers, an immigration lawyer, went on a shooting rampage. In 2006 four members of a Latino gang—Porfirio Avila, Gilbert Saldana, Alejandro Martinez, and Fernando Cazares—were convicted of the racially motivated assaults and murders of two African-Americans in Los Angeles.

Another famous case of racially motivated murder came to a close in 2005 after more than forty years. Edgar Ray Killen, a former Ku Klux Klan organizer, was convicted in June 2005 of three counts of manslaughter for his role in the deaths of civil rights activists Andrew Goodman, 20, Michael Schwerner, 24, and James Chaney, 21, in June 1964. The three young volunteers were murdered in Philadelphia, Mississippi, as they participated in the "Freedom Summer" campaign, an effort to register southern blacks to vote. The shocking disappearance and murder of these civil rights workers later became the subject of several books, movies, and criminal investigations, including the one by high school students in Illinois in 2004 that included an interview with Killen and ultimately led to his conviction. The eighty-year-old Killen was sentenced to the maximum sentence of sixty years in prison, twenty years for each manslaughter conviction, to be served consecutively.

In an incident that mayor Greg Nickels described as "a crime of hate," one woman was killed and five others were wounded in an assault on the Jewish Federation building in Seattle, Washington, on July 28, 2006 (http://www.cnn.com/2006/US/07/28/seattle.shooting/). In the attack Naveed Afzal Haq, a thirty-year-old U.S. citizen of Pakistani descent, fired randomly on employees before surrendering to police. He had held a thirteen-year-old girl at gunpoint in order to pass through the building's rigid security. Once inside he told his hostages that he was "a Muslim-American" who was "angry at Israel."

## Where Do Hate Crimes Occur?

In its annual report on hate crimes, the FBI assembles statistics on hate crime victims, perpetrators, motivation, and location. According to this data, bias incidents reported during 2005 were more likely to occur at the victim's home than at any other location, representing 2,148 of the 7,163 total incidents. The remainder occurred on highways, roads, alleys, and streets (1,314); in schools and colleges (967); in parking lots and garages (471); and in places of worship (310). (See Table 3.5.)

## Who Commits Hate Crimes?

Hate crimes are committed by individuals, groups of individuals, and organizations with a bias against certain races, religions, or societal groups. In "Hate Crimes" (2005, http://www.violence.neu.edu/in_the_news/past_news/hate_crimes/ ), Jack Levin and Jack McDevitt of Northeastern University describe three types of hate crimes based on the offender's motivation.

- *Thrill-seeking crimes*: Thrill crimes are committed by individuals who are out looking for excitement and who act out this desire in a violent or destructive way. According to Levin and McDevitt, "In the same way that some young men get together on a Saturday night

TABLE 3.5

**Hate crime incidents by bias motivation and location, 2005**

| Location | Total incidents | Bias motivation | | | | | Multiple-bias incidents* |
|---|---|---|---|---|---|---|---|
| | | Race | Religion | Sexual orientation | Ethnicity/ national origin | Disability | |
| Total | 7,163 | 3,919 | 1,227 | 1,017 | 944 | 53 | 3 |
| Air/bus/train terminal | 55 | 34 | 3 | 5 | 12 | 1 | 0 |
| Bank/savings and loan | 23 | 16 | 6 | 0 | 1 | 0 | 0 |
| Bar/nightclub | 138 | 76 | 7 | 31 | 23 | 1 | 0 |
| Church/synagogue/temple | 310 | 61 | 223 | 11 | 14 | 1 | 0 |
| Commercial office building | 152 | 86 | 29 | 11 | 25 | 1 | 0 |
| Construction site | 17 | 12 | 1 | 1 | 3 | 0 | 0 |
| Convenience store | 101 | 53 | 11 | 11 | 25 | 1 | 0 |
| Department/discount store | 45 | 30 | 8 | 2 | 5 | 0 | 0 |
| Drug store/doctor's office/hospital | 52 | 28 | 13 | 7 | 4 | 0 | 0 |
| Field/woods | 72 | 48 | 6 | 7 | 11 | 0 | 0 |
| Government/public building | 129 | 70 | 20 | 18 | 21 | 0 | 0 |
| Grocery/supermarket | 62 | 40 | 4 | 6 | 12 | 0 | 0 |
| Highway/road/alley/street | 1,314 | 778 | 93 | 254 | 183 | 6 | 0 |
| Hotel/motel/etc. | 45 | 28 | 5 | 5 | 5 | 2 | 0 |
| Jail/prison | 48 | 27 | 3 | 9 | 9 | 0 | 0 |
| Lake/waterway | 21 | 8 | 0 | 8 | 5 | 0 | 0 |
| Liquor store | 18 | 6 | 2 | 3 | 7 | 0 | 0 |
| Parking lot/garage | 471 | 264 | 46 | 69 | 89 | 3 | 0 |
| Rental storage facility | 7 | 5 | 1 | 1 | 0 | 0 | 0 |
| Residence/home | 2,148 | 1,216 | 313 | 328 | 270 | 21 | 0 |
| Restaurant | 110 | 59 | 15 | 14 | 19 | 3 | 0 |
| School/college | 967 | 519 | 208 | 123 | 113 | 3 | 1 |
| Service/gas station | 67 | 39 | 7 | 5 | 14 | 2 | 0 |
| Specialty store (tv, fur, etc.) | 78 | 45 | 10 | 11 | 11 | 1 | 0 |
| Other/unknown | 699 | 365 | 191 | 75 | 61 | 7 | 0 |
| Multiple locations | 14 | 6 | 2 | 2 | 2 | 0 | 2 |

*In a *multiple-bias incident* two conditions must be met: 1) more than one offense type must occur in the incident and 2) at least two offense types must be motivated by different biases.

SOURCE: "Table 10. Incidents: Bias Motivation, by Location, 2005," in *Hate Crime Statistics 2005*, U.S. Department of Justice, Federal Bureau of Investigation, October 2006, http://www.fbi.gov/ucr/hc2005/table10.htm (accessed January 10, 2007)

to play a game of cards, youthful hatemongers gather to destroy property or to bash minorities." Importantly, this type of hate crime is not triggered by a particular incident, usually is not directed at a particular individual (but at anyone who fits the target profile), and often occurs in a place frequented by the victim or victims rather than by the perpetrators.

- *Reactive crimes*: Reactive hate crimes are those that can typically be traced to a particular incident in which the perpetrators perceive a threat from an outsider. As examples of such triggering events Levin and McDevitt suggest a person of a different race moving into a racially segregated neighborhood or being promoted at work. In these cases, the victim is chosen specifically in response to this attempt to "invade" a specific area or assume a privileged position in the community. These hate crimes are the most common form.

- *Mission-oriented crimes*: The least common type of hate crime is the mission-oriented incident, according to Levin and McDevitt. Perpetrators of these crimes act on the basis of what they believe to be a moral mission. They often organize with others who share their beliefs in such organizations as the Ku Klux Klan and aim their crimes at a class of people rather than at a particular individual.

The FBI's UCR shows that in 2005 white people were the known perpetrators in 42.8% of all hate crimes (3,585 incidents), and African-Americans were the known offenders in 11.1% of cases (933 incidents). The offender's race was not reported in 751 cases (9%), and the offender was unknown in 2,784 cases (33.2%). The largest number of racially motivated crimes involved anti–African-American incidents committed by whites (1,803 hate crimes). Of the 484 racially motivated attacks by African-Americans, 368 were directed at whites. (See Table 3.6.)

## TERRORISM

The National Counterterrorism Center (NCTC) was established by President George W. Bush in 2004 to serve as the primary U.S. government organization for integrating and analyzing intelligence on terrorism and counterterrorism. The NCTC defines terrorism as "premeditated, politically motivated violence perpetrated against noncombatant targets by subnational groups or clandestine agents, usually intended to influence an audience" (Title 22 of the U.S. Code, Section 2656f[d]). Terrorism is domestic when it involves the citizens or residents of the country where the terrorist incident takes

TABLE 3.6

**Hate crime offenses by known offender's race and bias motivation, 2005**

| | | Known offender's race | | | | | | |
|---|---|---|---|---|---|---|---|---|
| Bias motivation | Total offenses | White | Black | American Indian/ Alaskan Native | Asian/ Pacific Islander | Multiple races, group | Unknown race | Unknown offender |
| **Total** | **8,380** | **3,585** | **933** | **68** | **44** | **215** | **751** | **2,784** |
| **Single-bias incidents** | 8,373 | 3,585 | 933 | 68 | 44 | 212 | 749 | 2,782 |
| Race: | 4,691 | 2,205 | 484 | 45 | 22 | 128 | 387 | 1,420 |
| Anti-white | 935 | 204 | 368 | 19 | 4 | 22 | 85 | 233 |
| Anti-black | 3,200 | 1,803 | 87 | 13 | 6 | 84 | 239 | 968 |
| Anti-American Indian/Alaskan Native | 95 | 40 | 6 | 12 | 0 | 1 | 11 | 25 |
| Anti-Asian/Pacific Islander | 231 | 88 | 11 | 1 | 8 | 11 | 29 | 83 |
| Anti-multiple races, group | 230 | 70 | 12 | 0 | 4 | 10 | 23 | 111 |
| Religion: | 1,314 | 306 | 42 | 6 | 5 | 11 | 132 | 812 |
| Anti-Jewish | 900 | 198 | 9 | 4 | 2 | 6 | 86 | 595 |
| Anti-Catholic | 61 | 8 | 4 | 0 | 0 | 0 | 5 | 44 |
| Anti-Protestant | 58 | 14 | 0 | 1 | 0 | 1 | 7 | 35 |
| Anti-Islamic | 146 | 52 | 20 | 1 | 1 | 2 | 14 | 56 |
| Anti-other religion | 102 | 25 | 5 | 0 | 2 | 2 | 16 | 52 |
| Anti-multiple religions, group | 42 | 9 | 4 | 0 | 0 | 0 | 3 | 26 |
| Anti-atheism/agnosticism/etc. | 5 | 0 | 0 | 0 | 0 | 0 | 1 | 4 |
| Sexual Orientation: | 1,171 | 502 | 220 | 6 | 11 | 35 | 108 | 289 |
| Anti-male homosexual | 713 | 303 | 141 | 4 | 8 | 22 | 72 | 163 |
| Anti-female homosexual | 180 | 67 | 33 | 0 | 2 | 7 | 11 | 60 |
| Anti-homosexual | 228 | 113 | 33 | 2 | 1 | 6 | 19 | 54 |
| Anti-heterosexual | 23 | 9 | 6 | 0 | 0 | 0 | 4 | 4 |
| Anti-bisexual | 27 | 10 | 7 | 0 | 0 | 0 | 2 | 8 |
| Ethnicity/national origin: | 1,144 | 548 | 179 | 9 | 5 | 35 | 116 | 252 |
| Anti-Hispanic | 660 | 340 | 115 | 3 | 1 | 18 | 50 | 133 |
| Anti-other ethnicity/national origin | 484 | 208 | 64 | 6 | 4 | 17 | 66 | 119 |
| Disability: | 53 | 24 | 8 | 2 | 1 | 3 | 6 | 9 |
| Anti-physical | 21 | 9 | 4 | 1 | 1 | 2 | 1 | 3 |
| Anti-mental | 32 | 15 | 4 | 1 | 0 | 1 | 5 | 6 |
| **Multiple-bias incidents*** | 7 | 0 | 0 | 0 | 0 | 3 | 2 | 2 |

*In a multiple-bias incident two conditions must be met: 1) more than one offense type must occur in the incident and 2) at least two offense types must be motivated by different biases.

SOURCE: "Table 5. Offenses: Known Offender's Race, by Bias Motivation, 2005," in *Hate Crime Statistics 2005*, U.S. Department of Justice, Federal Bureau of Investigation, October 2006, http://www.fbi.gov/ucr/hc2005/table5.htm (accessed January 10, 2007)

place. For example, a terrorist attack carried out on U.S. soil by Americans. Terrorism is international when it involves the citizens or territory of more than one country.

According to the NCTC, approximately 11,000 terrorist attacks occurred around the world and resulted in 14,600 deaths in 2005 (http://wits.nctc.gov/reports/crot2005nctcannexfinal.pdf). Slightly more than 30% of the attacks and 55% of the fatalities (approximately 8,300) occurred in Iraq. About 6,000 attacks (54% of all attacks) were against facilities and/or resulted in no deaths.

Between 2004 and 2005, the NCTC made significant changes to its methods for counting terrorist attacks. At the same time the level of effort to collect data on terrorist incidents increased. As a result the 2005 data cannot be directly compared with the 2004 data. However, the NCTC reported that attacks on noncombatants increased significantly in Iraq during 2005. Outside of Iraq, the total number of terrorist incidents with ten or more fatalities remained steady at seventy incidents in 2004 and 2005.

## INCIDENTS OF INTERNATIONAL TERRORISM

In 1993 the World Trade Center in New York City, a symbol of American financial wealth and power, was the target of international terrorists, who detonated a bomb in an underground parking garage, killing six people and injuring 1,000. On September 11, 2001, the World Trade Center's two 110-story office towers were once again the target of a Muslim terrorist group. At 7:59 a.m. on that day, American Airlines Flight 11 departed Logan International Airport in Boston bound for Los Angeles. Forty-six minutes later, at 8:45 a.m., the aircraft, diverted by hijackers, crashed into the North Tower of the World Trade Center in New York City. At 9:02 a.m., United Airlines Flight 175, also bound for Los Angeles from Boston and also diverted by hijackers, crashed into the South Tower of the World Trade Center. Both towers collapsed shortly thereafter, killing not only thousands of office workers and facility personnel trapped inside, but also more than 300 firefighters and rescue workers helping to evacuate them.

By 9:45 a.m., two more domestic airlines had been commandeered by hijackers and crashed. American Airlines Flight 77 crashed into the Pentagon, the headquarters of the U.S. military, killing over 100 people who were in that section of the building at the time. United Airlines Flight 93 crashed in a field on the outskirts of Pittsburgh, Pennsylvania, the result of an attempt by some passengers to wrest control of the aircraft from the hijackers. No one survived any of the flights. The 19 hijackers were associated with the al-Qaeda group. Al-Qaeda's leader, Osama Bin Laden, went into hiding after the United States launched attacks on al-Qaeda's bases in Afghanistan in October 2001.

The September 11th attacks were the worst acts of international terrorism on U.S. soil in the country's history. When the official cleanup and recovery efforts ended with a final ceremony on May 30, 2002, the New York City Office of Emergency Management gave the final tolls for the destruction caused by the attacks in that city. Of the 2,823 people killed in the World Trade Center, only 1,102 victims had been identified. An estimated 3.1 million hours of labor were spent on cleanup and 108,342 truckloads, over 1.8 million tons, of debris had been removed.

In addition to all those killed in New York, 64 passengers and crew from Flight 77 and 125 military and civilian personnel from the Pentagon were killed. All 44 passengers and crew on Flight 93 also died in the crash. The total death toll from the September 11th attacks was 3,056 people, including citizens of 78 different countries.

One of the most widely reported murders of a U.S. citizen by international terrorists happened early in 2002. On January 23, 2002, *Wall Street Journal* reporter Daniel Pearl was abducted in Pakistan while on his way to interview a Muslim fundamentalist leader. A month later the FBI confirmed that it had received a videotape containing "indisputable" confirmation that Pearl, 38, had been killed by his captors. Pearl's killing resulted in the arrest of several people believed to have been involved with the crime, including the alleged ringleader of the group, Ahmed Omar Saeed Sheikh, who had ties to radical Muslim extremist groups in the region.

The State Department confirmed in *Report on Incidents of Terrorism 2005* that 56 Americans were killed in international terrorist attacks in 2005 compared with 1,456 non-U.S. fatalities; 83% of the American victims were killed in Iraq (National Counterterrorism Center, April 11, 2006, http://wits.nctc.gov/reports/crot2005nct cannexfinal.pdf). (See Figure 3.1.) In addition to those who were killed in 2005, twenty-eight U.S. citizens were

**FIGURE 3.1**

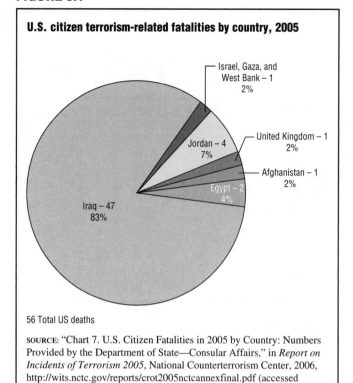

**U.S. citizen terrorism-related fatalities by country, 2005**

- Israel, Gaza, and West Bank – 1 / 2%
- United Kingdom – 1 / 2%
- Jordan – 4 / 7%
- Afghanistan – 1 / 2%
- Egypt – 2 / 4%
- Iraq – 47 / 83%

56 Total US deaths

SOURCE: "Chart 7. U.S. Citizen Fatalities in 2005 by Country: Numbers Provided by the Department of State—Consular Affairs," in *Report on Incidents of Terrorism 2005*, National Counterterrorism Center, 2006, http://wits.nctc.gov/reports/crot2005nctcannexfinal.pdf (accessed January 31, 2007)

injured or kidnapped as a result of international terrorism, including eleven in Iraq, six in Indonesia, and three in both Egypt and Jordan. (See Figure 3.2.)

The incidents involving U.S. citizens included three bombings at different points along the London, England, subway system and one explosive device detonated on a double-decker bus in that city on July 7, 2005. These attacks killed 52 people, including 1 U.S. citizen, and wounded another 700 people. The attacks occurred on the day the G8 Summit was scheduled to begin in Scotland. Abu Hafs al-Masri Brigades and the Secret Organization of al-Qaeda in Europe both claimed responsibility.

### Coordinating National Security after 9/11

As a result of the September 11th attacks, the Department of Homeland Security was established to coordinate federal, state, and local anti-terrorism efforts. The department focuses on detecting and preventing future terrorist attacks, as well as incident management and response and recovery in the event of an attack. In addition, the Homeland Security Council was established to advise the President on all aspects of homeland security. Council members include the Vice President and Attorney General of the United States as well as the Secretaries of Defense, Health and Human Services, Transportation, and the Treasury.

The National Commission on Terrorist Attacks Upon the United States (9/11 Commission), chaired by former New Jersey Governor Thomas Kean, was an independent,

FIGURE 3.2

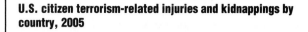

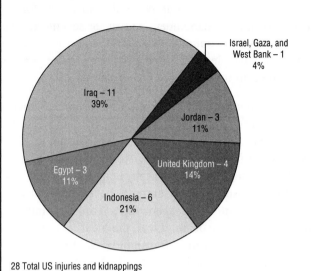

**U.S. citizen terrorism-related injuries and kidnappings by country, 2005**

Israel, Gaza, and West Bank – 1
4%

Iraq – 11
39%

Jordan – 3
11%

United Kingdom – 4
14%

Egypt – 3
11%

Indonesia – 6
21%

28 Total US injuries and kidnappings

SOURCE: "Chart 14. U.S. Citizen Terrorism Injuries/Kidnappings in 2005 by Country: U.S. Number Provided by the Department of State—Consular Affairs," in *Report on Incidents of Terrorism 2005*, National Counterterrorism Center, 2006, http://wits.nctc.gov/reports/crot2005nctcannexfinal.pdf (accessed January 31, 2007)

bipartisan commission created by congressional legislation in late 2002. The commission's charge was to prepare a complete account of the circumstances surrounding the September 11, 2001, terrorist attacks, including preparedness for and the immediate response to the attacks. The Commission released its public report on July 22, 2004. The report concluded that although the attacks were shocking, they should not have been a surprise. The authors argued that the 9/11 plot could have been stopped if security services had done their work more thoroughly. They praised the responses of first responders immediately after the attacks but found institutional weaknesses that made it easier for terrorists to attack and harder for authorities to respond adequately. The report includes several recommendations, including the creation of a national counterterrorism center, strengthened congressional oversight, and improved dialog between the West and the Islamic world.

On March 12, 2002, the Department of Homeland Security implemented a system of Threat Conditions as a way of providing uniform advisories of possible terrorist threats. The five threat-conditions range from Low (a low risk of terrorist attack) to Severe (a severe risk of terrorist attacks that may necessitate the closing of government offices and the deployment of emergency personnel). Intermediate threat conditions are Guarded (general risk of terrorist attacks), Elevated (significant risk of terrorist attacks), and High (high risk of terrorist attacks).

## Treatment of Terror Suspects

The Guantanamo Bay detention camp is a military prison located at the U.S. Navy base at Guantanamo Bay, Cuba. Since 2002 the camp has been used to confine people captured fighting against the United States military in Afghanistan and Iraq. Because the detainees were not members of a recognized military force, the United States did not provide them the protections afforded prisoners of war under the Geneva Conventions. These guidelines, according to the International Red Cross and Red Crescent organization, stipulate that prisoners of war "are entitled to respect for their lives, their dignity, their personal rights and their political, religious and other convictions. They must be protected against all acts of violence or reprisal. They are entitled to exchange news with their families and receive aid. They must enjoy basic judicial guarantees" (http://www.icrc.org/Web/Eng/siteeng 0.nsf/html/5ZMEEM).

It was not until February 2004 that the first Guantanamo detainees were charged with conspiracy to commit war crimes. They were to be tried by a military tribunal, but the tribunals were suspended when a U.S. court ruled them unconstitutional in November 2004, and the Supreme Court later declared them illegal.

In March 2004, the U.S. military released five British prisoners from Guantanamo and sent them back to the United Kingdom without charges. Three of the men later said that they had been abused while at Guantanamo; specifically, they said that they had been beaten, injected with drugs, deprived of sleep, hooded, and subject to sexual and religious humiliations. According to the U.S. State Department, about 520 detainees from more than 40 countries were at Guantanamo in April 2005. In May 2005, *Newsweek* magazine reported that U.S. interrogators at Guantanamo Bay had desecrated the Qur'an to get inmates to talk by placing the holy book on a toilet and even flushing the book down the toilet. The report led to anti-American riots in Afghanistan in which seventeen people died. The magazine later retracted the story. Although the Pentagon confirmed abuses to the Qur'an in June 2005, it referred to them as relatively minor.

In February 2006 a United Nations investigation concluded that the United States committed acts amounting to torture at Guantanamo Bay, including force-feeding detainees and subjecting them to prolonged solitary confinement. The investigators accused the United States of violating the detainees' rights to a fair trial, freedom of religion, and health. The report recommended that the United States close the facility. This recommendation was reiterated by UN Secretary-General Ban Ki-moon on January 8, 2007.

As of January 2007, the United States had released more than 300 inmates from Guantanamo but still held nearly 400 there. Charges were expected to be laid against

60 to 80 inmates and others were expected to be released. However, lawyers and activists were concerned about the fate of the remaining 200 to 300 detainees.

In another case that followed 9/11, Maher Arar, a Canadian citizen born in Syria in 1970, was detained by U.S. immigration officials during a stopover in New York as he was returning to Canada from a vacation in Tunisia in September 2002. Because he was on a terror watch list created by the Royal Canadian Mounted Police, the U.S. officials suspected that Arar had links to terrorists and deported him to Syria, even though he was carrying a Canadian passport. When Arar returned to Canada the following year, he reported that the Syrian government had chained him, beaten him, and confined him to a small cell. As a result of pressure from Canadian human rights organizations and private citizens, the Canadian government established a commission of inquiry into the case. In his final report in September 2006 the Commissioner of the Inquiry, Justice Dennis O'Connor, cleared Arar of all terrorism allegations. Arar filed suit against U.S. officials, including former Attorney General John Ashcroft, but a judge in the United States dismissed the case, invoking the "state secrets privilege." On September 19, 2006, U.S. Attorney General Alberto Gonzales denied wrongdoing on the part of the United States in Arar's transportation to Syria. Arar's case continued on appeal in 2007.

## INCIDENTS OF DOMESTIC TERRORISM

Several major U.S. domestic terrorism incidents occurred during the 1990s. On April 19, 1995, one of the most deadly acts of domestic terrorism occurred in Oklahoma City, Oklahoma, when a two-ton truck bomb exploded just outside the Alfred P. Murrah federal building, killing 168 people and injuring more than 800. The attack was perpetrated by Timothy McVeigh, a twenty-seven-year-old military veteran with ties to anti-government militia groups. McVeigh was executed by lethal injection in June 2001; Terry Nichols, an accomplice who helped McVeigh plan the attack and construct the bomb, was sentenced to life in prison without parole.

In July 1996, during the Olympic Summer Games in Atlanta, Georgia, a nail-packed pipe bomb exploded in a large common area. One person was killed, and more than 100 were injured. Although authorities had no leads at the time, similar explosive devices were later used in bomb attacks on a nightclub favored by homosexuals and two abortion clinics. These incidents led investigators to Eric Robert Rudolph, a Christian extremist whose views combined anti-government political sentiments with opposition to abortion and anti-homosexual bigotry. Rudolph eluded capture for five years before he surrendered to authorities in May 2003. Confessing to the Olympic bombing, he said he was motivated by anti-government

and anti-socialist beliefs. He is serving life imprisonment without possibility of parole.

In January 1998 Theodore Kaczynski was sentenced to life imprisonment with no possibility of parole for his actions as the "Unabomber." Over a seventeen-year period Kaczynski committed sixteen bombings in several states. Three people were killed and twenty-three persons were injured in the attacks.

On September 25, 2001, a letter postmarked September 20 from St. Petersburg, Florida, containing a white powdery substance, was handled by an assistant to NBC News anchorman Tom Brokaw. After complaining of a rash, the assistant consulted a physician and tested positive for exposure to the anthrax bacterium (*bacillus anthracis*), an infectious agent that, if inhaled into the lungs, can lead to death. Over the next two months, envelopes testing positive for anthrax were received by various news organizations in the United States and by government offices, including the offices of Senate Majority Leader Tom Daschle (D-South Dakota) and of New York Governor George Pataki. As a result of exposure to anthrax sent via the U.S. mail, five people died, including two postal workers who handled letters carrying the anthrax spores. Hundreds more who were exposed were placed on antibiotics as a preventive measure. Despite an intensive investigation by the FBI and other law enforcement agencies, no arrests in the case had been made as of May 2007.

In a spree that began on May 3, 2002, eighteen pipe bombs were found in rural mailboxes in Illinois, Iowa, Nebraska, Colorado, and Texas, injuring five people. Four days after the first bomb exploded, the FBI arrested twenty-one-year-old college student Luke J. Helder in connection with the bombings. Helder was charged by federal prosecutors in Iowa with using an explosive device to maliciously destroy property affecting interstate commerce and with using a destructive device to commit a crime of violence, punishable by up to life imprisonment. The pipe bombs, some of which did not detonate, were accompanied by letters warning of excessive government control over individual behavior.

Between February 2004 and September 2006, the NCTC recorded sixteen domestic terrorism incidents in the United States. (See Table 3.7.) None of these incidents resulted in fatalities or involved hostages. Most of these events did not result in any injuries, but nine people were injured when a man drove a sport utility vehicle through a crowd of students at the University of North Carolina—Chapel Hill. Other domestic terrorism incidents included arson attacks on several residences and bomb attacks on schools and the British consulate in New York City.

**TABLE 3.7**

**Incidents of domestic terrorism, January 1, 2004–September 30, 2006**

| Date | Subject | Fatalities | Injuries | Hostages | Total victims |
|------|---------|-----------|----------|----------|---------------|
| 2/2/2004 | U.S. Senate office attacked with the chemical/biological agent ricin in Washington, DC | 0 | 0 | 0 | 0 |
| 2/7/2004 | Construction site set ablaze by Earth Liberation Front (ELF) in Charlottesville, VA | 0 | 0 | 0 | 0 |
| 6/9/2004 | High school damaged by pipe bomb in Taconic, MA | 0 | 0 | 0 | 0 |
| 7/8/2004 | Animal Liberation Front (ALF) set fire to property belonging to Brigham Young University in Provo, UT | 0 | 0 | 0 | 0 |
| 2/7/2005 | Apartment complex damaged in arson attack by ELF arsonists in Sutter Creek, CA | 0 | 0 | 0 | 0 |
| 3/14/2005 | Trace amounts of potential anthrax found at Department of Defense mail facility in Washington, DC | 0 | 0 | 0 | 0 |
| 4/13/2005 | Elementary school targeted by detonation of an improvised explosive device (IED) in New Bedford, MA | 0 | 0 | 0 | 0 |
| 5/5/2005 | United Kingdom Consulate damaged in bomb attacks in New York, NY | 0 | 0 | 0 | 0 |
| 5/18/2005 | ELF suspected of burning 2 residences in Oyster Bay, NY | 0 | 0 | 0 | 0 |
| 11/21/2005 | 4 residences damaged in arson by ELF in Hagerstown, MD | 0 | 0 | 0 | 0 |
| 11/29/2005 | 2 vehicles damaged in incendiary attack by suspected ELF in San Diego, CA | 0 | 0 | 0 | 0 |
| 11/29/2005 | 7 vehicles damaged in incendiary attack by suspected ELF in San Diego, CA | 0 | 0 | 0 | 0 |
| 1/17/2006 | 1 residence destroyed in arson attack by suspected ELF in Coupeville, WA | 0 | 0 | 0 | 0 |
| 3/3/2006 | 9 civilians wounded in attack by lone wolf in Chapel Hill, NC | 0 | 9 | 0 | 9 |
| 5/26/2006 | Police disabled a bomb in St. Johns County, FL | 0 | 0 | 0 | 0 |
| 9/11/2006 | Health center damaged in incendiary attack by lone wolf in Davenport, IA | 0 | 0 | 0 | 0 |
| | **Grand total** | **0** | **9** | **0** | **9** |

SOURCE: Adapted from "United States," in *Worldwide Incidents Tracking System*, National Counterterrorism Center, 2007, http://wits.nctc.gov/RunSearchCountry.do?countryId=174 (accessed January 16, 2007).

## Eco-terrorism

Since the late 1970s some extremist environmental and animal rights groups have turned increasingly to criminal violence to promote their ideas and attack their perceived enemies. Eco-terrorism is the name given to these fringe actions. The FBI has defined eco-terrorism as "the use or threatened use of violence of a criminal nature against innocent victims or property by an environmentally-oriented, subnational group for environmental-political reasons, or aimed at an audience beyond the target, often of a symbolic nature" (http://www.fbi.gov/congress/congress02/jarboe021202.htm). Corporate and university research laboratories, clothing companies, fast food restaurants, real estate developers, automobile dealers, logging companies, and medical-supply firms have been some of their most frequent targets. Prominent eco-terrorist groups include the underground Earth Liberation Front (ELF), the related Animal Liberation Front (ALF), and the Stop Huntingdon Animal Cruelty (SHAC) campaign. According to the FBI, between 1990 and 2005 animal and environmental rights extremists claimed credit for more than 1,200 criminal incidents that resulted in millions of dollars of damage and monetary loss (http://www.fbi.gov/page2/may05/jlewis052305.htm).

The FBI reported in 2005 that although most animal rights and eco-extremists do not engage in violence aimed at killing people, this appears to be changing. Furthermore, the number and size of their attacks are growing. In addition to the harassing phone calls, e-mail campaigns, and acts of vandalism that eco-terrorists have carried on for several years, these groups now use improved explosive devices and make personal threats to employees of targeted companies.

The Animal Liberation Front is among the most notorious animal rights groups operating in the United States. In North America, cells operate independently and under the following guidelines published on the Web site of the North American ALF (http://www.animalliberation pressoffice.org/history.htm):

- "To liberate animals from places of abuse, i.e., laboratories, factory farms, fur farms, etc., and place them in good homes where they may live out their natural lives, free from suffering

- "To inflict economic damage to those who profit from the misery and exploitation of animals

- "To reveal the horror and atrocities committed against animals behind locked doors, by performing direct actions and liberations

- "To take all necessary precautions against harming any animal, human and non-human"

At various university laboratories in the United States ALF operatives have broken into research facilities to release animals, destroy computers and documents, and paint slogans on walls. In addition to research facilities, ALF has targeted businesses in the meat industry. For example, ALF has taken responsibility for firebombing a McDonald's restaurant in Tucson, Arizona, on September 11, 2001, causing some $500,000 in damages.

ALF activists are allied with SHAC. In 1998 a television documentary aired in the United Kingdom alleging mistreatment of animals by Huntingdon Life Sciences (HLS), a British-based research company. Outraged animal activists began pressuring financial institutions associated with HLS to stop supporting the company, thus forcing HLS to stop testing animals. The campaign was called Stop Huntingdon Animal Cruelty (SHAC). SHAC now has chapters in several countries, including the United States. After a U.S.-based company bought HLS, SHAC activists began targeting U.S. companies that did business with HLS. In 2002 SHAC members sent threatening letters to employees of Marsh, Inc., which insured HLS at the time. They also released smoke bombs in two Seattle buildings that housed Marsh offices. At the end of 2002, Marsh announced that it would stop insuring HLS.

The Earth Liberation Front (ELF) is ALF's environmental counterpart. The ELF has described its aim as inflicting "economic damage on those profiting from the destruction and exploitation of the natural environment." The group also aspires "to reveal and educate the public on the atrocities committed against the earth and all species that populate it." The ELF considers property destruction to be non-violent because no human beings or animals are targeted. Arsons and property destruction attributed to ELF include Two Elk Lodge in Vail, Colorado, in 1998; the destruction of the Center for Urban Horticulture at the University of Washington in Seattle on May 21, 2001; and burning a U.S. Forest Service Station in Irvine, Pennsylvania, in August 2002. In the most destructive act of eco-terrorism in U.S. history, ELF burned down a newly built San Diego, California, five-story apartment complex in August 2003, causing some $50 million in damage. The following month, group members burned four San Diego homes under construction, resulting in an estimated $1 million in damages. The group has vandalized sport utility vehicle (SUV) dealerships in Pennsylvania, California, and New Mexico, resulting in over $2.5 million in damages.

# CHAPTER 4

# WHITE-COLLAR CRIME

## A DEFINITION OF WHITE-COLLAR CRIME

The term "white-collar crime" was first used by the American criminologist Edwin H. Sutherland to define a violation of the criminal law committed by "a person of respectability and high social status in the course of his [or her] occupation" (*White Collar Crime*, 1949). In 1981 the U.S. Department of Justice developed a further definition, which included "nonviolent crime for financial gain utilizing deception and committed by anyone who has special technical and professional knowledge of business and government, irrespective of the person's occupation" (*Dictionary of Criminal Justice Data Terminology*, Bureau of Justice Statistics).

White-collar crimes include the following categories investigated by the Federal Bureau of Investigation (FBI):

- Money laundering, securities and commodities fraud, bank fraud and embezzlement, environmental crimes, fraud against the government, election law violations, copyright violations, and telemarketing fraud.

- International, national, and regional organized crime activities for which the FBI's expertise or capabilities increase the likelihood of a successful investigation and prosecution

- Health care fraud, especially systemic abuses, such as large-scale billing fraud and fraudulent activities that threaten patient safety

- Financial institution fraud involving $100,000 or more

- Telemarketing and insurance fraud where there is evidence of nationwide or international activities.

## HOW MANY CRIMES?

In *The 2005 National Public Survey on White Collar Crime* (2006, http://www.nw3c.org/research/national_public_survey.cfm), a report for the National White Collar Crime Center (NW3C), John Kane and April Wall detailed the results of interviews conducted with 1,605 adults. Survey participants were asked about their experiences and those of their households with white-collar crime during the previous twelve months.

Almost half (46.5%) of households and 36% of individuals surveyed reported that they had been a victim of white-collar crime during the previous year; 62.5% of individuals had experienced at least one type of white-collar crime in their lifetime. The most common white-collar crimes experienced by households included being misled about the price of a product or service (35.9% of reported incidents), having a credit card misused (24.5%), and being directly affected by a national corporate scandal (21.4%). Of households that experienced a white-collar crime, 67% reported the crime to at least one organization (such as a credit card company, business, or personal attorney), and 30.1% reported the crime to a law-enforcement or other crime-control agency. The most commonly reported crimes by individuals were pricing schemes (33.2%), credit card misuse (21.8%), and the effects of national corporate scandals (20.6%).

## PERCEPTIONS OF WHITE-COLLAR CRIMES

The NW3C survey included questions about the perceived seriousness of several types of crime, including white-collar crimes. The most serious crime according to respondents was carjacking and murder, which received a score of 6.89 on a scale of 0 ("not serious") to 7 ("very serious"). Car theft was perceived as the least serious crime, with a score of 4.0 out of 7. All of the white-collar crimes included in the survey were perceived to be more serious than car theft, including omission of a safety report (6.18), insurance fraud (5.83), hacking into a database (5.6), embezzlement (5.58), overcharging for insurance (5.49), submitting a false earnings report (5.4), and auction fraud (5.12).

## WHITE-COLLAR CRIME ARRESTS

The FBI reported in its Uniform Crime Reports (UCR) that of 14.1 million arrests for all crimes in the United States during 2005, 118,455 were for forgery and counterfeiting, 321,521 were for fraud, and 18,970 were for embezzlement. (See Table 1.4 in Chapter 1.) In an analysis of 10.4 million arrests processed by 10,974 agencies throughout the country in 2005, the FBI found that arrests for forgery and counterfeiting were most often reported in the South (37,328 arrests), followed by the West (23,410), Midwest (13,984), and Northeast (12,624) (http://www.fbi.gov/ucr/05cius/data/documents/05tbl30.xls). The largest number of arrests for fraud was also reported by southern agencies (140,271 arrests), followed by the Midwest (34,501), the Northeast (34,093), and the West (22,856). For embezzlement, the largest number of cases was also reported in the South (7,526), followed by the West (3,410), the Midwest (1,975), and the Northeast (1,186).

Among the 10,974 agencies reporting, most arrests for forgery and counterfeiting were made in cities (64,874 arrests), followed by suburban areas (34,552) and metropolitan counties (14,944) (http://www.fbi.gov/ucr/05cius/data/documents/05tbl31.xls). For fraud, arrests were also most common in cities (120,631), followed by suburban areas (115,295); 70,881 fraud arrests were made in metropolitan areas and 40,209 in non-metropolitan areas. There were 10,341 arrests for embezzlement in cities, 5,524 arrests for embezzlement in suburban areas, and 2,653 arrests for embezzlement in metropolitan areas.

## WHITE-COLLAR CRIME OFFENDERS AND VICTIMS

According to the FBI's UCR, most white-collar crime offenders are over the age of 18, and the number of offenders under 18 years old decreased between 1996 and 2005 (http://www.fbi.gov/ucr/05cius/data/table_33.html). In data from 8,009 agencies nationwide, 2,600 people under age 18 were arrested for forgery and counterfeiting during 2005, a 52.1% decrease from 5,433 in 1996. The number of individuals under age 18 who were arrested for fraud in 2005 was 4,779, a 31.2% decrease from 6,947 in 1996. The decrease in the number of arrests of those under 18 for embezzlement in 2005 was less dramatic—14.7% (from 880 in 1996 to 751 in 2005).

Although the 8,009 agencies reported more arrests of males than females for forgery/counterfeiting and fraud in 2005, they arrested more females than males for embezzlement. Specifically, 43,068 males were arrested in 2005 for forgery and counterfeiting, a 4.8% decrease from 45,250 in 1996; 104,201 were arrested for fraud (down 24.4% from 137,874 in 1996); and 5,979 were arrested for embezzlement (up 7.8% from 5,545 in 1996). For females, the arrest totals were 27,670 for for-gery/counterfeiting (up 3% from 26,853 in 1996), 89,338 for fraud (down 23.8% from 117,288 in 1996), and 6,108 for embezzlement (up 32.6% from 4,607 in 1996).

## IDENTITY THEFT

The incidence of identity theft has risen significantly in recent years as more and more transactions of every type are handled remotely using telephones, computers, and the Internet. Identity thieves steal personal information from victims, such as their social security, driver's license, credit card, or other identification numbers, and then set up new bank or credit card accounts or otherwise misrepresent themselves as their victims to obtain money, goods, or services fraudulently.

The Federal Trade Commission (FTC) was required by the Identity Theft and Assumption Deterrence Act of 1998 to form the FTC Identity Theft Hotline and Data Clearinghouse in 1999 to track incidents of this type of crime. The FTC reported in *Identity Theft Victim Complaint Data: Figures and Trends January 1–December 31, 2005* that 255,565 cases of identity theft were reported in 2005. This figure was 3.5% higher than in 2004 (246,847 complaints) and 18.8% higher than in 2003 (215,177 complaints). (See Figure 4.1.)

In 2005 personal information stolen from identity theft victims was used to set up new credit card accounts

**FIGURE 4.1**

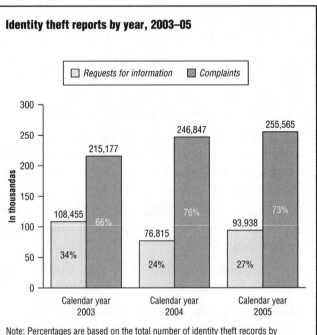

**Identity theft reports by year, 2003–05**

Note: Percentages are based on the total number of identity theft records by calendar year.

SOURCE: "Figure 3. Total Identity Theft Records by Calendar Year," in *Identity Theft Victim Complaint Data: Figures and Trends, January 1–December 31, 2005*, Federal Trade Commission, January 25, 2006, http://www.consumer.gov/idtheft/pdf/clearinghouse_2005.pdf (accessed January 15, 2007)

FIGURE 4.2

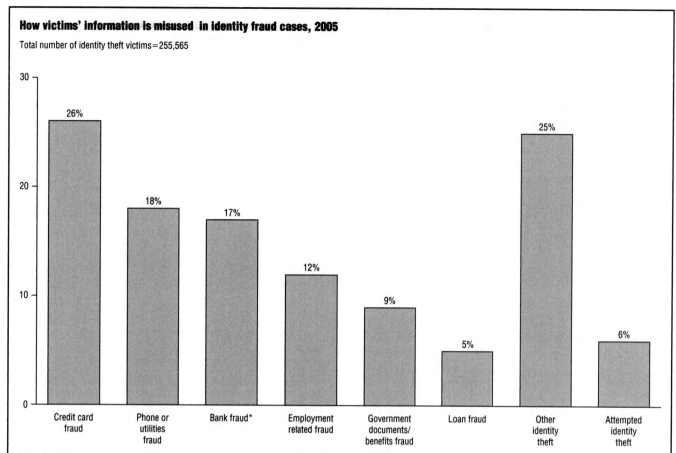

**How victims' information is misused in identity fraud cases, 2005**

Total number of identity theft victims=255,565

Notes: Percentages are based on the total number of identity theft complaints (255,565). Percentages add to more than 100 because approximately 20% of victims reported experiencing more than one type of identity theft. All victims reported experiencing at least one type of identity theft.
*Includes fraud involving checking and savings accounts and electronic fund transfers.

SOURCE: "Figure 4. How Victims' Information Is Misused," in *Identity Theft Victim Complaint Data: Figures and Trends, January 1–December 31, 2005,* Federal Trade Commission, January 25, 2006, http://www.consumer.gov/idtheft/pdf/clearinghouse_2005.pdf (accessed January 15, 2007)

or misuse existing accounts in 26% of the reported cases. Other identity theft crimes include unauthorized use of telephone, utility, and other communications services (18%), bank fraud (17%), and employment-related fraud (12%). (See Figure 4.2.)

According to the FTC, 29% of identity theft victims who reported the crimes were between 18 and 29 years old, 24% were 30 to 39 years old, and 20% were 40 to 49 years old. Those under the age of 18 and over age 60 were the least likely to be targets of identity theft. (See Figure 4.3.) The largest share of identity theft victims who reported the crimes (43%) discovered the theft within one month. Of the remainder, 16% learned of the theft within 6 months and 12% within 25 to 48 months. (See Figure 4.4.) The Bureau of Justice Statistics (BJS) reports that about one-third of households that experienced identity theft discovered the theft by missing money or noticing unfamiliar charges on an account; almost one-quarter learned of the theft when they were contacted by a credit bureau. (See Table 4.1.)

Overall, a third of the households participating in the National Crime Victimization Survey (NCVS) experienced one or more problems as a result of identity theft in 2004. According to Katrina Baum of the BJS in *Identity Theft, 2004* (April 2006, http://www.ojp.usdoj.gov/bjs/pub/pdf/it04.pdf), more than one-third (34.1%) were contacted by a debt collector or creditor, a slightly smaller percentage (30.5%) had banking problems, 25.8% had problems with their credit card accounts, and 15.4% had to pay higher interest rates as a result of identity theft. About one-third of households were able to resolve the problems associated with the theft in one day, and one-fifth spent two to seven days correcting the situation. For nearly fifteen out of a hundred victims, resolving identity theft problems took between one and two months. (See Figure 4.5.)

Seven out of ten identity theft victims were aware of personal monetary losses resulting from the crime, according to Baum, and total dollar losses among victims reached $3.2 billion in 2004. In households that were

**FIGURE 4.3**

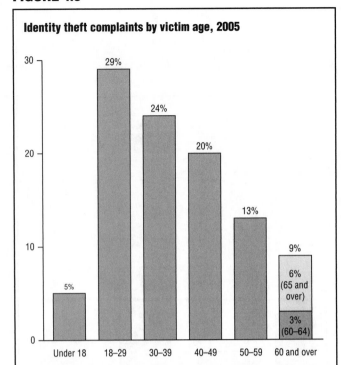

Identity theft complaints by victim age, 2005

Notes: Percentages are based on the total number of identity theft complaints where victims reported their age (239,277). 95% of the victims who contacted the Federal Trade Commission directly reported their age.

SOURCE: "Figure 6. Identity Theft Complaints by Victim Age," in *Identity Theft Victim Complaint Data: Figures and Trends, January 1–December 31, 2005*, Federal Trade Commission, January 25, 2006, http://www.consumer.gov/idtheft/pdf/clearinghouse_2005.pdf (accessed January 15, 2007)

**FIGURE 4.4**

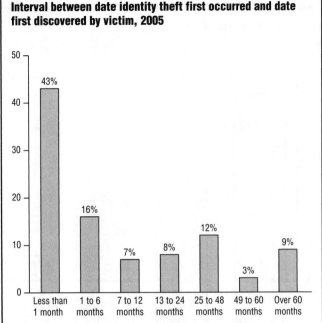

Interval between date identity theft first occurred and date first discovered by victim, 2005

Percentages are based on the total number of identity theft complaints where victims provided the dates on which the identity theft first occurred and they first discovered it (135,437). 54% of the victims who contacted the Federal Trade Commission directly reported this information. Because some victims experienced multiple instances where their information had been misused, these figures do not track the amount of time it took a victim to discover a particular instance of identity theft, but, rather, the amount of time between the initial misuse of the victim's information and when the victim first discovered that their information had been misused.

SOURCE: "Figure 8. Number of Months between Date Identity Theft First Occurred and Date First Discovered by Victim," in *Identity Theft Victim Complaint Data: Figures and Trends, January 1–December 31, 2005*, Federal Trade Commission, January 25, 2006, http://www.consumer .gov/idtheft/pdf/clearinghouse_2005.pdf (accessed January 15, 2007)

aware of the extent of the financial loss they experienced, more than half (55%) sustained losses less than $500. One victim in twenty lost $5,000 or more.

## CORPORATE CRIME

Tracking white-collar crime, especially corporate crime, is generally much more complicated than tracking other crimes. There often is no single offender or victim to report the crime. White-collar crime is often based on trust established between the victim and the offender before any crime is committed. Building trust expands the timeframe of the crime, permitting repeated thefts from an unsuspecting victim.

Different types of ethical violations linked to corporate crime include misrepresentation in advertising, deceptive packaging, socially irresponsible television commercials, sales of harmful and unsafe products, sales of virtually worthless products, environmental pollution, kickbacks and payoffs, unethical influences on government, unethical competitive practices, personal gain for management, unethical treatment of workers, trade secret theft, and victimization of local communities.

The tobacco industry offers an example of corporate crime. In November 1998, forty-six states collectively

settled lawsuits they had brought against cigarette manufacturers. They had sought to recoup the health care costs associated with smoking-related illnesses that were paid out by state Medicaid agencies. Although the sale of tobacco products was legal, the states alleged that tobacco firms knew about the highly addictive nature of smoking and deliberately concealed their research findings from the general public for decades while promoting tobacco use.

Since the 1990s, several rulings have been made against tobacco companies. In October 2006, for example, Judge Gladys Kessler of the Federal District Court for the District of Columbia issued a decision in the Department of Justice racketeering lawsuit. She ordered tobacco companies to stop labeling cigarettes as "low tar" or "light" to give the false impression that they are less dangerous than full-flavor cigarettes. In her decision, Judge Kessler stated:

"Over the course of more than fifty years, defendants lied, misrepresented and deceived the American public, including smokers and the young people they avidly sought as replacement smokers, about the devastating health effects of smoking."

TABLE 4.1

**How victims became aware of identity theft, by type of theft, July–December 2004**

| How theft was discovered | Total | Percent of thefts involving— | | | |
| --- | --- | --- | --- | --- | --- |
| | | Existing credit cards | Other existing accounts | Personal information | Multiple types of theft during the same episode |
| Issuer placed block on account | 3.8% | 4.5% | 3.3% | 1.0%* | 5.3%* |
| Missing money or noticed charges on account | 30.4 | 31.2 | 42.1 | 7.9 | 29.5 |
| Contacted about late/unpaid bills | 22.8 | 30.7 | 9.0 | 18.6 | 25.2 |
| Banking problems | 10.8 | 11.8 | 11.7 | 6.2 | 10.7 |
| Noticed credit card or checkbook was missing | 6.2 | 5.9 | 7.7 | 1.5* | 9.7 |
| Notified by police | 1.1 | 0.4* | 0.6* | 3.8* | 1.7* |
| Denied phone or utility service | 2.4 | 0.1* | 4.4 | 3.7* | 5.7* |
| Noticed an error in credit report | 5.6 | 4.4 | 3.0* | 13.0 | 6.7* |
| Other way | 28.6 | 19.3 | 35.2 | 49.0 | 27.5 |

Note: Table excludes 1% of households victimized by identity theft that did not provide an answer to how they became aware of the identity theft.
*Estimate based on 10 or fewer cases.

SOURCE: Katrina Baum, "Table 2. How Victim Became Aware of Identity Theft, by Type of Identity Theft," in *Identity Theft, 2004*, U.S. Department of Justice, Office of Justice Programs, Bureau of Justice Statistics, April 2006, http://www.ojp.usdoj.gov/bjs/pub/pdf/it04.pdf (accessed January 15, 2007)

**FIGURE 4.5**

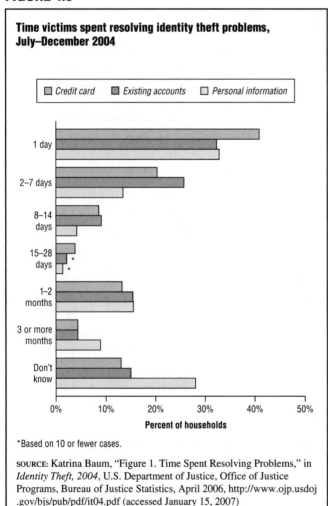

**Time victims spent resolving identity theft problems, July–December 2004**

☐ Credit card   ■ Existing accounts   ☐ Personal information

*Based on 10 or fewer cases.

SOURCE: Katrina Baum, "Figure 1. Time Spent Resolving Problems," in *Identity Theft, 2004*, U.S. Department of Justice, Office of Justice Programs, Bureau of Justice Statistics, April 2006, http://www.ojp.usdoj.gov/bjs/pub/pdf/it04.pdf (accessed January 15, 2007)

## FALSIFYING CORPORATE DATA

The collapse of the Enron Corporation is one of the most glaring examples of corporate crime and falsification of corporate data in recent history. Enron, based in Houston, Texas, was an energy broker trading in electricity and other energy commodities. In the late 1990s, however, instead of simply brokering energy deals, Enron devised increasingly complex contracts with buyers and sellers that allowed Enron to profit from the difference in the selling price and the buying price of commodities such as electricity. Enron executives created a number of "partnerships"—in effect, companies that existed only on paper whose sole function was to hide debt and make Enron appear to be much more profitable than it actually was.

On December 2, 2001, Enron filed for bankruptcy protection, listing some $13.1 billion in liabilities and $24.7 billion in assets—$38 billion less than the assets listed only two months earlier. As a result, thousands of Enron employees lost their jobs. In addition, many Enron staff—who had been encouraged by company executives to invest monies from their 401k retirement plans in Enron stock—had their retirement savings reduced to almost nothing as a result of the precipitous decline in value of Enron stock.

In the wake of Enron's collapse, several committees in the U.S. Senate and House of Representatives began to investigate whether Enron defrauded investors by deliberately concealing financial information. Numerous lawsuits were filed against Enron, its accounting firm Arthur Andersen, and former Enron executives including former chairman Kenneth L. Lay and former chief executive officer Jeffrey Skilling.

Enron treasurer Ben Glisan Jr. was convicted of conspiracy charges to commit wire and securities fraud. He was sentenced to five years in prison and was released January 19, 2007. Lay and Skilling went on trial in January 2006. Federal prosecutor Kathryn Ruemmler accused the men of using "accounting tricks, fiction, hocus-pocus, trickery, misleading statements, half-truths, omissions and outright lies" in committing their crimes, as reported by Kristen Hays in the *Chicago Sun-Times* ("Prosecutor Tells Jury of Lay, Skilling 'Hocus-Pocus,'" May 16, 2006). On May 25 a jury found Lay guilty of all six counts against him in the corporate trial; he was also convicted of four counts of fraud in a separate trial relating to his personal finances. He faced twenty to thirty years in prison but died of a heart attack on July 5, 2006, before the judge set his sentence. The jury found Skilling guilty of nineteen of the twenty-eight counts against him, and he was sentenced to twenty-four years and four months in federal prison. Skilling began serving his sentence at a low-security federal facility in Waseca, Minnesota, and is projected to be released in 2028.

On June 15, 2002, a New York jury found accounting firm Arthur Andersen guilty of obstructing justice in connection with the Enron collapse. Arthur Andersen was convicted of destroying Enron documents during an ongoing federal investigation of the company's accounting practices. As a result of the verdict, Andersen faced a fine of $500,000 and a probation term of up to five years. Although the conviction was overturned by the U.S. Supreme Court in 2005, the firm is effectively out of the accounting business with its few remaining U.S. employees responsible for administrating the many legal cases generated by the scandal.

The Enron scandal helped lead to the passage of the Sarbanes-Oxley Act (SOX), signed into law on July 30, 2002. The law was designed to rebuild public trust in the U.S. corporate sector by imposing new criminal and civil penalties for security violations and establishing a new certification system for internal audits. SOX also grants independent auditors more access to company data and requires increased disclosure of compensation methods and systems, especially for upper management.

## BANK FRAUD

The FBI investigates incidents of financial institution fraud, including insider fraud, check fraud, mortgage and loan fraud, and financial institution failures. According to the *Financial Institution Fraud and Failure Report, Fiscal Year 2005* (2005, http://www.fbi.gov/publications/financial/2005fif/fif05.pdf), the FBI has seen a marked decline in the number of financial institution fraud investigations since the early 1990s. At the end of fiscal year (FY) 2005, the FBI was conducting 5,041 financial institution fraud investigations; 62 of these cases (1.2%) involved criminal activity related to failed financial institutions. This reflects a 92% reduction in failure investigations since the July 1992 peak of 758 cases. However, although the number of failure investigations has declined, the FBI is still involved in a substantial number of major financial institution fraud investigations. Major

cases are defined as non-failure cases involving more than $100,000. In FY 2005, the FBI was investigating 4,135 major cases of institutional fraud. The number of major investigations underway had remained fairly stable during the period FY 2000 through FY 2005, with a high of 4,383 in FY 2001 and a low of 3,915 in FY 2004.

The U.S. Department of Justice reports in the *Sourcebook of Criminal Justice Statistics* (http://www.albany.edu/sourcebook/pdf/t31482005.pdf) that the number of convictions in financial institution fraud cases declined only slightly from 2000 (1,394 convictions) to 2005 (1,218 convictions). Almost $3.6 billion in restitution was reported in 2005, almost double the amount for 2002.

## FRAUD AGAINST INSURANCE COMPANIES

Annually, thousands of acts of fraud against insurance companies are reported. These include faking a death to collect life insurance, setting fire to a house to collect property insurance, or claiming injuries not actually suffered.

The Internal Revenue Service (IRS) reports that it initiated twenty-four investigations of insurance fraud in FY 2006, down slightly from twenty-eight investigations in FY 2005 and twenty-five investigations in FY 2004 (http://www.irs.gov/compliance/enforcement/article/0,,id=118213,00.html). Of people convicted of insurance fraud in FY 2006, 93.3% were incarcerated and were sentenced to serve an average fifty months in confinement.

In one case, business owner Fred Rich of Portland, Texas, pleaded guilty to a mail fraud and money laundering conspiracy in January 2006. An IRS investigation revealed that he had defrauded insurance companies by staging vehicle accidents and making phony property damage claims for mold and water damage to residences. People who owed Rich money participated with him in several staged motor vehicle accidents at his business and home. The co-conspirators then filed insurance claims and split the proceeds with Rich. Rich was sentenced on March 9, 2006, to fifty months in prison followed by three years of supervised release. He was also ordered to pay $629,000 in restitution and a $10,000 fine.

## FRAUD BY INSURANCE COMPANIES

Some insurance companies have been found guilty of defrauding their customers. For example, David Brabandt and his sister Barbara Del Aguila, who operated the Aguila Insurance Agency in Dallas, Texas, were charged in April 2005 with taking payments from over 300 people and not purchasing insurance for them. They pleaded guilty on February 1, 2006, to two felony charges, were sentenced to two years in prison, and were ordered to pay $183,861.29 in restitution.

In March 2006 Michael T. McRaith, director of insurance for the State of Illinois, issued a cease and desist order against the Safe Auto Insurance Company of Columbus, Ohio. According to McRaith, Safe Auto had not properly notified the Secretary of State's office of policies it held for drivers in Illinois. As a result, the state suspended the driver's licenses and vehicle registrations of several policyholders who had paid premiums to the company. The company was ordered to correct its notification procedures and pay customer expenses resulting from the improper filings.

## SECURITIES FRAUD

There are many laws regulating the securities markets—which include the New York Stock Exchange (NYSE) and the National Association of Securities Dealers Automated Quotation (NASDAQ)—and the corporations that sell "securities" on the markets. These regulations require corporations to be honest with their investors about the corporations; they also require stockbrokers to be forthcoming with their clients.

Despite these rules, both the corporate officials who release information about their companies and the stockbrokers who help people invest in securities sometimes knowingly lie to or hide information from consumers to raise a company's stock level for their own profit. Corporations commit this type of fraud by releasing false information to the financial markets through news releases, quarterly and annual reports, Securities and Exchange Commission (SEC) filings, market analyst conference calls, proxy statements, and prospectuses. Brokers commit this type of fraud by failing to follow clients' instructions when directed; misrepresenting or omitting information; or making unsuitable recommendations or investments, unauthorized trades, or excessive trades (churning). Because brokerage analysts' recommendations to clients can affect the fees earned by the firms' investment banking operations, analysts can profit by playing up the value of certain stocks.

The Stanford Law School Securities Class Action Clearinghouse, in cooperation with Cornerstone Research, tracks the number of securities fraud class action filings each year. In 2006 there were 118 filings (*Securities Class Action Case Filings, 2006: A Year in Review*, 2007, http://securities.stanford.edu/). The 2006 total was considerably lower than the ten-year average of 193 per year and was the lowest annual total since the Public Securities Litigation Reform Act was adopted in 1995. Filings were down by 38% from the 178 filed in 2005.

Of the 110 filings in 2006, almost one-third (36) involved the noncyclical consumer industry (agriculture, beverage, biotechnology, commercial services, cosmetics/personal care, food, healthcare products, healthcare services, household products/wares, and pharmaceuti-

cals). Twenty-one of the filings involved technology companies. The most common allegations made were misrepresentation in financial documents and accounting irregularities.

Cornerstone Research speculates that the dramatic drop in securities fraud class action filings in 2006 might be due in part to increased enforcement activities by the SEC and the Department of Justice as well as passage of the Sarbanes-Oxley Act of 2002. With heavy penalties involved for infractions, corporations appeared to have adopted a more conservative approach in accounting, which resulted in fewer filings.

In a suit resolved during 2006, Gladys Kessler, U.S. District Court Judge for the District of Columbia, approved a plan to distribute $300 million to investors of Time Warner Inc. to settle a lawsuit stemming from accounting fraud perpetrated by the company. In the suit, Time Warner was charged with overstating its online advertising revenue and the number of its Internet subscribers.

### Oil and Gas Investment Frauds

The U.S. Postal Inspection Service reports in *Oil and Gas Investment Frauds* (http://www.usps.com/postalinspectors/fraud/oil-gas.htm) that although many oil and gas investments are legitimate, this area is well known for fraudulent offers made to potential investors. Illegitimate solicitors operate what are known as "boiler rooms," hastily set-up business offices with few furnishings. From these locations telephone solicitors call consumers in an attempt to convince them to invest in bogus oil or gas drilling ventures. Typically, the phone solicitors guarantee high profits, stress that the offer is only available to a select group of investors, and insist on an immediate decision. According to Kathy Chu in *USA Today* ("Prices Prompt Oil, Gas Investment Scams," August 17, 2006), investors seeking to make quick profits in the energy sector have lost millions of dollars in illegitimate oil and gas investments. Oil and gas fraud was one of the top five investor scams in the state of Texas during 2006.

## TELEMARKETING FRAUD

Telemarketing is a form of direct marketing in which representatives from companies call consumers or other businesses in order to sell their goods and services. Telemarketing services can also be tied to other forms of direct marketing such as print, radio, or television marketing. For example, a television advertisement might ask the viewer to call a toll-free number. The overwhelming majority of telemarketing operations are legitimate and trustworthy.

The National Fraud Information Center (NFIC) is a project of the National Consumers League (NCL), a nonprofit organization. The NFIC reported that in 2006,

31% of all telemarketing complaints received by the NCL's Fraud Center involved false check scams, in which consumers received notification that they have won a prize along with a phony check and a phone number to call for instructions on how to pay taxes or fees associated with claiming the prize (http://fraud.org/stats/2006/telemarketing.pdf). The average loss from these scams was $3,278. Another common telemarketing scam involved requests for payment to claim prizes that were never sent; 26% of all complaints were in this category and these victims lost an average of $2,749.

On December 20, 2006, two co-owners and seven office managers of Gecko Communications Inc. were sentenced for participating in a scheme to defraud an estimated 83,000 people across the country of more than $15.6 million. The company made false offers to provide credit cards to people with poor credit and charged up to $229 for the cards. To execute their plan, the Gecko company purchased lists of consumers with low credit ratings. Misrepresenting themselves as a financial company with credit counselors on staff, Gecko convinced consumers to pay for the opportunity to receive a pre-approved credit card. In fact, those who paid were sent credit card applications. The defendants were sentenced to prison terms ranging from two to six years. They were also ordered to pay restitution.

## MAIL CRIME

The U.S. Postal Inspection Service (USPIS) investigates crimes involving the nation's mail, including mail fraud, mail theft, and the mailing of controlled substances. Postal inspections resulted in 6,788 arrests and 5,544 convictions for mail theft (theft and possession of stolen mail) during FY 2005 (http://www.usps.com/postalinspectors/05anrept.pdf). In addition, there were 1,855 arrests and 1,279 convictions for mailing controlled substances (such as narcotics, steroids, and drug paraphernalia) and 1,577 arrests and 1,264 convictions for mail fraud. In one notable case, a twenty-year-old man from Massachusetts was convicted on May 4, 2006, of wire and mail fraud charges. He had advertised Superbowl tickets on eBay, collected approximately $255,000 from customers, and never provided the tickets or refunds.

## COMPUTER CRIME
### Federal Computer Crime Legislation

The first state computer crime law took effect in Florida in 1978. Other states soon followed until all fifty states had computer crime provisions.

In 1986 Congress passed the Computer Fraud and Abuse Act (P.L. 99-474) that makes it illegal to perpetrate fraud on a computer. The Computer Abuse Amendments of 1994 (P.L. 103-322) make it a federal crime "through means of a computer used in interstate commerce of communication ... [to] damage, or cause damage to, a computer, computer system, network, information, data, or program ... with reckless disregard" for the consequences of those actions to the computer owner. This law pertains to maliciously destroying or changing computer records or knowingly distributing a virus that shuts down a computer system. A virus program resides inside another program and is activated by some predetermined code to create havoc in the host computer. Virus programs can be transmitted by sharing disks and programs or through e-mail.

The 2001 USA Patriot Act, which gave increased powers to U.S. government law enforcement and intelligence agencies to help prevent terrorist attacks, amended the Computer Fraud and Abuse Act. The act was expanded to include the types of electronic records that law enforcement authorities may obtain without a subpoena, including records of Internet session times and durations, as well as temporarily assigned network addresses. The Patriot Act was reauthorized on March 9, 2006, in the USA Patriot Improvement and Reauthorization Act of 2005 (HR 3199).

### Internet Fraud

The National White Collar Crime Center and the FBI reported that the Internet Crime Complaint Center (IC3) Web site received 231,493 complaints of Internet crime in 2005 (*IC3 2005 Internet Crime Report*, 2006, http://www.ic3.gov/media/annualreport/2005_IC3Report.pdf). This represents an 11.6% increase over 2004 when the center received 207,449 complaints. Of these complaints, IC3 referred 97,076 to federal, state, and local law enforcement agencies for further consideration. Almost all of these cases involved fraud leading to financial loss for the victim. The total dollar cost of all cases of Internet fraud referred to law enforcement agencies was $183.12 million, with a median loss of $424 per complaint. This is a significant increase from $68 million in losses reported in 2004.

The most frequently reported Internet offense (62.7% of complaints) involved Internet auction fraud. Other complaints were for nondelivered merchandise and/or payment (15.7% of complaints) and credit card fraud (6.8%). About three-quarters (75.4%) of offenders were male and half resided in just seven states (California, New York, Florida, Texas, Illinois, Pennsylvania, and Ohio). Fraudulent contacts took place primarily by e-mail and Web pages. Almost three-quarters (73.2%) of complainants had engaged in e-mail contact with the perpetrator compared with 16.5% through a Web page.

SPAM. The IC3 defines "spam" as unsolicited bulk e-mail. According to IC3, spam is widely used to commit traditional white-collar crimes, including financial institution fraud, credit card fraud, and identity theft. Spam messages are usually considered unsolicited because the recipients have not chosen to receive the messages. Generally, spam involves multiple identical messages sent simultaneously. Spam can also be used to access computers and servers without authorization and transmit viruses or forward spam. Spam senders often sell open proxy information, credit card information, and e-mail lists illegally.

The Controlling the Assault of Non-Solicited Pornography and Marketing Act of 2003 (CAN-SPAM Act, P.L. 108-187, S. 877) established requirements for those who send commercial e-mail. CAN-SPAM requires that all spam contain a legitimate return address as well as instructions on how to opt out of receiving additional spam from the sender. Spam must also state in the subject line if the e-mail is pornographic in nature. Violators of these rules are to be subject to heavy fines.

The law's main provisions include:

- *Banning false or misleading header information*—The "from," "to," and routing information (including the originating name and e-mail address) must be accurate and identify the person who initiated the e-mail.

- *Prohibiting deceptive subject lines*—The subject line must not mislead the recipient about the message's contents or subject matter.

- *Requiring an opt-out method*—Senders must provide a return e-mail address or another Internet-based way that allow the recipient to ask the sender not to send any more e-mail messages to them.

The first person convicted by a jury in a CAN-SPAM case was Jeffrey Brett Goodin of California. He was found guilty on January 12, 2007, of operating an Internet-based scheme to obtain personal and credit card information. Goodin sent e-mails to AOL users that appeared to be from AOL's billing department. The messages instructed recipients to "update" their AOL billing information or lose service. The Web pages were actually scam pages set up by Gooding to collect personal and credit card information on the users.

SPYWARE. The Anti-Spyware Coalition—a group composed of software manufacturers, academics, and consumer advocates—defines spyware as "Technologies deployed without appropriate user consent and/or implemented in ways that impair user control over:

- Material changes that affect their user experience, privacy, or system security

- Use of their system resources, including what programs are installed on their computers; and/or

- Collection, use, and distribution of their personal or other sensitive information" (http://www.antispywarecoalition.org/about/FAQ.html).

According to the National Conference of State Legislatures, four states—Hawaii, Louisiana, Rhode Island,

and Tennessee—had enacted or adopted anti-spyware legislation in 2006 and another eighteen states were considering such legislation. California's Consumer Protection Against Computer Spyware Act makes it illegal for anyone to install software on someone else's computer and use it to deceptively modify settings, including the user's home page, default search page, or bookmarks. The act also outlaws collecting, through intentionally deceptive means, personally identifiable information by logging keystrokes, tracking Web site visits, or extracting personal information from a user's hard drive.

In November 2006 the federal government reached a settlement in the case of Odysseus Marketing, Inc., a company that advertised a free file-sharing software program and then exploited consumers who downloaded the program. Odysseus intercepted and replaced search results of users, attacked them with numerous pop-up advertisements, and copied their keystrokes, including such information as names, addresses, and Internet browsing habits. In the settlement, the defendants agreed not to download spyware in the future or exploit security vulnerabilities in Internet Explorer or other browsers. In addition, the government imposed a fine of $50,000.

**Computer Hacking**

Computer hacking takes place when an outsider gains unauthorized access to a secure computer by identifying and exploiting system vulnerabilities. Criminal hackers use their software expertise to crack security codes in order to access stored information or "highjack" a computer (that is, take it over and instruct it to generate spam or perform other malicious actions). The Web Application Security Consortium tracks hacking incidents that have been reported in the media and that result from vulnerabilities in Web application security. The consortium reported that the number of Web hacking incidents has increased significantly in recent years, from just nine in 2003 to forty-four in 2006. However, the number of hacking incidents in 2006 did decrease from 2005, when sixty-one hacking incidents were reported (http://www.webappsec.org/projects/whid/statistics.shtml).

A survey of security executives and law enforcement personnel conducted by *CSO Magazine*, the U.S. Secret Service, and the CERT® Coordination Center found that in 2005 hackers were considered the greatest computer security threat to U.S. companies (www.cert.org/archive/pdf/ecrimesummary05.pdf). More than one-third (37%) of respondents identified hacking as the greatest computer security threat to their organizations. About half as many (18%) identified current employees as the greatest threat, and 5% listed former employees.

According to Ethan Butterfield in *Washington Technology*, state governments increased security activities in response to several hacking incidents in 2006 ("Fear Factor: Spike in Malicious Hacking Creates Need for

Vigorous Action at State Level." October 2, 2006, http://www.washingtontechnology.com/print/21_19/29418-1.html). Included in the high-profile incidents were attacks on the Nebraska state child-support payment system and the IT systems of Ohio University, leaving the personal information of hundreds of thousands of people at risk.

The federal government is also vulnerable to hackers. In November 2006 a federal grand jury indicted a Romanian man, Victor Faur, a citizen of Romania, who gained unauthorized access to more than 150 different government computers (http://oig.nasa.gov/press/pr2007-C.pdf). Faur targeted computers at the Jet Propulsion Laboratory, Goddard Space Flight Center, Sandia National Laboratories, and U.S. Naval Observatory. Prosecutors speculate that U.S. government computers were targeted because of their reputation for high security; once he had control of the computers, the hacker merely set up chat rooms and bragged about his accomplishment. If convicted, Faur faces a maximum sentence of fifty-four years in federal prison. The incident cost about $1.5 million in estimated repairs, data losses, and system improvements

## INTELLECTUAL PROPERTY

According to the World Intellectual Property Organization, "intellectual property" comprises "creations of the mind: inventions, literary and artistic works, and symbols, names, images, and designs used in commerce" (http://www.wipo.int/about-ip/en/). These include industrial property such as trademarks, chemical formulas, patents, and designs, and copyrighted material such as literary works, films, musical compositions and recordings, graphic and architectural designs, works of art in any medium, and domain names.

The Intellectual Property Owners Association reports that the number of intellectual property suits in the U.S. federal court system in 2006 included 4,944 copyright cases, 3,740 cases related to trademark infringement, and 2,830 patent cases (http://www.ipo.org/). Trademark infringements increased by 17.3% between 1997 and 2006, and by 2% between 2005 and 2006. The number of patent infringement suits increased by 34% between 1997 and 2006, and by 4% between 2005 and 2006. Most dramatically, the number of suits related to copyrights increased more than 119% between 1997 and 2006, and by 14.7% between 2005 and 2006.

In the United States intellectual property is protected by the joint efforts of the United States Patent and Trademark Office, the U.S. Copyright Office, the U.S. Department of Justice, U.S. Department of Commerce, and two agencies that focus on international aspects of intellectual property: the U.S. Customs Service, which monitors incoming goods arriving from other nations, and the Office of the U.S. Trade Representative, which negotiates on behalf of U.S interests and develops and implements trade agreements and policies.

In a speech before the U.S. Chamber of Commerce on June 20, 2006, U.S. Attorney General Alberto Gonzales reported that the costs of intellectual property theft to American businesses include $250 billion in financial losses and 750,000 lost jobs every year (http://www.usdoj.gov/ag/speeches/2006/ag_speech_060620.html). Gonzales stressed, however, that these figures do not include the costs of intellectual property theft to the nation's economy overall. In his remarks, Gonzales referred to the case of Danny Ferrer, who pleaded guilty in June 2006 to copyright infringement. Ferrer sold almost $2.5 million worth of pirated software through his Web site until the FBI shut it down in October 2005. Ferrer's sales resulted in almost $20 million in losses to the copyright holders of the products he copied illegally. Ferrer faced a maximum sentence of ten years in prison and a $500,000 fine.

## ANTITRUST VIOLATIONS

Antitrust violations include price fixing, bid rigging, and other conspiracies that artificially inflate prices and cheat consumers. Such schemes are illegal because they deprive consumers of fair access to products at reasonable prices. Market division, in which competitors agree to divide customers among themselves, is also illegal for the same reason. The Department of Justice reported that in 2006 the Antitrust Division obtained the second highest level of criminal fines in the division's history. For the fiscal year ending on September 30, 2006, the division obtained $473 million in criminal fines, a 40% increase over FY 2005, and filed 33 criminal cases, many of which involved several defendants. (See Figure 4.6.)

**FIGURE 4.6**

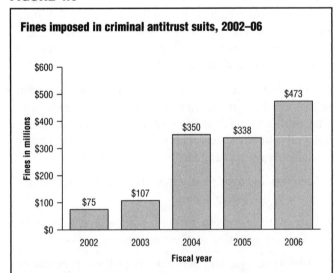

Fines imposed in criminal antitrust suits, 2002–06

SOURCE: "Criminal Antitrust Fines," in *Antitrust Division Ends the Year with Second-Highest Level of Criminal Fines, More Merger Challenges*, U.S. Department of Justice, December 21, 2006, http://www.usdoj.gov/atr/public/press_releases/2006/220465a.htm (accessed February 3, 2007)

**TABLE 4.2**

**Criminal investigations by the Internal Revenue Service, fiscal years 2004–06**

| | Fiscal year 2006 | Fiscal year 2005 | Fiscal year 2004 |
|---|---|---|---|
| Investigations initiated | 1863 | 1873 | 1736 |
| Prosecution recommendations | 1020 | 1157 | 1197 |
| Indictments/informations | 830 | 953 | 941 |
| Sentenced | 691 | 804 | 657 |
| Incarceration rate* | 75.10% | 79.10% | 83.60% |
| Average months to serve | 26 | 28 | 27 |

*Incarceration includes confinement to federal prison, halfway house, home detention, or some combination thereof.

SOURCE: "Statistical Data—General Tax Fraud," in *Criminal Investigations: Tax Fraud Alerts*, U.S. Department of the Treasury, Internal Revenue Service, 2007, http://www.irs.gov/compliance/enforcement/article/0,,id=106791,00.html (accessed January 21, 2007)

## TAX FRAUD

For most Americans, failure to pay the correct amount of taxes to the Internal Revenue Service (IRS) results in agreement to pay off the taxes in some manner. However, when the IRS believes it has found a pattern of deception designed to avoid paying taxes, criminal charges can be brought. In 2006 the Criminal Investigations Division of the IRS initiated 1,863 cases, slightly lower than 1,873 in 2005 but higher than 1,736 cases in 2004. (See Table 4.2.) Of cases investigated in 2006, the IRS recommended prosecution in 1,020 cases, and in 830 cases criminal charges were filed or brought by indictment. The IRS reported 691 convictions for tax fraud, and defendants were incarcerated in 75.1% of cases for an average of 26 months.

## FORGERY AND COUNTERFEITING

As technology advances, forgers can use sophisticated computers, scanners, and laser printers to make copies of more and more documents, including counterfeit checks, identification badges, driver's licenses, and money.

Making counterfeit U.S. currency or altering genuine currency to increase its value is punishable by a fine, imprisonment of up to fifteen years, or both. Possession of counterfeit U.S. currency is also a crime, punishable by a fine, imprisonment of up to fifteen years, or both. Counterfeiting is not limited to paper money. Manufacturing counterfeit U.S. coins in any denomination above five cents is subject to the same penalties as all other counterfeit activities. Anyone who alters a real coin to increase its value to collectors can be punished by a fine, imprisonment for up to five years, or both. The level of counterfeit bills in circulation worldwide is estimated to be less than 0.02% of all bills, about one to two counterfeit bills for every 10,000 genuine bills, according to the U.S. Bureau of Engraving and Printing (http://www.moneyfactory.gov/newmoney/main.cfm/media/releases102003newyork).

In response to the growing use of computer-generated counterfeit money, the U.S. Department of the Treasury redesigned the $50 and $100 bills in the 1990s and introduced new $5, $10, and $20 bills between 1998 and 2000. These bills contain a watermark making them harder to accurately copy. Another change in currency design was introduced in October 2003: a new $20 bill with shades of green, peach, and blue in the background. A blue eagle and metallic green eagle and shield have also been added to the bill's design. A new $50 note was issued on September 28, 2004, and a new $10 note was issued on March 2, 2006. On June 29, 2006, the U.S. government announced plans to redesign the $5 note and issue the new note in early 2008.

The Secret Service explains that many counterfeiters have abandoned the "traditional" method of offset printing, which requires specialized skills and machinery. Instead counterfeiters produce fake currency with basic computer training and typical office equipment. Although the number of counterfeit bills in circulation is likely to increase because more people have access to the machines and methods required to produce them, the security features added to the design and manufacture of U.S. currency have also made it easier to detect bogus bills.

The Department of the Treasury reports in *The Use and Counterfeiting of United States Currency Abroad, Part 3* (September 2006, http://www.federalreserve.gov/boarddocs/rptcongress/counterfeit/counterfeit2006.pdf), the value of U.S. currency determined to be counterfeit after entering circulation was $61 million in 2005, up by more than 50% since 1999, when $40.6 million in counterfeit was found in circulation. During this period, the value of counterfeit currency seized before entering circulation was $52.6 million, down from $140.3 million in 1999. (See Table 4.3.)

## MONEY LAUNDERING

The U.S. Government Accountability Office defines money laundering as "disguising or concealing illicit funds to make them appear legitimate" (http://www.gao.gov/new.items/d04710t.pdf). Money laundering involves transferring illegally received monies into legal accounts so that when money is withdrawn from those accounts, it appears to the police or other government authorities to be legal earnings of the account or the business. When a money-laundering scheme is successful, the criminals can spend their illegally acquired money with little fear

**TABLE 4.3**

**Counterfeit currency seized and passed, 1999–2005**

[Millions of dollars]

| Year | Passed | | | Seized | | |
|---|---|---|---|---|---|---|
| | Domestic | Foreign | Total | Domestic | Foreign | Total |
| 1999 | 39.2 | 1.4 | 40.6 | 13.7 | 126.6 | 140.3 |
| 2000 | 39.7 | 1.4 | 41.1 | 20.9 | 190.8 | 211.7 |
| 2001 | 47.5 | 1.5 | 49.0 | 12.6 | 54.0 | 66.6 |
| 2002 | 42.9 | 1.4 | 44.3 | 9.7 | 120.4 | 130.1 |
| 2003 | 36.6 | 1.5 | 38.1 | 10.7 | 52.2 | 62.9 |
| 2004 | 43.6 | 1.2 | 44.7 | 10.3 | 33.6 | 43.9 |
| 2005 | 56.2 | 4.8 | 61.0 | 14.7 | 37.9 | 52.6 |

Note: "seized" refers to counterfeit currency that was detected before being circulated, while "passed" indicates currency that was determined to be counterfeit after entering circulation. Only passed currency represents a loss to the public; seized counterfeits represent an averted threat.

SOURCE: "Table 6.2. Data on Counterfeit Currency, Fiscal Years 1999–2005," in *The Use and Counterfeiting of United States Currency Abroad, Part 3*, U.S. Department of the Treasury, September 2006, http://www.ustreas.gov/press/releases/reports/the%20use%20and%20counterfeiting%20of%20u.s.%20 currency%20abroad%20%20part%203%20september2006.pdf (accessed February 3, 2007)

of being caught. Many of the techniques that launderers use would be perfectly legal business transactions if the source of the cash were not illegal activities.

Over the years the federal government has enacted a number of laws to prevent money laundering. For example, the Uniting and Strengthening America Act by Providing Appropriate Tools Required to Intercept and Obstruct Terrorism (P.L. 107-56), known as the USA Patriot Act, fortified laws dealing with how U.S. banks use foreign banks to transfer money into and out of the country and the financing of terrorist organizations and activities. It also outlawed bulk cash smuggling, making it illegal to take more than $10,000 in concealed cash across the border to avoid reporting requirements.

On July 5, 2006, the Financial Crimes Enforcement Network, a section of the U.S. Department of the Treasury, issued final regulations for Section 312 of the USA Patriot Act. This section addresses correspondent accounts for foreign financial institutions as well as accounts opened in the United States by noncitizens. According to the new regulations, financial institutions are required to establish and implement policies to detect and report suspicious money-laundering activities. In addition to tighter controls at U.S. institutions, the federal government also extended its ability to obtain financial evidence abroad. As of March 2007 the U.S. Department of State and Department of Justice had entered into mutual legal assistance treaties (MLATs) with fifty-one countries. MLATs facilitate evidence gathering in international criminal cases, and make it possible to access banking and other financial records from foreign institutions in money-laundering cases.

Increased awareness of money laundering is reflected in the number of Suspicious Activity Reports (SAR) submitted by banks to the U.S. Department of the Treasury. Banks are required to submit these reports whenever they have reason to believe that a transaction of at least

$5,000 involves money derived from illegal activities. In the *SAR Activity Review: Trends, Tips, and Issues* (May 2006, http://www.fincen.gov/sarreviewissue10.pdf), the Treasury Department reported that it received 345 SARS regarding more than $1,000 in checks cashed by a single individual in one day, 309 suspicious money transfers, and 12 reports regarding suspected money laundering. (See Table 4.4.)

The number of money-laundering investigations initiated by the IRS has declined in recent years, from 1,789 in FY 2004 to 1,443 in FY 2006. Although the number of prosecutions has also decreased, from 1,515 in 2004 to 1,248 in 2006, the number of defendants sentenced has increased from 687 in FY 2004 to 800 in FY 2006. Similarly, the average number of months that those convicted serve in prison has increased from 63 months in FY 2004 to 74 months in FY 2006. (See Table 4.5.)

The U.S. Attorney's office in Seattle, Washington, reported the conclusion of one money laundering case in October 2006. The defendant in the case pleaded guilty to "willful failure to report a currency transaction in excess of $10,000," according to the U.S. Attorney's Office (http://www.usdoj.gov/usao/waw/press/2006/oct/plowman.html). The defendant, an attorney who represented a cocaine dealer, had accepted cashier's checks totaling $176,000 from his client to purchase a laundromat. The attorney did not document his receipt of this money, kept in a safe in his office, and failed to submit the required IRS forms recording large money transfers. According to the prosecutors, the attorney then used a $60,000 check and $100,000 in cash to purchase the business on behalf of his client, but wrote a sales document reflecting a purchase price of only $60,000, allowing $100,000 to transfer in the sale without documentation. Admitting this transaction was part of a pattern of similar unlawful actions. The attorney faced a sentence of ten years in prison.

**TABLE 4.4**

**Suspicious activity reports submitted to the U.S. Department of the Treasury, 2005**

| Activity | Occurrences | Percentage of total reported activities |
|---|---|---|
| Check cashing (over $1,000 aggregate for any person on any day) | 345 | 27.87% |
| Check cashing (non-specific) | 339 | 27.38% |
| Money transmission | 309 | 24.96% |
| Money services businesses activities (non-specific) | 131 | 10.58% |
| Informal value transfer systems (including hawala) | 49 | 3.96% |
| Arrests, indictments, and illicit activities associated with the operation of unregistered money services business | 15 | 1.21% |
| On money services business registration list without authorization date | 13 | 1.05% |
| No apparent money services business activity | 13 | 1.05% |
| Money laundering | 12 | 0.97% |
| Currency exchange | 7 | 0.57% |
| Black market peso exchange-like activity | 2 | 0.16% |
| Exchange of cashed third-party checks with related business for cash | 2 | 0.16% |
| Registered money services business facilitating transfers for related unregistered money services business | 1 | 0.08% |
| **Totals** | **1,238** | **100.00%** |

SOURCE: "Table 1. Types of Reported Activities," in "Section 2—Trends and Analysis," *SAR Activity Review: Trends, Tips, and Issues*, no. 10, May 2006, http://www.fincen.gov/sarreviewissue10.pdf (accessed February 4, 2007)

**TABLE 4.5**

**Money laundering and Bank Secrecy Act investigations by the Internal Revenue Service, fiscal years 2004–06**

| Money laundering investigations | Fiscal year 2006 | Fiscal year 2005 | Fiscal year 2004 |
|---|---|---|---|
| Investigations initiated | 1443 | 1639 | 1789 |
| Prosecution recommendations | 1248 | 1338 | 1515 |
| Indictments/informations | 1016 | 1147 | 1304 |
| Sentenced | 800 | 782 | 687 |
| Incarceration rate* | 88.10% | 88.40% | 89.10% |
| Average months to serve | 74 | 62 | 63 |
| **Bank Secrecy Act (BSA) investigations** | | | |
| Investigations initiated | 554 | 546 | 523 |
| Prosecution recommendations | 437 | 379 | 501 |
| Indictments/informations | 364 | 359 | 417 |
| Sentenced | 332 | 310 | 280 |
| Incarceration rate* | 75.30% | 83.20% | 83.20% |
| Average months to serve | 43 | 42 | 37 |

*Incarceration includes confinement to federal prison, halfway house, home detention, or some combination thereof.
Notes: Since actions on a specific investigation may cross fiscal years, the data shown in cases initiated may not always represent the same universe of cases shown in other actions within the same fiscal year. BSA statistics include investigations from Suspicious Activity Report (SAR) Review Teams, violations of BSA filing requirements, and all Title 31 and Title 18-1960 violations.

SOURCE: "Statistical Data—Money Laundering Enforcement," in *Criminal Investigations: Tax Fraud Alerts*, U.S. Department of the Treasury, Internal Revenue Service, 2007, http://www.irs.gov/compliance/enforcement/article/0,,id=113002,00.html (accessed February 4, 2007)

## RETAIL STORE THEFT

The *2005 National Retail Security Survey Final Report* (2006) by Richard Hollinger and Lynn Langton of the University of Florida is an annual survey of retail theft. The 2005 survey analyzed data from 156 of the largest U.S. retail chains. The survey found that retail shrinkage—a combination of employee theft, shoplifting, vendor fraud, and administrative error—represented about 1.6% of total annual sales in 2005, an increase from 1.5% in 2004 but a decrease from 1.8% in 1991. (See Figure 4.7.) Shrinkage rates were highest (4.7%) for accessories retailers, followed by home center/hardware/lumber/garden stores (3.2%) and craft/hobby stores (2.6%). (See Figure 4.8.)

According to the survey, employee theft accounts for more losses from retail theft than any other cause. (See Figure 4.9.) However, the average loss per employee-theft incident had decreased from $1,762 in 2003 to $1,053 in 2005. This is probably due to increased use of surveillance technology by retailers.

The *18th Annual Retail Theft Survey* conducted by Jack L. Hayes International, a retail security consulting firm, collected information from 24 large retail companies with 13,313 stores and $519 billion in 2005 retail sales (http://

**FIGURE 4.7**

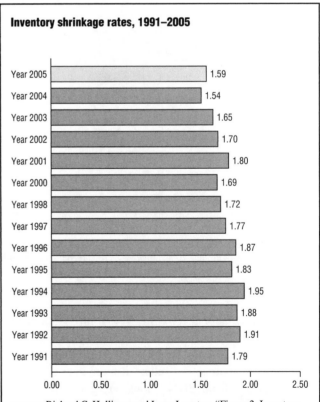

**Inventory shrinkage rates, 1991–2005**

| Year | Rate |
|---|---|
| Year 2005 | 1.59 |
| Year 2004 | 1.54 |
| Year 2003 | 1.65 |
| Year 2002 | 1.70 |
| Year 2001 | 1.80 |
| Year 2000 | 1.69 |
| Year 1998 | 1.72 |
| Year 1997 | 1.77 |
| Year 1996 | 1.87 |
| Year 1995 | 1.83 |
| Year 1994 | 1.95 |
| Year 1993 | 1.88 |
| Year 1992 | 1.91 |
| Year 1991 | 1.79 |

SOURCE: Richard C. Hollinger and Lynn Langton, "Figure 2. Inventory Shrinkage Rates," in *2005 National Retail Security Survey Final Report*, University of Florida, 2006, http://www.crim.ufl.edu/research/srp/finalreport_2005.pdf (accessed February 7, 2007)

FIGURE 4.8

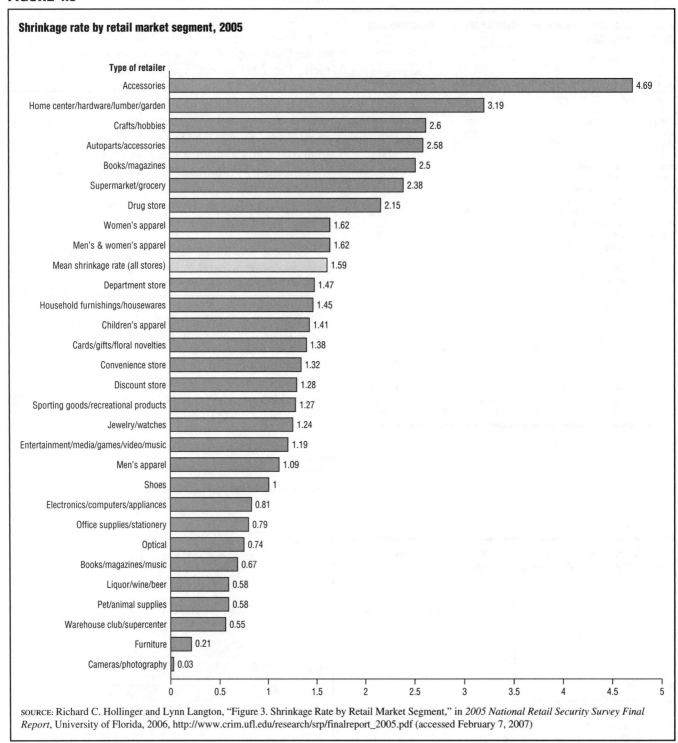

**Shrinkage rate by retail market segment, 2005**

| Type of retailer | Rate |
|---|---|
| Accessories | 4.69 |
| Home center/hardware/lumber/garden | 3.19 |
| Crafts/hobbies | 2.6 |
| Autoparts/accessories | 2.58 |
| Books/magazines | 2.5 |
| Supermarket/grocery | 2.38 |
| Drug store | 2.15 |
| Women's apparel | 1.62 |
| Men's & women's apparel | 1.62 |
| Mean shrinkage rate (all stores) | 1.59 |
| Department store | 1.47 |
| Household furnishings/housewares | 1.45 |
| Children's apparel | 1.41 |
| Cards/gifts/floral novelties | 1.38 |
| Convenience store | 1.32 |
| Discount store | 1.28 |
| Sporting goods/recreational products | 1.27 |
| Jewelry/watches | 1.24 |
| Entertainment/media/games/video/music | 1.19 |
| Men's apparel | 1.09 |
| Shoes | 1 |
| Electronics/computers/appliances | 0.81 |
| Office supplies/stationery | 0.79 |
| Optical | 0.74 |
| Books/magazines/music | 0.67 |
| Liquor/wine/beer | 0.58 |
| Pet/animal supplies | 0.58 |
| Warehouse club/supercenter | 0.55 |
| Furniture | 0.21 |
| Cameras/photography | 0.03 |

SOURCE: Richard C. Hollinger and Lynn Langton, "Figure 3. Shrinkage Rate by Retail Market Segment," in *2005 National Retail Security Survey Final Report*, University of Florida, 2006, http://www.crim.ufl.edu/research/srp/finalreport_2005.pdf (accessed February 7, 2007)

www.hayesinternational.com/thft_srvys.html). Nationwide these retailers apprehended more than 670,000 corrupt employees and shoplifters in 2005. Merchandise recovered through these captures was valued at more than $127 million, up 17.3% from 2004. However, goods recovered amounted to less than 3% of losses. The survey indicates that for every dollar recovered by retailers, $37.05 was lost to theft. Furthermore, the companies reported one out of every 26.5 employees was caught stealing. On average, employee thieves stole more than their shoplifting counterparts, with an average $724.15 stolen by employees and $126.87 stolen by shoppers.

## PUBLIC CORRUPTION

Abuse of public trust may be found wherever the interest of individuals or businesses overlaps with government interest. It ranges from the health inspector who

**FIGURE 4.9**

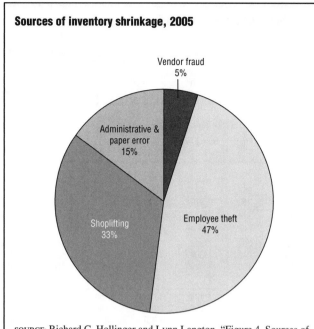

**Sources of inventory shrinkage, 2005**

Vendor fraud
5%

Administrative &
paper error
15%

Shoplifting
33%

Employee theft
47%

SOURCE: Richard C. Hollinger and Lynn Langton, "Figure 4. Sources of Inventory Shrinkage," in *2005 National Retail Security Survey Final Report*, University of Florida, 2006, http://www.crim.ufl.edu/research/srp/finalreport_2005.pdf (accessed February 7, 2007)

accepts a bribe from a restaurant owner or the police officer who "shakes down" the drug dealer, to the council member or legislator who accepts money to vote a certain way. These crimes are often difficult to uncover, as often few willing witnesses are available.

The U.S. Department of Justice reports in its *Report to Congress on the Activities and Operations of the Public Integrity Section for 2005* (2006, http://www.usdoj.gov/criminal/pin/docs/AnnReport_05.pdf) that the number of persons indicted for offenses involving the abuse of public office increased steadily from 1973 to 1983 and has remained relatively stable since that time. In 2005, 1,163 people were indicted and 1,027 were convicted in public corruption cases. Of those indicted, 445 were elected or appointed federal officials, 96 were state officials, 309 were local officials, and the remaining 313 were private citizens not employed by the government. (See Table 4.6.)

### Bribes, Kickbacks, and Racketeering

In one of the most notable cases involving bribery and kickbacks, Jack Abramoff, a prominent lobbyist in Washington, D.C., pleaded guilty to fraud, tax evasion, and conspiracy to bribe public officials in January 2006. He was sentenced to five years and ten months in prison and ordered to pay $21 million in restitution.

Abramoff received kickbacks from his former business partner, Michael Scanlon, in a conspiracy to defraud

Native American tribes who sought government approval to operate casinos. The tribes hired Abramoff to represent their interests, and he then recommended Scanlon's public relations firm to the tribes. Abramoff received a kickback from Scanlon for the referral. Abramoff and Scanlon supplied financial incentives, trips, and entertainment expenses to public officials whose support was needed for the projects they represented.

Abramoff was also listed as a co-conspirator in the charges against former Rep. Robert W. Ney (R-OH), who was sentenced in January 2007 to thirty months in prison and two years of supervised release. In addition Ney was ordered to serve 100 hours of community service for each year of supervised release and pay a $6,000 fine. Ney pleaded guilty on October 13, 2006, to honest services fraud, lobbying violations, and making false statements to the U.S. House of Representatives. Ney represented the 18th District of Ohio from 1995 through 2006. He admitted that he accepted international and domestic trips, meals, sports and concert tickets, and other incentives from Abramoff and others in exchange for his support on matters before the House of Representatives. In addition to Abramoff and Scanlon, a foreign businessman also provided financial incentives to Ney in return for his support in obtaining a travel visa and an exemption from legal restrictions against foreign nationals selling U.S. aircraft abroad.

### SCAMS ON THE ELDERLY

Because senior citizens are often retired and living on fixed incomes and savings, the promise of economic security can be very alluring. As a consequence, the elderly can be particularly vulnerable to economic crimes such as fraud and confidence schemes.

Seniors are particularly vulnerable to con artists. Often, they are lonely, isolated from their families, and sometimes more willing than in earlier years to believe what they are told. Some suffer mental or physical frailties that leave them less able to defend themselves against high-pressure tactics. In addition, they may be financially insecure and may want to believe the con artist's promises of future wealth and security. Since many elderly are too embarrassed to admit that they have been fooled, many of these crimes are not reported.

Statistics on fraud against the elderly, sometimes called elder scams, are not collected by the major crime reporting agencies. Surveys conducted by the AARP (formerly the American Association of Retired Persons) indicated that most victims of telemarketing fraud were fifty years of age or older. Top frauds committed against those sixty or older involved prizes/sweepstakes, lotteries/lottery clubs, and magazine sales.

One popular scam involves con artists calling or mailing information to elderly people announcing that

**TABLE 4.6**

**Number of officials and private citizens prosecuted in public corruption cases, selected years 1986–2005**

| | 1986 | 1987 | 1989 | 1991 | 1993 | 1995 | 1997 | 1999 | 2001 | 2003 | 2004 | 2005 |
|---|---|---|---|---|---|---|---|---|---|---|---|---|
| **Federal officials** | | | | | | | | | | | | |
| Charged | 596 | 651 | 695 | 803 | 627 | 527 | 459 | 480 | 502 | 479 | 424 | 445 |
| Convicted | 523 | 545 | 610 | 665 | 595 | 438 | 392 | 460 | 414 | 421 | 381 | 390 |
| Awaiting trial as of 12/31 | 83 | 118 | 126 | 149 | 133 | 120 | 83 | 101 | 131 | 129 | 98 | 118 |
| **State officials** | | | | | | | | | | | | |
| Charged | 88 | 102 | 71 | 115 | 113 | 61 | 51 | 115 | 95 | 94 | 111 | 961 |
| Convicted | 71 | 76 | 54 | 77 | 133 | 61 | 49 | 80 | 61 | 87 | 81 | 94 |
| Awaiting trial as of 12/31 | 24 | 26 | 18 | 42 | 39 | 23 | 20 | 44 | 75 | 38 | 48 | 51 |
| **Local officials** | | | | | | | | | | | | |
| Charged | 232 | 246 | 269 | 242 | 309 | 236 | 255 | 237 | 224 | 259 | 268 | 309 |
| Convicted | 207 | 204 | 201 | 180 | 272 | 191 | 169 | 219 | 184 | 119 | 252 | 232 |
| Awaiting trial as of 12/31 | 55 | 89 | 122 | 88 | 132 | 89 | 118 | 95 | 110 | 106 | 105 | 148 |
| **Private citizens** | | | | | | | | | | | | |
| Charged | 292 | 277 | 313 | 292 | 322 | 227 | 292 | 302 | 266 | 318 | 410 | 313 |
| Convicted | 225 | 256 | 284 | 272 | 362 | 188 | 243 | 306 | 261 | 241 | 306 | 311 |
| Awaiting trial as of 12/31 | 84 | 135 | 109 | 67 | 99 | 91 | 106 | 89 | 121 | 139 | 168 | 134 |
| **Totals** | | | | | | | | | | | | |
| Charged | 1,208 | 1,276 | 1,348 | 1,452 | 1,371 | 1,051 | 1,057 | 1,134 | 1,087 | 1,150 | 1,213 | 1,163 |
| Convicted | 1,026 | 1,081 | 1,149 | 1,194 | 1,362 | 878 | 853 | 1,065 | 920 | 868 | 1,020 | 1,027 |
| Awaiting trial as of 12/31 | 246 | 368 | 375 | 346 | 403 | 32 | 327 | 329 | 437 | 412 | 419 | 451 |

SOURCE: Adapted from "Table II. Progress over the Last Two Decades: Federal Prosecutions of Public Corruption by U.S. Attorneys' Offices," in *Report to Congress on the Activities and Operations of the Public Integrity Section for 2005*, U.S. Department of Justice—Criminal Division, 2006, http://www.usdoj .gov/criminal/pin/AnnReport_05.pdf (accessed January 17, 2007)

they have won a free prize, but must pay postage and handling to receive it. They are told a credit card number is needed to pay these costs. The thieves then use the credit card number to buy items and to get cash. The elderly are also susceptible to repairmen who stop by and say they can fix their homes. The workers may do the repair work, but it is shoddy and overpriced. If the elderly try to complain, the repairmen are no longer in the area, possibly not even in the state.

A more elaborate scam involves a con artist, acting as a bank official, telling the elderly person that a particular bank teller is giving out counterfeit bills and that the bank needs help in catching the teller. The elderly person goes to the teller's window and withdraws a large sum of money. The victim then gives the money to the "bank official" to be examined. The "bank official" assures the customer that the money will be redeposited in his or her account; of course, it never is.

## ENVIRONMENTAL CRIME

Environmental crime involves illegally polluting the air, water, or ground. Sometimes firms dump hazardous materials and waste. To investigate properly, local, state, national, and international agencies often need to cooperate. It is not unusual for environmental criminals to transport hazardous waste across state or international borders for disposal in places with less stringent environ-

mental enforcement. Even when a problem is known to exist, environmental crime cases are often difficult to prosecute due to their complex nature. The ramifications of pollution may take years to realize as pollutants become dispersed in the environment. In addition, financial penalties are often low enough to make it worth the risk for companies to flout the regulations. The more common means of enforcing environmental laws is through regulatory action by government agencies and the application of civil penalties to those who violate the regulations.

During fiscal year 2006 the Environmental Protection Agency (EPA) initiated 305 criminal complaint cases and charged 278 defendants with environmental crimes ("EPA Enforcement Cuts Total Pollution by Record 3 Billion Pounds Over Last Three Years—Air Pollution Reductions Alone Result in Health Benefits of $3.5 Billion Yearly," November 15, 2006, http://yosemite.epa .gov/). Together these defendants received a total 154 months in prison and were required to pay $43 million in fines in addition to $29 million for environmental rehabilitation. Additional enforcement actions resulted in agreements to pay $391 million to clean up 15 million cubic yards of contaminated soil and approximately 1.3 billion cubic yards of contaminated groundwater at waste sites and $4.9 billion to reduce pollution and achieve compliance with environmental laws.

# CHAPTER 5
# CONTROLLING CRIME

Systems are in place in the United States to prevent and deter crime. When these efforts fall short and a crime is committed, the justice system of the United States goes into action. The system has three major components that work together:

- Law enforcement agencies gather evidence and capture suspected perpetrators.

- The judicial system tries perpetrators in a court of law and, if they are found guilty, sentences them to a period of incarceration or some other form of punishment, restitution, and/or treatment.

- Correction agencies house convicted criminals in prisons, jails, treatment centers, or other places of confinement.

## CITY, COUNTY, AND STATE LAW ENFORCEMENT

The vast majority of law enforcement in the United States is carried out by local and state agencies. According to the Federal Bureau of Investigation (FBI) in its Uniform Crime Reporting (UCR) program, in 2005 the United States had 14,291 city, county, and state police agencies. (See Table 5.1.) In 2005 the United States had 969,070 full-time law enforcement employees, including 673,146 sworn police officers and 295,924 civilian employees. A significant majority (88.4%) of police officers were male, while 61.8% of civilian employees were female. Suburban counties employed 438,747 law enforcement personnel, and all cities with populations of 250,000 or more employed 202,230 law enforcement personnel. All cities with populations of one million or more employed 110,340 law enforcement personnel.

### Killed in the Line of Duty

From 1996 through 2005, felons killed 575 law enforcement officers. This excludes those who were killed in the terrorist attacks of September 11, 2001. (See Table 5.2.) Although the number of officers killed increased in 1997 and 2001, in general the number of law enforcement murders has declined, from 61 in 1996 to 55 in 2005.

## FEDERAL LAW ENFORCEMENT

According to Brian A. Reaves of the Bureau of Justice Statistics (BJS) in *Federal Law Enforcement Officers, 2004* (June 2006, http://www.ojp.usdoj.gov/bjs/pub/pdf/fleo04.pdf), federal agencies in September 2004 employed about 105,000 full-time officers who were authorized to make arrests and carry guns. This figure reflects a 13% increase from 2002. Of the major federal law enforcement employers in 2005, the U.S. Customs and Border Protection employed the highest number (27,705), followed by the Federal Bureau of Prisons (15,214) and the FBI (12,242). (See Table 5.3.)

The BJS reports that in 2005 about 84% of federal officers were male. Of agencies employing five hundred or more full-time officers with arrest and firearm authority, the Administrative Office of the U.S. Courts employed the highest percentage of women, 44.2%, and the U.S. Fish and Wildlife Service had the smallest proportion, 8.7%, of female officers. (See Table 5.4.) The U.S. Customs and Border Protection had the largest minority percentage, 46.8%. About two-fifths of the officers at the Veterans Health Administration (40.1%) and the Federal Bureau of Prisons (39.7%) were members of a racial or ethnic minority group.

## GOALS OF THE CORRECTIONS SYSTEM

The corrections system operates prisons, oversees parole, and administers probation. Parole and probation are systems for monitoring and controlling criminals without removing them from the general population. According to the Civic Practices Network (CPN) in *Balancing Justice: Setting Citizen Priorities for the Corrections System* (1996,

# TABLE 5.1

**Full-time law enforcement employees by status, population group, and sex, 2005**

| Population group | Total law enforcement employees | Percent law enforcement employees | | Total officers | Percent officers | | Total civilians | Percent civilians | | Number of agencies | 2005 estimated population |
|---|---|---|---|---|---|---|---|---|---|---|---|
| | | Male | Female | | Male | Female | | Male | Female | | |
| **Total agencies:** | **969,070** | **73.1** | **26.9** | **673,146** | **88.4** | **11.6** | **295,924** | **38.2** | **61.8** | **14,291** | **279,200,617** |
| **Total cities:** | **561,844** | **74.9** | **25.1** | **431,590** | **88.3** | **11.7** | **130,254** | **30.6** | **69.4** | **10,832** | **187,432,928** |
| Group I (250,000 and over) | 202,230 | 70.4 | 29.6 | 151,870 | 83.0 | 17.0 | 50,360 | 32.6 | 67.4 | 70 | 53,583,154 |
| 1,000,000 and over (group I subset) | 110,340 | 69.0 | 31.0 | 81,899 | 81.8 | 18.2 | 28,441 | 32.0 | 68.0 | 10 | 24,885,884 |
| 500,000 to 999,999 (group I subset) | 52,384 | 73.2 | 26.8 | 40,358 | 83.9 | 16.1 | 12,026 | 37.4 | 62.6 | 23 | 15,331,041 |
| 250,000 to 499,999 (group I subset) | 39,506 | 70.8 | 29.2 | 29,613 | 84.8 | 15.2 | 9,893 | 28.8 | 71.2 | 37 | 13,366,229 |
| Group II (100,000 to 249,999) | 66,461 | 73.3 | 26.7 | 50,111 | 88.7 | 11.3 | 16,350 | 26.1 | 73.9 | 180 | 27,066,683 |
| Group III (50,000 to 99,999) | 63,134 | 76.1 | 23.9 | 48,687 | 90.8 | 9.2 | 14,447 | 26.4 | 73.6 | 411 | 28,032,707 |
| Group IV (25,000 to 49,999) | 61,199 | 77.9 | 22.1 | 48,052 | 91.5 | 8.5 | 13,147 | 28.0 | 72.0 | 769 | 26,455,091 |
| Group V (10,000 to 24,999) | 68,958 | 79.3 | 20.7 | 54,925 | 92.7 | 7.3 | 14,033 | 26.9 | 73.1 | 1,791 | 28,385,387 |
| Group VI (under 10,000) | 99,862 | 79.4 | 20.6 | 77,945 | 91.6 | 8.4 | 21,917 | 36.2 | 63.8 | 7,611 | 23,909,906 |
| Metropolitan counties | 280,410 | 69.7 | 30.3 | 165,011 | 86.8 | 13.2 | 115,399 | 45.4 | 54.6 | 1,264 | 63,938,833 |
| Nonmetropolitan counties | 126,816 | 72.1 | 27.9 | 76,545 | 92.3 | 7.7 | 50,271 | 41.5 | 58.5 | 2,195 | 27,828,856 |
| Suburban area* | 438,747 | 73.1 | 26.9 | 288,835 | 88.9 | 11.1 | 149,912 | 42.7 | 57.3 | 7,354 | 118,418,670 |

*Suburban area includes law enforcement agencies in cities with less than 50,000 inhabitants and county law enforcement agencies that are within a metropolitan statistical area. Suburban area excludes all metropolitan agencies associated with a principal city. The agencies associated with suburban areas also appear in other groups within this table.

SOURCE: Table 74. Full-time Law Enforcement Employees, by Population Group, Percent Male and Female, 2005, in *Crime in the United States, 2005*, U.S. Department of Justice, Federal Bureau of Investigation, September 2006, http://www.fbi.gov/ucr/05cius/data/table_74.html (accessed January 18, 2007)

TABLE 5.2

**Law enforcement officers feloniously killed, by circumstances at scene of incident, 1996–2005**

| Circumstance | Total | 1996 | 1997 | 1998 | 1999 | 2000 | 2001* | 2002 | 2003 | 2004 | 2005 |
|---|---|---|---|---|---|---|---|---|---|---|---|
| **Total** | 575 | 61 | 70 | 61 | 42 | 51 | 70 | 56 | 52 | 57 | 55 |
| **Disturbance calls** | 95 | 4 | 13 | 16 | 5 | 8 | 13 | 9 | 10 | 10 | 7 |
| Bar fights, person with firearm, etc. | 36 | 1 | 3 | 7 | 4 | 4 | 5 | 4 | 5 | 1 | 2 |
| Family quarrels | 59 | 3 | 10 | 9 | 1 | 4 | 8 | 5 | 5 | 9 | 5 |
| **Arrest situations** | 147 | 26 | 22 | 15 | 9 | 12 | 24 | 10 | 8 | 13 | 8 |
| Burglaries in progress/pursuing burglary suspects | 18 | 3 | 5 | 0 | 0 | 3 | 3 | 0 | 1 | 2 | 1 |
| Robberies in progress/pursuing robbery suspects | 50 | 12 | 11 | 3 | 3 | 1 | 4 | 4 | 1 | 7 | 4 |
| Drug-related matters | 28 | 3 | 1 | 7 | 2 | 3 | 8 | 3 | 1 | 0 | 0 |
| Attempting other arrests | 51 | 8 | 5 | 5 | 4 | 5 | 9 | 3 | 5 | 4 | 3 |
| **Civil disorders (mass disobedience, riot, etc.)** | 0 | 0 | 0 | 0 | 0 | 0 | 0 | 0 | 0 | 0 | 0 |
| **Handling, transporting, custody of prisoners** | 18 | 1 | 3 | 4 | 2 | 2 | 2 | 0 | 2 | 1 | 1 |
| **Investigating suspicious persons/circumstances** | 71 | 13 | 8 | 5 | 7 | 6 | 8 | 6 | 4 | 7 | 7 |
| **Ambush situations** | 102 | 6 | 12 | 10 | 6 | 10 | 9 | 17 | 9 | 15 | 8 |
| Entrapment/premeditation | 40 | 2 | 5 | 4 | 4 | 2 | 3 | 4 | 6 | 6 | 4 |
| Unprovoked attacks | 62 | 4 | 7 | 6 | 2 | 8 | 6 | 13 | 3 | 9 | 4 |
| **Investigative activities (surveillance, searches, interviews, etc.)** | 8 | 0 | 2 | 0 | 0 | 0 | 0 | 0 | 2 | 0 | 4 |
| **Handling mentally deranged persons** | 13 | 1 | 1 | 0 | 0 | 0 | 3 | 4 | 0 | 2 | 2 |
| **Traffic pursuits/stops** | 102 | 10 | 8 | 10 | 8 | 13 | 8 | 10 | 14 | 6 | 15 |
| Felony vehicle stops | 42 | 6 | 3 | 5 | 4 | 4 | 5 | 6 | 4 | 0 | 5 |
| Traffic violation stops | 60 | 4 | 5 | 5 | 4 | 9 | 3 | 4 | 10 | 6 | 10 |
| **Tactical situations (barricaded offender, hostage taking, high-risk entry, etc.)** | 19 | 0 | 1 | 1 | 5 | 0 | 3 | 0 | 3 | 3 | 3 |

*The 72 deaths that resulted from the events of September 11, 2001, are not included in this table.

SOURCE: Table 20. Law Enforcement Officers Feloniously Killed: Circumstance at Scene of Incident, 1996–2005, in *Law Enforcement Officers Killed and Assaulted 2005*, U.S. Department of Justice, Federal Bureau of Investigations, October 2006, http://www.fbi.gov/ucr/killed/2005/table20.htm (accessed January 22, 2007)

http://www.cpn.org/tools/manuals/Community/balancing justice.html), the role of the correctional system is to carry out the sentence that the criminal court system gives to the offender. CPN lists five goals for the system:

- "Punishment—Making criminals suffer for their crimes"

- "Incapacitation—Keeping criminals from committing other crimes by keeping them off the streets"

- "Restitution—Ensuring that criminals pay a debt to victims and to society as a whole"

- "Deterrence—Preventing crime by making it clear to potential criminals that the consequences of committing a crime are severe"

- "Rehabilitation—Helping criminals become productive, responsible citizens who can contribute to society and avoid committing crimes once they are released"

There is considerable disagreement over which of these goals should be emphasized, and how to do so. The issue of how best to keep prisoners who have completed their sentences from committing new crimes after their release (recidivism) is especially controversial. Another area of much dispute is how severe of a punishment is merited by particular crimes.

## Effectiveness of Prisons

The BJS reported in *Reentry Trends in the U.S.: Recidivism* (2002, http://www.ojp.usdoj.gov/bjs/reentry/recidivism.htm#recidivism) that slightly more than two-thirds (67.5%) of prisoners released from state prison in fifteen states in 1994 were rearrested within three years. (See Table 5.5.) This rate was higher than in 1983, when 62.5% of released prisoners were arrested again within three years. The rearrest rate for drug offenders increased most dramatically, from 50.4% in 1983 to 66.7% in 1994. However, the BJS notes that reconviction rates did not change significantly from 1983, when 46.8% were reconvicted, and 1994, when the rate was 46.9%.

In a study of maximum-security—"supermax"—prisons, Daniel P. Mears (*Evaluating the Effectiveness of Supermax Prisons*, Urban Institute, March 2006, http://www.urban.org/publications/411326.html) reported that these prisons have a broad range of unintended effects, including increased mental illness. However, noted Mears, there also were "positive unintended effects of supermaxes, such as improving living conditions and outcomes for general population inmates." Prison wardens generally agree that supermax prisons are effective in "increasing safety, order, and control throughout prison

**TABLE 5.3**

**Federal agencies employing 500 or more full-time law enforcement officers authorized to carry firearms and make arrests, September 2004**

| Agency | Full-time officers |
|---|---|
| U.S. Customs and Border Protection | 27,705 |
| Federal Bureau of Prisons | 15,214 |
| Federal Bureau of Investigation | 12,242 |
| U.S. Immigration and Customs Enforcement | 10,399 |
| U.S. Secret Service | 4,769 |
| Drug Enforcement Administration[a] | 4,400 |
| Administrative Office of the U.S. Courts[b] | 4,126 |
| U.S. Marshals Service | 3,233 |
| U.S. Postal Inspection Service | 2,976 |
| Internal Revenue Service, Criminal Investigation | 2,777 |
| Veterans Health Administration | 2,423 |
| Bureau of Alcohol, Tobacco, Firearms and Explosives | 2,373 |
| National Park Service[c] | 2,148 |
| U.S. Capitol Police | 1,535 |
| Bureau of Diplomatic Security, Diplomatic Security Service[a] | 825 |
| U.S. Fish and Wildlife Service, Division of Law Enforcement | 708 |
| USDA Forest Service, Law Enforcement & Investigations | 600 |

Note: Table excludes employees based in U.S. territories or foreign countries.
[a]Data are estimates based on information provided by the agency.
[b]Includes all federal probation officers employed in federal judicial districts that allow officers to carry firearms.
[c]Includes 1,536 park rangers and 612 U.S. park police officers.

SOURCE: Brian A. Reaves, "Table 1. Federal Agencies Employing 500 or More Full-Time Officers with Authority to Carry Firearms and Make Arrests, September 2004," in *Federal Law Enforcement Officers, 2004*, U.S. Department of Justice, Office of Justice Programs, Bureau of Justice Statistics, July 2006, http://www.ojp.usdoj.gov/bjs/pub/pdf/fleo04.pdf (accessed January 22, 2007)

systems and incapacitating violent or disruptive inmates." Nonetheless, studies have not been done to determine if the cost of running these prisons justifies the benefits.

Although some people, like the prison wardens who participated in the Urban Institute study above, think that our nation's prisons are achieving their goals, others believe that the nation's prison system needs some major reforms. Writing in the *San Francisco Chronicle*, Mark Martin ("Prison Reform Needs Reform. Corrections System Can't Do Task Alone," March 12, 2006, http://www.sfgate.com/cgi-bin/article.cgi?f=/c/a/2006/03/12/ING6N HHM0U1.DTL) reported that, according to those who have studied California's prison system (the country's largest):

> Sentencing laws enacted more than 30 years ago, and repeatedly described as a failure, require nothing of inmates, who sit in cells or on yards instead of entering drug treatment or vocational education programs. Corrections administrators have little power to determine when an inmate is truly ready to leave prison, and that results in the daily release of dangerous people back into the neighborhoods they previously terrorized. Overburdened parole agents are required to monitor virtually every parolee, leaving the agents little time to concentrate on the parolees most likely to pose a threat to citizens. That has resulted in this shocking fact: More than 20,000 California parolees are unaccounted for on any given day.

**TABLE 5.4**

**Gender and race or ethnicity of full-time federal officers with arrest and firearm authority in agencies employing 500 or more full-time officers, September 2004**

| Agency | Number of officers | Female | Percent of full-time federal officers with arrest and firearm authority | | | | | |
|---|---|---|---|---|---|---|---|---|
| | | | Racial/ethnic minority | | | | | |
| | | | Total minority | American Indian | Black or African American | Asian or Pacific Islander | Hispanic or Latino any race | Other race |
| U.S. Customs and Border Protection | 28,200 | 15.3% | 46.8% | 0.6% | 5.0% | 4.2% | 36.9% | 0.0% |
| Federal Bureau of Prisons | 15,361 | 13.3 | 39.7 | 1.3 | 24.2 | 1.5 | 12.7 | 0.0 |
| Federal Bureau of Investigation | 12,414 | 18.5 | 17.2 | 0.4 | 5.8 | 3.6 | 7.4 | 0.0 |
| U.S. Immigration and Customs Enforcement | 10,691 | 13.7 | 33.9 | 0.6 | 8.6 | 2.7 | 22.0 | 0.0 |
| U.S. Secret Service | 4,780 | 10.5 | 19.6 | 0.6 | 11.2 | 2.6 | 5.2 | 0.0 |
| Drug Enforcement Administration | 4,500 | 8.9 | 19.4 | 0.4 | 7.6 | 2.5 | 8.9 | 0.0 |
| Administrative Office of the U.S. Courts | 4,166 | 44.2 | 32.2 | 0.5 | 15.3 | 1.6 | 14.1 | 0.6 |
| U.S. Marshals Service | 3,233 | 10.2 | 20.0 | 0.7 | 7.3 | 2.3 | 9.6 | 0.1 |
| U.S. Postal Inspection Service | 2,999 | 19.6 | 36.4 | 0.5 | 21.6 | 4.7 | 9.6 | 0.0 |
| Internal Revenue Service, Criminal Investigation | 2,791 | 30.0 | 24.0 | 0.8 | 10.2 | 4.5 | 8.1 | 0.4 |
| Veterans Health Administration | 2,474 | 6.9 | 40.1 | 0.9 | 26.8 | 2.5 | 10.0 | 0.0 |
| Bureau of Alcohol, Tobacco, Firearms & Explosives | 2,398 | 13.3 | 19.9 | 1.1 | 9.3 | 2.1 | 7.5 | 0.0 |
| National Park Service-Ranger Division | 1,547 | 18.2 | 10.3 | 2.1 | 2.5 | 2.4 | 3.0 | 0.3 |
| U.S. Capitol Police | 1,535 | 18.8 | 34.7 | 0.3 | 28.9 | 1.2 | 4.2 | 0.0 |
| Bureau of Diplomatic Security, Diplomatic Security Service | 825 | 11.8 | 20.0 | 0.7 | 9.7 | 3.4 | 5.5 | 0.7 |
| U.S. Fish and Wildlife Service | 713 | 8.7 | 13.6 | 3.5 | 1.7 | 1.4 | 7.0 | 0.0 |
| National Park Service-U.S. Park Police | 612 | 11.4 | 18.8 | 0.0 | 10.9 | 2.8 | 5.1 | 0.0 |
| USDA Forest Service | 604 | 17.5 | 17.4 | 6.5 | 3.3 | 1.3 | 6.3 | 0.0 |

Note: Table includes employees in U.S. territories.

SOURCE: Brian A. Reaves, "Table 4. Gender and Race or Ethnicity of Federal Officers with Arrest and Firearm Authority, Agencies Employing 500 or More Full-Time Officers, September 2004," in *Federal Law Enforcement Officers, 2004*, U.S. Department of Justice, Office of Justice Programs, Bureau of Justice Statistics, July 2006, http://www.ojp.usdoj.gov/bjs/pub/pdf/fleo04.pdf (accessed January 22, 2007)

**TABLE 5.5**

**Percent of prisoners released in 15 states and rearrested within 3 years, by offense, 1983 and 1994**

| | All released prisoners | Violent | Property | Drug | Public-order |
|---|---|---|---|---|---|
| 1983 | 62.5 | 59.6 | 68.1 | 50.4 | 54.6 |
| 1994 | 67.5 | 61.7 | 73.8 | 66.7 | 62.2 |

SOURCE: Percent of Released Prisoners Rearrested within 3 years, by Offense, 1983 and 1994, in *Reentry Trends in the U.S.: Recidivism*, U.S. Department of Justice, Office of Justice Programs, Bureau of Justice Statistics, 2002, http://www.ojp.usdoj.gov/bjs/reentry/recidivism.htm#recidivism (accessed February 7, 2007)

## When Prisoners Reenter the Community

What happens to prisoners after they leave prison is an important measure of the corrections system's effectiveness. In *Returning Home: Understanding the Challenges of Prisoner Reentry* (Urban Institute, January 24, 2004, http://www.urban.org/publications/410974.html), Christy Visher et al. studied the experiences of inmates who left prisons in Maryland and returned to the community. They found that about 40% of respondents were working full time thirty to ninety days after their release from prison. About half (51%) relied on their families for financial support. During the first few months after release, 32.6% used drugs or got drunk. Although 45% of respondents had participated in a post-release program, few found the programs useful in their transition to community life. Nonetheless, even though participants had extensive criminal histories and family members with criminal records, 78% thought that they would be able to stay out of prison.

## PRISON SENTENCES

After a person is found guilty of a crime, he or she is often sentenced to a period of incarceration. Sentencing policies in the United States have changed since the 1970s. According to historical BJS records (http://www.albany.edu/sourcebook/pdf/t6282004.pdf), prison populations began increasing in 1973, when the rate was 96 prisoners per 100,000 adult residents in the United States; in 2005 the rate was an estimated 491 per 100,000, according to the BJS statisticians Paige M. Harrison and Allen J. Beck in *Prisoners in 2005* (November 2006, http://www.ojp.usdoj.gov/bjs/pub/pdf/p05.pdf). The total number of inmates in federal or state prisons in 2005 was 1.5 million, an increase from 1.2 million in 1995. From 2004 to 2005 the prison population increased by 1.9%.

The period of expanding incarceration coincided with emphasis at state and federal levels on controlling the use and distribution of drugs. The modern "war on drugs" began in the early 1970s under President Richard Nixon. The Drug Enforcement Agency was created to spearhead anti-drug efforts and federal funding for drug control increased substantially. Many state and local governments also cracked down on drug use and trafficking. The result was a substantial increase in the number of people sentenced for drug crimes, which in turn put a strain on the U.S. criminal justice system and created controversies that persisted into the twenty-first century.

It is against this background that new sentencing policies developed. BJS statisticians Paula M. Ditton and Doris James Wilson (*Truth in Sentencing in State Prisons*, January 1999, http://www.ojp.usdoj.gov/bjs/pub/pdf/tssp.pdf) summarize the situation beginning with the 1970s as follows:

> In the early 1970s, states generally permitted parole boards to determine when an offender would be released from prison. In addition, good-time reductions for satisfactory prison behavior, earned-time incentives for participation in work or educational programs, and other time reductions to control prison crowding resulted in the early release of prisoners. These policies permitted officials to individualize the amount of punishment or leniency an offender received and provided means to manage the prison population.

> Such discretion in sentencing and release policies led to criticism that some offenders were punished more harshly than others for similar offenses and to complaints that overall sentencing and release laws were too soft on criminals. By the late 1970s and early 1980s, States began developing sentencing guidelines, enacting mandatory minimum sentences and adopting other sentencing reforms to reduce disparity in sentencing and to toughen penalties for certain offenses, specifically drug offenses (as part of the "war on drugs"), offenses with weapons, and offenses committed by repeat or habitual criminals.

## TRUTH-IN-SENTENCING

Sentence reforms enacted by states came to be known as "truth-in-sentencing" statutes. The first such statute was enacted by the state of Washington in 1984. Also that year, Congress established the U.S. Sentencing Commission (USSC) in the Sentencing Reform Act. Congress charged this new federal agency with developing sentencing guidelines for federal courts. The Sentencing Reform Act was the federal enactment of truth-in-sentencing.

Truth-in-sentencing is intended to tell the public that a sentence announced by the court will actually be served—rather than the criminal serving only some small fraction of the sentence, the prisoner being released on parole, or the individual having the sentence commuted to probation and serving no time at all. Under truth-in-sentencing statutes, offenders are required to spend substantial portions of their sentences in prison.

With truth-in-sentencing came the distinction between *indeterminate* and *determinate* sentencing. Indeterminate sentencing gives parole boards the authority to release offenders at their option after a process of review.

Determinate sentencing takes decision-making power away from parole boards, fixes the term to be served, and provides or denies the means to shorten the sentence by good behavior or other "earned" time. Part of the truth-in-sentencing statutes are mandatory minimum sentences for specific offenses and circumstances. Guidelines define the range of sentences the judge may apply, again governed by the offense and the prior history of the offender (for example, first-time or repeat-offender, severity of the offense, etc.).

Setting uniform sentences for offenses and requiring that fixed proportions of them be served by those convicted put pressure on prison and jail capacities. In response, Congress passed the Violent Crime Control and Law Enforcement Act of 1994, known as the 1994 Crime Act. The Crime Act included the authority for the federal government to offer grants to states to expand their prison capacity if they imposed truth-in-sentencing requirements on violent offenders. To qualify for the grants, the states had to pass laws requiring that serious violent offenders serve at least 85% of their imposed sentences in prison.

### Impact of Truth-in-Sentencing Laws

Katherine J. Rosich and Kamala Mallik Kane ("Truth in Sentencing and State Sentencing Practices," *NIJ Journal*, No. 252, July 2005, http://www.ojp.usdoj.gov/nij/journals/252/sentencing_print.html) summarized the results of a study by the Urban Institute's Justice Policy Center on the impact of truth-in-sentencing practices. According to the researchers, when the federal truth-in-sentencing incentive grant program was implemented, many states were already changing their sentencing structures and practices. State truth-in-sentencing reforms varied greatly, and many were in place before the federal grant program was enacted. Most states (forty-one plus the District of Columbia) had some type of truth-in-sentencing activity by the end of the 1990s. More than half of all states (twenty-eight) and the District of Columbia had received federal grants; another thirteen states with some truth-in-sentencing activity did not receive federal truth-in-sentencing grants.

The Urban Institute study found that, overall, federal truth-in-sentencing grants led to relatively few state truth-in-sentencing reforms. Many states had already adopted some form of truth-in-sentencing by the time the federal truth-in-sentencing program was implemented, and there was relatively little reform activity after 1994. In addition, according to Rosich and Mallik Kane, state truth-in-sentencing "practices generally increased the expected length of time to be served, but these increases were rarely the main contributor to increases in prison populations. Changes in crime rates, arrests, and prison admissions were often more influential."

## FEDERAL SENTENCING GUIDELINES

The Sentencing Reform Act of 1984 is the federal approach to truth-in-sentencing, or determinate sentencing. The USSC's publication *Fifteen Years of Guidelines Sentencing* (November 2004, http://www.ussc.gov/15_year/15year.htm) lists the goals of the Sentencing Reform Act:

1. Elimination of unwarranted disparity

2. Transparency, certainty, and fairness

3. Proportionate punishment; and

4. Crime control through deterrence, incapacitation, and the rehabilitation of offenders

The act was designed to eliminate the unregulated power of federal judges to impose sentences of indeterminate length. Because of this unregulated power, some people were convicted of the same crime but sentenced by different judges to receive wildly different terms of incarceration. The USSC developed federal guidelines to give a range of sentencing options to federal judges while guaranteeing minimum and maximum sentencing lengths.

The USSC continues to update the guidelines as laws administered by the federal courts are changed or new laws are passed. The USSC also issues supplemental volumes. The latest edition of the guidelines was published in 2006 (*Federal Sentencing Guidelines Manual*, November 2006, http://www.ussc.gov/2006guid/gl2006.pdf).

At the core of the guidelines are offenses as defined by federal statutes. The USSC assigns an "offense level" to each offense, known as the "base offense level," which ranges from one to forty-three. The lowest actual offense for which the USSC has a level is trespass. Trespass is level four. First-degree murder has a base offense level of forty-three. Based on the circumstances associated with an offense, additional levels can be added or taken away until a particular offense has been assigned to the appropriate level. Judges and prosecutors use the levels to find the relevant sentence, in months of imprisonment, in the federal "sentencing table."

An illustration is provided for kidnapping, abduction, and unlawful restraint in Table 5.6. The table displays the USSC's guideline for this offense. The offense has a base offense level of thirty-two, but additional levels can be added. For example, if the victim sustained serious bodily injury, the level is increased by four, to thirty-six. If the victim was sexually exploited, the level is increased by six levels, to thirty-eight. If the victim was not released before seven days had passed, the level is increased by one, to thirty-three.

In the USSC's 2006 sentencing table, level twenty-eight, for example, points to six columns of sentence ranges indicating a minimum and a maximum sentence in each column. (See Table 5.7.) The first column, where the sentence range is seventy-eight to ninety-seven months,

## TABLE 5.6

**Federal sentencing guidelines on kidnapping, 2006**

(a) Base offense level: 32

(b) Specific offense characteristics

    (1) If a ransom demand or a demand upon government was made, increase by 6 levels.

    (2) (A) If the victim sustained permanent or life-threatening bodily injury, increase by 4 levels;
        (B) if the victim sustained serious bodily injury, increase by 2 levels; or
        (C) if the degree of injury is between that specified in subdivisions (A) and (B), increase by 3 levels.

    (3) If a dangerous weapon was used, increase by 2 levels.

    (4) (A) If the victim was not released before thirty days had elapsed, increase by 2 levels.
        (B) If the victim was not released before seven days had elapsed, increase by 1 level.

    (5) If the victim was sexually exploited, increase by 6 levels.

    (6) If the victim is a minor and, in exchange for money or other consideration, was placed in the care or custody of another person who had no legal right to such care or custody of the victim, increase by 3 levels.

    (7) If the victim was kidnapped, abducted, or unlawfully restrained during the commission of, or in connection with, another offense or escape therefrom; or if another offense was committed during the kidnapping, abduction, or unlawful restraint, increase to—
        (A) the offense level from the chapter two offense guideline applicable to that other offense if such offense guideline includes an adjustment for kidnapping, abduction, or unlawful restraint, or otherwise takes such conduct into account; or
        (B) 4 plus the offense level from the offense guideline applicable to that other offense, but in no event greater than level 43, in any other case, if the resulting offense level is greater than that determined above.

SOURCE: "§2A4.1. Kidnapping, Abduction, Unlawful Restraint," in *2006 Federal Sentencing Guidelines Manual*, U.S. Sentencing Commission, November 1, 2006, http://www.ussc.gov/2006guid/2a4_1.html (accessed January 23, 2007)

applies to offenders with no prior convictions or one prior conviction. The sixth column, where the sentence is 140 to 175 months, provides sentencing guidelines for offenders with thirteen or more prior convictions. A single level thus provides six different levels of confinement, and, within each level, a minimum and maximum number of months of imprisonment. This leaves judges with some discretion to determine sentencing.

Level twenty-eight falls into the sentencing table's Zone D. (See Table 5.7.) Individuals in this zone are not permitted to receive any probation and must serve at least the minimum sentence shown in the applicable column. A three-time offender would be sentenced to a minimum of eighty-seven months in prison and, under the USSC guidelines, could receive at most fifty-four days off per year for good behavior. Thus, this offender would serve at least 85% of the minimum sentence. If a case of kidnapping involved sexual exploitation, the offender would also be charged with criminal sexual abuse (a base offense level of twenty-four) or sexual abuse of a minor (level eighteen to twenty-four depending on whether the abuse was attempted or committed). Parole is not available in any of the guideline cases.

Property crimes are handled in the USSC guidelines in a similar manner. The base level is increased with the

amount of property involved. For larceny, embezzlement, and other forms of theft, for instance, the base offense level is six in cases where the loss to the victim is $5,000 or less. If the loss is greater than $5,000 but less than $10,000, the level rises to eight and continues to rise as the amount of the loss rises. If the loss is more than $200,000 but less than $400,000, the level is eighteen. If the loss is greater than $100 million, the level is thirty-two—which will result in a mandatory sentence of at least ten years in prison for a first-time offender. A person who earned the maximum days for good behavior could expect to be out of incarceration in eight years and seven months if he or she received the minimum sentence. Fines and restitution of stolen money or property would also be required.

## "Departures" from the Guidelines

"Departures" mean that the guidelines are applied to a majority but not to all persons charged with federal offenses—and they vary by category of offense. According to the USSC, in an analysis of cases decided between October 1, 2004, and January 11, 2005, 28.4% of offenders received departures below the guideline range and 0.7% received departures above the guideline range. (See Table 5.8.) All six offenders convicted of antitrust violations (100%) received sentences below the guideline range, while 12.5% of those convicted for manslaughter received sentences above the guideline range.

U.S. Supreme Court decisions in 2004 and 2005 modified sentencing guidelines. In 2004 the Supreme Court ruled in *Blakely v. Washington* that a state judge cannot impose a longer sentence when the basis for the enhanced sentence was not admitted by the subject or found by a jury. In the Blakely case the subject admitted to kidnapping his estranged wife. The maximum sentence for the crime was fifty-three months in prison, but the judge imposed a sentence of ninety months after determining that Blakely had acted with deliberate cruelty, a factor that allowed a longer sentence under existing statutes. However, the charge of deliberate cruelty had not been part of Blakely's plea, and it had not been determined by a jury. The Supreme Court found that the Sixth Amendment right to a trial by jury had thus been violated. The Blakely ruling means that only facts proved to a jury can justify an enhanced sentence.

The Supreme Court made a related ruling in January 2005 in *United States v. Booker*. In this case the subject had been charged with possession with intent to distribute fifty grams of crack cocaine, a crime for which the federal sentencing guidelines set a twenty-one-year, ten-month sentence. However, the judge later determined that Booker had possessed ninety-two grams of crack cocaine and had obstructed justice as well. Because of these additional offenses, the judge sentenced Booker to thirty years in prison. In language similar to the *Blakely* ruling,

TABLE 5.7

## Federal sentencing table, 2006

[In months of imprisonment]

| | | Criminal history category (criminal history points) | | | | | |
|---|---|---|---|---|---|---|
| Offense level | I (0 or 1) | II (2 or 3) | III (4, 5, 6) | IV (7, 8, 9) | V (10, 11, 12) | VI (13 or more) |
| 1 | 0–6 | 0–6 | 0–6 | 0–6 | 0–6 | 0–6 |
| 2 | 0–6 | 0–6 | 0–6 | 0–6 | 0–6 | 7–Jan |
| 3 | 0–6 | 0–6 | 0–6 | 0–6 | 8–Feb | 9–Mar |
| 4 | 0–6 | 0–6 | 0–6 | 8–Feb | 10–Apr | 12–Jun |
| 5 | 0–6 | 0–6 | 7–Jan | 10–Apr | 12–Jun | 15–Sep |
| 6 | 0–6 | 7–Jan | 8–Feb | 12–Jun | 15–Sep | 18–Dec |
| 7 | 0–6 | 8–Feb | 10–Apr | 14–Aug | 18–Dec | 15–21 |
| 8 | 0–6 | 10–Apr | 12–Jun | 16–Oct | 15–21 | 18–24 |
| 9 | 10–Apr | 12–Jun | 14–Aug | 18–Dec | 18–24 | 21–27 |
| 10 | 12–Jun | 14–Aug | 16–Oct | 15–21 | 21–27 | 24–30 |
| 11 | 14–Aug | 16–Oct | 18–Dec | 18–24 | 24–30 | 27–33 |
| 12 | 16–Oct | 18–Dec | 15–21 | 21–27 | 27–33 | 30–37 |
| 13 | 18–Dec | 15–21 | 18–24 | 24–30 | 30–37 | 33–41 |
| 14 | 15–21 | 18–24 | 21–27 | 27–33 | 33–41 | 37–46 |
| 15 | 18–24 | 21–27 | 24–30 | 30–37 | 37–46 | 41–51 |
| 16 | 21–27 | 24–30 | 27–33 | 33–41 | 41–51 | 46–57 |
| 17 | 24–30 | 27–33 | 30–37 | 37–46 | 46–57 | 51–63 |
| 18 | 27–33 | 30–37 | 33–41 | 41–51 | 51–63 | 57–71 |
| 19 | 30–37 | 33–41 | 37–46 | 46–57 | 57–71 | 63–78 |
| 20 | 33–41 | 37–46 | 41–51 | 51–63 | 63–78 | 70–87 |
| 21 | 37–46 | 41–51 | 46–57 | 57–71 | 70–87 | 77–96 |
| 22 | 41–51 | 46–57 | 51–63 | 63–78 | 77–96 | 84–105 |
| 23 | 46–57 | 51–63 | 57–71 | 70–87 | 84–105 | 92–115 |
| 24 | 51–63 | 57–71 | 63–78 | 77–96 | 92–115 | 100–125 |
| 25 | 57–71 | 63–78 | 70–87 | 84–105 | 100–125 | 110–137 |
| 26 | 63–78 | 70–87 | 78–97 | 92–115 | 110–137 | 120–150 |
| 27 | 70–87 | 78–97 | 87–108 | 100–125 | 120–150 | 130–162 |
| 28 | 78–97 | 87–108 | 97–121 | 110–137 | 130–162 | 140–175 |
| 29 | 87–108 | 97–121 | 108–135 | 121–151 | 140–175 | 151–188 |
| 30 | 97–121 | 108–135 | 121–151 | 135–168 | 151–188 | 168–210 |
| 31 | 108–135 | 121–151 | 135–168 | 151–188 | 168–210 | 188–235 |
| 32 | 121–151 | 135–168 | 151–188 | 168–210 | 188–235 | 210–262 |
| 33 | 135–168 | 151–188 | 168–210 | 188–235 | 210–262 | 235–293 |
| 34 | 151–188 | 168–210 | 188–235 | 210–262 | 235–293 | 262–327 |
| 35 | 168–210 | 188–235 | 210–262 | 235–293 | 262–327 | 292–365 |
| 36 | 188–235 | 210–262 | 235–293 | 262–327 | 292–365 | 324–405 |
| 37 | 210–262 | 235–293 | 262–327 | 292–365 | 324–405 | 360–life |
| 38 | 235–293 | 262–327 | 292–365 | 324–405 | 360–life | 360–life |
| 39 | 262–327 | 292–365 | 324–405 | 360–life | 360–life | 360–life |
| 40 | 292–365 | 324–405 | 360–life | 360–life | 360–life | 360–life |
| 41 | 324–405 | 360–life | 360–life | 360–life | 360–life | 360–life |
| 42 | 360–life | 360–life | 360–life | 360–life | 360–life | 360–life |
| 43 | Life | Life | Life | Life | Life | Life |

Zone A — Zone B — Zone C — Zone D

SOURCE: "Sentencing Table," in *2006 Federal Sentencing Guidelines Manual*, U.S. Sentencing Commission, November 1, 2006, http://www.ussc.gov/2006guid/5a.html (accessed January 23, 2007)

the U.S. Supreme Court ruled that federal judges cannot determine facts that are used to increase a defendant's punishment beyond what is authorized by a jury verdict or the defendant's own admissions. In its ruling the court struck down the mandatory application of sentencing guidelines, and instructed courts to apply reasonableness in determining sentences. Guidelines should be considered, but judges are not required to follow them. The legal impact of these two decisions continued to be worked out in the courts.

In its *Final Report on the Impact of* United States v. Booker *on Federal Sentencing* (March 2006, http://www.ussc.gov/booker_report/Booker_Report.pdf), the USSC found that most federal cases are sentenced according to the sentencing guidelines. "When within-range sentences and government-sponsored, below-range sentences are combined, the rate of sentencing in conformance with the sentencing guidelines is 85.9%," the USSC concluded. The report also concluded that the average sentence length since *Booker* has increased.

**TABLE 5.8**

**Sentences within and departing from U.S. Sentencing Commission guidelines, October 1, 2004–January 11, 2005**

| Primary offense | Total | Sentenced within guideline range | | Departures below the guideline range | | Departures above the guideline range | |
|---|---|---|---|---|---|---|---|
| | | Number | Percent | Number | Percent | Number | Percent |
| Total | 17,484 | 12,396 | 70.9 | 4,960 | 28.4 | 128 | 0.7 |
| Murder | 26 | 17 | 65.4 | 8 | 30.8 | 1 | 3.8 |
| Manslaughter | 8 | 6 | 75.0 | 1 | 12.5 | 1 | 12.5 |
| Kidnapping/hostage taking | 18 | 10 | 55.6 | 7 | 38.9 | 1 | 5.6 |
| Sexual abuse | 91 | 74 | 81.3 | 15 | 16.5 | 2 | 2.2 |
| Assault | 118 | 103 | 87.3 | 13 | 11.0 | 2 | 1.7 |
| Robbery | 332 | 258 | 77.7 | 72 | 21.7 | 2 | 0.6 |
| Arson | 10 | 8 | 80.0 | 2 | 20.0 | 0 | 0.0 |
| Drugs-trafficking | 5,796 | 3,695 | 63.8 | 2,088 | 36.0 | 13 | 0.2 |
| Drugs-communication facility | 78 | 60 | 76.9 | 18 | 23.1 | 0 | 0.0 |
| Drugs-simple possession | 151 | 138 | 91.4 | 5 | 3.3 | 8 | 5.3 |
| Firearms | 2,201 | 1,719 | 78.1 | 461 | 20.9 | 21 | 1.0 |
| Burglary/B&E | 10 | 8 | 80.0 | 2 | 20.0 | 0 | 0.0 |
| Auto theft | 20 | 16 | 80.0 | 4 | 20.0 | 0 | 0.0 |
| Larceny | 437 | 381 | 87.2 | 52 | 11.9 | 4 | 0.9 |
| Fraud | 1,595 | 1,207 | 75.7 | 377 | 23.6 | 11 | 0.7 |
| Embezzlement | 159 | 142 | 89.3 | 17 | 10.7 | 0 | 0.0 |
| Forgery/counterfeiting | 265 | 206 | 77.7 | 55 | 20.8 | 4 | 1.5 |
| Bribery | 39 | 22 | 56.4 | 16 | 41.0 | 1 | 2.6 |
| Tax | 134 | 96 | 71.6 | 38 | 28.4 | 0 | 0.0 |
| Money laundering | 213 | 134 | 62.9 | 79 | 37.1 | 0 | 0.0 |
| Racketeering/extortion | 186 | 121 | 65.1 | 64 | 34.4 | 1 | 0.5 |
| Gambling/lottery | 23 | 16 | 69.6 | 7 | 30.4 | 0 | 0.0 |
| Civil rights | 23 | 18 | 78.3 | 5 | 21.7 | 0 | 0.0 |
| Immigration | 4,598 | 3,167 | 68.9 | 1,396 | 30.4 | 35 | 0.8 |
| Pornography/prostitution | 291 | 240 | 82.5 | 38 | 13.1 | 13 | 4.5 |
| Prison offenses | 85 | 74 | 87.1 | 9 | 10.6 | 2 | 2.4 |
| Administration of justice offenses | 242 | 184 | 76.0 | 54 | 22.3 | 4 | 1.7 |
| Environmental/wildlife | 39 | 32 | 82.1 | 7 | 17.9 | 0 | 0.0 |
| National defense | 8 | 6 | 75.0 | 2 | 25.0 | 0 | 0.0 |
| Antitrust | 6 | 0 | 0.0 | 6 | 100.0 | 0 | 0.0 |
| Food & drug | 19 | 14 | 73.7 | 5 | 26.3 | 0 | 0.0 |
| Other miscellaneous offenses | 263 | 224 | 85.2 | 37 | 14.1 | 2 | 0.8 |

Note: Of the 18,788 cases, 1,304 were excluded due to one or both of the following reasons: missing primary offense (30) or missing/inapplicable departure information (1,284).

SOURCE: "Table 27. Offenders Receiving Departures in Each Primary Offense Category, Fiscal Year 2005, Pre-*Booker* (October 1, 2004, through January 11, 2005)," in *Sourcebook of Federal Sentencing Statistics*, U.S. Sentencing Commission, 2006, http://www.ussc.gov/ANNRPT/2005/table27_pre.pdf (accessed January 23, 2007)

Experiencing a minor increase since *Booker* was the rate of government-sponsored, below-range sentences. These below-range sentences are permissible because of stipulations in the guidelines for so-called "departures" from the guidelines' provisions. Departures may be "upward" for cases where special circumstances merit longer incarceration than the maximum sentence in the guidelines; "downward" departures authorize shorter sentences than the minimum for extenuating circumstances or because the defendant provided "substantial assistance" to federal authorities, typically by helping with a broader investigation or providing testimony against other suspects.

According to the USSC in its *Sourcebook of Federal Sentencing Statistics* (2005, http://www.ussc.gov/ANNRPT/ 2005/table13_post.pdf), in 53,556 federal cases determined after the *Booker* decision (between January 12, 2005, and September 30, 2005), prisoners received an average sentence of 51.1 months. The highest average sentence was 228.4 months for murder, followed by 224.6 months for kidnapping/hostage taking, 100.4 months for national

defense crimes, and 93.5 months for robbery. The shortest average sentences were 3.8 months for environmental/wildlife crimes, 5.1 months for gambling/lottery crimes, 5.5 months for food and drug crimes, and 7 months for simple drug possession.

## STATE SENTENCES AND TIME SERVED

The adoption of truth-in-sentencing statutes appears to have resulted, at the state level, in a decrease in the *length* of sentences imposed but an increase in the total *time served*, including the percentage of the sentence imposed that is actually spent in prison.

Average sentence lengths can decline while time served stays the same or increases if mandatory time in prison, as a percentage of the sentence, increases. Thus, a person sentenced to five years serving 60% of his or her sentence serves as long as a person sentenced to four years who serves 75% of his or her sentence. In both cases time served will be three years. Table 5.9 shows

## TABLE 5.9

**Average felony sentence lengths in state courts, by offense and type of sentence, 2002**

| Most serious conviction offense | Maximum sentence length (in months) for felons sentenced to— | | | |
| | Incarceration | | | Probation |
| | Total | Prison | Jail | |
|---|---|---|---|---|
| **Mean** | | | | |
| **All offenses** | 36 mo | 53 mo | 7 mo | 38 mo |
| **Violent offenses** | 62 mo | 84 mo | 8 mo | 43 mo |
| Murder[a] | 217 | 225 | 10 | 76 |
| Sexual assault[b] | 78 | 100 | 8 | 54 |
|    Rape | 104 | 132 | 9 | 65 |
|    Other sexual assault | 65 | 84 | 8 | 51 |
| Robbery | 79 | 1 | 11 | 52 |
| Aggravated assault | 37 | 54 | 7 | 39 |
| Other violent[c] | 33 | 51 | 8 | 37 |
| **Property offenses** | 28 mo | 41 mo | 7 mo | 37 mo |
| Burglary | 36 | 0 | | 40 |
| Larceny[d] | 22 | 34 | 6 | 36 |
|    Motor vehicle theft | 18 | 30 | 6 | 33 |
| Fraud[e] | 24 | 38 | 6 | 36 |
| **Drug offenses** | 32 mo | 48 mo | 6 mo | 36 mo |
| Possession | 22 | 35 | 5 | 33 |
| Trafficking | 38 | 55 | 7 | 39 |
| **Weapon offenses** | 28 mo | 38 mo | 7 mo | 35 mo |
| **Other offenses[f]** | 23 mo | 38 mo | 6 mo | 37 mo |

Note: For persons receiving a combination of sentences, the sentence designation came from the most severe penalty imposed, prison being the most severe, followed by jail, then probation. Prison includes death sentences. Felons receiving a sentence other than incarceration or probation are classified under "probation." Means exclude sentences to death or to life in prison. This table is based on an estimated 945,167 cases.
[a]Includes nonnegligent manslaughter.
[b]Includes rape.
[c]Includes offenses such as negligent manslaughter and kidnapping.
[d]Includes motor vehicle theft.
[e]Includes forgery and embezzlement.
[f]Composed of nonviolent offenses such as receiving stolen property and vandalism.

SOURCE: Matthew R. Durose and Patrick A. Langan, "Table 3. Average Felony Sentence Lengths in State Courts, by Offense and Type of Sentence, 2002," in *Felony Sentences in State Courts, 2002*, U.S. Department of Justice, Bureau of Justice Statistics, December 2004, www.ojp.usdoj.gov/bjs/pub/pdf/fssc02.pdf (accessed February 28, 2007)

average sentence lengths for those convicted of felony offenses in state courts during 2002.

## "THREE STRIKES, YOU'RE OUT"

Nine years after passing the first truth-in-sentencing law, the state of Washington passed the first of the so-called "three-strikes" laws in December 1993. The measure took effect in the wake of a voter initiative, which passed by a three-to-one margin. Three-strikes laws are the functional equivalent of sentencing guidelines in that they mandate a fixed sentence length for repeat offenders for specified crimes or a mix of crimes—but their formulation in public debate, using the baseball analogy, is much easier to understand than the complexities of thick books of codes and sentencing tables. Under three-strikes laws, the offender receives a mandatory sentence upon conviction for the third offense—life imprisonment with-

out parole (as in Washington State), twenty-five years without parole (as in California), or some variant of a long sentence. These laws are designed to remove the criminal from society for a long period of time or, in some instances, for life.

The Washington law identifies specific offenses that are "strikable." California, which passed its own (and more famous) three-strikes law just months after Washington passed its measure, specifies the categories of offenses that must precede the third felony conviction. The sentence of a convicted felon in California is doubled if his or her record has a prior serious or violent felony conviction. The convict receives a twenty-five-year-to-life sentence upon conviction of any third felony if the previous two convictions were for serious or violent felony offenses. All persons convicted under the California three-strikes law must serve 80% of their sentence before they are eligible for parole.

### Tightening Preexisting Statutes

In all but one of the states with three-strikes statutes (Kansas is the exception), legislation was already on the books when the popularity of three-strikes laws led almost half the states—and the federal government—to enact laws pioneered on the West Coast. California, for instance, already had a law on its books that was very similar to those that passed later as three-strikes statutes in other states.

As reported by John Clark, James Austin, and D. Alan Henry in NIJ's "'Three Strikes and You're Out': A Review of State Legislation" (September 1997, http://www.ncjrs.gov/pdffiles/165369.pdf), even before its three-strikes law became effective, California required:

Life with no parole eligibility before 20 years for third violent felony conviction where separate prison terms were served for the first two convictions; life without parole for fourth violent felony conviction.

California's statute, therefore, represented a tightening and modification of existing law so that the triggering offense for life imprisonment was not the fourth but the third felony—which did not have to be violent.

Much the same pattern, with variations, characterized the introduction of three-strikes laws in other states. Prior to enacting a three-strikes law, Louisiana required a mandatory life term for the fourth felony conviction if two previous convictions had been violent or drug offenses. The state's new three-strikes law imposed the sentence after the third offense. In Tennessee the preexisting law required mandatory life without parole for the third violent felony conviction. Tennessee's new law imposed the same requirement for the second violent felony. Like Louisiana, Vermont replaced a "four-strikes" law with a three-strikes law. In some states the tightening was more stringent. In New Mexico the preexisting law imposed an increased sentence of one year for the second, four years for the third, and eight years for the fourth felony. The new law imposed a life sentence after the third violent felony but permitted parole after thirty years.

## Opposition and Challenges to Three-Strikes Laws

Opponents of three-strikes laws charge that the laws unfairly target African-Americans, who are disproportionately represented among felony convicts. They also argue that three-strikes laws remove proportion and reasonableness from sentencing by making all third strikes punishable by the same prison sentence, whether it be stealing a small item or killing someone. Opponents also note that incarcerating more people for longer periods requires more prisons and increases corrections costs for maintaining prisoners. Reducing the possibility of parole results in an increasing number of elderly prisoners, who are statistically much less likely to commit crimes than younger prisoners, and who have increasing health-care needs. Finally, some critics of the laws suggest that the finality of three-strikes laws may make active criminals more desperate and thus, more violent. According to this view, if criminals know they will be sentenced to life in prison, then they have nothing to lose and might be more likely to kill witnesses or to resist arrest through violent means.

On April 1, 2002, the United States Supreme Court agreed to consider whether California's three-strikes law, considered to be one of the toughest in the country, violates the Eighth Amendment's ban against cruel and unusual punishment. More than half of California prisoners sentenced under the three-strikes law were convicted of nonviolent third-strike felonies, including drug possession and petty theft, and are serving mandatory sentences of twenty-five years to life without the possibility of parole. In *Lockyer v. Andrade* (538, U.S. 63 [2003]), the Supreme Court considered the case of Leandro Andrade, an inmate serving two consecutive twenty-five-year sentences in California for stealing videotapes valued at $150 from two different video stores. Because each theft counted as an offense and Andrade had two prior convictions, the new crimes counted as his third and fourth strikes for purposes of sentencing. In March 2003 the Supreme Court, in a five–four decision, upheld the sentence imposed on Andrade and thereby upheld the right of states to impose lengthy sentences on repeat felony offenders, regardless of the relative seriousness of the third-strike felony.

## Impact and Effectiveness of Three-Strikes Laws

Vincent Schiraldi, Jason Colburn, and Eric Lotke reported in *An Examination of the Impact of 3-Strike Laws 10 Years after Their Enactment* (Justice Policy Institute, September 23, 2004, http://www.justicepolicy.org/downloads/JPIOUTOFSTEPREPORTFNL.doc) that twenty-two states followed California's lead by passing three-strikes laws.

According to Schiraldi, Colburn, and Lotke, the three-strikes laws have had little impact on state prison populations since they were enacted, except for California, Florida, and Georgia. Of the twenty-one three-strikes states (out of twenty-three) on which data on the number of people incarcerated were available, fourteen had incarcerated fewer than one hundred people under three strikes. Only three states had more than four hundred people imprisoned under three strikes: California (42,322 inmates), Georgia (7,631), and Florida (1,628). Altogether, the twenty-one states with available imprisonment data had a total population of 112 million and 10,624 people in prison under three strikes.

Schiraldi, Colburn, and Lotke also report that between 1993 and 2002, states with three-strikes laws experienced only a slightly greater decline in serious crime rates (26.8%) than states without three-strikes laws (22.3%).

California is unique because it is the only state in which a three-strikes sentence can be imposed for any felony offense. Schiraldi, Colburn, and Lotke point to California Department of Corrections data indicating that almost two-thirds (65%) of those sentenced under the state's three-strikes laws are incarcerated for nonviolent offenses. California experienced a 38.8% drop in serious crime rates between 1993 and 2002. However, New York, a large state without three-strikes laws, had a 49.6% decrease in serious crimes during this period. It is possible that the improved job market in each state, as opposed to specific criminal justice policies, was responsible for the decline in serious crime rates. While crime rates were dropping, unemployment rates declined by 35% in California and 24% in New York between 1994 and 2002. The national decrease during this period was 9%.

The three-strikes laws in Florida and Georgia apply only to people convicted of violent offenses. These states experienced a smaller decline in violent crime rates than neighboring Alabama, which does not have a three-strikes law.

Since 2000 several states have loosened their mandatory minimum sentencing laws or taken other measures to reduce their prison populations. For example, in 2001 Mississippi adopted an early-release provision for nonviolent offenders, and states such as California, Texas, North Carolina, Connecticut, Idaho, and Arkansas have passed legislation mandating the diversion of nonviolent drug offenders to community-based treatment programs.

## ALTERNATIVE SENTENCING

Forms of sentencing other than probation, prison, or a combination of the two (split sentences) are widely used in virtually every state. The Institute of Public Policy at the Truman School of Public Affairs, University of

Missouri, reported in *Alternative Sentencing & Strategies for Successful Prisoner Reentry* (June 30, 2006, http://www.mosac.mo.gov/Documents/alternative-sentencing.pdf) that sometimes, the best way to prevent an offender from re-offending is not through a traditional sentence (for example, a prison term or probation and parole). In certain cases it is better—for the offenders and for society—to impose alternative sentences that provide job skills, drug and alcohol counseling, and other rehabilitation-focused interventions. Alternative sentencing usually involves life skills training, job skills training, and/or offender rehabilitation through drug counseling and alcohol counseling.

State departments of correction, the District of Columbia, and the Federal Bureau of Prisons offer a range of alternative sentencing options for criminal offenders. Although programs can vary among regions, those options include work-release and weekend sentencing, shock incarceration (sometimes called boot camp), community service programs, day fines, day reporting centers, electronic monitoring and house arrest, residential community corrections, and diversionary treatment programs. Other types of alternative sentencing options, such as mediation and restitution, are sometimes available (see below).

Oregon has one of the most successful and comprehensive alternative sentencing systems. As reported by the Institute of Public Policy in *Alternative Sentencing & Strategies for Successful Prisoner Reentry*, the state's model has six parts:

1. Criminal Risk Factor Assessment and Case Planning. Every inmate received by the Department of Corrections is assessed and a plan is developed for that individual to help him through prison and guide a successful reentry back into the community.

2. Staff/Inmate Interactions. This step in the process acknowledges that prison staff interaction with inmates can shape positive behavior. Prison staff are encouraged to offer positive feedback to inmates and provide incentives for good behavior.

3. Work and Programs. Part of the plan each prisoner receives upon prison entry includes prison programs that would best mitigate the risks that inmate may be subject to. Most prisoners also have jobs and responsibilities in the prison.

4. Children and Families. This program seeks to work with the children of inmates in an attempt to break the cycle of family incarceration (children of the incarcerated are 7 times more likely to end up in prison than the rest of the population.)

5. Reentry. Oregon has 7 facilities physically located in areas most likely to receive the inmates upon exit from prison. This allows relatively easy access for the pris-oner to partially reenter the community. These facilities also are specifically focused on reentry and assist the inmate with housing, jobs, and other things he may need to make the transition into society.

6. Community Supervision and Programs. The Department of Corrections works intimately with the community based programs including the faith based community, other government agencies, and nonprofits to offer technical assistance and resources in order to support their work. The goal of the Department of Corrections between steps 5 and 6 is to offer a seamless transition for offenders so that they have the best chance possible to become productive citizens.

In "The Effectiveness of Community-Based Sanctions in Reducing Recidivism" (*Corrections Today*, February 2003, http://www.aca.org/publications/ctarchivespdf/feb03/martin.pdf), Ginger Martin surveyed recidivism rate data for alternative forms of sentencing in Oregon. (Recidivism is relapse into criminal behavior.) The study included 13,219 prisoners released from January 1999 to December 2001. Martin found that community service programs, work release, and electronic monitoring were cheaper than incarceration, and, when these methods were used, levels of recidivism declined after twelve months. The addition of a treatment component, such as a drug treatment program, to the community-based option produced a further 10% reduction in recidivism.

## Mediation and Restitution

Mediation began in Canada in 1974 and was later adopted in the United States, where more than twenty states were using mediation by the beginning of the twenty-first century. In mediation the victim and the offender meet under the auspices of a community worker and work out a "reconciliation," usually involving some type of restitution and requiring offenders to take responsibility for their actions. This technique is used mainly for minor crimes and often involves private organizations; therefore, the judiciary does not always accept its resolution. Most often restitution is not considered the complete punishment but part of a broader punishment, such as probation or working off the restitution dollar amount while in prison.

## Work Release and Weekend Sentencing

Work-release programs permit selected prisoners nearing the end of their terms to work in the community and return to prison facilities or community residential facilities during nonworking hours. Such programs are designed to prepare inmates to return to the community in a relatively controlled environment while they are learning how to work productively. Work release also allows inmates to earn income, reimburse the state for part of their confinement costs, build up savings for their eventual full release, and acquire more positive living habits. Those on weekend sentencing programs spend certain days in prison, usually weekends, but are free the remainder of the time. Both of these types of sentences are known as "intermittent incarceration." Violent offenders and those convicted of drug offenses are usually excluded from such programs by the courts.

Work-release programs seem to help prisoners once they return to society. In the study *Baltimore Prisoners' Experiences Returning Home* (Urban Institute, March 2004, http://www.urban.org/UploadedPDF/310946_BaltimorePrisoners.pdf), Christy Visher et al. found that "those who found jobs after release were more likely to have participated in work release jobs while incarcerated than those who did not find jobs." Nancy G. LaVigne et al. in a related Urban Institute publication, *Chicago Prisoners' Experiences Returning Home* (December 2004, http://www.urban.org/UploadedPDF/311115_ChicagoPrisoners. pdf), found similar benefits from work release participation.

## Shock Incarceration (Boot Camps)

Shock incarceration is another name for reformatories or "boot camps" that use military discipline for juveniles and adults. The name comes from former British Home Secretary William Whitelaw, who called for a "short, sharp shock" that would end teenagers' criminal careers. Boot camps established in Great Britain attracted youths who liked the challenge. Robert Winnett reported in the *Sunday Times* that, according to the British government, boot camps are effective ("Crime Record Shows Boot Camps Work," June 12, 2005, http://www.timesonline.co.uk/tol/news/uk/article532517.ece). Statistics showed that the reconviction rate of offenders who attended a particularly regimented institution, the Thorn Cross boot camp in Cheshire, England, was considerably lower than average for similar institutions.

According to Alexander W. Pisciotta in *Benevolent Repression* (1994), the prototype of such a facility in the United States was established at the Elmira Reformatory in New York as far back as 1876. The first modern, correctional boot camp was established in Georgia in 1983. Faced with unprecedented overcrowding in its prisons and jails, Georgia was looking for alternatives to incarceration for adult offenders. Oklahoma began its program in 1984 and, by the end of 1988, fifteen programs were operating in nine states. The majority of programs started in the 1990s. By 1998, thirty-three correctional agencies (state and federal) operated forty-nine camps for adult inmates. Sentences are usually short (three to five months).

Many adult boot camps claim to offer programs aimed at offender rehabilitation. Typically, boot camp programs include physical training and regular drill-type exercise, housekeeping and maintenance of the facility, and often hard labor. Some programs include vocational, educational, or treatment programs. Drug and alcohol counseling, reality therapy, relaxation therapy, individual counseling, and recreation therapy are often incorporated into such programs. Because some offenders in boot camps have drug problems, many programs devote time to drug treatment each week. Programs closely regulate dress, talking, movement, eating, hygiene, and other behaviors. Obedience to rules reinforces submission to authority and forces the prisoners to handle a challenge that is both tedious and demanding.

Boot camps are intended to be both punitive in their rigid discipline and rehabilitative by enhancing self-esteem upon successful completion of the program. Shock incarceration is intended to motivate prisoners, teach respect for themselves and others, and break destructive cycles of behavior. Virtually all of these programs are based on the assumption that a military regimen is beneficial.

The major selling points for boot camps have been cost savings and reductions in prison crowding. However, the major reason boot camps appear to cost less and be less crowded is that their programs last less time than traditional sentences. In addition, studies of boot camps have indicated that the facilities have not had a major effect on recidivism.

## Community Service Programs

Begun in the United States in Alameda County, California, in 1966 as a penalty for traffic offenses, community service has spread throughout the United States. The penalty is most often a supplement to other penalties and mainly given to "white-collar" criminals, juvenile delinquents, and those who commit nonserious crimes. Offenders are usually required to work for government or private nonprofit agencies cleaning parks, collecting roadside trash, setting up chairs for community events, community painting projects, and helping out at nursing homes.

The BJS in *State Court Organization 1998* (David B. Rottman et al., June 2000, http://www.ojp.usdoj.gov/bjs/pub/pdf/sco98.pdf) labeled community service "an exception to unconstitutional servitude," indirectly referring to the thirteenth amendment to the Constitution, which states, in Section 1: "Neither slavery nor involuntary servitude, except as a punishment for crime whereof the party shall have been duly convicted, shall exist within the United States, or any place subject to their jurisdiction." By exempting the involuntary servitude of convicted criminals, the Constitution makes both community service and chain gangs possible.

## Day Fines

Under the day fines type of alternative sentence, the offender pays a monetary sum rather than spending time in jail or prison. Most judges assess fixed, flat-fee fines sparingly. The fees are tied to the seriousness of the crimes and the criminal records of the offenders, and they bear no relationship to the offender's wealth. As a result, judges often think the fixed fines are too lenient for wealthy offenders and too harsh for poor ones.

When setting a day fine, the judge first determines how much punishment an offender deserves. For example, a judge decides that the gravity of the offense is worth 15, 60, or 120 punishment units, without regard to income. The value of each unit is set at a percentage of the offender's daily income, and the total fine amount is determined by simple multiplication. The fine is paid into the jurisdiction's treasury. Day fines are also used in Europe.

## Day Reporting Centers

Day reporting centers (DRCs) were developed in Great Britain and first instituted in the United States during the 1980s. These programs allow offenders to reside in the community. Paige M. Harrison and Allen J. Beck report in the BJS's *Prison and Jail Inmates at Midyear 2005* (May 2006, http://www.ojp.usdoj.gov/bjs/pub/pdf/pjim05.pdf) that 4,747 DRCs were operating in the United States by the middle of 2005.

According to Patrick Hyde in "Day Reporting Eases Jail Overcrowding" (*American City and County*, September 1, 2006, http://www.bi.com/content.php?section=news&page=news&detail=09212006), "through treatment and training, the centers provide an intermediate sanction for, and reduce recidivism by, low-risk offenders." Designed for persons on pretrial release, probation, or parole, DRCs are mostly populated by people with drug and alcohol problems and require offenders to appear on a frequent and regular basis to participate in services or activities provided by the center or other community agencies. Random drug screening and breathalyzers are used at the centers. According to Hyde, in addition to providing employment and educational training, the centers conduct classes in such things as anger management, substance abuse, life skills, and cognitive skills. Failure to adhere to program requirements or to report at stated intervals can lead to commitment to prison or jail. DRC participation can also be terminated if the offender is charged with a new crime.

DRCs monitor offenders on the road to rehabilitation. They are also intended to relieve jail or prison overcrowding. Offenders often move from higher to lower levels of control at DRCs based on their progress in treatment and compliance with supervisory guidelines. Many programs last 90 or 180 days. DRCs do not generally exclude serious offenders, although many programs include only nonserious drug- and alcohol-using offenders. Some DRCs require offenders to perform community service; the level and type of community service varies by jurisdiction.

## Intensive Probation Supervision

Intensive Probation Supervision (IPS) is another method of closely supervising offenders while they reside in the community. Increasingly, offenders who have been convicted of felonies (rather than misdemeanors) are being sentenced to probation. Routine probation, however, is not designed or structured to handle high-risk probationers. Therefore, IPS was developed as an alternative that is stricter than routine probation.

Caseloads of officers assigned to IPS offenders are kept low. In typical programs, the offender must contact a supervising officer frequently, pay restitution to victims, participate in community service, have and keep a job, and, if appropriate, undergo random and unannounced drug testing. Offenders are often required to pay a probation fee.

## House Arrest and Electronic Monitoring Program

Some nonviolent offenders are sentenced to house arrest (or home confinement), which means that they are legally required to remain confined in their own homes. They are allowed to leave only for medical purposes or to go to work, although some curfew programs permit offenders to work during the day and have a specified number of hours of free time before returning home. The idea began as a way to keep drunk drivers off the street, but it quickly expanded to include other nonviolent offenders.

The most severe type of house arrest is home incarceration, where the offender's home actually becomes a prison that he or she cannot leave except for very special reasons, such as medical emergencies. Home-detention programs require the offender to be at home when he or she is not working. Some offenders are required to perform a certain number of hours of community service and, if they are employed, to repay the cost of probation and/or restitution.

An electronic monitoring program (EMP), used in tandem with house arrest, involves attaching a small radio transmitter to the offender in a nonremovable bracelet or anklet. Some systems send a signal to a small monitoring box, which is programmed to call a Department of Corrections computer if the signal is broken; other systems randomly call probationers and the computer verifies the prisoner's identity through voice recognition software. In some cases, a special device in the electronic monitor sends a confirmation to the computer. Some systems have global positioning system (GPS) technologies, which use satellites to locate offenders, to help corrections officers ensure that offenders are not violating any territorial restrictions.

EMPs are often used to monitor the whereabouts of those under house arrest and permitted to be only at home or at work. Electronic monitoring is sometimes used to ensure that child molesters stay a specified distance from schools. EMPs cost much less than building new prison cells or housing more inmates. However, close supervision by officers is crucial to the success of any home confinement or electronic monitoring. Officers must ensure that the participants are indeed working when they leave the house and that they are not using illegal drugs. Electronic monitoring equipment must also be checked periodically to determine whether the offender has attempted to disable the equipment.

## Residential Community Corrections

Residential community corrections facilities are known less formally as "halfway houses," because they are designed to help prisoners reintegrate into community life. Some offenders are sentenced to halfway houses directly in lieu of incarceration if their offenses and general profile indicate that they will benefit from the structure and counseling available in such facilities. Many states frequently use halfway houses to relieve prison overcrowding.

Residential programs house offenders in a structured environment. Offenders work full time, maintain the residence center, perform community service, and sometimes attend educational or counseling programs. They may leave the centers only for work or approved programs such as substance-abuse treatment. One type of residential program, called the restitution center, allows offenders to work to pay restitution and child support. The centers regularly test the residents for drugs.

## Diversionary Treatment Programs

Probation combined with mandatory treatment programs is used as an alternative sentence for nonviolent offenders convicted of drug offenses, alcohol abuse, or sex offenses. Sentenced individuals are free on probation but typically are required to attend group therapy and supervised professional treatment sessions.

## THE FEAR OF CRIME

The fear of becoming a victim of crime can undermine community relationships. People may withdraw physically and emotionally, losing contact with their neighbors and weakening the social fabric of their lives and communities. The 2006 Gallup Poll "Americans' Crime Worries" found that 20% of those surveyed frequently or occasionally worried about being murdered, 33% worried about being mugged, 50% worried about their home being burglarized while they were not there, 21% worried about being sexually assaulted, 47% worried about having their car broken into, 40% worried about having a school-aged child physically harmed while attending school, and 44% worried about being a victim of terrorism.

**TABLE 5.10**

**Public opinion on level of crime in the United States, selected years 1989–2006**

IS THERE MORE CRIME IN THE U.S. THAN THERE WAS A YEAR AGO, OR LESS?

|      | More | Less | Same (vol.) | No opinion |
|------|------|------|-------------|------------|
|      | %    | %    | %           | %          |
| 1989 | 84   | 5    | 5           | 6          |
| 1990 | 84   | 3    | 7           | 6          |
| 1992 | 89   | 3    | 4           | 4          |
| 1993 | 87   | 4    | 5           | 4          |
| 1996 | 71   | 15   | 8           | 6          |
| 1997 | 64   | 25   | 6           | 5          |
| 1998 | 52   | 35   | 8           | 5          |
| 2000 | 47   | 41   | 7           | 5          |
| 2001 | 41   | 43   | 10          | 6          |
| 2002 | 62   | 21   | 11          | 6          |
| 2003 | 60   | 25   | 11          | 4          |
| 2004 | 53   | 28   | 14          | 5          |
| 2005 | 67   | 21   | 9           | 3          |
| 2006 | 68   | 16   | 8           | 8          |

SOURCE: Adapted from "Is there more crime in the U.S. than there was a year ago, or less?" in *Crime*, The Gallup Organization, 2007, http://www.galluppoll.com/content/default.aspx?ci=1603 (accessed January 17, 2007). Copyright © 2007 by The Gallup Organization. Reproduced by permission of The Gallup Organization.

## More Crime or Less Crime Today?

Another Gallup Poll reported that 68% of Americans thought there was more crime in the United States in 2006 than in 2005. (See Table 5.10.) This percentage has risen significantly since 2000, when 47% of those surveyed thought that there was more crime in the nation than in the previous year. However, a smaller proportion of people in 2006 thought that the country's crime level has increased over the last year than in 1992, when 89% of those surveyed had this opinion.

Some 51% of respondents in the Gallup Poll said that they believed there was more crime in their area (that is, within a mile of their home) in 2006 than a year earlier. This is the same percentage that believed their neighborhoods were experiencing increased crime in 1972. However, this level is higher than the 26% with this opinion in 2001 and lower than the 54% in 1992 who reported an increase in crime in their area. (See Table 5.11.)

## Feeling Afraid

In a 2006 Gallup Poll, 37% of those surveyed said that they would be afraid to walk alone at night in their own area. This percentage has remained relatively stable since 1965, when 34% of survey respondents said that they would be afraid to walk alone at night in their own neighborhoods. (See Table 5.12.)

When asked if they engaged in certain protective behaviors because of concern over crime, 47% of Gallup Poll respondents in 2005 reported avoiding going to

**TABLE 5.11**

**TABLE 5.12**

**Public opinion on level of crime in own area, selected years 1972–2006**

IS THERE MORE CRIME IN YOUR AREA THAN THERE WAS A YEAR AGO, OR LESS?

| | More | Less | Same (vol.) | No opinion |
|---|---|---|---|---|
| | % | % | % | % |
| 2006 Oct 9–12 | 51 | 30 | 15 | 4 |
| 2005 Oct 13–16 | 47 | 33 | 18 | 2 |
| 2004 Oct 11–14 | 37 | 37 | 22 | 4 |
| 2003 Oct 6–8 | 40 | 39 | 19 | 2 |
| 2002 Oct 14–17 | 37 | 34 | 24 | 5 |
| 2001 Oct 11–14 | 26 | 52 | 18 | 4 |
| 2000 Aug 29–Sep 5 | 34 | 46 | 15 | 5 |
| 1998 Oct 23–25 | 31 | 48 | 16 | 5 |
| 1997 Aug 22–25 | 46 | 32 | 20 | 2 |
| 1996 Jul 25–28 | 46 | 24 | 25 | 5 |
| 1992 Feb 28–Mar 1 | 54 | 19 | 23 | 4 |
| 1990 Sep 10–11 | 51 | 18 | 24 | 8 |
| 1989 Jun 8–11 | 53 | 18 | 22 | 7 |
| 1989 Jan 24–28 | 47 | 21 | 27 | 5 |
| 1983 Jan 28–31 | 37 | 17 | 36 | 10 |
| 1981 Jan 9–12 | 54 | 8 | 29 | 9 |
| 1977 Nov 18–21 | 43 | 17 | 32 | 8 |
| 1975 Jun 27–30 | 50 | 12 | 29 | 9 |
| 1972 Dec 8–11 | 51 | 10 | 27 | 12 |

SOURCE: Adapted from "Is there more crime in your area than there was a year ago, or less?" in *Crime*, The Gallup Organization, 2007, http://www.galluppoll.com/content/default.aspx?ci=1603 (accessed January 17, 2007). Copyright © 2007 by The Gallup Organization. Reproduced by permission of The Gallup Organization.

**Public opinion on fear of walking alone at night in area of own residence, selected years 1965–2006**

IS THERE ANY AREA NEAR WHERE YOU LIVE—THAT IS, WITHIN A MILE—WHERE YOU WOULD BE AFRAID TO WALK ALONE AT NIGHT?

| | Yes | No |
|---|---|---|
| | % | % |
| 1965 | 34 | 66 |
| 1967 | 31 | 67 |
| 1968 | 35 | 62 |
| 1972 | 42 | 57 |
| 1975 | 45 | 55 |
| 1977 | 45 | 55 |
| 1979 | 42 | 58 |
| 1981 | 45 | 55 |
| 1982 | 48 | 52 |
| 1983 | 45 | 55 |
| 1989 | 43 | 57 |
| 1990 | 40 | 59 |
| 1992 | 44 | 56 |
| 1993 | 43 | 56 |
| 1994 | 39 | 60 |
| 1996 | 39 | 60 |
| 1997 | 38 | 61 |
| 2000 | 34 | 66 |
| 2001 | 30 | 69 |
| 2002 | 35 | 64 |
| 2003 | 36 | 64 |
| 2004 | 32 | 67 |
| 2005 | 38 | 62 |
| 2006 | 37 | 63 |

SOURCE: Adapted from "Is there any area near where you live—that is, within a mile—where you would be afraid to walk alone at night?" in *Crime*, The Gallup Organization, 2007, http://www.galluppoll.com/content/default.aspx?ci=1603 (accessed January 17, 2007). Copyright © 2007 by The Gallup Organization. Reproduced by permission of The Gallup Organization.

certain places or neighborhoods, 31% kept a dog for protection, 29% had a burglar alarm, and 23% reported buying a gun for protection. (See Table 5.13.)

## THE DEATH PENALTY

The death penalty is in place in thirty-seven states and is seen by some as a deterrent to committing crime. The 2006 Gallup study *Death Penalty* found that although a majority of Americans (67%) favored the death penalty for people convicted of murder, the percentage of those supporting the death penalty had decreased from a high of 80% in 1994. (See Table 5.14.) According to the same poll, 60% believed the death penalty was applied fairly, an increase from 51% in 2000.

Almost half (47%) of survey respondents thought that the death penalty is a better penalty for murder than life imprisonment; a similar percentage (48%) believed that life imprisonment is better than a death sentence. About one-fifth (21%) said that the death penalty is imposed too often; 25% thought that it is imposed about the right amount and 51% believed that it is not imposed frequently enough. Although many believed that the death penalty is not imposed frequently enough, most (63%) respondents said they believed that a person has been executed under the death penalty even though this individual was innocent of the crime with which he or she was charged.

## CONFIDENCE IN THE CRIMINAL JUSTICE SYSTEM

Each year the Gallup Organization asks the American people about their confidence in society's major institutions. Gallup reports in *Confidence in Institutions* that, of those polled in 2006, one-quarter (25%) had "a great deal" or "quite a lot" of confidence in the criminal justice system (see Figure 5.1), and, in the same poll, 43% reported at least some confidence. Almost one-third (31%) of respondents said they had little or no confidence in the criminal justice system. Of the institutions considered by poll respondents, the criminal justice system ranked above organized labor, the U.S. Congress, big business, and health maintenance organizations (HMOs), but inspired less confidence than the military, the police, organized religion, banks, the media, and public education, among others.

## CONFIDENCE IN THE POLICE

In Gallup's 2006 *Confidence in Institutions*, Americans expressed much more confidence in the police than they did in the criminal justice system. Fifty-eight percent stated they had a great deal or quite a lot of confidence in the police (see Figure 5.1), and 29% said they

TABLE 5.13

## Public opinion on selected crime protection behaviors, 2000 and 2005

NEXT, I'M GOING TO READ SOME THINGS PEOPLE DO BECAUSE OF THEIR CONCERN OVER CRIME. PLEASE TELL ME WHICH, IF ANY, OF THESE THINGS YOU, YOURSELF, DO OR HAVE DONE.

| | 2000 | | 2005 | |
|---|---|---|---|---|
| | Yes | No | Yes | No |
| | % | % | % | % |
| Keep a dog for protection | 32 | 68 | 31 | 69 |
| Bought a gun for protection of yourself or your home | 22 | 78 | 23 | 77 |
| Carry a gun for defense | 12 | 87 | 11 | 89 |
| Carry a knife for defense | 10 | 90 | 11 | 89 |
| Had a burglar alarm installed in your home | 23 | 76 | 29 | 70 |
| Carry mace or pepper spray | 18 | 82 | 18 | 82 |
| Avoid going to certain places or neighborhoods you might otherwise want to go to | 56 | 44 | 47 | 53 |

SOURCE: Adapted from "Next, I'm Going to Read Some Things People Do Because of Their Concern over Crime. Please Tell Me Which, if Any, of These Things You, Yourself, Do or Have Done. First,... Next,... [RANDOM ORDER]." in *Crime*, The Gallup Organization, 2007, http://www.galluppoll.com/content/default.aspx?ci=1603 (accessed January 17, 2007). Copyright © 2007 by The Gallup Organization. Reproduced by permission of The Gallup Organization.

TABLE 5.14

## Public opinion on the death penalty, selected years, 1936–2006

ARE YOU IN FAVOR OF THE DEATH PENALTY FOR A PERSON CONVICTED OF MURDER?

| | For | Against | No opinion |
|---|---|---|---|
| | % | % | % |
| 2006 Oct 9–12 | 67 | 28 | 5 |
| 2006 May 5–7* | 65 | 28 | 7 |
| 2005 Oct 13–16 | 64 | 30 | 6 |
| 2004 Oct 11–14 | 64 | 31 | 5 |
| 2003 Oct 6–8 | 64 | 32 | 4 |
| 2003 May 19–21 | 70 | 28 | 2 |
| 2002 Oct 14–17 | 70 | 25 | 5 |
| 2001 Oct 11–14 | 68 | 26 | 6 |
| 2001 Feb 19–21* | 67 | 25 | 8 |
| 2000 Aug 29–Sep 5 | 67 | 28 | 5 |
| 2000 Jun 23–25 | 66 | 26 | 8 |
| 2000 Feb 14–15 | 66 | 28 | 6 |
| 1999 Feb 8–9 | 71 | 22 | 7 |
| 1995 May 11–14 | 77 | 13 | 10 |
| 1994 Sep 6–7 | 80 | 16 | 4 |
| 1991 Jun 13–16 | 76 | 18 | 6 |
| 1988 Sep 25–Oct 1 | 79 | 16 | 5 |
| 1988 Sep 9–11 | 79 | 16 | 5 |
| 1986 Jan 10–13 | 70 | 22 | 8 |
| 1985 Jan 11–14 | 72 | 20 | 8 |
| 1985 Nov 11–18 | 75 | 17 | 8 |
| 1981 Jan 30–Feb 2 | 66 | 25 | 9 |
| 1978 Mar 3–6 | 62 | 27 | 11 |
| 1976 Apr 9–12 | 66 | 26 | 8 |
| 1972 Nov 10–13 | 57 | 32 | 11 |
| 1972 Mar 3–5 | 50 | 41 | 9 |
| 1971 Oct 29–Nov 2 | 49 | 40 | 11 |
| 1969 Jan 23–28 | 51 | 40 | 9 |
| 1967 Jun 2–7 | 54 | 38 | 8 |
| 1966 May 19–24 | 42 | 47 | 11 |
| 1965 Jan 7–12 | 45 | 43 | 12 |
| 1960 Mar 2–7 | 53 | 36 | 11 |
| 1957 Aug 29–Sep 4 | 47 | 34 | 18 |
| 1956 Mar 29–Apr 3 | 53 | 34 | 13 |
| 1953 Nov 1–5 | 68 | 25 | 7 |
| 1937 Dec 1–6 | 60 | 33 | 7 |
| 1936 Dec 2–7 | 59 | 38 | 3 |

*Based on half sample.

SOURCE: "Are you in favor of the death penalty for a person convicted of murder?" in *Death Penalty*, The Gallup Organization, 2006, http://www.galluppoll.com/content/?ci=1606&pg=1 (accessed February 5, 2007). Copyright © 2007 by The Gallup Organization. Reproduced by permission of The Gallup Organization.

had some confidence. Only 12% claimed to have little or no confidence in the police.

A 2005 Gallup Poll found that the percentage of people expressing confidence in local police in 2005, 53%, had decreased from 2004, when the level was 61%, and from 1999, when 70% had confidence in local police. (See Table 5.15.) Half of the men surveyed (50%) expressed confidence in local police, compared with 56% of women. Whites were most likely (57%) to express confidence in local police; only 40% of non-whites and 32% of African-Americans had confidence. Those aged sixty-five and older had the highest confidence levels in the police, with 72% reporting favorable opinions, compared with just 43% of those aged eighteen to twenty-nine.

**FIGURE 5.1**

### Public opinion on confidence in institutions, 2006

I AM GOING TO READ YOU A LIST OF INSTITUTIONS IN AMERICAN SOCIETY. PLEASE TELL ME HOW MUCH CONFIDENCE YOU, YOURSELF, HAVE IN EACH ONE—A GREAT DEAL, QUITE A LOT, SOME OR VERY LITTLE?

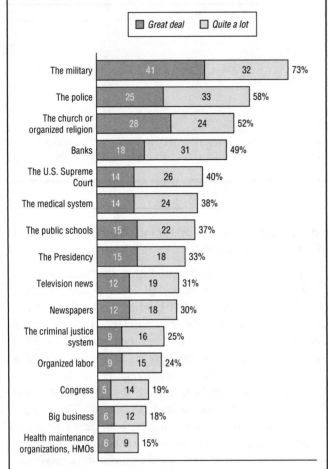

SOURCE: "I am going to read you a list of institutions in American society. Please tell me how much confidence you, yourself, have in each one—a great deal, quite a lot, some or very little?" in *Confidence in Institutions*, The Gallup Organization, June 8, 2006, http://www.galluppoll.com/content/?ci=1597&pg=1 (accessed January 22, 2007). Copyright © 2007 by The Gallup Organization. Reproduced by permission of The Gallup Organization.

**TABLE 5.15**

### Public opinion on confidence in local police, 1999, 2004, and 2005

[By demographic subgroup]

|  | 1999 | 2004 | 2005 |
|---|---|---|---|
|  | % | % | % |
| Overall | 70 | 61 | 53 |
| **Sex** |  |  |  |
| Men | 68 | 58 | 50 |
| Women | 71 | 64 | 56 |
| **Race** |  |  |  |
| White | 73 | 66 | 57 |
| Non-white | 57 | 44 | 40 |
| Black | 54 | 32 | 32 |
| **Age** |  |  |  |
| 18- to 29-year-olds | 66 | 51 | 43 |
| 30- to 49-year-olds | 68 | 61 | 56 |
| 50- to 64-year-olds | 71 | 60 | 46 |
| 65 years old and older | 76 | 74 | 72 |
| **Region** |  |  |  |
| East | 69 | 65 | 57 |
| Midwest | 71 | 62 | 52 |
| South | 67 | 58 | 52 |
| West | 73 | 62 | 54 |
| **Community** |  |  |  |
| Urban | N/A | 55 | 54 |
| Suburban | N/A | 66 | 54 |
| Rural | N/A | 59 | 50 |
| **Education** |  |  |  |
| High school grad or less | 68 | 59 | 52 |
| Some college | 67 | 60 | 49 |
| College grad | 77 | 64 | 59 |
| Post-grad | 78 | 68 | 59 |
| **Income** |  |  |  |
| Less than $30,000 | 66 | 52 | 50 |
| $30,000 to $74,999 | 71 | 63 | 52 |
| $75,000 or more | 79 | 67 | 57 |
| **Politics** |  |  |  |
| Liberal | 64 | 57 | 40 |
| Moderate | 72 | 61 | 57 |
| Conservative | 71 | 66 | 58 |
| Democrat | 68 | 58 | 52 |
| Independent | 65 | 48 | 49 |
| Republican | 79 | 78 | 60 |
| **Family status** |  |  |  |
| Married | N/A | 68 | 58 |
| Not married | N/A | 53 | 48 |
| Children under age 18 | N/A | 58 | 54 |
| No children under age 18 | N/A | 63 | 54 |
| **Employment status** |  |  |  |
| Employed | N/A | 60 | 49 |
| Not employed | N/A | 64 | 60 |
| **Religious service attendance** |  |  |  |
| Attend church weekly | N/A | 66 | 61 |
| Attend church nearly weekly/monthly | N/A | 68 | 57 |
| Seldom/never attend | N/A | 55 | 48 |

**TABLE 5.15**

**Public opinion on confidence in local police, 1999, 2004, and 2005** [CONTINUED]

[By demographic subgroup]

| | 1999 | 2004 | 2005 |
|---|---|---|---|
| | % | % | % |
| **Gun ownership** | | | |
| Gun in household | N/A | 63 | 52 |
| No gun | N/A | 61 | 54 |
| **Victim status** | | | |
| Crime victim, last 12 months | N/A | 48 | 46 |
| Not crime victim | N/A | 67 | 56 |

SOURCE: Jeffrey M. Jones, "Confidence in Police, Selected Years, by Demographic Subgroup," in *Confidence in Local Police Drops to 10-Year Low*, The Gallup Organization, November 10, 2005, http://www.galluppoll.com/content/?ci=19783 (accessed January 22, 2007). Copyright © 2007 by The Gallup Organization. Reproduced by permission of The Gallup Organization.

# CHAPTER 6
# CORRECTIONAL FACILITIES: PRISONS AND JAILS

Public views of crime and punishment have changed over the centuries. Yet in general most societies have moved from the extraction of personal or family justice—vengeful acts such as blood feuds or the practice of taking "an eye for an eye"—toward formal systems based on written codes and orderly processes. Jails and prisons have changed from being holding places where prisoners awaited deportation, maiming, whipping, or execution to places of extended—even lifelong—incarceration. Confinement itself has become the punishment.

## HISTORY OF CORRECTIONS IN THE UNITED STATES

During the colonial period in the United States physical punishment was more common than incarceration. Stocks, pillories, branding, flogging, and maiming—such as cutting off an ear or slitting nostrils—were typical punishments meted out to offenders. The death penalty, too, was used frequently. In 1636 the Massachusetts Bay Colony listed thirteen crimes that warranted execution, including murder, practicing witchcraft, and worshipping idols. In early New York State, 20% of offenses, including pocket picking, horse stealing, and robbery, were capital crimes (warranting the death penalty). Jails were used to hold prisoners awaiting trial or sentencing or as debtors' prisons, but a stay in jail was not considered a punishment itself.

The Puritans of Massachusetts believed that humans were naturally depraved, which made it easier for some of the colonies and the first states to enforce harsh punishments. In addition, since Puritans maintained the view that individuals had no control over their fate (predestination), few early Americans supported the idea that criminals could be rehabilitated.

The Quakers, led by William Penn, made colonial Pennsylvania an exception to the harsh practices often found in the other colonies. The early criminal code of colonial Pennsylvania abolished executions for all crimes except homicide, replaced physical punishments with imprisonment and hard labor, and did not charge the prisoners for their food and housing.

### The Reform Movement

The idea of individual freedom and the concept that people could change society for the better by using reason permeated American society during the 1800s. Reformers worked to abolish slavery, secure women's rights, and prohibit liquor, as well as to change the corrections system. Rehabilitation of prisoners became the goal of criminal justice, and inmates were given work to keep them busy and to defray the cost of their confinement. Prison administrators began constructing factories within prison walls or hiring inmates out as laborers in "chain gangs." In rural areas inmates worked on prison-owned farms. In the South prisoners—most of whom were African-American—were often leased out to local farmers. Prison superintendents justified the hard labor by arguing that it taught the offenders the value of work and self-discipline. Many free citizens, after all, earned their livings doing such work in factories and fields.

With the rise of labor unions in the North, the 1930s saw an end to the large-scale prison industry. Unions complained about competing with the inmates' free labor, especially amid the rising unemployment of the Great Depression. By 1940 the states had limited what inmates could produce. By 1970 the number of prison farms had decreased substantially because they were expensive to operate and the prisons found it cheaper to purchase food. In addition, agricultural work no longer prepared inmates for employment outside prison. Since the 1970s, however, support has grown for prison industries as a way to train inmates for outside jobs.

As crime increased during the late 1980s, criminal justice practices such as indeterminate sentencing, probation, parole, and treatment programs came under attack. Support decreased for rehabilitative programs and increased for keeping offenders incarcerated; many people subscribed to the idea that keeping criminals off the streets is the surest way to keep them from committing more crimes. As a result, the federal government and a growing number of states introduced mandatory sentencing and life terms for habitual criminals (often called "three strikes" laws after a baseball analogy, meaning that after three convictions "you're out"). They also limited the use of probation, parole, and time off for good behavior.

## PRISONS AND JAILS COMPARED

Corrections institutions are organized in tiers by level of government and, at each level (federal, state, and local), specific types of institutions provide corrections functions based on the relative severity of the offenses committed. The most restrictive form of corrections is incarceration in a prison. Both the federal and the state governments operate their own prison systems; within the federal government, the military maintains its own prisons. Prison inmates serve time for serious offenses and are incarcerated for a year or longer.

Most people sentenced to jail serve less than a year for misdemeanors and offenses against the public order. Jails are operated at the local level—by cities and counties. The federal government operates some jails as well, and within the federal government, the Bureau of Immigration and Customs Enforcement (ICE) has its own detention facilities. In some states, jails and prisons are operated under a single state authority but still maintain the distinction—prisons for long terms and for serious offenses, jails for lesser terms and less serious offenses.

## FEDERAL CORRECTIONS

The U.S. Bureau of Prisons (BOP) maintains institutions at five different security levels, and prisoners are assigned based on their offenses and behavioral history:

- *Minimum Security*: At the lowest security level are Federal Prison Camps (FPCs), such as those in Yankton, South Dakota, and Montgomery, Alabama. These facilities have dormitory housing, a relatively low staff-to-inmate ratio, and limited or no perimeter fencing. They are located on or near larger institutions or military bases, where the inmates participate in work programs.

- *Low Security Federal Correctional Institutions (FCIs)*: FCIs have fenced perimeters and dormitory cubicle housing. Inmates are typically involved in work programs.

- *Medium Security FCIs*: These facilities feature reinforced perimeter fencing, usually a double fence with an electronic detection system. In addition, inmates are

housed in cells and have access to work and treatment programs.

- *High Security United States Penitentiaries (USPs)*: The most secure environment in the federal prison system includes highly secured perimeters with walls and reinforced fences. Inmates are held in multiple- or single-occupant cells, are closely watched, and do not have freedom to move around within the facility without supervision.

- *Administrative Facilities*: These facilities hold offenders awaiting trial or treat inmates with serious medical needs. Special facilities also may be used to house the most dangerous, violent, or escape-prone inmates. These include Metropolitan Correctional Centers (MCCs), Metropolitan Detention Centers (MDCs), Federal Detention Centers (FDCs), Federal Medical Centers (FMCs), the Federal Transfer Center (FTC), and the Administrative-Maximum USP (ADX).

The BOP administered 174 facilities as of 2007, including twenty-one high security penitentiaries, sixty-eight federal correctional institutions, and six minimum-security prison camps. At that time nearly six out of ten federal prisoners (57%) were held in low or minimum-security facilities, with 28% in medium-security institutions, and 11% maintained under high security. The remainder had not been assigned a security level.

### Federal Inmate Populations

Paige M. Harrison and Allen J. Beck of the Bureau of Justice Statistics (BJS) report in *Prison and Jail Inmates at Midyear 2005* (May 2006, http://www.ojp.usdoj.gov/bjs/pub/pdf/pjim05.pdf) that since 1995, the federal prison population has grown more quickly than the state prison population. The rate of growth in the federal prison population averaged 3% between 1995 and 2005 and reached its peak of 6% in the first six months of 1999. In the first six months of 2005 the number of federal inmates increased by 2.3%, more than twice the increase experienced at the state level.

The number of noncitizens held in federal prisons increased by 30% from 1998 to 2000 before falling in 2001; between 2001 and 2005, however, the number of noncitizens held in federal prisons increased by about 4%. (See Table 6.1.) In 2005 federal prisons held 35,285 noncitizen inmates in custody, representing about 19% of all prisoners in federal custody. In many cases these are individuals who were caught violating immigration and border security laws.

Harrison and Beck report in *Prison and Jail Inmates at Midyear 2005* that federal admissions (the number of new inmates added to the federal prison population) increased 21.2% from 43,732 in 2000 to 52,982 in 2004. During this period, the number of releases increased 32.2%, from 35,259 in 2000 to 46,624 in 2004. The number of

## TABLE 6.1

**Noncitizens held in federal prisons, 1998–2005**

| Year | Total | Federal | State |
|------|-------|---------|-------|
| 2005 | 91,117 | 35,285 | 55,832 |
| 2004 | 91,815 | 34,422 | 57,393 |
| 2003 | 90,568 | 34,456 | 56,112 |
| 2002 | 88,677 | 33,873 | 54,804 |
| 2001 | 87,917 | 33,886 | 54,031 |
| 2000 | 89,676 | 36,090 | 53,586 |
| 1999 | 88,811 | 33,765 | 55,046 |
| 1998 | 77,099 | 27,682 | 49,417 |
| Percent change, 2004–2005 | −0.8% | 2.5% | −2.7% |

SOURCE: Paige M. Harrison and Allen J. Beck, "Table 6. Number of Noncitizens Held in State or Federal Prisons at Midyear, 1998–2005," in *Prison and Jail Inmates at Midyear 2005*, U.S. Department of Justice, Office of Justice Programs, Bureau of Justice Statistics, May 2006, http://www.ojp.usdoj.gov/bjs/pub/pdf/pjim05.pdf (accessed January 17, 2007)

admissions was higher in 2004 than the number of releases, resulting in an increase in the federal prison population that year of more than 6,300 inmates.

In *Prisoners in 2005* (November 2006, http://www.ojp.usdoj.gov/bjs/pub/pdf/p05.pdf), Harrison and Beck report that more than half (55%) of all federal inmates were sentenced for drug offenses. This rate is down from 60% in 1995. Between 1995 and 2003, the number of federal inmates convicted of public-order offenses increased by 170%; most of this growth was due to a 394% increase in immigration offenses.

### Federal Facilities and Staffing

The Federal Bureau of Prisons reports that in January 2007 federal prisons had 35,198 staff members (http://www.bop.gov/news/quick.jsp). Almost three-quarters (72.6%) of federal prison staff members were male. A majority (64.1%) were white; most of the remainder were African-American (21%), Hispanic (11.3%), Asian (2.1%), or Native American (1.5%). The federal government's total corrections payroll was $165.4 million in March 2003.

## STATE CORRECTIONS

There are more than 1,300 state prisons in the United States, where inmates are housed whose crimes do not fall under the jurisdiction of the federal justice system. States administer their own sentences and budget for corrections based on their own laws and regulations. Most prison inmates in the United States are held in a state prison. In 2005, for example, according to *Prisoners in 2005*, roughly 1.3 million people were incarcerated in state prisons, compared with 179,000 held in federal custody.

### State Inmate Populations

State prison populations have increased each year since 1995. On June 30, 2005, state prisons held 1,255,514 inmates, an increase of 1.3% since 2004 and of 2.5% since 1995, according to Harrison and Beck in *Prison and Jail Inmates at Midyear 2005*. (See Table 6.2.)

In *Prisoners in 2005* the researchers report that between January 1 and December 31, 2005, the largest increase (11.9%) in prison population occurred in South Dakota, followed by Montana (10.9%), Kentucky (10.4%), and Nebraska (7.9%). During this period, state prison populations declined in eleven states led by

## TABLE 6.2

**Number of persons held in state or federal prisons or in local jails, selected years 1995–2005**

| Year | Total inmates in custody | Prisoners in custody | | Inmates held in local jails | Total incarceration rate[a] |
|------|------|------|------|------|------|
| | | Federal | State | | |
| 1995 | 1,585,586 | 89,538 | 989,004 | 507,044 | 601 |
| 2000[b] | 1,935,753 | 133,921 | 1,176,269 | 621,149 | 683 |
| 2001[b] | 1,961,247 | 143,337 | 1,180,155 | 631,240 | 685 |
| 2002[b] | 2,033,331 | 151,618 | 1,209,640 | 665,475 | 701 |
| 2003[b] | 2,081,580 | 161,673 | 1,222,135 | 691,301 | 712 |
| 2004[b] | | | | | |
| June | 2,129,802 | 169,370 | 1,239,656 | 713,990 | 725 |
| December | | | | | |
| 2005[b] | — | 170,535 | 1,244,311 | — | |
| June 30 | 2,186,230 | 175,954 | 1,255,514 | 747,529 | 738 |
| Percent change, 6/30/04–6/30/05 | 2.6% | 3.9% | 1.3% | 4.7% | |
| Annual average change, 12/31/95–6/30/05 | 3.4% | 7.4% | 2.5% | 3.9% | |

Note: Jail counts are for midyear (June 30) and exclude persons who were supervised outside of a jail facility. State and federal prisoner counts for 1995–2003 are for December 31.
—Not available.
[a]Persons in custody per 100,000 residents in each reference year.
[b]Total counts include federal inmates in non-secure privately operated facilities: 6,143 in 2000, 6,192 in 2001, 6,598 in 2002, 6,471 in 2003, 6,786 (June) and 7,065 (December) in 2004, and 7,233 in June, 2005.

SOURCE: Paige M. Harrison and Allen J. Beck, "Table 1. Number of Persons Held in State or Federal Prisons or in Local Jails, 1995–2005," in *Prison and Jail Inmates at Midyear 2005*, U.S. Department of Justice, Office of Justice Programs, Bureau of Justice Statistics, May 2006, http://www.ojp.usdoj.gov/bjs/pub/pdf/pjim05.pdf (accessed January 17, 2007)

Georgia (down 4.6%), Maryland (2.4%), Louisiana (2.3%), and Mississippi (2.2%).

The number of state inmates under age 18 decreased from 2,485 on June 30, 2004, to 2,266 one year later, as reported in *Prison and Jail Inmates at Midyear 2005*. The number of minors in state prisons reached its peak in 1995, when 5,309 juveniles were imprisoned, and has decreased every year since. However, the number of noncitizens held in state prisons increased by 13% between 1998 and 2005, from 49,417 to 55,832, even though a drop of 2.7% was registered between 2004 and 2005. (See Table 6.1.)

State prison admissions increased 11.5% from 625,219 in 2000 to 697,066 in 2004, according to Harrison and Beck in *Prison and Jail Inmates at Midyear 2005*. Admissions outpaced releases during this period, with 672,202 prisoners released from state prisons during 2004, up from 604,858 in 2000.

## State Facilities and Staffing

Various factors, many out of the control of prison officials, influence the costs of running a state prison. Among these variables are climate (heating costs in the Northeast are generally more expensive than in the South), local wage rates, and local cost of living. However, other costs are within the control of prison officials. State prisons with a high inmate-to-staff ratio, or fewer guards per prisoner, reported lower costs than those with large staffs, which had as many as one staff member for every 1.7 inmates. States with a few large prison facilities tended to have lower overall operating costs than those with many smaller facilities.

According to James J. Stephan of the Bureau of Justice Statistics in *State Prison Expenditures 2001* (June 2004, http://www.ojp.usdoj.gov/bjs/pub/pdf/spe01.pdf), salaries, wages, and benefits for state prison employees made up about two-thirds of state prison operating expenditures in 2001. Operating costs include supplies, maintenance, and contractual services. About 4% was spent on new construction, renovations, major repairs, equipment, land, or buildings. Expenditures for new prison construction declined from $1.5 billion in 1996 to $1.1 billion in 2001.

Other operating costs for state prisons include medical care, food service, and utilities. By far the largest of these costs in 2001 was some $3.3 billion spent on prisoner medical care, followed by $1.2 billion for prisoner food, and $996 million for utilities. Nationwide, the average annual amount spent for medical care per prisoner was $2,625 (in comparison, U.S. citizens spent an average $4,370 per year on their own health care). The amount spent on prisoner medical care varied widely by state. Having a high number of inmates with drug and alcohol abuse problems can raise costs; operating larger prison facilities and thereby raising the average inmate-to-doctor ratio can save money. In 2001 Maine spent the most on prisoner medical care per inmate ($5,601), while Louisiana spent the least ($860). By region, the West averaged the most spent on medical care per inmate ($3,672), and the South averaged the least ($2,025). Annual food service costs tended to be lowest in those states, such as Mississippi ($297 per prisoner) and North Carolina ($191 per prisoner), where prisons operated their own farms and grew their own fruits and vegetables. In addition, North Carolina prisoners operate their own cannery and meat processing plant.

## State and Federal Prisoners Held Elsewhere

IN PRIVATELY RUN PRISONS. According to the BJS in *Prisoners in 2005* 107,447 prisoners under the jurisdiction of federal and state correctional authorities were housed in private correctional facilities in 2005. This was an increase from 98,628 in 2004 and accounted for 6% of all state inmates and 14.4% of federal prisoners.

The number of state inmates in privately operated prisons increased from 73,860 to 80,401 between 2004 and 2005, an 8.8% increase. In comparison, the number of federal inmates in private facilities increased from 24,768 to 27,046, an increase of 9.2%. The states with the highest percentage of prisoners under private management were New Mexico (43%), Wyoming (41%), Hawaii (31%), Alaska (28%), and Montana (26%). Seventeen states had no prisoners in privately operated facilities in 2005: Arkansas, Connecticut, Delaware, Illinois, Iowa, Kansas, Massachusetts, Michigan, Missouri, Nebraska, Nevada, New Hampshire, New York, Oregon, Rhode Island, Utah, and West Virginia.

IN LOCAL JAILS. Local jails held 747,529 inmates as of 2005, according to Harrison and Beck in *Prison and Jail Inmates at Midyear 2005*. Of these, 73,097 were state or federal prisoners who were being housed in a local facility.

## JAILS

In addition to confining offenders for short terms (usually a sentence of less than one year), jails administer community justice programs that offer alternatives to incarceration and hold:

- Suspects pending arraignment, trial, or sentencing or awaiting transfer to federal or state authorities

- Inmates unable to transfer to other jurisdictions because of overcrowding at those facilities

- Juveniles awaiting transfer to a juvenile detention facility

- Mental patients being transferred to a medical facility

TABLE 6.3

**Persons under jail supervision, by confinement status and type of program, midyear, selected years 1995–2005**

| Confinement status and type of program | 1995 | 2000 | 2004 | 2005 |
|---|---|---|---|---|
| Total | 541,913 | 687,033 | 784,538 | 819,434 |
| Held in jail | 507,044 | 621,149 | 713,990 | 747,529 |
| Supervised outside of a jail facility[a] | 34,869 | 65,884 | 70,548 | 71,905 |
| Weekender programs | 1,909 | 14,523 | 11,589 | 14,110 |
| Electronic monitoring | 6,788 | 10,782 | 11,689 | 11,403 |
| Home detention[b] | 1,376 | 332 | 1,173 | 1,497 |
| Day reporting | 1,283 | 3,969 | 6,627 | 4,747 |
| Community service | 10,253 | 13,592 | 13,171 | 15,536 |
| Other pretrial supervision | 3,229 | 6,279 | 14,370 | 15,458 |
| Other work programs[c] | 9,144 | 8,011 | 7,208 | 5,796 |
| Treatment programs[d] | — | 5,714 | 2,208 | 1,973 |
| Other | 887 | 2,682 | 2,513 | 1,385 |

—Not available.
[a]Excludes persons supervised by a probation or parole agency.
[b]Includes only those without electronic monitoring.
[c]Includes persons in work release programs, work gangs, and other work alternative programs.
[d]Includes persons under drug, alcohol, mental health, and other medical treatment.

SOURCE: Paige M. Harrison and Allen J. Beck, "Table 8. Persons under Jail Supervision, by Confinement Status and Type of Program, Midyear 1995, 2000, and 2004–05," in *Prison and Jail Inmates at Midyear 2005*, U.S. Department of Justice, Office of Justice Programs, Bureau of Justice Statistics, May 2006, http://www.ojp.usdoj.gov/bjs/pub/pdf/pjim05.pdf (accessed January 17, 2007)

- Military detainees being transferred to military authorities

- Individuals under protective custody or being held as trial witnesses

## Local Inmate Populations

According to Harrison and Beck in *Prison and Jail Inmates at Midyear 2005*, on June 30, 2005, the nation's jails held or supervised 819,434 inmates; 91% (747,592 inmates) of whom were behind bars and the rest (71,905 inmates) were supervised outside the jail in community service, work release, weekend reporting, electronic monitoring, and other alternative programs. The jail population increased by 4.7% between 2004 and 2005. (See Table 6.3.) This rate of increase was higher than the average annual growth of 3.9% between 1995 and 2005.

According to Harrison and Beck, the jail inmate population rose from 193 per 100,000 U.S. residents in 1995 to 252 per 100,000 in 2005. (See Table 6.4.) The average daily jail population for 2005 was 733,442, an increase of 3.9% from 706,242 in 2004 and of 43.9% from 509,828 in 1995. (See Table 6.5.)

Significant changes have occurred in the profile of the jail population in the ten-year period shown in Table 6.5. Men represented the overwhelming majority of jail inmates throughout the period, but the proportion of women has increased. In 1995, 51,300 women were incarcerated, representing 10.1% of the local jail population; in 2005,

TABLE 6.4

**Number of offenders held in jail and incarceration rate, 1995 and 2000–05**

| Year | Number held in jail | Jail incarceration rate* |
|---|---|---|
| 2005 | 747,529 | 252 |
| 2004 | 713,990 | 243 |
| 2003 | 691,301 | 238 |
| 2002 | 665,475 | 231 |
| 2001 | 631,240 | 222 |
| 2000 | 621,149 | 220 |
| 1995 | 507,044 | 193 |

*Number of jail inmates per 100,000 U.S. residents on July 1 of each year.

SOURCE: Paige M. Harrison and Allen J. Beck, "At Mid-Year, the Nation's Jails Supervised 819,434 Persons," in *Prison and Jail Inmates at Midyear 2005*, U.S. Department of Justice, Office of Justice Programs, Bureau of Justice Statistics, May 2006, http://www.ojp.usdoj.gov/bjs/pub/pdf/pjim05.pdf (accessed January 17, 2007)

TABLE 6.5

**Average daily population and the number of men, women, and juveniles in local jails, midyear, selected years 1995–2005**

| | 1995 | 2000 | 2004 | 2005 |
|---|---|---|---|---|
| Average daily population[a] | 509,828 | 618,319 | 706,242 | 733,442 |
| Number of inmates, June 30 | 507,044 | 621,149 | 713,990 | 747,529 |
| Adults | 499,300 | 613,534 | 706,907 | 740,770 |
| Male | 448,000 | 543,120 | 619,908 | 646,807 |
| Female | 51,300 | 70,414 | 86,999 | 93,963 |
| Juveniles[b] | 7,800 | 7,615 | 7,083 | 6,759 |
| Held as adults[c] | 5,900 | 6,126 | 6,159 | 5,750 |
| Held as juveniles | 1,800 | 1,489 | 924 | 1,009 |

Note: Data are for June 30. Detailed data for 1995 were estimated and rounded to the nearest 100.
[a]The average daily population is the sum of the number of inmates in a jail each day for a year, divided by the total number of days in the year.
[b]Juveniles are persons held under the age of 18.
[c]Includes juveniles who were tried or awaiting trial as adults.

SOURCE: Paige M. Harrison and Allen J. Beck, "Table 9. Average Daily Population and the Number of Men, Women, and Juveniles in Local Jails, Midyear 1995, 2000, and 2004–05," in *Prison and Jail Inmates at Midyear 2005*, U.S. Department of Justice, Office of Justice Programs, Bureau of Justice Statistics, May 2006, http://www.ojp.usdoj.gov/bjs/pub/pdf/pjim05.pdf (accessed January 17, 2007)

93,963 women were incarcerated, representing 12.6% of local jail inmates, as reported in *Prison and Jail Inmates at Midyear 2005*. In addition, the female jail population grew at an average annual rate of 6.2% between 1995 and 2005, compared with 3.7% for males. Although the overall number of inmates in local jails has been rising, the number of juveniles in adult jails has dropped from 7,800 in 1995 to 6,759 in 2005. (See Table 6.5.)

## Facilities and Staffing

According to the *Sourcebook of Criminal Justice Statistics 2003*, local jurisdictions had 3,376 jails in 1999, the last time the BJS conducted a jail census (http://www.albany.edu/sourcebook/pdf/t198.pdf). There are 3,043 counties in the United States. The number of jails, therefore, is roughly equivalent to one per county plus additional jails in large urban areas. Their rated capacity was 660,361 in 1999, and 93% of this capacity was occupied. The South had the highest number of jails (1,623), followed by the Midwest (977), West (538), and Northeast (227). Texas had the highest number of jails in any state (271), followed by Georgia (204), California (145), and Alabama (155). These numbers include only facilities that hold inmates beyond their initial arraignment; local police lock-ups, for example, where suspects are held overnight awaiting formal charges, are not included in the count.

Two-thirds of jail staff members in 1999 were male; 66% of staffers were white, 24% were African-American, 8% were Hispanic, and 2% were of other races. Eighty-nine percent of inmates in 1999 were male; 41% of inmates were white, 42% African-American, 15% Hispanic (Hispanics may be of any race), and 2% of other races.

## Privately Operated Jails

In 1993 the United States had seventeen privately operating jails. By 1999, according to the *Sourcebook of Criminal Justice Statistics 2003*, the number had increased to 47 jails, with 16,656 offenders. Of these, 13,814 were inmates in the private jails and 2,842 were supervised by these facilities but not confined.

On average, private jails were bigger than those operated by public agencies. Excluding offenders supervised but not confined, the average population of the 47 private jails in 1999 was 294 inmates. Most inmates (89%) were male, as in the public jails. The racial composition was somewhat different from public facilities: 31.7% of inmates were white, 38% were African-American, 16% were Hispanic, and 14.2% were of other races.

Women accounted for nearly half of private jail staff members (46.3% of total staff, 40.8% of correctional officers). Private jail staff supervised 3.3 inmates per person, a somewhat higher workload than in publicly run jails (2.9 inmates per staff). Private correctional officers supervised 5.3 inmates each, one more than publicly employed guards (4.3).

## Federal Jails

The federal government operated eleven jails in 1999, according to the *Sourcebook of Criminal Justice Statistics 2003*. These facilities held nearly as many inmates as private jails—11,209, up from 5,899 in 1993. Federal jail inmates were overwhelmingly male (93%). The majority, 63%, were white; 32% were African-American, and 5% were of all other races. Federal jail staff was 74.5% male. The total employee-to-inmate ratio in 1999 was 3.6, and each correctional officer supervised 6.7 inmates. Federal

jails were crowded; they operated at 39% above rated capacity—but the 1999 results were better than in 1993 when federal jails were 55% above capacity.

## PRIVATE CORRECTIONAL FACILITIES

Rising prison populations and the need to expand the prison system in the states has led to calls for privatization. The basic assumption behind this idea is that the private sector is inherently more efficient and flexible than public bureaucracies because it is less constrained by regulations and is more cost effective. Private facilities also save the public the initial costs of prison construction, since those costs are assumed by private contractors. This saves the government from taking on long-term debt in order to build housing for more prisoners. In this view, a privatized or even a partially privatized corrections system would cost taxpayers less money. Corrections functions, however, are ultimately vested in governmental hands, and private prisons must operate under established rules and regulations. The complexity of corrections activities is such that comparisons between private and public facilities are very difficult to make, and the cost savings achieved by private corrections are in dispute because the evidence is inconclusive.

A 2002 report by Geoffrey F. Segal and Adrian T. Moore for the Reason Foundation (*Weighing the Watchmen: Evaluating the Costs and Benefits of Outsourcing Correctional Services*, http://www.reason.org/ps289.pdf) summarized twenty-eight previous studies comparing the costs of government-run and private prisons. Of the twenty-eight studies, which were conducted by government agencies, universities, auditors, and research organizations, twenty-two found significant cost savings from privatization. Segal and Moore also found that private facilities provide at least the same quality of services as government-run facilities.

However, the Federal Bureau of Prisons found that at least one private facility experienced many more problems than comparable public facilities. In *Evaluation of the Taft Demonstration Project: Performance of a Private-Sector Prison and the BOP* (October 7, 2005, http://www.bop.gov/news/research_projects/published_reports/pub_vs_priv/orelappin2005.pdf) the Bureau reported on a federal prison in Taft, California, that has operated as a demonstration of prison privatization since 1996. According to the report, the Taft Correctional Institution (TCI) had higher numbers than expected of most types of misconduct and a higher number than anticipated of positive results for random drug tests. TCI has also experienced particularly serious incidents of prisoner misconduct, including two escapes from inside the secure-perimeter fences and one general disturbance involving up to 1,000 inmates. During the same period, the BOP had three escapes altogether from the more than 100 public prisons it operates.

Despite the uncertainty, the privately run prison population has grown at a faster rate than the correctional population as a whole. At year-end in 2005, according to the BJS (*Prisoners in 2005*), 107,447 state and federal prisoners were in privately operated facilities. (See Table 6.6.) This is an increase of 7% from 2004, when 98,628 inmates were held in private facilities and of 18.7% since 2000, when private facilities had 90,542 inmates.

The *Sourcebook of Criminal Justice Statistics 2003* reported that there were 264 private prisons in 2000, more than twice the number (110) of such facilities in 1995 (http://www.albany.edu/sourcebook/pdf/t1102.pdf). The rated capacity of these facilities was 105,133 in 2000 and 89% of this capacity was occupied. In 1995, total private prison capacity was 19,294 and 86% of this capacity was occupied. Of the 264 private prisons in 2000, 4 were maximum security, 65 were medium security, and 195 were minimum or low security. Most were relatively small—132 held fewer than 100 inmates, 46 had 250 to 749 inmates, and 43 had 100 to 249 inmates.

## INCREASING PRISON POPULATIONS

Overall, crime in the United States has decreased since the 1990s, and yet the prison and jail populations have been increasing rapidly. The inmate population in the United States is measured by the rate of incarceration—that is, the number of people sent by the courts to prisons and jails per 100,000 people in the general population. As reported by The Sentencing Project, an advocacy group promoting alternatives to incarceration, in *New Incarceration Figures: Thirty-three Consecutive Years of Growth* (December 2006, http://www.sentencingproject.org/Admin/Documents/publications/inc_newfigures.pdf), the United States had the highest incarceration rate in the world in 2005 with 737 individuals confined in prisons or jails per 100,000 population. This rate was higher than in Russia (611), Cuba (487), Israel (209), England (148), China (118), Germany (95), or Japan (62).

Some reasons for high rates of incarceration in the United States include:

- More people are being sent to prison; that is, fewer convicts are getting off with probation or parole.

- Mandatory sentencing rules require that some criminals be held for longer periods.

- Some courts are requiring stiffer sentences.

## COMPARING THE CRIME RATE AND INCARCERATION RATE

The official crime rate, reported by the Federal Bureau of Investigation in its Uniform Crime Reports, has been in decline for more than a decade. In 1991, 758.2 violent crimes were committed for every 100,000 people; this rate dropped to 469.2 per 100,000 in 2005. The property crime rate also peaked in 1991 at 5,140.2 per 100,000 population; by 2005 the rate had fallen to 3,429.8 per 100,000. During the same period, however, the incarceration rate as reported by the BJS increased from 313 per 100,000 population in 1991 to 491 per 100,000 in 2005 (http://www.ojp.usdoj.gov/bjs/glance/tables/incrttab.htm).

The incarceration rate for federal and state prisoners in the United States, excluding those in jail, has risen from a low of 79 per 100,000 in 1925 to 488 in 2005, according to the *Sourcebook of Criminal Justice Statistics 2003* (http://www.albany.edu/sourcebook/pdf/t6282005.pdf). Beginning in 1925, the rate of incarceration of U.S. prisoners rose steadily for 15 years to a peak of 137 in 1939. The rate declined somewhat and more or less leveled out to between 100 and 120 for the next 35 years. Then, in the early 1970s, the rate began to rise steadily. From 1974 to 2002, the rate increased more than four-fold. The rate for males jumped from about 200 inmates per 100,000 people in the mid-1970s to over 900 per 100,000 at the turn of the twenty-first century. Female incarceration rates began to rise in the 1980s, from a steady rate of 10 per 100,000 population during the late 1970s to 65 per 100,000 by 2005.

Excluding inmates held in local jails, at midyear 2005 the United States had 488 prisoners per 100,000 population, an 18.7% increase from 411 in 1995 (*Prison and Jail Inmates at Midyear 2005*). The rate of sentenced federal inmates increased by 72%, from 32 per 100,000 in 1995 to 55 per 100,000 in 2005. The rate for state prisoners increased 14%, from 379 per 100,000 in 1995 to 433 per 100,000 in 2005. (See Table 6.7.)

These two trends appear paradoxical. Part of the explanation is that the official crime rate does not track drug offenses—or related money laundering offenses and illegal weapons violations—which have been growing at high rates. As a result, the official crime rate and the incarceration rate do not always move in parallel because they do not reflect the same facts.

In *Prisoners in 2005* Harrison and Beck report that the prison population increased 1.9% between 2004 and 2005; this growth rate was lower than the average annual growth rate of 3.1% since 1995. According to the BJS researchers, the number of inmates in state facilities grew 1.3% from 1,243,745 to 1,259,905 between December 31, 2004, and yearend 2005. The number of those under federal jurisdiction rose from 170,535 to 179,220 (5.1%). Overall, the annual rate of increase of prisoners under state and federal jurisdiction in 2005 (1.9%) was significantly lower than the increase experienced in 1995 (6.7%).

**TABLE 6.6**

## State and federal prisoners held in private facilities or local jails, by jurisdiction, yearend 2004 and 2005

| Region and jurisdiction | Private facilities | | | Local jails | | |
|---|---|---|---|---|---|---|
| | 2005 | 2004 | Percent of inmates[a] | 2005 | 2004 | Percent of inmates[a] |
| U.S. total | 107,447 | 98,628 | 7.0% | 73,097 | 74,445 | 4.8% |
| Federal[b] | 27,046 | 24,768 | 14.4 | 1,044 | 1,199 | 0.6 |
| State | 80,401 | 73,860 | 6.0 | 72,053 | 73,246 | 5.4 |
| **Northeast** | 3,571 | 3,347 | 2.1% | 1,990 | 1,555 | 1.2% |
| Connecticut | 0 | 0 | 0 | — | — | — |
| Maine | 20 | 32 | 1.0 | 0 | 0 | 0.0 |
| Massachusetts | 0 | 0 | 0 | 212 | 236 | 2.0 |
| New Hampshire | 0 | 0 | 0 | 13 | 9 | 0.5 |
| New Jersey | 2,600 | 2,510 | 9.5 | 1,754 | 1,258 | 6.4 |
| New York | 0 | 0 | 0 | 11 | 52 | 0.0 |
| Pennsylvania | 503 | 366 | 1.2 | 0 | 0 | 0.0 |
| Rhode Island | 0 | 0 | 0 | — | — | — |
| Vermont | 448 | 439 | 21.6 | — | — | — |
| **Midwest** | 3,030 | 3,477 | 1.2% | 3,171 | 3,267 | 1.2% |
| Illinois | 0 | 0 | 0 | 0 | 0 | 0.0 |
| Indiana | 115 | 641 | 0.5 | 1,695 | 2,024 | 6.9 |
| Iowa | 0 | 0 | 0 | 0 | 0 | 0.0 |
| Kansas | 0 | 0 | 0 | 0 | 0 | 0.0 |
| Michigan | 0 | 480 | 0 | 53 | 52 | 0.1 |
| Minnesota | 760 | 307 | 8.2 | 674 | 484 | 7.3 |
| Missouri | 0 | 0 | 0 | 0 | 0 | 0.0 |
| Nebraska | 0 | 0 | 0 | 0 | 0 | 0.0 |
| North Dakota | 47 | 35 | 3.4 | 45 | 43 | 3.2 |
| Ohio | 2,075 | 1,929 | 4.5 | 0 | 0 | 0.0 |
| South Dakota | 10 | 6 | 0.3 | 99 | 42 | 2.9 |
| Wisconsin | 23 | 79 | 0.1 | 605 | 622 | 2.7 |
| **South** | 51,823 | 48,267 | 8.5% | 60,621 | 62,966 | 10.0% |
| Alabama | 320 | 244 | 1.1 | 2,281 | 1,645 | 8.2 |
| Arkansas | 0 | 0 | 0 | 1,056 | 1,230 | 7.8 |
| Delaware | 0 | 0 | 0 | — | — | — |
| Florida | 6,261 | 4,328 | 7.0 | 41 | 42 | 0.0 |
| Georgia | 4,778 | 4,693 | 9.8 | 4,948 | 5,117 | 10.1 |
| Kentucky | 2,224 | 1,746 | 11.3 | 5,674 | 5,084 | 28.9 |
| Louisiana | 2,952 | 2,921 | 8.2 | 16,183 | 17,469 | 44.8 |
| Maryland | 129 | 127 | 0.6 | 142 | 135 | 0.6 |
| Mississippi | 4,779 | 4,744 | 23.3 | 4,426 | 4,624 | 21.6 |
| North Carolina | 210 | 212 | 0.6 | 0 | 0 | 0.0 |
| Oklahoma | 5,908 | 5,905 | 23.8 | 1,850 | 1,807 | 7.5 |
| South Carolina | 14 | 6 | 0.1 | 384 | 429 | 1.7 |
| Tennessee | 5,162 | 5,105 | 19.6 | 7,112 | 6,577 | 27.0 |
| Texas | 17,517 | 16,668 | 10.4 | 10,569 | 13,228 | 6.3 |
| Virginia | 1,569 | 1,568 | 4.4 | 4,679 | 4,502 | 13.2 |
| West Virginia | 0 | 0 | 0 | 1,276 | 1,077 | 24.0 |
| **West** | 21,977 | 18,769 | 7.2% | 6,271 | 5,458 | 2.1% |
| Alaska | 1,365 | 1,392 | 28.4 | — | — | — |
| Arizona | 4,800 | 4,176 | 14.3 | 185 | 186 | 0.6 |
| California | 2,801 | 2,989 | 1.6 | 2,518 | 2,452 | 1.5 |
| Colorado | 4,039 | 2,819 | 18.8 | 393 | 638 | 1.8 |
| Hawaii | 1,902 | 1,666 | 30.9 | — | — | — |
| Idaho | 1,596 | 1,263 | 23.4 | 569 | 133 | 8.3 |
| Montana | 895 | 895 | 25.5 | 687 | 687 | 19.6 |
| Nevada | 0 | 0 | 0 | 148 | 153 | 1.3 |
| New Mexico | 2,843 | 2,686 | 43.3 | 122 | 0 | 1.9 |
| Oregon | 0 | 0 | 0 | 48 | 18 | 0.4 |
| Utah | 0 | 0 | 0 | 1,246 | 1,189 | 19.6 |
| Washington | 890 | 327 | 5.1 | 332 | 1 | 1.9 |
| Wyoming | 846 | 556 | 41.3 | 23 | 1 | 1.1 |

—Not applicable. Prison and jails form an integrated system.
[a]Based on the total number of inmates under state or federal jurisdiction, by jurisdiction and region.
[b]Includes federal inmates held in non-secure privately operated facilities (7,065 in 2004 and 7,144 in 2005).

SOURCE: Paige M. Harrison and Allen J. Beck, "Table 7. State and Federal Prisoners Held in Private Facilities or Local Jails, by Jurisdiction, Yearend 2004 and 2005," in *Prisoners in 2005*, U.S. Department of Justice, Office of Justice Programs, Bureau of Justice Statistics, November 2006, http://www.ojp.usdoj.gov/bjs/pub/pdf/p05.pdf (accessed January 12, 2007)

**TABLE 6.7**

Rates of sentenced federal and state prisoners per 100,000 U.S. residents, selected years 1995–2005

|  | State | Federal | Total* |
|---|---|---|---|
| 1995 | 379 | 32 | 411 |
| 2000 | 426 | 42 | 469 |
| 2001 | 422 | 48 | 470 |
| 2002 | 427 | 49 | 476 |
| 2003 | 430 | 52 | 482 |
| 2004 | 432 | 54 | 486 |
| 2005, midyear | 433 | 55 | 488 |

*Totals may not add due to rounding.

SOURCE: Paige M. Harrison and Allen J. Beck, "Number of Sentenced Inmates per 100,000 U.S. Residents on December 31," in *Prison and Jail Inmates at Midyear 2005*, U.S. Department of Justice, Office of Justice Programs, Bureau of Justice Statistics, May 2006, http://www.ojp.usdoj.gov/bjs/pub/pdf/pjim05.pdf (accessed January 17, 2007)

**TABLE 6.8**

Sentenced inmates in state and federal prisons, by gender, 1995, 2004, and 2005

|  | Male | Female |
|---|---|---|
| **All inmates** | | |
| 6/30/2005 | 1,406,649 | 106,174 |
| 6/30/2004 | 1,389,143 | 102,691 |
| 12/31/1995 | 1,057,406 | 68,468 |
| Percent change, 2004–2005 | 1.3% | 3.4% |
| Average annual change, 1995–2005 | 3.0% | 4.7% |
| **Sentenced to more than 1 year** | | |
| 6/30/2005 | 1,349,223 | 96,778 |
| 6/30/2004 | 1,332,571 | 93,632 |
| 12/31/1995 | 1,021,059 | 63,963 |
| **Incarceration rate*** | | |
| 6/30/2005 | 925 | 64 |
| 6/30/2004 | 922 | 63 |
| 12/31/1995 | 789 | 47 |

*The total number of prisoners with a sentence of more than 1 year per 100,000 U.S. residents.

SOURCE: Paige M. Harrison and Allen J. Beck, "Table 4. Number of Prisoners under the Jurisdiction of State or Federal Correctional Authorities, by Gender, 1995, 2004, and 2005," in *Prison and Jail Inmates at Midyear 2005*, U.S. Department of Justice, Office of Justice Programs, Bureau of Justice Statistics, May 2006, http://www.ojp.usdoj.gov/bjs/pub/pdf/pjim05.pdf (accessed January 17, 2007)

One trend that has contributed to the growth of prison populations is the rise in female populations in state and federal prison. Although state prisons hold many fewer females than males, the rate of growth in the female state prison population is higher than that of the male populations. Between 2004 and 2005 the female population grew by 3.4%, from 102,691 to 106,174; between 1995 and 2005 the female prison population increased by an average of 4.7% annually. (See Table 6.8.) The number of male state inmates increased by 1.3% between 2004 and 2005, from 1,389,143 to 1,406,649, and averaged an annual increase rate of 3% between 1995 and 2005.

The average percent change among sentenced prisoners in state or federal custody between 1995 and 2005 was highest in the western United States, where the average increase was 3.6% and the number of prisoners grew from 207,661 to 296,341. (See Table 6.9.) The average change between 1995 and 2005 was lowest, 2.7%, in the South, where the population of sentenced prisoners grew from 446,491 to 583,132.

Prison populations vary widely by state and region of the country. In 2005 some smaller states experienced the largest growth rate in their prison populations, according to Harrison and Beck. Among the states, the average percentage change was highest in North Dakota, where the number of prisoners increased an average of 9.3% per year from 1995 to 2005, followed by West Virginia (7.9%), Oregon (7.5%), and Idaho and Wisconsin (both at 7.4%).

**Crowding in Prisons**

From 1995 to 2005 overall capacity in the state and federal prison systems increased as the prison population grew. Old prisons were replaced with new ones; more prisoners were housed in privately operated prisons; and additions to capacity at existing sites added new beds.

These additions have failed to keep up with the demand for prison space, however. According to Harrison and Beck in *Prisoners in 2005*, the federal system was operating at 134% of its rated capacity in 2005. In 2005, twenty-three states and the federal government were operating prisons at or above their highest capacity. The most overcrowded systems included Massachusetts and Illinois, which operated at 133% of their rated capacity, followed by Wisconsin (127%) and North Dakota (126%). (See Table 6.10.)

What does crowding mean? The American Correctional Association guidelines, *Standards for Adult Correctional Institutions* (2003), specify that a standard cell area should measure sixty square feet, and inmates should spend no more than ten hours per day in their cells. When crowding occurs, two inmates are often assigned to a cell designed for one person, or temporary housing units are set up to take prison overflow. Overcrowding makes it more likely that disagreements will rise between inmates, leading to violence and injuries. In addition, diseases are more likely to spread among the prison population.

**Jail Capacity**

"Rated capacity" is the maximum number of beds or inmates that may be housed in a jail. In 2005 U.S. jails added 33,398 beds to total jail capacity, bringing it to 789,001, according to Harrison and Beck in *Prison and Jail Inmates at Midyear 2005*. (See Table 6.11.) This was the highest annual increase since 1995. Capacity use had dropped to 90% in 2001 but increased to 95% in 2005.

TABLE 6.9

**Sentenced state and federal prisoners, by jurisdiction, year end 1995, 2004 and 2005**

| Region and jurisdiction | 12/31/2005 | 12/31/2004 | 12/31/1995 | Percent change, 2004–05 | Average change, 1995–05[a] | Incarceration rate, 2005 |
|---|---|---|---|---|---|---|
| U.S. total | 1,461,132 | 1,433,728 | 1,085,022 | 1.9% | 3.0% | 491 |
| Federal | 166,173 | 159,137 | 83,663 | 4.4 | 7.1 | 56 |
| State | 1,294,959 | 1,274,591 | 1,001,359 | 1.6 | 2.6 | 435 |
| **Northeast** | 162,641 | 161,121 | 155,030 | 0.9% | 0.5% | 298 |
| Connecticut[b] | 13,121 | 13,240 | 10,419 | −0.9 | 2.3 | 373 |
| Maine | 1,905 | 1,961 | 1,326 | −2.9 | 3.7 | 144 |
| Massachusetts[c] | 9,081 | 8,688 | 10,427 | 4.5 | −1.4 | 239 |
| New Hampshire | 2,520 | 2,448 | 2,015 | 2.9 | 2.3 | 192 |
| New Jersey[d] | 27,359 | 26,757 | 27,066 | 2.2 | 0.1 | 313 |
| New York | 62,743 | 63,751 | 68,486 | −1.6 | −0.9 | 326 |
| Pennsylvania | 42,345 | 40,931 | 32,410 | 3.5 | 2.7 | 340 |
| Rhode Island[b] | 2,025 | 1,894 | 1,833 | 6.9 | 1.0 | 189 |
| Vermont[b] | 1,542 | 1,451 | 1,048 | 6.3 | 3.9 | 247 |
| **Midwest** | 252,845 | 249,545 | 192,177 | 1.3% | 2.8% | 383 |
| Illinois[d] | 44,919 | 44,054 | 37,658 | 2.0 | 1.8 | 351 |
| Indiana | 24,416 | 23,939 | 16,046 | 2.0 | 4.3 | 388 |
| Iowa[d] | 8,737 | 8,525 | 5,906 | 2.5 | 4.0 | 294 |
| Kansas[d] | 9,068 | 8,966 | 7,054 | 1.1 | 2.5 | 330 |
| Michigan | 49,546 | 48,883 | 41,112 | 1.4 | 1.9 | 489 |
| Minnesota | 9,281 | 8,758 | 4,846 | 6.0 | 6.7 | 180 |
| Missouri[d] | 30,803 | 31,061 | 19,134 | −0.8 | 4.9 | 529 |
| Nebraska | 4,330 | 4,038 | 3,006 | 7.2 | 3.7 | 245 |
| North Dakota | 1,327 | 1,238 | 544 | 7.2 | 9.3 | 208 |
| Ohio[d] | 45,854 | 44,806 | 44,663 | 2.3 | 0.3 | 400 |
| South Dakota | 3,454 | 3,088 | 1,871 | 11.9 | 6.3 | 443 |
| Wisconsin | 21,110 | 22,189 | 10,337 | −4.9 | 7.4 | 380 |
| **South** | 583,132 | 576,292 | 446,491 | 1.2% | 2.7% | 539 |
| Alabama | 27,003 | 25,257 | 20,130 | 6.9 | 3.0 | 591 |
| Arkansas | 13,383 | 13,668 | 8,520 | −2.1 | 4.6 | 479 |
| Delaware[b] | 3,972 | 4,087 | 3,014 | −2.8 | 2.8 | 467 |
| Florida | 89,766 | 85,530 | 63,866 | 5.0 | 3.5 | 499 |
| Georgia[e] | 48,741 | 51,089 | 34,168 | −4.6 | 3.6 | 533 |
| Kentucky | 19,215 | 17,140 | 12,060 | 12.1 | 4.8 | 459 |
| Louisiana | 36,083 | 36,939 | 25,195 | −2.3 | 3.7 | 797 |
| Maryland | 22,143 | 22,696 | 20,450 | −2.4 | 0.8 | 394 |
| Mississippi | 19,335 | 19,469 | 12,251 | −0.7 | 4.7 | 660 |
| North Carolina | 31,522 | 30,683 | 27,914 | 2.7 | 1.2 | 360 |
| Oklahoma[d] | 23,245 | 22,913 | 18,151 | 1.4 | 2.5 | 652 |
| South Carolina | 22,464 | 22,730 | 19,015 | −1.2 | 1.7 | 525 |
| Tennessee[d] | 26,369 | 25,884 | 15,206 | 1.9 | 5.7 | 440 |
| Texas | 159,255 | 157,617 | 127,766 | 1.0 | 2.2 | 691 |
| Virginia | 35,344 | 35,564 | 27,260 | −0.6 | 2.6 | 464 |
| West Virginia | 5,292 | 5,026 | 2,483 | 5.3 | 7.9 | 291 |
| **West** | 296,341 | 287,633 | 207,661 | 3.0% | 3.6% | 431 |
| Alaska[b] | 2,781 | 2,632 | 2,042 | 5.7 | 3.1 | 414 |
| Arizona[e] | 31,411 | 31,106 | 20,291 | 1.0 | 4.5 | 521 |
| California | 168,982 | 164,933 | 131,745 | 2.5 | 2.5 | 466 |
| Colorado[d] | 21,456 | 20,293 | 11,063 | 5.7 | 6.8 | 457 |
| Hawaii[b] | 4,422 | 4,174 | 2,590 | 5.9 | 5.5 | 340 |
| Idaho | 6,818 | 6,375 | 3,328 | 6.9 | 7.4 | 472 |
| Montana | 3,509 | 3,164 | 1,999 | 10.9 | 5.8 | 373 |
| Nevada | 11,644 | 11,280 | 7,713 | 3.2 | 4.2 | 474 |
| New Mexico | 6,292 | 6,111 | 3,925 | 3.0 | 4.8 | 323 |
| Oregon | 13,390 | 13,167 | 6,515 | 1.7 | 7.5 | 365 |
| Utah | 6,269 | 5,915 | 3,447 | 6.0 | 6.2 | 252 |
| Washington | 17,320 | 16,503 | 11,608 | 5.0 | 4.1 | 273 |
| Wyoming | 2,047 | 1,980 | 1,395 | 3.4 | 3.9 | 400 |

[a]The average annual percentage increase from 1995 to 2005.
[b]Prisons and jails form one integrated system. Data include total jail and prison population.
[c]The incarceration rate includes an estimated 6,200 inmates sentenced to more than one year but held in local jails or houses of correction.
[d]Includes some inmates sentenced to one year or less.
[e]Population figures based on custody counts.

SOURCE: Paige M. Harrison and Allen J. Beck, "Table 4. Sentenced Prisoners under the Jurisdiction of State or Federal Correctional Authorities, Yearend 1995, 2004, and 2005," in *Prisoners in 2005*, U.S. Department of Justice, Office of Justice Programs, Bureau of Justice Statistics, November 2006, http://www.ojp.usdoj.gov/bjs/pub/pdf/p05.pdf (accessed January 12, 2007)

**TABLE 6.10**

## Federal and state prison capacities, yearend 2005

| Region and jurisdiction | Type of capacity measure | | | Custody population as a percent of— | |
|---|---|---|---|---|---|
| | Rated | Operational | Design | Highest capacity[a] | Lowest capacity[a] |
| Federal | 119,371 | — | — | 134% | 134% |
| **Northeast** | | | | | |
| Connecticut[b] | — | — | — | — | — |
| Maine | 1,897 | 1,897 | 1,897 | 103% | 103% |
| Massachusetts | — | — | 7,778 | 133 | 133 |
| New Hampshire | 2,419 | 2,238 | 2,213 | 100 | 109 |
| New Jersey | — | 25,949 | — | 89 | 89 |
| New York | 59,904 | 61,330 | 53,843 | 103 | 117 |
| Pennsylvania | 38,347 | 38,347 | 38,347 | 108 | 108 |
| Rhode Island | 3,861 | 3,861 | 4,054 | 84 | 88 |
| Vermont | 1,716 | 1,716 | 1,355 | 94 | 120 |
| **Midwest** | | | | | |
| Illinois | 33,801 | 33,801 | 29,861 | 133% | 150% |
| Indiana | 17,590 | 24,167 | — | 94 | 129 |
| Iowa | — | — | 7,238 | 121 | 121 |
| Kansas | 9,357 | — | — | 97 | 97 |
| Michigan | — | 49,837 | — | 99 | 99 |
| Minnesota | — | 8,203 | — | 97 | 97 |
| Missouri | — | 30,788 | — | 99 | 99 |
| Nebraska | — | 3,969 | 3,175 | 111 | 139 |
| North Dakota | 1,005 | 952 | 1,005 | 126 | 134 |
| Ohio | 35,531 | — | — | 121 | 121 |
| South Dakota | — | 3,445 | — | 97 | 97 |
| Wisconsin[c] | — | 17,325 | — | 127 | 127 |
| **South** | | | | | |
| Alabama[d] | — | 25,206 | 12,444 | 95% | 193% |
| Arkansas | 13,500 | 13,283 | 12,610 | 92 | 99 |
| Delaware | 6,679 | 6,665 | 5,475 | 102 | 124 |
| Florida | — | 88,156 | 66,641 | 98 | 130 |
| Georgia | — | 47,542 | — | 103 | 103 |
| Kentucky | 12,301 | 12,301 | 12,301 | 103 | 103 |
| Louisiana | 19,371 | 20,050 | — | 97 | 100 |
| Maryland | — | 22,647 | — | 100 | 100 |
| Mississippi[e] | 22,403 | — | — | 72 | 72 |
| North Carolina[f] | — | — | 31,500 | 116 | 116 |
| Oklahoma[e] | 24,145 | 24,145 | 24,145 | 95 | 95 |
| South Carolina | — | 23,169 | — | 97 | 97 |
| Tennessee | 20,122 | 19,670 | — | 96 | 98 |
| Texas[c] | 162,075 | 158,024 | 162,075 | 86 | 88 |
| Virginia | 31,358 | — | — | 93 | 93 |
| West Virginia | 3,655 | 4,226 | 3,655 | 96 | 110 |
| **West** | | | | | |
| Alaska | 3,098 | 3,206 | — | 107 | 111% |
| Arizona | 28,077 | 33,938 | 30,051 | 84 | 102 |
| California | — | 164,159 | 87,250 | 102 | 193 |
| Colorado | — | 14,153 | 12,836 | 120 | 133 |
| Hawaii | — | 3,487 | 2,451 | 110 | 157 |
| Idaho | 5,845 | 5,553 | 5,845 | 80 | 84 |
| Montana[e] | — | 1,591 | — | 121 | 121 |
| Nevada[e] | 11,063 | 20,895 | 7,766 | 56 | 150 |
| New Mexico[e] | — | 6,713 | 6,227 | 98 | 106 |
| Oregon | — | 12,646 | 12,646 | 102 | 102 |
| Utah | — | 6,203 | 6,411 | 79 | 82 |
| Washington | 12,992 | 15,014 | 15,014 | 112 | 129 |
| Wyoming | 1,283 | 1,260 | 1,231 | 97 | 102 |

— Data not available.

[a]Population counts are based on the number of inmates held in facilities operated by the jurisdiction. Excludes inmates held in local jails, in other states, or in private facilities.
[b]Connecticut no longer reports capacity because of a law passed in 1995.
[c]Excludes capacity of county facilities and inmates housed in them.
[d]Design capacity defined as the original design capacity.
[e]Includes capacity of private and contract facilities and inmates housed in them.
[f]Reported standard operating capacity.

SOURCE: Paige M. Harrison and Allen J. Beck, "Table 8. Reported Federal and State Prison Capacities, Yearend 2005," *Prisoners in 2005*, U.S. Department of Justice, Office of Justice Programs, Bureau of Justice Statistics, November 2006, http://www.ojp.usdoj.gov/bjs/pub/pdf/p05.pdf (accessed January 12, 2007)

## TABLE 6.11

**Capacity of local jails and percent of capacity occupied, 1995–2005**

| Year | Rated capacity[a] | Amount of capacity added[b] | Percent of capacity occupied[c] |
|------|-------------------|------------------------------|----------------------------------|
| 2005 | 789,001 | 33,398 | 95% |
| 2004 | 755,603 | 19,132 | 94 |
| 2003 | 736,471 | 22,572 | 94 |
| 2002 | 713,899 | 14,590 | 93 |
| 2001 | 699,309 | 21,522 | 90 |
| 2000 | 677,787 | 25,466 | 92 |
| 1999 | 652,321 | 39,541 | 93 |
| 1998 | 612,780 | 26,216 | 97 |
| 1997 | 586,564 | 23,593 | 97 |
| 1996 | 562,971 | 17,208 | 92 |
| 1995 | 545,763 | | 93 |
| Average annual increase, 1995–2005 | 3.8% | 24,229 | |

Note: Capacity data for 1995–98, and 2000–04 are survey estimates subject to sampling error.

[a]Rated capacity is the number of beds or inmates assigned by a rating official to facilities within each jurisdiction.

[b]The number of beds added during the 12 months ending June 30 of each year.

[c]The number of inmates divided by the rated capacity times 100.

SOURCE: Paige M. Harrison and Allen J. Beck, "Table 11. Rated Capacity of Local Jails and Percent of Capacity Occupied, 1995–2005," in *Prison and Jail Inmates at Midyear 2005*, U.S. Department of Justice, Office of Justice Programs, Bureau of Justice Statistics, May 2006, http://www.ojp.usdoj.gov/bjs/pub/pdf/pjim05.pdf (accessed January 17, 2007)

## FACTORS THAT IMPACT INMATE POPULATION GROWTH

As noted above, the number of inmates in state and federal prisons has risen steadily for more than two decades. Between 1980 and 1990 the prison population more than doubled from 319,598 to 743,382, according to the BJS (http://www.ojp.usdoj.gov/bjs/glance/tables/corr2tab.htm). By 2005 it had doubled again to 1,525,924. When the number of jail inmates is added, nearly 2.2 million inmates were being held in U.S. prisons and jails as of December 31, 2005. To put it another way, in 1980 the U.S. incarceration rate was 139 sentenced inmates per 100,000 residents. By 2005 the rate was at its highest ever: 491 sentenced prison or jail inmates per 100,000 population. Some factors that have contributed to the rise in inmate population include increases in arrests, convictions, and the lengths of prison stays for certain types of crime and repeat offenders.

### Arrest Rate

According to the FBI in *Crime in the United States*, total estimated arrests rose from 14.2 million in 1990 to a peak of 15.3 million in 1997. However, the number of arrests has since returned to earlier levels, declining to 14.1 million in 2005. The arrest rate itself, therefore, cannot explain the increase in prison populations or the incarceration rate. The impact of arrests on prison population figures depends on the types of crimes for which people have been detained and whether or not they are subsequently convicted and sentenced for those crimes.

Table 1.4 in Chapter 1 shows arrests by categories for 2005. More people (1,846,351) were arrested for drug abuse violations than any other specific type of crime. Arrests for drug abuse violations were up by 24.6% in between 1996 and 2005. Other categories of offenses showed a decline during this period. Arrests for murder were down by 16.5%, robbery by 16.2%, and forcible rape by 19.3%. More rigorous prosecution of drug violations may, in part, explain why the rate of growth in prison populations is higher than the growth rate of total arrests. During the 1980s and 1990s many states made drug crimes punishable by mandatory prison terms rather than probation. Prosecutions for drug offenses grew from 21% of federal defendants in 1982 to 35% in 2004, according to BJS (http://www.ojp.usdoj.gov/bjs/dcf/ptrpa.htm).

### Sentencing Status and Procedural Delays

According to Doris J. James of the Bureau of Justice Statistics in *Profile of Jail Inmates, 2002* (July 2004, http://www.ojp.usdoj.gov/bjs/pub/pdf/pji02.pdf), 28.2% of jail inmates in 2002 were detained while awaiting arraignment or trial, and about 15% were held on a prior sentence but also awaiting arraignment or trial on a new charge.

These percentages are in line with data reported in the Bureau's publication *Felony Sentences in State Courts, 2002* (http://www.ojp.gov/bjs/pub/pdf/fssc02.pdf) by Matthew R. Durose and Patrick A. Langan. Between 1992 and 2002, the median number of days required to dispose of all cases increased from 138 to 184 days. In 2002 the median time between arrest and sentencing for violent offenses was 218 days; for property offenses, 172 days; and for drug offenses, 175 days. Of all persons convicted of a felony in state courts, 78% were sentenced within one year following arrest. Increased time spent by inmates waiting in jail for arraignment or trial is another factor that raises the count of prisoners incarcerated at any given time.

### Drug Offenses

The rise in drug offenders confined by the states and federal government has contributed dramatically to crowding in prisons. According to data issued by the U.S. Bureau of Prisons (http://www.albany.edu/sourcebook/pdf/t657.pdf), of 20,686 total sentenced federal prisoners in 1970, some 3,384, or 16.3%, were drug offenders. As the "war on drugs" gained in force in subsequent years, more and more people were sent to prison for drug offenses, and they received longer sentences as well. This was especially true in the 1980s. By 1990, the number of sentenced federal prisoners had more than doubled, to 46,575 people. Nearly all of the increase could be attributed to drug offenders, as over that same period the number of drug offenders in federal prison had increased by over 700%, to 24,297. In fact, by 1990 more than half (52.2%) of all federal prisoners were

## TABLE 6.12

**Number and percentage of federal prisoners sentenced for drug offenses, 1970–2004**

| | Total sentenced and unsentenced population | Sentenced population | | |
|---|---|---|---|---|
| | | | Drug offenses | |
| | | Total | Number | Percent of total |
| 1970 | 21,266 | 20,686 | 3,384 | 16.3% |
| 1971 | 20,891 | 20,529 | 3,495 | 17.0 |
| 1972 | 22,090 | 20,729 | 3,523 | 16.9 |
| 1973 | 23,336 | 22,038 | 5,652 | 25.6 |
| 1974 | 23,690 | 21,769 | 6,203 | 28.4 |
| 1975 | 23,566 | 20,692 | 5,540 | 26.7 |
| 1976 | 27,033 | 24,135 | 6,425 | 26.6 |
| 1977 | 29,877 | 25,673 | 6,743 | 26.2 |
| 1978 | 27,674 | 23,501 | 5,981 | 25.4 |
| 1979 | 24,810 | 21,539 | 5,468 | 25.3 |
| 1980 | 24,252 | 19,023 | 4,749 | 24.9 |
| 1981 | 26,195 | 19,765 | 5,076 | 25.6 |
| 1982 | 28,133 | 20,938 | 5,518 | 26.3 |
| 1983 | 30,214 | 26,027 | 7,201 | 27.6 |
| 1984 | 32,317 | 27,622 | 8,152 | 29.5 |
| 1985 | 36,042 | 27,623 | 9,491 | 34.3 |
| 1986 | 37,542 | 30,104 | 11,344 | 37.7 |
| 1987 | 41,609 | 33,246 | 13,897 | 41.8 |
| 1988 | 41,342 | 33,758 | 15,087 | 44.7 |
| 1989 | 47,568 | 37,758 | 18,852 | 49.9 |
| 1990 | 54,613 | 46,575 | 24,297 | 52.2 |
| 1991 | 61,026 | 52,176 | 29,667 | 56.9 |
| 1992 | 67,768 | 59,516 | 35,398 | 59.5 |
| 1993 | 76,531 | 68,183 | 41,393 | 60.7 |
| 1994 | 82,269 | 73,958 | 45,367 | 61.3 |
| 1995 | 85,865 | 76,947 | 46,669 | 60.7 |
| 1996 | 89,672 | 80,872 | 49,096 | 60.7 |
| 1997 | 95,513 | 87,294 | 52,059 | 59.6 |
| 1998 | 104,507 | 95,323 | 55,984 | 58.7 |
| 1999 | 115,024 | 104,500 | 60,399 | 57.8 |
| 2000 | 123,141 | 112,329 | 63,898 | 56.9 |
| 2001 | 131,419 | 120,829 | 67,037 | 55.5 |
| 2002 | 139,183 | 128,090 | 70,009 | 54.7 |
| 2003 | 148,731 | 137,536 | 75,801 | 55.1 |
| 2004* | 154,706 | 143,864 | 77,867 | 54.1 |

Note: These data represent prisoners housed in Federal Bureau of Prisons facilities; prisoners housed in contract facilities are not included. Data for 1970–76 are for June 30; beginning in 1977, data are for September 30.

*As of November 2004.

SOURCE: Ann L. Pastore and Kathleen Maguire, editors, "Table 6.57. Federal Prison Population, and Number and Percent Sentenced for Drug Offenses," in *Sourcebook of Criminal Justice Statistics 2003*, 31st ed., U.S. Department of Justice, Office of Justice Programs, Bureau of Justice Statistics, 2005, http://www.albany.edu/sourcebook/pdf/t657.pdf (accessed February 13, 2007)

drug offenders. This trend continued through 2004, when 77,867 drug offenders were in federal prison, out of 143,864 federal prisoners under sentence. (See Table 6.12.)

At the state level at yearend 2003, according to the BJS, about 20% of prison inmates (250,900 prisoners) were serving time because of a conviction involving drug possession, manufacture, or trafficking. Drug convictions at the state level exploded 682% during the 1980s, from 19,000 prisoners in 1980 to 148,600 in 1990 according to the BJS (http://www.ojp.usdoj.gov/bjs/glance/tables/corr typtab.htm). Increases continued through 2002, when state prisoners incarcerated for drug offenses peaked at 265,100.

Drug offenses at the local level also contributed to increases in the number and rate of U.S. incarcerations. According to the BJS in "Correctional Populations and Facilities" (http://www.ojp.usdoj.gov/bjs/dcf/correct.htm), an estimated 155,900 jail inmates were held for a drug offense in 2002, an increase from 114,100 in 1996. Drug trafficking accounted for most of the increase.

### Time Served

Prison populations are influenced both by the length of the sentences imposed by the courts and the percentage of the sentence that felons actually serve. Beginning in the mid-1980s, the federal government and many states passed truth-in-sentencing laws as part of a widespread movement to "get tough on crime." The idea behind these laws was to ensure that all or a substantial portion of each sentence imposed would actually be served. States operating under federal truth-in-sentencing guidelines require that 85% of sentences be served. Most states, the District of Columbia, and the federal government operate under such statutes. Their effect has been longer retention of prisoners and thus a growth in prison populations.

As reported by Durose and Langan in *Felony Sentences in State Courts, 2002*, between 1994 and 2002 the average sentence imposed for all offenses fell from seventy-one months to fifty-three months. At the same time, however, the percentage of time actually served increased from 38% in 1994 to 51% in 2002. The net effect of these averages was to increase the time actually served for several important categories of crime. The percentage of sentenced time actually served for murder, for example, rose from 47% in 1994 to 63% in 2002, and the actual time served for murder rose from 127 months in 1994 to 142 months in 2002. Therefore, inmates are serving a higher percentage of sentenced time in the most serious crime categories; in short, the inmate population has grown because the most serious offenders are staying longer.

### Parole Violations

The rising incidence of rearrest of those who have been paroled is yet another cause of the rising prison population. In 1990, 29.1% of all admissions to state prison systems were parole violators. According to *Prison and Jail Inmates Midyear 2005*, that proportion had increased to 34% of all admissions by 2004—219,033 prisoners out of 644,084.

### COSTS OF CORRECTIONS

The costs of corrections in the United States have been rising in absolute terms, even after the country's growing population has been taken into account. Between 1980 and 1999 the number of people held behind bars would have increased more than three-fold even if the U.S. population had remained unchanged. In 1980, 139 people were in state and federal prisons for every 100,000 U.S. residents. By 2005 that ratio had increased to 491 people per 100,000 population, according to *Prisoners in 2005*, and costs have escalated to keep pace.

Kristen A. Hughes of the Bureau of Justice Statistics indicates in *Justice Expenditure and Employment in the United States, 2003* (May 2006, http://www.ojp.usdoj. gov/bjs/pub/pdf/jeeus03.pdf) that the total amount spent on corrections at the federal, state, and local levels rose by more than 500% from about $9.6 billion in 1982 to $63.4 billion in 2003. During this period, total expenditures for police protection also increased—from $19.5 billion to $89 billion. Total judicial and legal costs rose from $7.9 billion in 1982 to $42.9 billion in 2003. Local governments paid $93.9 billion of the $185.5 billion in total U.S. justice expenditures in 2003, including $57.5 billion spent on police. State governments paid $39.2 billion of the $63.4 billion spent on corrections in the United States. Figure 6.1 shows the increase in direct justice expenditures and a breakdown by level of government from 1982 through 2003.

Total spending on corrections in 1982 equaled $40 for each U.S. resident. By 2003 that figure had risen more than 400% to $209 per person. (See Table 6.13.) By comparison, the per capita cost of police protection, after inflation, rose by 240%, from $84 to $286, and judicial and legal costs rose by 320%, from $34 to $143.

## Federal Prison Expenditures

Between 1982 and 2003, according to Hughes, the federal government increased its spending on corrections by 925%, from $541 million to $5.5 billion. In comparison, state expenditures for corrections increased 550.9% and local jurisdictions increased spending by 519.6%. The federal government spent more than state and local governments on intergovernmental grants-in-aid, shared revenues, and amounts paid to other governments for services performed. (See Table 6.14.)

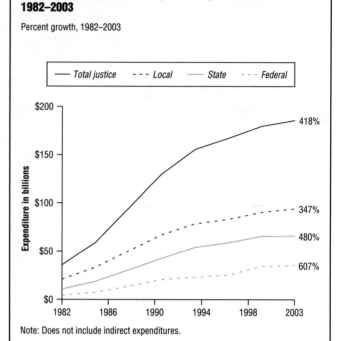

**FIGURE 6.1**

**Direct justice expenditures by level of government, 1982–2003**

Percent growth, 1982–2003

Note: Does not include indirect expenditures.

SOURCE: Kristen A. Hughes, "Figure 2. The Total Direct Justice Expenditure for All Levels of Government Grew from $36 Billion in 1982 to $185 Billion in 2003, a 418% Increase," in *Justice Expenditure and Employment in the United States, 2003*, U.S. Department of Justice, Office of Justice Programs, Bureau of Justice Statistics, April 2006, http://www.ojp.usdoj.gov/bjs/pub/pdf/jeeus03.pdf (accessed January 23, 2007)

*The Budget of the United States for Fiscal Year 2008* proposes $5.4 billion for the BOP and $1.3 billion for the Office of the Federal Detention Trustee (Office of Management and Budget, February 2007). The proposal includes $169 million to expand prison capacity by completing the first phase of a new prison in Pollock, Louisiana; completing a prison in Mendota, California; and expanding the number of contract prison beds by more

**TABLE 6.13**

**Total and per capita justice expenditure across government and by function, selected years 1982–2003**

| Year | Population | Justice expenditure across government and function Total (in millions) | Per capita | Police protection expenditure Total (in millions) | Per capita | Judicial and legal expenditure Total (in millions) | Per capita | Corrections expenditure Total (in millions) | Per capita |
|---|---|---|---|---|---|---|---|---|---|
| 2003 | 290,850,000 | $185,490 | $638 | $83,089 | $286 | $41,545 | $143 | $60,855 | $209 |
| 2002 | 287,985,000 | 179,580 | 624 | 79,540 | 276 | 40,431 | 140 | 59,609 | 207 |
| 1997 | 267,784,000 | 129,793 | 485 | 57,754 | 216 | 28,529 | 107 | 43,511 | 162 |
| 1992 | 245,807,000 | 93,777 | 382 | 41,327 | 168 | 20,989 | 85 | 31,461 | 128 |
| 1987 | 243,400,000 | 58,871 | 242 | 28,778 | 118 | 12,555 | 52 | 17,549 | 72 |
| 1982 | 226,548,000 | 35,842 | 158 | 19,022 | 84 | 7,771 | 34 | 9,049 | 40 |

Note: Using the consumer price index (CPI) to adjust the 2003 per capita figure of $638 for inflation would yield approximately $335 in 1982 dollars.

SOURCE: Kristen A. Hughes, "Appendix Table. Direct and per Capita Expenditure across Government and by Function, Selected Years, 1982–2003," in *Justice Expenditure and Employment in the United States, 2003*, U.S. Department of Justice, Office of Justice Programs, Bureau of Justice Statistics, April 2006, http://www.ojp.usdoj.gov/bjs/pub/pdf/jeeus03.pdf (accessed January 23, 2007)

**TABLE 6.14**

Justice expenditures, by level of government and justice activity, selected years 1982–2003

| | Federal | | | | State | | | | Local | | | |
|---|---|---|---|---|---|---|---|---|---|---|---|---|
| | Total | Police protection | Judicial and legal | Corrections | Total | Police protection | Judicial and legal | Corrections | Total | Police protection | Judicial and legal | Corrections |
| **Expenditure (in millions)** | | | | | | | | | | | | |
| 1982 | $4,458 | $2,527 | $1,390 | $541 | $11,602 | $2,833 | $2,748 | $6,020 | $20,968 | $14,172 | $3,784 | $3,011 |
| 1987 | 7,496 | 4,231 | 2,271 | 994 | 20,157 | 4,067 | 4,339 | 11,691 | 33,265 | 21,089 | 6,230 | 5,947 |
| 1992 | 17,423 | 7,400 | 7,377 | 2,646 | 33,755 | 5,593 | 7,723 | 20,439 | 50,115 | 29,659 | 10,052 | 10,404 |
| 1997 | 27,065 | 12,518 | 10,651 | 3,896 | 46,444 | 7,501 | 9,803 | 29,141 | 67,083 | 40,976 | 13,101 | 13,007 |
| 2000 | 27,820 | 13,999 | 9,353 | 4,467 | 58,165 | 9,787 | 13,249 | 35,129 | 78,995 | 48,219 | 14,842 | 15,934 |
| 2001 | 30,443 | 15,014 | 10,230 | 5,199 | 63,372 | 10,497 | 14,444 | 38,432 | 83,377 | 50,718 | 15,938 | 16,721 |
| 2002 | 34,346 | 17,626 | 11,013 | 5,707 | 65,508 | 11,081 | 15,365 | 39,062 | 90,485 | 55,086 | 17,042 | 18,358 |
| 2003 | 35,323 | 20,422 | 9,356 | 5,545 | 66,114 | 11,144 | 15,782 | 39,187 | 93,877 | 57,503 | 17,718 | 18,656 |
| Percent change 1982–2003 | 692.4% | 708.2% | 573.1% | 925.0% | 469.9% | 293.4% | 474.3% | 550.9% | 347.7% | 305.8% | 368.2% | 519.6% |
| Average annual percent change, 1982–2003 | 9.9% | 10.0% | 9.1% | 11.2% | 8.2% | 6.4% | 8.3% | 8.9% | 7.1% | 6.6% | 7.3% | 8.6% |

Note: Detail may not add to total because of rounding.

SOURCE: Kristen A. Hughes, "Table 2. Total Direct and Intergovernmental Expenditure of Federal, State, and Local Governments for Each Justice Function, and Percent Change, Fiscal Years 1982–2003," in *Justice Expenditure and Employment in the United States, 2003*, U.S. Department of Justice, Office of Justice Programs, Bureau of Justice Statistics, April 2006, http://www.ojp.usdoj.gov/bjs/pub/pdf/jeeus03.pdf (accessed January 23, 2007)

than 1,100. Historically, actual outlays tend to be slightly lower than the amount requested as Congress debates the amounts to be spent.

## Corrections Expenditures by States

Based on data from the BJS in *Justice Expenditure and Employment in the United States, 2003*, corrections represented about 2.6% of state and local direct expenditures in 2005. The criminal and justice system as a whole accounted for some 7.2% of state and local budgets; another 29% went to education, 14% to public welfare, and 7% to health and hospitals. These percentages have been remarkably steady since 1977. (See Figure 6.2.)

Total state expenditures for corrections have increased steadily over the past few decades, from $4.3 billion in 1980 to $36.9 billion in 2003, according to the *Sourcebook of Criminal Justice Statistics 2003* (http://www.albany.edu/sourcebook/pdf/t192003.pdf). Of this amount, states spent $30.2 billion on institutions, including $1.1 billion on construction. The percentage of state corrections budgets spent on correctional facilities has increased from 67.4% in 1980 to 77.9% in 2003. Overall, California spent the most ($5.5 billion) on corrections in 2003, followed by Texas ($3 billion), New York ($2.4 billion), and Florida ($2.2 billion). States with the lowest direct spending on corrections during fiscal year 2002 included North Dakota ($36.8 million), South Dakota ($66.9 million), New Hampshire ($79.5 million), Vermont ($79.5 million), and Wyoming ($82.8 million).

## Local Jail Expenditures by Counties and Municipalities

According to *Justice Expenditure and Employment in the United States, 2003*, governments on the local level

**FIGURE 6.2**

State and local expenditures on selected government functions, 1977–2003

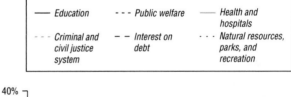

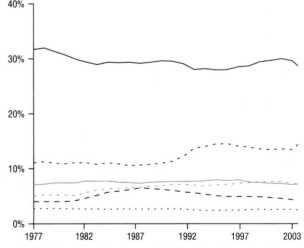

Note: The government functions included will not sum to 100% of government spending, because some functions were excluded for display purposes. Figures may not match those from the expenditure and employment extracts because of definitional difference.

SOURCE: Kristen A. Hughes, "Figure 3. Percent of State and Local Direct Expenditures for Selected Functions, 1977–2003," in *Justice Expenditure and Employment in the United States, 2003*, U.S. Department of Justice, Office of Justice Programs, Bureau of Justice Statistics, April 2006, http://www.ojp.usdoj.gov/bjs/pub/pdf/jeeus03.pdf (accessed January 23, 2007)

TABLE 6.15

**Employment and monthly payroll of the justice system, by activity and level of government, March 2003**

| Activity | All governments | Federal | State | Local | Percent distribution | | | |
| --- | --- | --- | --- | --- | --- | --- | --- | --- |
| | | | | | Total | Federal | State | Local |
| **Total justice system** | | | | | | | | |
| Total employees | 2,361,193 | 253,367 | 733,570 | 1,374,256 | 100% | 10.7% | 31.1% | 58.2% |
| 2003 March payroll* | $9,041 | $1,279 | $2,639 | $5,123 | 100 | 14.1 | 29.2 | 56.1 |
| **Police protection** | | | | | | | | |
| Total employees | 1,118,936 | 156,607 | 105,933 | 856,396 | 100% | 14.0% | 9.5% | 76.5% |
| 2003 March payroll* | $4,545 | $760 | $438 | $3,347 | 100 | 16.7 | 9.6 | 73.6 |
| **Judicial and legal** | | | | | | | | |
| Total employees | 494,007 | 61,984 | 164,051 | 267,972 | 100% | 12.5% | 33.2% | 54.2% |
| 2003 March payroll* | $1,969 | $353 | $682 | $934 | 100 | 17.9 | 34.6 | 47.4 |
| **Corrections** | | | | | | | | |
| Total employees | 748,250 | 34,776 | 463,586 | 249,888 | 100% | 4.6% | 62.0% | 33.4% |
| 2003 March payroll* | $2,526 | $165 | $1,519 | $842 | 100 | 6.5 | 60.1 | 33.3 |

Note: Detail may not add to total because of rounding. These data are based on a summation of responses from individual state and local government agencies. Local government data are estimates subject to sampling variability.
*Payroll is in millions.

SOURCE: Kristen A. Hughes, "Table 5. Employment and Monthly Payroll of the Justice System, by Activity and Level of Government, March 2003," in *Justice Expenditure and Employment in the United States, 2003*, U.S. Department of Justice, Office of Justice Programs, Bureau of Justice Statistics, April 2006, http://www.ojp.usdoj.gov/bjs/pub/pdf/jeeus03.pdf (accessed January 23, 2007)

**FIGURE 6.3**

**Expenditures for justice functions by level of government, 1982–2003**

Percent growth, 1982–2003

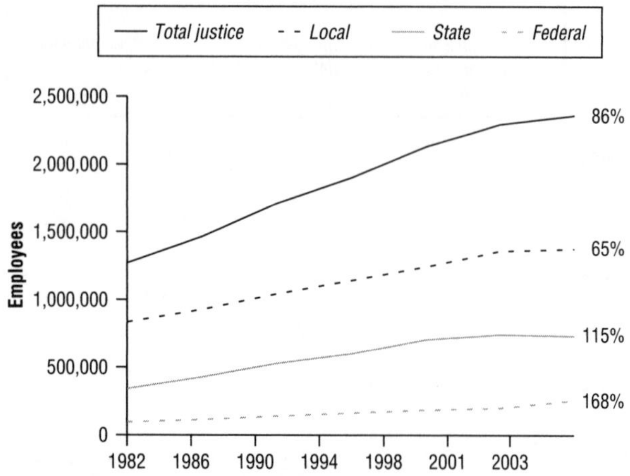

SOURCE: Kristen A. Hughes, "Highlights: Expenditure for Justice Functions Varies by Level of Government," in *Justice Expenditure and Employment in the United States, 2003*, U.S. Department of Justice, Office of Justice Programs, Bureau of Justice Statistics, April 2006, http://www.ojp.usdoj.gov/bjs/pub/pdf/jeeus03.pdf (accessed January 23, 2007)

Harrison and Beck report in *Prison and Jail Inmates at Midyear 2005* that between 1995 and 2005, the number of inmates in local jails rose from 507,044 to 733,442. (See Table 6.5.) The number of people held in local jails grew by 4.7%, from 713,990 to 747,529, between July 1, 2004, and June 30, 2005. However, at the end of June 2005, local jails were operating at 5% below their rated capacity. The researchers also indicate that local authorities supervised an additional 71,905 offenders in alternative programs such as work release, weekend reporting, electronic monitoring, and community service.

## PRISON WORK PROGRAMS AND INDUSTRIES

Work in fields, laundries, and kitchens has always been a part of many inmates' lives; some even participate in work-release programs. According to James J. Stephan and Jennifer C. Karburg of the Bureau of Justice Statistics in *Census of State and Federal Correctional Facilities, 2000* (October 16, 2003, http://www.ojp.usdoj.gov/bjs/pub/pdf/csfcf00.pdf), the last such census published, 91% of all correctional facilities had some type of work program. Furthermore, 92% of state and federal facilities operated work programs, compared with 73% of private facilities.

The most common type of work program involved facility support; 100% of federal facilities had this type of program. The second most common work programs were public works programs; 66% of state and 47% of private facilities had these types of programs. About 46% of confinement facilities had prison industries, 29% operated farms and other agricultural activities, and 60% were involved in outside public works projects, such as road and park maintenance.

carry the bulk of justice system costs because police protection is primarily the responsibility of local communities. Some 58.2% of all justice system employees (1,374,256) are employed at the local level. (See Table 6.15.) In 2003, $57.5 billion, 69.2% of all funds spent on police protection, came from county or municipal governments. (See Figure 6.3.)

## Work in Federal Prisons

According to the Federal Bureau of Prisons, federal prison inmates are required to work if they are medically able to do so (http://www.bop.gov/inmate_programs/work_prgms.jsp). Their work assignments typically contribute to the facility operations and maintenance in such areas as food service, plumbing, painting, or landscaping. Inmates earn $0.12 to $0.40 per hour for these in-house work assignments. The BOP also reports that 17% of federal prison inmates work in Federal Prison Industries (FPI) factories. This program provides slightly higher wages to inmates, from $0.23 to $1.15 per hour as of fiscal year 2006. Work includes manufacturing jobs in such areas as furniture, electronics, textiles, and graphic arts. With a high school diploma or its equivalent inmates can be promoted to a managerial role.

**UNICOR** UNICOR is the trade name for Federal Prison Industries, Inc., the government corporation that employs inmates in federal prisons. UNICOR should not be confused with state prison industry programs administered by the states. Under UNICOR, established in 1934, federal inmates get job training by producing goods and services for federal agencies. In 2007 items produced by inmates included clothing and textiles (military items and apparel, protective clothing for law enforcement, mattresses, medical textiles), electronics (circuit boards, electrical cables, outdoor lighting systems/flood lights), industrial products (prescription and non-prescription safety eyewear, traffic and safety signage, license plates, air filters, perimeter fencing), office furniture (systems furniture, seating, and office furniture, filing and storage products). Inmates also provide fleet management and vehicular components (fleet vehicle and vehicular component remanufacturing, fleet vehicle uplifting, and fleet management services), recycling (computers and electronic equipment), and other services (data services, printing and binding, contact center/help desk support).

UNICOR products and services must be purchased by federal agencies and are not for sale in interstate commerce or to nonfederal entities. UNICOR is not permitted to compete with private industry. If UNICOR cannot make the needed product or provide the required service, federal agencies may buy the product from the private sector through a waiver issued by UNICOR.

According to the FPI *FY 2006 Annual Report*, UNICOR employed 21,205 inmates in 108 factories at 79 prison locations in 2006 (http://www.unicor.gov/information/publications/pdfs/corporate/catar2006.pdf). Approximately 18% of all eligible inmates in BOP facilities worked for UNICOR that year. The agency's goal is to employ 25% of all work-eligible prisoners who have no existing job skills.

UNICOR is a self-supporting government corporation that may borrow funds from the U.S. Treasury and use the proceeds to purchase equipment, pay wages to inmates and staff, and invest in expansion of facilities. However, no funds are appropriated for UNICOR operations. During fiscal year 2006 its sales topped $717.5 million.

## Work in State Prisons

State and local governments prevent prisoners from working at some jobs because they would be in competition with private enterprise or workers. In 1936 Congress barred convicts from working on federal contracts worth more than $10,000. In 1940 Congress made it illegal to transport convict-made goods through interstate commerce. These rules were changed in 1979 when Congress established the Prison Industry Enhancement Certification Program (PIECP). The PIECP allows state correctional industries that meet certain requirements to sell inmate-produced goods to the federal government and in interstate commerce.

Some private industries pay inmates minimum wage, but many prisons take most of prisoners' wages to pay for room and board, restitution, family support, and taxes. The Bureau of Justice Assistance reported that from December 1979 through June 30, 2003, PIECP participants had paid wages of $264 million (http://www.ncjrs.gov/html/bja/piecp/bja-prison-industr.html#background). After deductions for victims programs ($24.5 million), room and board ($70.6 million), family support ($15.7 million), and taxes ($35.6 million), inmates had earned $117.8 million.

Many prison administrators generally favor work programs. Some believe that work keeps prisoners productive and occupied, thus leading to a safer prison environment. Another cited benefit is that work programs prepare prisoners for re-entry into the non-institutionalized world by helping them develop job skills and solid work habits that will be needed for post-incarceration employment. Some prisons report that inmates who work in industry are less likely to cause problems in prison or be rearrested after release than convicts who do not participate in work programs.

In addition, many inmates report that they like the opportunity to work. They assert that it provides relief from boredom and gives them some extra money. Inmates find that the money they earn helps them to meet financial obligations for their families even while they are in prison.

# CHAPTER 7
# CHARACTERISTICS AND RIGHTS OF INMATES

## RACE, ETHNICITY, AGE, AND GENDER

### State and Federal Prison Inmates

According to Paige M. Harrison and Allen J. Beck of the Bureau of Justice Statistics (BJS) in *Prisoners in 2005* (November 2006, http://www.ojp.usdoj.gov/bjs/pub/pdf/p05.pdf), in 2005 over 1.3 million men and 98,600 women were serving sentences in state and federal prisons. (See Table 7.1.) Of these prisoners, 459,700 males and 45,800 females were white, 547,200 males and 29,900 females were African-American, and 279,000 males and 15,900 females were Hispanic.

Table 7.1 shows that the largest proportion of male prisoners (244,800) was aged twenty-five to twenty-nine. Among women the largest number (19,400) were between the ages of thirty-five and thirty-nine. Among men the largest number of white prisoners were aged forty-five to fifty-four years (76,300), whereas more African-American (106,600) and Hispanic (59,600) prisoners were twenty-five to thirty-nine years old.

The largest overall number of prisoners were African-American. Among men African-Americans outnumbered whites in every age group except those aged forty-five to fifty-four and those aged fifty-five and older. Among women whites were more numerous than African-Americans in every age category.

According to Harrison and Beck, there were 471 white males per 100,000 residents aged eighteen and older in prison in 2005. (See Table 7.2.) For Hispanics, this rate was 1,244, and for African-Americans it was 3,145. The rates for women were 45 for whites, 76 for Hispanics, and 156 for African-Americans. Harrison and Beck estimate that in 2005, 8.1% of African-American males aged twenty-five to twenty-nine were in prison, compared to 1.1% of white males and 2.6% of Hispanic males.

Harrison and Beck note that over 1.4 million men and 107,000 women made up the correctional population in 2005. The number of male inmates increased 1.9% from

2004 to 2005 and by an average annual rate of 3% from 1995 to 2005. The female correctional population increased by 2.6% from 2004 to 2005 and grew 4.6% on average each year from 1995 to 2005. The number of male prisoners sentenced to more than one year grew 1.9% from 2004 to 2005, and the female population increased by 2.7%. The incarceration rate for men was 781 per 100,000 residents in 1995 and 929 per 100,000 residents in 2005. The corresponding rate for women was 47 per 100,000 residents in 1995 and 65 per 100,000 residents in 2005.

### Jail Inmates

According to Harrison and Beck of the BJS, in *Prison and Jail Inmates at Midyear 2005* (May 2005, http://www.ojp.gov/bjs/pub/pdf/pjim05.pdf), at midyear 2005 the jail incarceration rate for women was 63 per 100,000 female residents, whereas the rate for men was 447 per 100,000 male residents. (See Table 7.3.) In 2005, 12.7% of jail inmates were female, compared to 10.2% of jail inmates who were female ten years earlier in 1995.

Most local jail inmates in 2005 were members of racial and ethnic minority groups. Table 7.4 shows that the percentage of whites in jails increased from 40.1% in 1995 to 44.3% in 2005. The proportion of Hispanics increased slightly, from 14.7% to 15%, whereas the proportion of African-Americans decreased from 43.5% to 38.9%.

African-Americans were more than four times more likely than whites, three times more likely than Hispanics, and nine times more likely than other ethnic groups to be held in jail. On a per capita basis, men were more than seven times more likely than women to have been in a jail in 2005.

## TYPES OF CRIMES

### Federal Prisons

In *Federal Bureau of Prisons Quick Facts* (December 30, 2006, http://www.bop.gov/news/quick.jsp), the Federal Bureau of Prisons reports that more than half (53.7%) of all federal prison inmates were sentenced for drug violations in

**TABLE 7.1**

**Number of state or federal prisoners, by gender, race, Hispanic origin, and age, 2005**

| | Number of sentenced prisoners | | | | | | | |
| | Males | | | | Females | | | |
| Age | Total[a] | White[b] | Black[b] | Hispanic | Total[a] | White[b] | Black[b] | Hispanic |
|---|---|---|---|---|---|---|---|---|
| Total | 1,362,500 | 459,700 | 547,200 | 279,000 | 98,600 | 45,800 | 29,900 | 15,900 |
| 18–19 | 26,300 | 7,200 | 11,800 | 5,600 | 1,200 | 500 | 400 | 200 |
| 20–24 | 218,700 | 62,700 | 94,200 | 50,400 | 11,900 | 5,300 | 3,600 | 2,300 |
| 25–29 | 244,800 | 67,000 | 106,600 | 59,600 | 15,300 | 6,700 | 4,700 | 2,900 |
| 30–34 | 224,200 | 69,800 | 92,000 | 51,100 | 17,400 | 8,100 | 5,100 | 2,900 |
| 35–39 | 207,200 | 72,300 | 81,600 | 41,600 | 19,400 | 9,000 | 6,000 | 3,000 |
| 40–44 | 185,200 | 70,900 | 71,000 | 31,600 | 16,500 | 7,800 | 5,100 | 2,400 |
| 45–54 | 189,800 | 76,300 | 71,100 | 29,500 | 13,800 | 6,500 | 4,300 | 1,800 |
| 55 or older | 63,500 | 32,900 | 17,600 | 9,000 | 3,000 | 1,800 | 700 | 300 |

Note: Based on estimates by gender, race, Hispanic origin, and age from the 2004 Survey of Inmates in State Correctional Facilities and updated from jurisdiction counts by gender at year end 2005. Estimates were rounded to the nearest 100.
[a]Includes American Indians, Alaska Natives, Asians, Native Hawiians, other Pacific Islanders, and persons identifying two or more races.
[b]Excludes Hispanics and persons identifying two or more races.

SOURCE: Paige M. Harrison and Allen J. Beck, "Table 10. Number of Sentenced Prisoners under State or Federal Jurisdiction, by Gender, Race, Hispanic Origin, and Age, Yearend 2005," in *Prisoners in 2005*, U.S. Department of Justice, Office of Justice Programs, Bureau of Justice Statistics, November 2006, http://www.ojp.usdoj.gov/bjs/pub/pdf/p05.pdf (accessed January 12, 2007)

**TABLE 7.2**

**Number of sentenced state or federal prisoners per 100,000 residents, by gender, race, Hispanic origin, and age, 2005**

| | Number of sentenced prisoners pre 100,000 residents | | | | | | | |
| | Males | | | | Females | | | |
| Age | Total[a] | White[b] | Black[b] | Hispanic | Total[a] | White[b] | Black[b] | Hispanic |
|---|---|---|---|---|---|---|---|---|
| Total | 929 | 471 | 3,145 | 1,244 | 65 | 45 | 156 | 76 |
| 18–19 | 619 | 274 | 1,920 | 791 | 29 | 20 | 61 | 38 |
| 20–24 | 2,016 | 948 | 6,345 | 2,493 | 118 | 85 | 248 | 137 |
| 25–29 | 2,342 | 1,098 | 8,082 | 2,618 | 153 | 113 | 339 | 158 |
| 30–34 | 2,234 | 1,172 | 7,726 | 2,450 | 177 | 138 | 391 | 165 |
| 35–39 | 1,953 | 1,067 | 6,630 | 2,255 | 185 | 134 | 435 | 184 |
| 40–44 | 1,641 | 923 | 5,472 | 1,975 | 145 | 102 | 345 | 164 |
| 45–54 | 899 | 493 | 3,136 | 1,327 | 63 | 41 | 163 | 85 |
| 55 or older | 208 | 135 | 697 | 416 | 8 | 6 | 19 | 13 |

Note: Based on estimates of the U.S. resident population on January 1, 2006, by gender, race, Hispanic origin, and age. Detailed categories exclude persons identifying with two or more races.
[a]Includes American Indians, Alaska Native, Asians, Native Hawaiians, other Pacific Islanders, and persons identifying two or more races.
[b]Excludes Hispanics and persons identifying two or more races.

SOURCE: Paige M. Harrison and Allen J. Beck, "Table 11. Number of Sentenced Prisoners under State or Federal Jurisdiction per 100,000 Residents, by Gender, Race, Hispanic Origin, and Age, Yearend 2005," in *Prisoners in 2005*, U.S. Department of Justice, Office of Justice Programs, Bureau of Justice Statistics, November 2006, http://www.ojp.usdoj.gov/bjs/pub/pdf/p05.pdf (accessed January 12, 2007)

2006. (See Table 7.5.) After drug offenses, the most common offenses of federal prisoners were weapons violations, explosives charges, and arson (14.2% of offenders), immigration violations (10.7%), and robbery (5.4%).

According to *Federal Bureau of Prisons Quick Facts*, most federal inmates in April 2007 were male (93.2%). Of all federal inmates at that time, 56.4% were white, 40.2% were African-American, 1.7% were Native American, and 1.6% were Asian. The Federal Bureau of Prisons reports that among those incarcerated in federal prisons, 73.5%

were U.S. citizens, 16.8% were citizens of Mexico, 1.6% were Colombian citizens, 1.6% were citizens of the Dominican Republic, and 0.8% were Cuban citizens. The remaining 5.7% were of unknown or other citizenship.

**State Prisons**

In *Key Facts at a Glance* (October 23, 2005, http://www.ojp.usdoj.gov/bjs/glance/tables/corrtyptab.htm), Beck and Harrison of the BJS report that between 1980 and 2003 the number of people in the state correctional system

TABLE 7.3

**Gender and race of jail inmates, 2005**

|  | Estimated count | Jail incarceration rate[a] |
|---|---|---|
| **Total** | **747,529** | **252** |
| **Gender** | | |
| Male | 652,958 | 447 |
| Female | 94,571 | 63 |
| **Race/Hispanic origin** | | |
| White[b] | 331,000 | 166 |
| Black[b] | 290,500 | 800 |
| Hispanic/Latino | 111,900 | 268 |
| Other[c] | 13,000 | 88 |
| Two or more | 1,000 | * |

Note: Inmate counts by race/Hispanic origin were estimated and rounded to the nearest 100. Resident population figures were estimated for July 1, 2005, based on the *2000 Census of Population and Housing.*
*Not calculated.
[a]Number of jail inmates per 100,000 residents in each group.
[b]Non-Hispanic only.
[c]Includes American Indians, Alaska Natives, Asians, Native Hawaiians, and other Pacific Islanders.

SOURCE: Paige M. Harrison and Allen J. Beck, "Jail Incarceration Rates Rose in the Last 12-month Period," in *Prison and Jail Inmates at Midyear 2005,* U.S. Department of Justice, Office of Justice Programs, Bureau of Justice Statistics, May 2006, http://www.ojp.usdoj.gov/bjs/pub/pdf/pjim05.pdf (accessed February 13, 2007)

TABLE 7.4

**Gender, race, Hispanic origin, and conviction status of local jail inmates, midyear, selected years 1995–2005**

| Characteristic | 1995 | 2000 | 2004 | 2005 |
|---|---|---|---|---|
| **Total** | **100%** | **100%** | **100%** | **100%** |
| **Gender** | | | | |
| Male | 89.8% | 88.6% | 87.7% | 87.3% |
| Female | 10.2 | 11.4 | 12.3 | 12.7 |
| **Race/Hispanic origin** | | | | |
| White[a] | 40.1% | 41.9% | 44.4% | 44.3% |
| Black[a] | 43.5 | 41.3 | 38.6 | 38.9 |
| Hispanic | 14.7 | 15.1 | 15.2 | 15.0 |
| Other[b] | 1.7 | 1.6 | 1.8 | 1.7 |
| Two or more races[c] | | | | 0.1 |
| **Conviction status** | | | | |
| Convicted | 44.0% | 44.0% | 39.7% | 38.0% |
| Male | 39.7 | 39.0 | 34.8 | 33.2 |
| Female | 4.3 | 5.0 | 4.9 | 4.8 |
| Unconvicted | 56.0 | 56.0 | 60.3 | 62.0 |
| Male | 50.0 | 50.0 | 53.0 | 54.2 |
| Female | 6.0 | 6.0 | 7.3 | 7.7 |

Note: Detail may not add to total because of rounding.
[a]Non-Hispanic only.
[b]Includes American Indians, Alaska Natives, Asians, Native Hawaiians, and other Pacific Islanders.
[c]More than one race was not requested prior to 2005.

SOURCE: Paige M. Harrison and Allen J. Beck, "Table 10. Gender, Race, Hispanic Origin, and Conviction Status of Local Jail Inmates, Midyear 1995, 2000, and 2004–05," in *Prison and Jail Inmates at Midyear 2005,* U.S. Department of Justice, Office of Justice Programs, Bureau of Justice Statistics, May 2006, http://www.ojp.usdoj.gov/bjs/pub/pdf/pjim05.pdf (accessed January 17, 2007)

TABLE 7.5

**Federal prisoners by type of offense, 2006**

| | | |
|---|---|---|
| Drug offenses: | 95,689 | 53.7% |
| Weapons, explosives, arson: | 25,316 | 14.2% |
| Immigration: | 19,054 | 10.7% |
| Robbery: | 9,630 | 5.4% |
| Burglary, larceny, property offenses: | 6,800 | 3.8% |
| Extortion, fraud, bribery: | 7,401 | 4.2% |
| Homicide, aggravated assault, and kidnapping offenses: | 5,544 | 3.1% |
| Miscellaneous: | 2,183 | 1.2% |
| Sex offenses: | 4,083 | 2.3% |
| Banking and insurance, counterfeit, embezzlement: | 994 | 0.6% |
| Courts or corrections: | 735 | 0.4% |
| Continuing criminal enterprise: | 579 | 0.3% |
| National security: | 105 | 0.1% |

SOURCE: "Types of Offenses," in *Federal Bureau of Prisons Quick Facts,* U.S. Department of Justice, Federal Bureau of Prisons, December 30, 2006, http://www.bop.gov/news/quick.jsp (accessed January 17, 2007)

increased by 325%, from 294,000 to over 1.2 million. Most inmates were in state prisons rather than in federal facilities or local jails. Figure 7.1 shows a twenty-three-year history of state incarcerations divided by type of crime committed. The largest category was violent crime, which accounted for more than half of the increase in the state prison population since 1980. The number of prisoners incarcerated for drug offenses grew from 19,000 in 1980 to 250,900 in 2004, as measured by state prison population. Between 1980 and 2003 the number of prisoners confined for crimes against the public order increased from 12,400 to 86,400. These crimes include illegal weapons possession, drunken driving, flight to escape prosecution, obstruction of justice, and liquor law violations.

According to Harrison and Beck, in *Prisoners in 2005,* 51.8% of all state prison inmates (250,900) were serving time for violent crimes in 2003. A fifth (20.2%) of all prisoners were serving for drug offenses, and another fifth (20.9%) for property crimes. The remaining 6.9% had been convicted of offenses against the public order.

Beck and Harrison note that the distribution of offenses has changed somewhat over the period shown in Figure 7.1. The inmates incarcerated for drug offenses in 1980 accounted for about 6% of total state prisoners; by 1990 they reached a peak of 22%, declining slightly thereafter; in 2003 drug offenders accounted for 20% of all inmates. Violent crimes represented 59% of all state prison incarcerations in 1980, dropped to a low of 46% in 1990, but have been increasing in share of total offenses since, reaching 52% in 2003. The largest drop has been in property crime. This category dropped from 30% in 1980 to 25% in 1990 and finally to 21% of total inmates in 2003.

## Jails

In the *Sourcebook of Criminal Justice Statistics 2003* (2005, http://www.albany.edu/sourcebook/), Ann L. Pastore

FIGURE 7.1

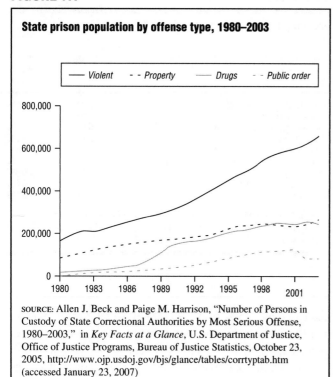

**State prison population by offense type, 1980–2003**

SOURCE: Allen J. Beck and Paige M. Harrison, "Number of Persons in Custody of State Correctional Authorities by Most Serious Offense, 1980–2003," in *Key Facts at a Glance*, U.S. Department of Justice, Office of Justice Programs, Bureau of Justice Statistics, October 23, 2005, http://www.ojp.usdoj.gov/bjs/glance/tables/corrtyptab.htm (accessed January 23, 2007)

and Kathleen Maguire of the Utilization of Criminal Justice Statistics Project note that between 1983 and 2002 the number of jail inmates increased by 184%, from 219,573 to 623,492. (See Table 7.6.) In 1983 the largest proportion of jail inmates had been convicted of property offenses (38.6%), followed by violent offenses (30.7%), public-order offenses (20.6%), and drug offenses (9.3%). The distribution of offenses had changed drastically by 2002, when approximately equal proportions of prisoners had been convicted of violent offenses (25.4%), property offenses (24.4%), drug offenses (24.7%), and public-order offenses (24.9%).

A majority (87.3%) of jail inmates were male in 2005. This figure is down slightly from 1990, when 90.8% of jail inmates were male. (See Table 7.7.) In 2005 white, non-Hispanics made up the largest proportion of jail inmates (44.3%); almost as many were African-American, non-Hispanic (38.9%), followed by Hispanic (15%) and other races (1.8%).

## EDUCATION OF PRISON AND JAIL INMATES

In *Education and Correctional Populations* (January 2003, http://www.ojp.gov/bjs/pub/pdf/ecp.pdf), Caroline Wolf Harlow of the BJS reports on the educational attainment of prison and jail inmates. Harlow summarizes the results of surveys of inmates in correctional facilities in 1991 and 1997, surveys of local jail inmates in 1989 and 1996, *Current Population Survey* data for 1997, and data from the 1992 *Adult Literacy Survey*, which was spon-

sored by the National Center of Educational Statistics. Even though the data are somewhat dated, this study is the most recent to offer a comprehensive consideration of the education of inmates.

### Educational Attainment

Harlow reports that in 1997, 11.4% of state prisoners and 23.9% of federal prisoners had "postsecondary/some college" education or were "college graduates or more." In contrast, 48.4% of the general population had postsecondary education or a college degree or higher. Prisoners with less than a high school education comprised 39.7% of the state prison population and 26.5% of the federal prison population in 1997, compared to only 18.4% of the general population.

In 1997, 33.2% of the general population had achieved a high school diploma as its highest level of education. In contrast, only 20.5% of the state prison population and 27% of the federal prison population were high school graduates. More than a fifth of the prison population had a general education diploma (GED)—28.5% in state prisons and 22.7% in federal prisons. No comparable data for the general population were available.

### Women and Men

According to Harlow, among state prison inmates in 1997, 41.8% of women and 39.6% of men had not completed high school. Almost 44% of women and 49.3% of men had a high school diploma or GED but no postsecondary education, whereas 14.3% of women and 11.1% of men had completed some college courses or were college graduates.

A slightly smaller percentage of women (50.1%) participated in educational programs offered in state prisons than men (52%).

### Education by Race and Ethnicity

Harlow indicates that a breakdown of the state prison population by race and ethnicity shows that 27.2% of whites, 44.1% of African-Americans, and 53% of Hispanics had less than a high school education in 1997—all significantly higher than the same group in the general population (18.4%). For 58% of the white prison population, a high school diploma or GED was their highest educational attainment and 14.9% had at least some college education. Among African-American prisoners, 45.8% had a high school diploma or GED as their highest educational attainment and 10% had at least some college. Among Hispanics 39.6% had a high school diploma or GED but no further education and 7.4% had at least some college education.

### Education Programs

Richard Coley and Paul Barton of the Educational Testing Service report in *Locked Up and Locked Out: An*

**TABLE 7.6**

**Jail inmates by type of offense, 1983, 1989, 1996, 2002**

| Most serious offense | Percent of jail inmates | | | | | | |
| --- | --- | --- | --- | --- | --- | --- | --- |
| | | | | 2002 | | | |
| | 1983 | 1989 | 1996 | Total | Convicted | Unconvicted | Both[a] |
| **Number of jail inmates** | 219,573 | 380,160 | 496,752 | 623,492 | 342,372 | 178,035 | 100,348 |
| Violent offenses | 30.7% | 22.5% | 26.3% | 25.4% | 21.6% | 34.4% | 22.3% |
| Murder, nonnegligent manslaughter | 4.1 | 2.8 | 2.8 | 2.0 | 0.9 | 5.3 | NA |
| Negligent manslaughter | 0.6 | 0.5 | 0.4 | 0.5 | 0.7 | 0.4 | 0.3 |
| Kidnapping | 1.3 | 0.8 | 0.5 | 0.7 | 0.4 | 1.4 | 0.6 |
| Rape | 1.5 | 0.8 | 0.5 | 0.6 | 0.6 | 0.8 | 0.4 |
| Other sexual assault | 2.0 | 2.6 | 2.7 | 2.8 | 2.7 | 3.6 | 1.5 |
| Robbery | 11.2 | 6.7 | 6.5 | 5.6 | 3.9 | 8.7 | 5.5 |
| Assault | 8.6 | 7.2 | 11.6 | 11.7 | 10.9 | 12.5 | 12.7 |
| Other violent[b] | 1.3 | 1.1 | 1.3 | 1.4 | 1.4 | 1.6 | 1.1 |
| Property offenses | 38.6 | 30.0 | 26.9 | 24.4 | 24.9 | 21.5 | 27.4 |
| Burglary | 14.3 | 10.7 | 7.6 | 6.7 | 6.4 | 6.8 | 8.0 |
| Larceny/theft | 11.7 | 7.9 | 8.0 | 7.0 | 7.6 | 5.3 | 7.6 |
| Motor vehicle theft | 2.3 | 2.8 | 2.6 | 2.0 | 2.0 | 1.6 | 2.6 |
| Arson | 0.8 | 0.7 | 0.4 | 0.3 | 0.3 | 0.5 | 0.1 |
| Fraud | 5.0 | 4.0 | 4.6 | 4.9 | 5.3 | 4.2 | 4.7 |
| Stolen property | 2.5 | 2.4 | 2.1 | 1.7 | 1.6 | 1.4 | 2.5 |
| Other property[c] | 1.9 | 1.6 | 1.6 | 1.8 | 1.8 | 1.7 | 1.9 |
| Drug offenses | 9.3 | 23.0 | 22.0 | 24.7 | 24.0 | 23.4 | 30.2 |
| Possession | 4.7 | 9.7 | 11.5 | 10.8 | 10.0 | 10.4 | 14.6 |
| Trafficking | 4.0 | 12.0 | 9.2 | 12.1 | 12.6 | 10.6 | 13.5 |
| Other drug | 0.6 | 1.3 | 1.3 | 1.8 | 1.5 | 2.3 | 2.1 |
| Public-order offenses | 20.6 | 22.8 | 24.4 | 24.9 | 29.1 | 20.2 | 19.2 |
| Weapons | 2.3 | 1.9 | 2.3 | 2.0 | 2.1 | 1.9 | 2.2 |
| Obstruction of justice | 2.0 | 2.8 | 4.9 | 3.9 | 3.5 | 5.4 | 2.7 |
| Traffic violations | 2.2 | 2.7 | 3.2 | 3.7 | 4.7 | 2.3 | 2.5 |
| Driving while intoxicated[d] | 7.0 | 8.8 | 7.4 | 6.4 | 8.9 | 2.3 | 5.1 |
| Drunkenness, morals[e] | 3.4 | 1.7 | 2.0 | 1.7 | 1.8 | 1.5 | 1.8 |
| Violation of parole, probation[f] | 2.3 | 3.0 | 2.6 | 2.9 | 3.5 | 1.5 | 3.3 |
| Immigration violations | NA | NA | 0.2 | 1.8 | 1.8 | 2.5 | 0.3 |
| Other public-order[g] | 1.6 | 1.8 | 1.8 | 2.5 | 2.8 | 2.8 | 1.2 |
| Other offenses[h] | 0.8 | 1.6 | 0.5 | 0.5 | 0.4 | 0.6 | 0.9 |

[a]Includes inmates with a prior conviction, but no new conviction for the current charge.
[b]Includes blackmail, extortion, hit-and-run driving with bodily injury, child abuse, and criminal endangerment.
[c]Includes destruction of property, vandalism, hit-and-run driving without bodily injury, trespassing, and possession of burglary tools.
[d]Includes driving while intoxicated and driving under the influence of drugs or alcohol.
[e]Includes drunkenness, vagrancy, disorderly conduct, unlawful assembly, morals, and commercialized vice.
[f]Includes parole or probation violations, escape, absence without leave (AWOL), and flight to avoid prosecution.
[g]Includes rioting, abandonment, nonsupport, invasion of privacy, liquor law violations, and tax evasion.
[h]Includes juvenile offenses and other unspecified offenses.

SOURCE: Ann L. Pastore and Kathleen Maguire, editors, "Table 6.19. Most Serious Current Offense of Jail Inmates, by Conviction Status, 1983, 1989, 1996, and 2002," in *Sourcebook of Criminal Justice Statistics 2003*, 31st ed., U.S. Department of Justice, Office of Justice Programs, Bureau of Justice Statistics, 2005, http://www.albany.edu/sourcebook/pdf/t619.pdf (accessed February 13, 2007)

*Educational Perspective on the U.S. Prison Population* (February 2006, http://www.ets.org/Media/Research/pdf/PIC-LOCKEDUP.pdf) that spending for state and federal correctional education programs subsided during the 1980s and 1990s. More recently, several states, including California, Florida, and Illinois, have cut their prison education budgets even more. Furthermore, the number of prison staff providing education has decreased, from 4.1% in 1990 to 3.2% of the total staff in 2000.

Many prisons offer educational programs to inmates, including basic adult education, secondary education, college courses, special education, vocational training, and study release programs. All federal prison inmates who lack a high school diploma or GED must participate in literacy programs for at least 240 hours or until they obtain a GED.

According to *State of the Bureau 2005* (2006, http://bop.gov/news/PDFs/sob05.pdf), the Federal Bureau of Prisons reports that 22,600 federal prisoners were enrolled in GED programs in 2005 and that 6,265 inmates earned a GED.

In addition, the Bureau of Prisons oversaw or funded 340 occupational training programs, 540 apprenticeship programs, and 150 advanced occupational training programs in 2005. Eleven thousand federal prisoners were enrolled in these educational programs during 2005. The bureau estimates that on any given day in 2005, 35% of all federal prisoners were enrolled in at least one educational program.

According to Coley and Barton, 90% of state prisons and 80% of private prisons offered some kind of educational program in 2000. Most state prisons offered adult

**TABLE 7.7**

**Jail inmates by sex, race, and type of offense, 1990–2005**

| | Percent of jail inmates | | | | | | | | | | | | | | | |
|---|---|---|---|---|---|---|---|---|---|---|---|---|---|---|---|---|
| | 1990 | 1991 | 1992 | 1993 | 1994 | 1995 | 1996[a] | 1997 | 1998 | 1999 | 2000 | 2001 | 2002 | 2003 | 2004 | 2005 |
| Total | 100% | 100% | 100% | 100% | 100% | 100% | 100% | 100% | 100% | 100% | 100% | 100% | 100% | 100% | 100% | 100% |
| **Sex** | | | | | | | | | | | | | | | | |
| Male | 90.8 | 90.7 | 90.8 | 90.4 | 90.0 | 89.8 | 89.2 | 89.4 | 89.2 | 88.8 | 88.6 | 88.4 | 88.4 | 88.1 | 87.7 | 87.3 |
| Female | 9.2 | 9.3 | 9.2 | 9.6 | 10.0 | 10.2 | 10.8 | 10.6 | 10.8 | 11.2 | 11.4 | 11.6 | 11.6 | 11.9 | 12.3 | 12.7 |
| **Race, Hispanic origin** | | | | | | | | | | | | | | | | |
| White, non-Hispanic | 41.8 | 41.1 | 40.1 | 39.3 | 39.1 | 40.1 | 41.6 | 40.6 | 41.3 | 41.3 | 41.9 | 43.0 | 43.8 | 43.6 | 44.4 | 44.3 |
| Black, non-Hispanic | 42.5 | 43.4 | 44.1 | 44.2 | 43.9 | 43.5 | 41.1 | 42.0 | 41.2 | 41.5 | 41.3 | 40.6 | 39.8 | 39.2 | 38.6 | 38.9 |
| Hispanic | 14.3 | 14.2 | 14.5 | 15.1 | 15.4 | 14.7 | 15.6 | 15.7 | 15.5 | 15.5 | 15.1 | 14.7 | 14.7 | 15.4 | 15.2 | 15.0 |
| Other[b] | 1.3 | 1.2 | 1.3 | 1.3 | 1.6 | 1.7 | 1.7 | 1.8 | 2.0 | 1.7 | 1.6 | 1.6 | 1.6 | 1.8 | 1.8 | 1.8 |
| **Conviction status[c]** | | | | | | | | | | | | | | | | |
| Convicted | 48.5 | NA | NA | NA | NA | 44.0 | NA | NA | 43.2 | 45.9 | 44.0 | 41.5 | 40.0 | 39.4 | 39.7 | 38.0 |
| Male | 44.1 | NA | NA | NA | NA | 39.7 | NA | NA | 38.4 | 40.8 | 39.0 | 36.6 | 35.4 | 34.7 | 34.8 | 33.2 |
| Female | 4.5 | NA | NA | NA | NA | 4.3 | NA | NA | 4.8 | 5.1 | 5.0 | 4.9 | 4.6 | 4.7 | 4.9 | 4.8 |
| Unconvicted | 51.5 | NA | NA | NA | NA | 56.0 | NA | NA | 56.8 | 54.1 | 56.0 | 58.5 | 59.9 | 60.6 | 60.3 | 62.0 |
| Male | 46.7 | NA | NA | NA | NA | 50.0 | NA | NA | 50.6 | 48.0 | 50.0 | 51.9 | 53.0 | 53.5 | 53.0 | 54.2 |
| Female | 4.8 | NA | NA | NA | NA | 6.0 | NA | NA | 6.1 | 6.1 | 6.0 | 6.6 | 6.9 | 7.1 | 7.3 | 7.7 |

Note: Percents may not add to total because of rounding.
[a]Based on all persons under jail supervision; not limited to inmates confined in jail facilities.
[b]Includes Asians, American Indians, Alaska Natives, Native Hawaiians, and other Pacific Islanders. Beginning in 2005, category also includes persons reporting two or more races.
[c]Data for conviction status include adults only with the exception of 1999, which includes adults and juveniles.

SOURCE: Ann L. Pastore and Kathleen Maguire, editors, "Table 6.17. Jail Inmates, by Sex, Race, Hispanic Origin, and Conviction Status, United States, 1990–2005," in *Sourcebook of Criminal Justice Statistics 2003*, 31st ed., U.S. Department of Justice, Office of Justice Programs, Bureau of Justice Statistics, 2005, http://www.albany.edu/sourcebook/pdf/t6172005.pdf (accessed February 13, 2007)

basic education (80%) and adult secondary education (83%). They also offered vocational training (55%), special education (39%), and college courses (26%).

However, federal support for state prison education programs has dropped in recent years. Before 1998 the federal government required states to spend at least 10% of their basic state grant for adult education in state institutions, including prisons. The law has changed to require states to spend no more than 10%. As part of the "get tough on crime" movement, inmates are no longer eligible for Pell grants to support the costs of postsecondary education.

Coley and Barton report that, according to several studies, inmates who participate in education are less likely to commit crimes after they are released than other prisoners. Several studies also show that when prisoners participate in vocational or college education programs, they are more likely to get a job after they are released and less likely to have disciplinary problems.

## PRISONERS WITH CHILDREN

Jeremy Travis, Elizabeth Cincotta McBride, and Amy L. Solomon of the Urban Institute report in *Families Left Behind: The Hidden Costs of Incarceration and Reentry* (June 2005, http://www.urban.org/UploadedPDF/310882_families _left_behind.pdf) that over 1.4 million state and federal pris-

oners are parents of children younger than eighteen. Most incarcerated parents are male (93%) and 89% are in state prisons. Some 65% of women, who make up 6% of the state prison population, have minor children. More than half (58%) of the minor children of parents in prison are younger than ten years.

In many cases parents are incarcerated far away from their children. According to Travis, McBride, and Solomon, female prisoners are in facilities that are, on average, 160 miles away from their children, and men are 100 miles away. These distances make it difficult for family members to visit inmates. More than half of all incarcerated parents say that they never receive a personal visit from their children. However, almost 60% of mothers and 40% of fathers have weekly telephone or mail contact with their children while in prison, in spite of the limits on calls and letters set by prisons and the high cost of collect phone calls.

Travis, McBride, and Solomon note that most parents of young children are in prison for having committed violent offenses (46% of fathers and 26% of mothers) or drug offenses (23% of fathers and 35% of mothers). Parents are sentenced to state prison for an average term of eighty months for their current offense. Over three-quarters of parents who are incarcerated in state prison have been convicted previously and more than half have been in prison before.

## MENTAL HEALTH PROBLEMS

A movement began in the 1970s to deinstitutionalize the mentally ill and reintegrate them into society. This widespread trend resulted in the closing of many large-scale mental hospitals and treatment centers. With fewer options open to them, the mentally ill came into contact with law enforcement authorities more often. Holly Hills, Christine Siegfried, and Alan Ickowitz, in *Effective Prison Mental Health Services: Guidelines to Expand and Improve Treatment* (May 2004, http://www.nicic .org/pubs/2004/018604.pdf), state: "Since the early 1990s, an increasing number of adults with mental illness have become involved with the criminal justice system. State and federal prisons, in particular, have undergone a dramatic transformation, housing a growing number of inmates with serious mental disorders. Complicating this situation is the high proportion of mentally ill inmates who have co-occurring substance use disorders."

According to the National Institute of Mental Health (January 22, 2007, http://www.nimh.nih.gov/healthinfor mation/statisticsmenu.cfm), 26.2% of Americans aged eighteen and older have a diagnosable mental disorder. The prevalence of mental illness in the state prison population is higher than that of the general population.

In *Mental Health Problems of Prison and Jail Inmates* (September 2006, http://www.ojp.usdoj.gov/bjs/ pub/pdf/mhppji.pdf), Doris J. James and Lauren E. Glaze of the BJS report that more than half of all prison and jail inmates had a mental health problem at midyear 2005. Specifically, 705,600 inmates in state prisons (56% of all state prison inmates), 78,800 in federal prisons (45% of all federal prison inmates), and 479,900 in local jails (64% of all local jail inmates) reported symptoms of a mental health problem. Forty-three percent of state prisoners and 54% of jail inmates reported symptoms of mania, 23% of state prisoners and 30% of jail inmates reported symptoms of major depression, and 15% of state prisoners and 24% of jail inmates reported symptoms of a psychotic disorder.

### Differences by Gender

James and Glaze indicate that female inmates have much higher rates of mental health problems than male inmates. In midyear 2005, 73% of female state prison inmates had a mental health problem, compared to 55% of male inmates. Similarly, 61% of female federal inmates reported a mental health problem, compared to 44% of males, and 75% of female jail inmates had a mental health problem, compared to 63% of male inmates.

### History of Homelessness and Foster Care

State prison and local jail inmates who reported a mental health problem were more likely than other inmates to have been homeless in the year before they entered prison or jail. Specifically, 13.2% of state prisoners and 17.2% of jail inmates had both a mental health problem and a recent experience of homelessness, compared to 6.3% of state prisoners and 8.8% of jail inmates who did not have a mental health problem but said they had been homeless in the year before they were incarcerated. (See Table 7.8.) Some 18.5% of state prisoners who had a mental health problem had lived in a foster home, agency, or institution while growing up, compared to 9.5% of state prisoners who did not report a mental health problem. Similarly, 14.5% of jail inmates who had a mental health problem had lived in a foster home, agency, or institution, compared to 6% of inmates who did not have a mental health problem.

## HIV/AIDS

According to Laura M. Maruschak of the BJS, in *HIV in Prisons, 2004* (November 2006, http://www.ojp.us doj.gov/bjs/pub/pdf/hivp04.pdf), the number of inmates who were diagnosed with the human immunodeficiency virus (HIV) in federal and state prisons reached a record high of 25,807 in 1999. (See Table 7.9.) Since then, the numbers have been declining. In 2004, 23,046 prisoners were HIV positive. Nearly half of the HIV-positive prisoners were located in three states: New York (4,500), Florida (3,250), and Texas (2,405). A larger percentage of female prisoners were HIV positive (2.6%) than were male prisoners (1.8%). Concerning prison inmates who were diagnosed with the acquired immunodeficiency syndrome (AIDS), the rate was 0.5%, compared to the rate for the general U.S. population, 0.2%.

In 2004 there were 203 prisoner deaths (185 state inmates and 18 federal inmates) that were AIDS related. The number of AIDS-related deaths in state prisons has declined 82% between 1995 and 2004. (See Table 7.10.) In every year since 1991 the rate of confirmed AIDS cases has been higher among prison inmates than the general population. At the end of 2004 the rate of confirmed AIDS cases in state and federal prisons (about 50 per 10,000 inmates) was more than three times higher than in the total U.S. population (15 per 10,000 people).

## DRUG USE

In *Drug Use and Dependence, State and Federal Prisoners, 2004* (October 2006, http://www.ojp.usdoj .gov/bjs/pub/pdf/dudsfp04.pdf), Christopher J. Mumola and Jennifer C. Karberg of the BJS note that in 2004, 56% of all state prisoners reported drug use in the month before the offense. This percentage changed little from 1997, when 57% of state prisoners reported previous drug use. A slightly lower percentage of federal prison inmates, 50%, reported drug use in the month before their offense in 2004, compared to 45% in 1997.

TABLE 7.8

**Homelessness, employment status, and family background of prison and jail inmates, by mental health status, midyear 2005**

| | Percent of inmates in— | | | | | |
| | State prison | | Federal prison | | Local jail | |
| Characteristic | With mental problem | Without | With mental problem | Without | With mental problem | Without |
|---|---|---|---|---|---|---|
| Homelessness in past year | 13.2% | 6.3% | 6.6% | 2.6% | 17.2% | 8.8% |
| Employed in month before arrest[a] | 70.1% | 75.6% | 67.7% | 76.2% | 68.7% | 75.9% |
| **Ever physically or sexually abused before admission** | 27.0% | 10.5% | 17.0% | 6.4% | 24.2% | 7.6% |
| Physically abused | 22.4 | 8.3 | 13.7 | 5.4 | 20.4 | 5.7 |
| Sexually abused | 12.5 | 3.8 | 7.3 | 1.7 | 10.2 | 3.2 |
| **While growing up—** | | | | | | |
| Ever received public assistance[b] | 42.5% | 30.6% | 33.3% | 24.9% | 42.6% | 30.3% |
| Ever lived in foster home, agency or institution | 18.5 | 9.5 | 9.8 | 6.3 | 14.5 | 6.0 |
| **Lived most of the time with—** | | | | | | |
| Both parents | 41.9% | 47.7% | 45.4% | 50.5% | 40.5% | 49.1% |
| One parent | 43.8 | 40.8 | 39.8 | 38.8 | 45.4 | 40.4 |
| Someone else | 11.6 | 10.2 | 13.5 | 10.3 | 12.0 | 9.4 |
| **Parents or guardians ever abused—** | 39.3 | 25.1 | 33.3 | 20.0 | 37.3 | 18.7 |
| Alcohol | 23.6 | 16.9 | 21.7 | 15.4 | 23.2 | 14.1 |
| Drugs | 3.1 | 1.9 | 2.2 | 1.4 | 2.7 | 1.1 |
| Both alcohol and drugs | 12.7 | 6.2 | 9.4 | 3.2 | 11.5 | 3.4 |
| Neither | 60.7 | 74.9 | 66.7 | 80.0 | 62.7 | 81.3 |
| **Family member ever incarcerated—** | 51.7% | 41.3% | 44.6% | 38.9% | 52.1% | 36.2% |
| Mother | 7.2 | 4.0 | 5.0 | 3.2 | 9.4 | 3.4 |
| Father | 20.1 | 13.4 | 15.3 | 9.9 | 22.1 | 12.6 |
| Brother | 35.5 | 29.4 | 29.4 | 27.0 | 34.8 | 25.8 |
| Sister | 7.0 | 5.1 | 5.5 | 4.2 | 11.3 | 5.1 |
| Child | 2.7 | 2.3 | 3.4 | 2.8 | 4.0 | 2.6 |
| Spouse | 1.7 | 0.9 | 2.6 | 1.8 | 2.4 | 0.9 |

[a]The reference period for jail inmates was in the month before admission.
[b]Public assistance includes public housing, Aid to Families with Dependent Children, food stamps, Medicaid, Women, Infants and Children, and other welfare programs.

SOURCE: Doris J. James and Lauren E. Glaze, "Table 4. Homelessness, Employment before Arrest, and Family Background of Prison and Jail Inmates, by Mental Health Status," in *Mental Health Problems of Prison and Jail Inmates*, U.S. Department of Justice, Office of Justice Programs, Bureau of Justice Statistics, September 2006, http://www.ojp.usdoj.gov/bjs/pub/pdf/mhppji.pdf (accessed January 23, 2007)

One-third (83.2%) of state prison inmates in 2004 said that they had committed their current offense while under the influence of drugs. (See Table 7.11.) The most common drug used by state prisoners is marijuana; 77.6% of state prisoners in 2004 reported they had used marijuana at some time in their lives. The percentage of prisoners who said they used cocaine or crack cocaine in the month before their offense declined from 25% in 1997 to 21.4% in 2004. During this period the use of heroin and other opiates in the month preceding the offense dropped slightly from 9.2% in 1997 to 8.2% in 2004, whereas the use of hallucinogens rose slightly from 4% to 5.9%.

According to Mumola and Karberg, 26% of federal prison inmates reported using drugs at the time of their offense in 2004, an increase from 22% in 1997. Between 1997 and 2004 marijuana use increased from 30.4% to 36.2%. However, the percentage of federal prisoners who reported using cocaine or crack cocaine in the month before their offense fell from 20% to 18%, and use at the time of the offense dropped from 9.3% to 7.4%.

Pastore and Maguire report that in 2002, 82.2% of jail inmates reported using drugs at some point in their lives. (See Table 7.12.) This percentage changed only slightly from 1996, when 82.4% reported previous drug use. The most commonly used drug was marijuana, which 75.7% reported using in 2002. Almost half (48.1%) reported using cocaine or crack cocaine in 2002; this percentage dropped slightly from 1996, when 50.4% reported using cocaine-based products.

## MEDICAL PROBLEMS IN JAIL INMATES

In *Medical Problems of Jail Inmates* (November 2006, http://www.ojp.usdoj.gov/bjs/pub/pdf/mpji.pdf), Laura M. Maruschak of the BJS indicates that an estimated 229,000 jail inmates said that they had a current medical problem other than a cold or virus in 2002. The medical problems they reported included arthritis (12.9%), hypertension (11.2%), asthma (9.9%), and heart problems (5.9%). (See Table 7.13.) Female inmates were more likely (53%) to report a medical problem than male

TABLE 7.9

**Number of HIV-positive prison inmates, 1998–2004 and jurisdictions with the largest HIV-positive populations, 2004**

| | HIV-positive prison inmates | |
|---|---|---|
| Year end | Number | Percent of custody population |
| 1998 | 25,680 | 2.2% |
| 1999 | 25,807 | 2.1 |
| 2000 | 25,333 | 2.0 |
| 2001 | 24,147 | 1.9 |
| 2002 | 23,866 | 1.9 |
| 2003 | 23,663 | 1.9 |
| 2004 | 23,046 | 1.8 |
| **Jurisdictions with largest HIV-positive population** | | |
| New York | 4,500 | 7.0% |
| Florida | 3,250 | 3.9 |
| Texas | 2,405 | 1.7 |
| Federal system | 1,680 | 1.1 |
| California | 1,212 | 0.7 |
| Georgia | 1,109 | 2.2 |

SOURCE: Laura M. Maruschak, "Highlights: Number of HIV-Infected Inmates Steadily Decreasing since 1999," in *HIV in Prisons, 2004*, U.S. Department of Justice, Bureau of Justice Statistics, November 2006, http://www.ojp.usdoj.gov/bjs/pub/pdf/hivp04.pdf (accessed January 23, 2007)

**TABLE 7.10**

**Number of AIDS-related deaths in state prisons, 1995–2004**

| | AIDS-related deaths in state prisons | | |
|---|---|---|---|
| | Number | | Rate per 100,000 inmates |
| Year | Reported in NPS-1 | Total* | |
| 1995 | 1,010 | | 100 |
| 1996 | 907 | | 90 |
| 1997 | 538 | | 48 |
| 1998 | 350 | | 30 |
| 1999 | 242 | | 20 |
| 2000 | 185 | | 15 |
| 2001 | 256 | 311 | 25 |
| 2002 | 215 | 283 | 22 |
| 2003 | 213 | 268 | 21 |
| 2004 | 128 | 185 | 14 |

*Total number of deaths for 2001–04 are based on a combination of the National Prisoners Statistics (NPS-1) and Deaths in Custody Reporting Program (DCRP) data.

SOURCE: Laura M. Maruschak, "Highlights: Rate of AIDS-Related Deaths in State Prisons Decreased in 2004," in *HIV in Prisons, 2004*, U.S. Department of Justice, Office of Justice Programs, Bureau of Justice Statistics, November 2006, http://www.ojp.usdoj.gov/bjs/pub/pdf/hivp04.pdf (accessed January 23, 2007)

inmates (35%). A majority (60.5%) of those over age forty-five reported a medical problem, compared to a quarter (25%) of those aged twenty-four or younger.

Maruschak notes that in 2002 an estimated 82,900 jail inmates (13.4%) reported that they had been injured since their admission to jail. About 7.4% said that they had been injured in an accident, and 7% said they had been injured in a fight. (See Table 7.14.) A higher percentage of men (13.8%) than women (10.1%) reported

being injured while in jail. About 7.4% of males and 4.1% of females said they had been injured in a fight. Those aged twenty-four or younger (17.4%) were more than twice as likely to have been injured since entering jail than those aged forty-five or older (7.8%). They were also much more likely to report being in a fight (10.6% versus 2.5% for those forty-five or older).

## CONVICTION STATUS

Convicted inmates include those awaiting sentencing, serving a sentence, or returned to jail for a violation of probation or parole. In *Prison and Jail Inmates at Midyear 2005*, Harrison and Beck explain that jails hold people who have not been convicted of a crime, including:

- People who are waiting for arraignment (brought before the court to hear the charges against them and to plead guilty or not guilty), conviction, or sentencing.

- People who have violated probation, parole, or bail bonds.

- Juveniles who are to be transferred to juvenile authorities.

- Mentally ill people before they are moved to appropriate mental health facilities.

- People held for the military, for protective custody, for contempt, and for the courts as witnesses.

Table 7.4 indicates that less than half (38%) of all adults under supervision by jail authorities had been convicted of current charges in 2005. This figure is down from 44% in 1995. Convicted female inmates comprised 4.8% of the inmate population in 2005, up from 4.3% in 1995. The percentage of adult male jail inmates who have been convicted of a current offense has dropped in recent years, from 39.7% in 1995 to 33.2% in 2005.

## CONFINEMENT STATUS

Harrison and Beck note in *Prison and Jail Inmates at Midyear 2005* that jails sometimes operate community-based programs as alternatives to incarceration. Of the 819,434 people supervised by jails in 2005, 747,529 were held in jails and the remaining 71,905 were supervised outside a jail facility. (See Table 6.3 in Chapter 6.) The highest number, 15,536, were sentenced to perform community service. Another 15,458 were supervised while awaiting trial, and 14,110 were participating in weekend reporting programs.

## PRISONERS' RIGHTS UNDER THE LAW

In 1871 a Virginia court, in *Ruffin v. Commonwealth* (62 Va. 790, 1871), commented that a prisoner "has, as a consequence of his crime, not only forfeited his liberty,

**TABLE 7.11**

**Drugs used by state prisoners, 1997 and 2004**

| | Percent of state prisoners who used drugs— | | | | | | | |
|---|---|---|---|---|---|---|---|---|
| | Ever | | Regularly[a] | | In the month before offense | | At the time of offense | |
| Type of drug | 2004 | 1997 | 2004 | 1997 | 2004 | 1997 | 2004 | 1997 |
| Any drug[b] | 83.2% | 83.0% | 69.2% | 69.6% | 56.0% | 56.5% | 32.1% | 32.6% |
| Marijuana/hashish | 77.6 | 77.0 | 59.0 | 58.3 | 40.3 | 39.2 | 15.4 | 15.1 |
| Cocaine/crack | 46.8 | 49.2 | 30.0 | 33.6 | 21.4 | 25.0 | 11.8 | 14.8 |
| Heroin/opiates | 23.4 | 24.5 | 13.1 | 15.0 | 8.2 | 9.2 | 4.4 | 5.6 |
| Depressants[c] | 21.3 | 23.7 | 9.9 | 11.3 | 5.4 | 5.1 | 2.0 | 1.8 |
| Stimulants[d] | 28.6 | 28.3 | 17.9 | 16.3 | 12.2 | 9.0 | 6.7 | 4.2 |
| Methamphetamine | 23.5 | 19.4 | 14.9 | 11.2 | 10.8 | 6.9 | 6.1 | 3.5 |
| Hallucinogens[e] | 32.9 | 28.7 | 13.3 | 11.3 | 5.9 | 4.0 | 2.0 | 1.8 |
| Inhalants | 13.6 | 14.4 | 4.5 | 5.4 | 1.0 | 1.0 | — | — |

Note: Detail adds to more than total because prisoners may have used more type of drug.
— Not reported.
[a]Used drugs at least once a week for at least a month.
[b]Other unspecified drugs are included in the totals.
[c]Includes barbiturates, tranquilizers, and quaalude.
[d]Includes amphetamine and methamphetamine.
[e]Includes LSD, PCP, and ecstasy.

SOURCE: Christopher J. Mumola and Jennifer C. Karberg, "Table 1. Drug Use by State Prisoners, 1997 and 2004," in *Drug Use and Dependence, State and Federal Prisoners, 2004*, U.S. Department of Justice, Office of Justice Programs, Bureau of Justice Statistics, October 2006, http://www.ojp.usdoj.gov/bjs/pub/pdf/dudsfp04.pdf (accessed February 13, 2007)

**TABLE 7.12**

**Drugs used by jail inmates, 1996 and 2002**

| | All inmates | | | | Convicted inmates[a] | | | |
|---|---|---|---|---|---|---|---|---|
| | Ever used drugs | | Ever used drugs regularly[b] | | Used drugs in the month before the offense | | Used drugs at the time of the offense | |
| Type of drug | 1996 | 2002 | 1996 | 2002 | 1996 | 2002 | 1996 | 2002 |
| Any drug | 82.4% | 82.2% | 64.2% | 68.7% | 54.0% | 52.6% | 34.9% | 28.8% |
| Marijuana or hashish | 78.2 | 75.7 | 54.9 | 57.6 | 36.0 | 37.5 | 18.0 | 13.6 |
| Cocaine or crack | 50.4 | 48.1 | 31.0 | 30.5 | 22.8 | 20.7 | 14.3 | 10.6 |
| Heroin or opiates | 23.9 | 20.7 | 11.8 | 11.9 | 7.9 | 7.8 | 5.1 | 4.1 |
| Depressants[c] | 29.9 | 21.6 | 10.4 | 10.6 | 5.3 | 6.1 | 2.2 | 2.4 |
| Stimulants[d] | 33.6 | 27.8 | 16.5 | 16.8 | 9.6 | 11.4 | 5.6 | 5.2 |
| Hallucinogens[e] | 32.2 | 32.4 | 10.5 | 13.2 | 4.2 | 5.9 | 1.4 | 1.6 |
| Inhalants | 16.8 | 12.7 | 4.8 | 4.1 | 0.9 | 1.0 | 0.3 | 0.2 |

[a]Includes all inmates with a current conviction or with a prior conviction, but no new conviction for the current charge.
[b]Used drugs at least once a week for at least a month.
[c]Includes barbiturates, tranquilizers, and quaaludes.
[d]Includes amphetamines and methamphetamine.
[e]Includes LSD, ecstasy, and PCP.

SOURCE: Ann L. Pastore and Kathleen Maguire, editors, "Table 6.21. Percent of Jail Inmates Reporting Drug Use, by Type of Drug and Frequency of Use, United States, 1996 and 2002," in *Sourcebook of Criminal Justice Statistics 2003*, 31st ed., U.S. Department of Justice, Office of Justice Programs, Bureau of Justice Statistics, 2005, http://www.albany.edu/sourcebook/pdf/t621.pdf (accessed February 14, 2007)

but all his personal rights except those which the law in its humanity accords to him. He is for the time being the slave of the state." Eighty years later, in *Stroud v. Swope* (187 F. 2d. 850, 1951), the Ninth Circuit Court asserted that "it is well settled that it is not the function of the courts to superintend the treatment and discipline of prisoners in penitentiaries, but only to deliver from imprisonment those who are illegally confined." The American Correctional Association, in *Legal Responsi-*

*bility and Authority of Correctional Officers* (1987), explains that correctional administrators held that prisoners lost all their constitutional rights after conviction. Prisoners had privileges, not rights, and privileges could be taken away arbitrarily.

A significant change in this legal view came in the 1960s. In *Cooper v. Pate* (378 U.S. 546, 1964), the U.S. Supreme Court held that the Civil Rights Act of 1871

TABLE 7.13

**Jail inmates reporting specific current medical problems, by gender and age, 2002**

| Current medical problem | All inmates | Gender | | Age | | | |
|---|---|---|---|---|---|---|---|
| | | Male | Female | 24 or younger | 25–34 | 35–44 | 45 or older |
| Arthritis | 12.9% | 12.0% | 19.4% | 5.3% | 9.4% | 16.6% | 32.5% |
| Asthma | 9.9 | 8.7 | 19.4 | 10.9 | 10.8 | 8.9 | 7.3 |
| Cancer | 0.7 | 0.5 | 2.5 | 0.2 | 0.7 | 0.6 | 2.2 |
| Diabetes | 2.7 | 2.5 | 4.1 | 0.6 | 2.3 | 2.9 | 8.4 |
| Heart problem | 5.9 | 5.5 | 9.2 | 4.4 | 4.6 | 6.4 | 11.7 |
| Hypertension | 11.2 | 10.8 | 14.1 | 5.3 | 8.5 | 14.3 | 26.1 |
| Kidney problems | 3.7 | 3.0 | 8.9 | 2.3 | 4.0 | 4.4 | 4.8 |
| Liver problems | 0.9 | 0.8 | 1.6 | 0.1 | 0.4 | 1.3 | 3.4 |
| Paralysis | 1.3 | 1.3 | 1.3 | 0.3 | 1.3 | 1.7 | 3.1 |
| Stroke | 3.2 | 3.2 | 3.3 | 1.3 | 2.9 | 4.9 | 4.8 |
| Hepatitis | 2.6 | 2.3 | 5.0 | 0.4 | 1.4 | 4.6 | 7.2 |
| HIV | 1.3 | 1.2 | 2.3 | 0.2 | 1.1 | 2.1 | 2.7 |
| Sexually transmitted disease | 0.9 | 0.8 | 2.0 | 0.7 | 0.7 | 1.0 | 1.7 |
| Tuberculosis (TB)* | 4.3 | 4.3 | 4.0 | 2.2 | 3.8 | 5.3 | 8.6 |

*Includes all inmates who reported ever having TB.

SOURCE: Laura M. Maruschak, "Table 2. Percent of Jail Inmates Reporting Specific Current Medical Problems, by Gender and Age, 2002," in *Medical Problems of Jail Inmates*, U.S. Department of Justice, Office of Justice Programs, Bureau of Justice Statistics, November 2006, http://www.ojp.usdoj.gov/bjs/pub/pdf/mpji.pdf (accessed January 23, 2007)

TABLE 7.14

**Injuries reported by jail inmates, by conviction status, gender, and age, 2002**

| Characteristics | Percent of inmates who reported an injury since admission | | |
|---|---|---|---|
| | Total | In an accident | In a fight |
| Total | 13.4% | 7.4% | 7.0% |
| **Conviction status** | | | |
| Convicted | 12.6% | 7.9% | 5.9% |
| Unconvicted | 15.6 | 7.5 | 8.8 |
| Both | 12.1 | 5.5 | 7.7 |
| **Gender** | | | |
| Male | 13.8% | 7.5% | 7.4% |
| Female | 10.1 | 6.7 | 4.1 |
| **Age** | | | |
| 24 or younger | 17.4% | 8.2% | 10.6% |
| 25–34 | 13.6 | 7.5 | 7.2 |
| 35–44 | 11.2 | 7.1 | 4.8 |
| 45 or older | 7.8 | 5.8 | 2.5 |

SOURCE: Laura M. Maruschak, "Table 6. Percent of Jail Inmates Who Reported an Injury since Admission, by Conviction Status, Gender and Age, 2002," in *Medical Problems of Jail Inmates*, U.S. Department of Justice, Office of Justice Programs, Bureau of Justice Statistics, November 2006, http://www.ojp.usdoj.gov/bjs/pub/pdf/mpji.pdf (accessed January 23, 2007)

granted protection to prisoners. The code states that "every person who, under color of any statute, ordinance, regulation, custom, or usage, of any State or Territory or the District of Columbia, subjects, or causes to be subjected, any citizen of the United States or other person within the jurisdiction thereof to the deprivation of any rights, privileges, or immunities secured by the Constitution and laws, shall be liable to the party injured in an action at law, suit in equity, or other proper proceeding for redress."

With the *Cooper* decision, the Court announced that prisoners had rights guaranteed by the Constitution and could ask the judicial system for help in challenging the conditions of their imprisonment.

## PRODUCE THE BODY

In *Cooper v. Pate*, the Supreme Court relied on civil rights. Another source of prisoners' rights arose from the Court's reliance on habeas corpus. This Latin phrase means "Have the body …" with the rest of the phrase, "brought before me," implied. A writ of habeas corpus is therefore the command issued by one court to another court (or lesser authority) to produce a person and to explain why that person is being detained. Habeas corpus dates back to an act of the British Parliament passed in 1679. Congress enacted the Judiciary Act of 1789 and gave federal prisoners the right to habeas corpus review. The Habeas Act of 1867 later protected the rights of newly freed slaves and extended habeas corpus protection to state prisoners. The effective meaning of habeas corpus for prisoners is that it enables them to petition federal courts to review any aspect of their cases.

After the Military Commissions Act of 2006, which authorized military trials of enemy combatants, was signed by President George W. Bush, the administration announced that the U.S. District Court in Washington, D.C., no longer had the authority to consider the habeas corpus petitions filed by prison inmates in Guantánamo Bay in Cuba. Karen DeYoung reports in "Court Told It

Lacks Power in Detainee Cases" (*Washington Post*, October 20, 2006) that the Justice Department posted a notice that "listed 196 pending habeas cases, some of which cover groups of detainees. The new Military Commissions Act ... it said, provides that 'no court, justice, or judge' can consider those petitions or other actions related to treatment or imprisonment filed by anyone designated as an enemy combatant, now or in the future." Besides those already imprisoned at Guantánamo Bay or elsewhere, the law applies to all non-U.S. citizens, including permanent U.S. residents.

## FIRST AMENDMENT CASES

The First Amendment of the Constitution guarantees that "Congress shall make no law respecting an establishment of religion, or prohibiting the free exercise thereof; or abridging the freedom of speech, or of the press; or the right of the people peaceably to assemble, and to petition the government for a redress of grievances."

### Censorship

In *Procunier v. Martinez* (416 U.S. 396, 1973), the Supreme Court ruled that prison officials cannot censor inmate correspondence unless they "show that a regulation authorizing mail censorship furthers one or more of the substantial governmental interests of security, order, and rehabilitation. Second, the limitation of First Amendment freedoms must be no greater than is necessary or essential to the protection of the particular governmental interest involved."

Prison officials may refuse to send letters that detail escape plans or encoded messages but may not censor inmate correspondence simply to "eliminate unflattering or unwelcome opinions or factually inaccurate statements." Because prisoners retain rights "when a prison regulation or practice offends a fundamental constitutional guarantee, federal courts will discharge their duty to protect constitutional rights."

However, the Court recognized that it was "ill equipped to deal with the increasingly urgent problems of prison administration and reform." Running a prison takes expertise and planning, all of which, the Court explained, is part of the responsibility of the legislative and executive branches. The task of the judiciary branch is to establish a standard of review for prisoners' constitutional claims that is responsive to both the need to protect inmates' rights and the policy of judicial restraint.

In *Pell v. Procunier* (417 U.S. 817, 1974), the Court ruled that federal prison officials could prohibit inmates from having face-to-face media interviews. The Court reasoned that judgments regarding prison security "are peculiarly within the province and professional expertise of corrections officials, and, in the absence of substantial evidence in the record to indicate that the officials have exaggerated their response to these considerations, courts should ordinarily defer to their expert judgment in such matters."

In *Nolan v. Fitzpatrick* (451 F. 2d 545, 1985), the First Circuit Court ruled that inmates had the right to correspond with newspapers. The prisoners were limited only in that they could not write about escape plans or include contraband material in their letters.

The Missouri Division of Corrections permitted correspondence between immediate family members who were inmates at different institutions and between inmates writing about legal matters, and allowed other inmate correspondence only if each prisoner's "classification/treatment team" thought it was in the best interests of the parties. Another Missouri regulation permitted an inmate to marry only with the superintendent's permission, which can be given only when there were "compelling reasons" to do so, such as a pregnancy. In *Turner v. Safley* (482 U.S. 78, 1987), the Supreme Court found the first regulation constitutional and the second one unconstitutional.

The Court held that the "constitutional right of prisoners to marry is impermissibly burdened by the Missouri marriage regulation." The Supreme Court had ruled earlier in *Zablocki v. Redhail* (434 U.S. 374, 1978) that prisoners had a constitutionally protected right to marry, subject to restrictions because of incarceration such as time and place and prior approval of a warden. However, the Missouri regulation practically banned all marriages.

The findings in *Turner v. Safley* have become a guide for prison regulations in the United States. In its decision, the Court observed that:

> When a prison regulation impinges on inmates' constitutional rights, the regulation is valid if it is reasonably related to legitimate penological interests.... First, there must be a "valid, rational connection" between the prison regulation and the legitimate governmental interest put forward to justify it.... Moreover, the governmental objective must be a legitimate and neutral one.... A second factor relevant in determining the reasonableness of a prison restriction...is whether there are alternative means of exercising the right that remain open to prison inmates.... A third consideration is the impact accommodation of the asserted constitutional right will have on guards and other inmates, and on the allocation of prison resources generally.

### Religious Beliefs

Even though inmates retain their First Amendment right to practice their religion, the courts have upheld restrictions on religious freedom when corrections departments need to maintain security, when economic considerations are involved, and when the regulation is reasonable.

In September 2000 the Religious Land Use and Institutionalized Persons Act was signed into law by President Bill Clinton. The act limits the ability of local governments to use zoning laws against religious institutions. Section 3 of the law requires that prison officials accommodate inmates' religious needs in certain cases, even if this means exempting the inmates from general prison rules. The state of Ohio challenged the act's constitutionality and argued that it violates the First Amendment's prohibition on the establishment of religion. Because the law does not require prison officials to accommodate inmates' secular needs or desires in similar ways, Ohio claimed the statute impermissibly advances religion. The state also argued that the law creates incentives for prisoners to feign religious belief to gain privileges. The Supreme Court upheld the constitutionality of the act in *Cutter v. Wilkinson* (544 U.S. 709, 2005), reversing a ruling by the Sixth Circuit Court of Appeals, which had agreed with the Ohio decision.

## FOURTH AMENDMENT

The Fourth Amendment guarantees the "right of the people to be secure . . . against unreasonable searches and seizures . . . and no warrants shall issue, but upon probable cause." The courts have not been as active in protecting prisoners under the Fourth Amendment as under the First and Eighth amendments. In *Bell v. Wolfish* (441 U.S. 520, 1979), the Supreme Court asserted that:

> simply because prison inmates retain certain constitutional rights does not mean that these rights are not subject to restrictions and limitations. . . . Maintaining institutional security and preserving internal order and discipline are essential goals that may require limitation or retraction of the retained constitutional rights of both convicted prisoners and pretrial detainees. Since problems that arise in the day-to-day operation of a corrections facility are not susceptible of easy solutions, prison administrators should be accorded wide-ranging deference in the adoption and execution of policies and practices that in their judgment are needed to preserve internal order and discipline and to maintain institutional security.

Based on this reasoning, the Court ruled that body searches did not violate the Fourth Amendment. "Balancing the significant and legitimate security interests of the institution against the inmates' privacy interests, such searches can be conducted on less than probable cause and are not unreasonable."

In another Fourth Amendment case, *Hudson v. Palmer* (468 U.S. 517, 1984), the Supreme Court upheld the right of prison officials to search a prisoner's cell and seize property:

> The recognition of privacy rights for prisoners in their individual cells simply cannot be reconciled with the concept of incarceration and the needs and objectives of penal institutions. . . . [However, the fact that a prisoner does not have a reasonable expectation of privacy] does not mean that he is without a remedy for calculated harassment unrelated to prison needs. Nor does it mean that prison attendants can ride roughshod over inmates' property rights with impunity. The Eighth Amendment always stands as a protection against "cruel and unusual punishments."

## Sexual Misconduct

Sexual misconduct by corrections personnel refers to any type of improper conduct of a sexual nature directed at prisoners. Given the control and power imbalance inherent between a corrections officer and a prison inmate, there is widespread consensus within society that this sort of misconduct should not be tolerated.

According to the National Institute of Corrections, all fifty states had custodial misconduct laws as of June 2006. (See Figure 7.2.) Most states defined sexual misconduct of inmates as a felony, four defined it as a misdemeanor, and five defined it as either a felony or misdemeanor, depending on the nature and severity of the assault.

In response to continuing concerns about sexual misconduct in prisons, President Bush signed into law the Prison Rape Elimination Act in September 2003. As part of this legislation, the BJS is charged with developing a national data collection on the incidence and prevalence of sexual assault within correctional facilities. Few studies have been conducted on the subject, and most of those focused on only a limited number of prisons and prisoners.

The legislation required the BJS to collect national data on sexual violence in correctional facilities. *Sexual Violence Reported by Correctional Authorities, 2005* (July 2006, http://ovc.gov/bjs/pub/pdf/svrca05.pdf) by BJS researchers Beck and Harrison is part of the bureau's response to the legislation. This report summarizes the results of the first-ever national survey of administrative records on sexual violence in adult and juvenile correctional facilities. According to Beck and Harrison, in 2005 there were 6,241 reported allegations of sexual violence in prisons and jails, up from 5,386 in 2004. Of these allegations, 1,829 involved staff sexual misconduct, 1,443 were for nonconsensual sexual acts between inmates, 914 were for staff sexual harassment, and 423 involved abusive sexual contact between inmates. (See Table 7.15.) In 2005, 885 of these incidents of sexual violence were substantiated by correctional authorities.

## EIGHTH AMENDMENT

The Eighth Amendment guarantees that "cruel and unusual punishment [not be] inflicted." The Eighth Amendment has been used to challenge the death penalty, three-strikes laws, crowded prisons, lack of health or

**FIGURE 7.2**

**States with criminal laws prohibiting sexual abuse of people in custody, 2006**

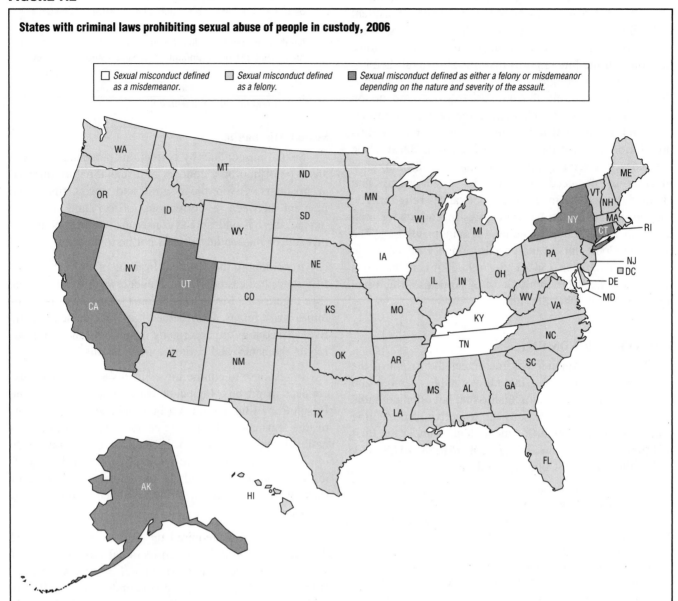

☐ *Sexual misconduct defined as a misdemeanor.*   ☐ *Sexual misconduct defined as a felony.*   ■ *Sexual misconduct defined as either a felony or misdemeanor depending on the nature and severity of the assault.*

SOURCE: United States. US Department of Justice/National Institute of Corrections. Maps: State Laws Prohibiting the Sexual Abuse of Individuals in Custody. Comp by Brenda V. Smith under NIC Cooperative Agreement 06S20GJJ1, Washington, DC. June 2006. Found at http://www.wcl.american. edu/nic/responses.cfm (last viewed February 14, 2007).

safety in prisons, and excessive violence by the guards. The Supreme Court has established several tests to determine whether conditions or actions violate the Eighth Amendment:

- Did the actions or conditions offend concepts of "decency and human dignity and precepts of civilization which [Americans] profess to possess"?

- Was it "disproportionate to the offense"?

- Did it violate "fundamental standards of good conscience and fairness"?

- Was the punishment unnecessarily cruel?

- Did the punishment go beyond legitimate penal purposes?

**Isolation**

Several landmark cases changed the way prisoners can be held in isolation. In *Holt v. Sarver* (300 F. Supp 825, 1969), a U.S. District Court in Arkansas found "solitary confinement or close confinement in isolation units of prisons not unconstitutional per se, but, depending on circumstances, it may violate the Eighth and Fourteenth Amendments." Isolation cells in an Arkansas prison were used for prisoners who broke rules, those who needed protective custody to separate them from other inmates, and those who were "general escape or security risks or who were awaiting trial on additional charges.... Confinement in isolation cells was not 'solitary confinement' in the conventional sense of the term. On the contrary, the cells

TABLE 7.15

**Sexual violence allegations in prisons and jails, 2005**

| | State and federal prisons | | Local jails | | Private prisons and jails | |
|---|---|---|---|---|---|---|
| | Number | Percent* | Number | Percent* | Number | Percent* |
| **Inmate-on-inmate non-consensual sexual acts** | 1,443 | 100.0 % | 263 | 100.0% | 34 | 100.0% |
| Substantiated | 163 | 13.7 | 32 | 15.8 | 7 | 31.8 |
| Unsubstantiated | 582 | 49.0 | 94 | 46.3 | 13 | 59.1 |
| Unfounded | 442 | 37.2 | 78 | 37.9 | 2 | 9.1 |
| Investigation ongoing | 236 | | 32 | | 12 | |
| **Inmate-on-inmate abusive sexual contacts** | 423 | 100.0% | 57 | 100.0% | 3 | 100.0% |
| Substantiated | 103 | 25.8 | 12 | 22.6 | 0 | 0 |
| Unsubstantiated | 235 | 58.8 | 17 | 32.1 | 3 | 100.0 |
| Unfounded | 62 | 15.5 | 24 | 45.3 | 0 | 0 |
| Investigation ongoing | 13 | | 4 | | 0 | |
| **Staff sexual misconduct** | 1,829 | 100.0 % | 184 | 100.0% | 29 | 100.0% |
| Substantiated | 195 | 14.9 | 53 | 36.5 | 6 | 20.7 |
| Unsubstantiated | 867 | 66.4 | 50 | 34.5 | 18 | 62.1 |
| Unfounded | 243 | 18.6 | 42 | 29.0 | 5 | 17.2 |
| Investigation ongoing | 519 | | 39 | | 0 | |
| **Staff sexual harassment** | 914 | 100.0% | 39 | 100.0% | 7 | 100.0% |
| Substantiated | 39 | 5.7 | 3 | 10.0 | 0 | 0 |
| Unsubstantiated | 478 | 69.4 | 12 | 40.0 | 7 | 100.0 |
| Unfounded | 172 | 25.0 | 15 | 50.0 | 0 | 0 |
| Investigation ongoing | 226 | | 8 | | 0 | |

Note: Excludes facilities operated by the U.S. military, the Bureau of Immigration and Customs Enforcement, tribal authorities and the Bureau of Indian Affairs.
*Percents based on allegations of which investigations had been completed.

SOURCE: Allen J. Beck and Paige M. Harrison, "Table 3. Allegations of Sexual Violence in Federal and State Prisons, Local Jails, and Private Prisons and Jails, 2005," in *Sexual Violence Reported by Correctional Authorities, 2005*, U.S. Department of Justice, Office of Justice Programs, Bureau of Justice Statistics, July 2006, http://www.ojp.usdoj.gov/bjs/pub/pdf/svrca05.pdf (accessed February 14, 2007)

are substantially overcrowded.... The average number of men confined in a single cell seems to be four, but at times the number has been much higher (up to ten and eleven)."

The court agreed that "if confinement of that type is to serve any useful purpose, it must be rigorous, uncomfortable, and unpleasant. However, there are limits to the rigor and discomfort of close confinement which a state may not constitutionally exceed."

The court found that the confinement of inmates in these isolation cells, which were "overcrowded, dirty, unsanitary, and pervaded by bad odors from toilets, constituted cruel and unusual punishment." The court also asserted that "prolonged confinement" of numbers of men in the same cell under unsanitary, dangerous conditions was "mentally and emotionally traumatic as well as physically uncomfortable. It is hazardous to health. It is degrading and debasing; it offends modern sensibilities, and, in the Court's estimation, amounts to cruel and unusual punishment."

## Death Penalty

Three Supreme Court cases, all decided in the 1970s, have produced the current interpretation of the Eighth Amendment relative to the death penalty. In *Furman v. Georgia* (408 U.S. 238, 1972), the Court held that the death penalty in three cases under review was "cruel and unusual" because under the then-prevailing statutes juries had "untrammeled discretion...to pronounce life

or death in capital cases." Due process required procedural fairness, including consideration of the severity of the crime and the circumstances. In the three cases decided in *Furman*, three individuals were condemned to die, two for rape and one for murder. All three of the offenders were black.

In response to *Furman*, states modified their statutes. North Carolina imposed a mandatory death sentence for first-degree murder. This law was tested in the Supreme Court in *Woodson v. North Carolina* (428 U.S. 280, 1976). The Court held that even though the death penalty was not cruel and unusual punishment in every circumstance, a mandatory death sentence did not satisfy the requirements laid down in *Furman*. The Court said: "North Carolina's mandatory death penalty statute for first-degree murder departs markedly from contemporary standards respecting the imposition of the punishment of death, and thus cannot be applied consistently with the Eighth and Fourteenth Amendments' requirement that the State's power to punish 'be exercised within the limits of civilized standards.'" The Court overturned the North Carolina law.

*Woodson* was decided on July 2, 1976. On the same day the Court rendered its judgment in the case of *Gregg v. Georgia*, the case of a man sentenced to death for murder and robbery under new legislation passed in Georgia following *Furman*. In this case the Court upheld the death penalty saying, in part:

The Georgia statutory system under which petitioner was sentenced to death is constitutional. The new procedures on their face satisfy the concerns of *Furman*, since before the death penalty can be imposed there must be specific jury findings as to the circumstances of the crime or the character of the defendant, and the State Supreme Court thereafter reviews the comparability of each death sentence with the sentences imposed on similarly situated defendants to ensure that the sentence of death in a particular case is not disproportionate. Petitioner's contentions that the changes in Georgia's sentencing procedures have not removed the elements of arbitrariness and capriciousness condemned by *Furman* are without merit.

## Death Penalty for Juveniles

In *Roper v. Simmons* (543 U.S. 551, 2005), the Supreme Court ruled that the death penalty for minors is cruel and unusual punishment. In a five to four ruling, the Court found it unconstitutional to sentence someone to death for a crime he or she committed when he or she was younger than eighteen. As a result of the ruling, seventy-three prisoners were removed from death row.

As part of its argument for outlawing the death penalty for minors, the Court cited scientific opinion that teenagers are too immature to be held accountable in the same way as adults for the crimes they commit. Justice Anthony M. Kennedy, speaking for the majority, explained: "From a moral standpoint it would be misguided to equate the failings of a minor with those of an adult, for a greater possibility exists that a minor's character deficiencies will be reformed."

## Three Strikes

In 2003 the Supreme Court ruled on the constitutionality of the California three-strikes law. The case involved the defendant Gary Albert Ewing, who had been sentenced to twenty-five years to life for a third offense, the theft of three golf clubs, with each valued at $399. His previous offenses included (among others) a burglary and a robbery while threatening his victim with a knife. *Ewing v. California* (538 U.S. 11, 2003) was a good test of the California statute because neither of Ewing's first two offenses were seriously violent and the third, the triggering offense, was what is known under California law as a "wobbler," namely an offense that can be tried, at the prosecutor's option, as either a felony or a misdemeanor.

The petition in *Ewing* argued that the punishment was "cruel and unusual" and disproportionate to the offense committed. In effect, Ewing had the profile of a habitual but petty criminal whose theft of golf clubs should have been tried as a misdemeanor. In this case the Court dismissed the proportionality argument and, instead, affirmed the state's right to set policy for the protection of the public. Quoting from another case, the Court said that "the Eighth Amendment does not require

strict proportionality between crime and sentence [but] forbids only extreme sentences that are 'grossly disproportionate' to the crime." California had the right to incapacitate repeat offenders by incarcerating them. According to the Court, the Constitution did not mandate that the states apply any one penological theory.

## Prison Conditions and Medical Care

In *Rhodes v. Chapman* (452 U.S. 337, 1981), the Supreme Court ruled that housing prisoners in double cells was not cruel and unusual punishment. The justices maintained that "conditions of confinement, as constituting the punishment at issue, must not involve the wanton and unnecessary infliction of pain, nor may they be grossly disproportionate to the severity of the crime warranting imprisonment. But conditions that cannot be said to be cruel and unusual under contemporary standards are not unconstitutional. To the extent such conditions are restrictive and even harsh, they are part of the penalty that criminals pay for their offenses against society."

The Court concluded that the Constitution "does not mandate comfortable prisons" and that only those deprivations denying the "minimal civilized measure of life's necessities" violate the Eighth Amendment.

Furthermore, a federal judge ruled in *Hadix v. Caruso* (case no. 4:92-CV-110) that officials at the Southern Michigan Correctional Facility had to stop using nonmedical restraints on prisoners because the "practice constitutes torture and violates the Eighth Amendment." On November 13, 2006, Judge Richard Enslen of the U.S. District Court issued the opinion in the case of Timothy Souders, a mentally ill detainee who died after spending four days nude and shackled in an isolated cell. Judge Enslen ordered the prison to "immediately cease and desist from the practice of using any form of punitive mechanical restraints [and] develop practices, protocols and policies to enforce this limitation."

## Guards Using Force

In *Whitney v. Albers* (475 U.S. 312, 1986), the Supreme Court ruled that guards, during prison disturbances or riots, must balance the need "to maintain or restore discipline" through force against the risk of injury to inmates. These situations require prison officials "to act quickly and decisively" and allow guards and administrators leeway in their actions. In *Whitney*, a prisoner was shot in the knee during an attempt to rescue a hostage. The Court found that the injury suffered by the prisoner was not cruel and unusual punishment under the circumstances.

In 1983 Keith Hudson, an inmate at the state penitentiary in Angola, Louisiana, argued with Jack McMillian, a guard. McMillian placed the inmate in handcuffs and shackles to take him to the administrative lockdown area.

On the way, Hudson stated that McMillian punched him in the mouth, eyes, chest, and stomach. Another guard held him while the supervisor on duty watched. Hudson sued, accusing the guards of cruel and unusual punishment.

A magistrate found that the guards used "force when there was no need to do so," and the supervisor allowed their conduct, thus violating the Eighth Amendment. The Court of Appeals for the Fifth Circuit, however, reversed the decision, ruling in *Hudson v. McMillian* (929 F. 2d 1014, 1990) that "inmates alleging use of excessive force in violation of the Eighth Amendment must prove: (1) significant injury; (2) resulting 'directly and only from the use of force that was clearly excessive to the need'; (3) the excessiveness of which was objectively unreasonable; and (4) that the action constituted an unnecessary and wanton infliction of pain."

The court agreed that the use of force was unreasonable and was a clearly excessive and unnecessary infliction of pain. However, the court found against Hudson because his injuries were "minor" and "required no medical attention."

## DUE PROCESS COMPLAINTS

The Fifth Amendment provides that no person should be deprived of life, liberty, or property by the federal government "without due process of the law." The Fourteenth Amendment reaffirms this right and explicitly applies it to the states. Due process complaints brought by prisoners under the Fourteenth and Fifth amendments are generally centered on questions of procedural fairness. Most of the time disciplinary action in prison is taken on the word of the guard or the administrator, and the inmate has little opportunity to challenge the charges. Rules are often vague or not formally written out. Disrespect toward a guard tends to be defined by the guards themselves.

The Supreme Court, however, has affirmed that procedural fairness should be used in some institutional decisions. In *Wolff v. McDonnell* (418 U.S. 539, 1974), the Supreme Court declared that a Nebraska law providing for sentences to be shortened for good behavior created a "liberty interest." Thus, if an inmate met the requirements, prison officials could not deprive him of the shortened sentence without due process, according to the Fourteenth Amendment.

At the Metropolitan Correctional Center, a federally operated short-term custodial facility in New York City designed mainly for pretrial detainees, inmates challenged the constitutionality of the facility's conditions. As this was a pretrial detention center, the challenge was brought under the due process clause of the Fifth Amendment. The District Court and the Court of Appeals found for the inmates, but the Supreme Court disagreed in *Bell v. Wolfish*.

## EARLY RELEASE

Beginning in 1983 the Florida legislature enacted a series of laws authorizing the awarding of early release credits to prison inmates when the state prison population exceeded predetermined levels. In 1986 Kenneth Lynce received a twenty-two-year prison sentence on a charge of attempted murder. He was released in 1992, based on the determination that he had accumulated five different types of early release credits totaling 5,668 days, including 1,860 days of "provisional credits" awarded as a result of prison overcrowding.

Shortly thereafter, the state attorney general issued an opinion interpreting a 1992 statute as having retroactively canceled all provisional credits awarded to inmates convicted of murder and attempted murder. Lynce was rearrested and returned to custody. He filed a habeas corpus petition alleging that the retroactive cancellation of provisional credits violated the ex post facto ("from a thing done afterward") clause of the Constitution.

The Supreme Court agreed with Lynce. In *Lynce v. Mathis* (519 U.S. 443, 1997), the Court ruled that to fall within the ex post facto prohibition a law must be "retrospective" and "disadvantage the offender affected by it." The 1992 statute was clearly retrospective and disadvantaged Lynce by increasing his punishment.

## THE COURT GOES BACK TO BASICS

In 1995 the Supreme Court made it harder for prisoners to bring constitutional suits to challenge due process rights. In a five to four decision in the case of *Sandin v. Conner* (515 U.S. 472), the majority asserted that it was frustrated with the number of due process cases, some of which, it felt, clogged the judiciary with unwarranted complaints, such as claiming a "liberty interest" in not being transferred to a cell with an electrical outlet for a television set.

*Sandin* concerned an inmate in Hawaii who was not allowed to call witnesses at a disciplinary hearing for misconduct that had placed him in solitary for thirty days. The Court of Appeals of the Ninth Circuit had held in 1993 that the inmate, Demont Conner, had a liberty interest, allowing him a range of procedural protections in remaining free from solitary confinement. The Supreme Court overruled the Court of Appeals, stating that the inmate had no liberty interest. Due process protections play a role only if the state's action has infringed on some separate, substantive right that the inmate possesses. For example, Wolff's loss of good-time credit was a substantive right that he possessed. The punishment Conner had received "was within the range of confinement to be normally expected" because he was serving thirty years to life for a number of crimes, including murder.

"States may under certain circumstances create liberty interests which are protected by the Due Process Clause," but these will be limited to actions that "[impose] atypical and significant hardship on the inmate in relation to the ordinary incidents of prison life." Being put in solitary confinement in a prison where most inmates are limited to their cells most of the day anyway is not a liberty-interest issue. Because there was no liberty interest involved, how the hearing was handled was irrelevant.

Based on this ruling, the Court held that a federal court should consider a complaint to be a potential violation of a prisoner's due process rights only when prison staff imposed "atypical and significant hardship on the inmate." Mismanaged disciplinary hearings or temporary placement in solitary were just "ordinary incidents of prison and life" and should not be considered violations of the Constitution.

Chief Justice Rehnquist asserted that past Supreme Court decisions have "led to the involvement of federal courts in the day-to-day management of prisons, often squandering judicial resources with little offsetting benefit to anyone." Judges should allow prison administrators the flexibility to fine-tune the ordinary incidents of prison life.

This decision continues the more conservative trend of the Supreme Court. Before the 1960s prisoners had few rights. A climate of reform beginning in the 1960s brought about a rash of cases that extended prisoners'

rights over time. The pendulum has swung back since the 1980s. A more conservative approach has led to more judicial restraint as the courts seek to balance the constitutional rights of the prisoners with the security interests of the correctional administrators.

## INNOCENCE PROTECTION ACT

Deoxyribonucleic acid (DNA) testing has emerged as a powerful tool capable of establishing the innocence of a person in cases where organic matter from the perpetrator of a crime (e.g., blood, skin, and semen) has been obtained by law enforcement officials. This organic matter can be tested against DNA samples taken from an accused or convicted person. If the two samples do not match, then they came from different people and the person being tested is innocent.

The Innocence Protection Act became law in 2004 as part of the Justice for All Act. The act enables people who are "convicted and imprisoned for federal offenses" and who claim to be innocent to have DNA testing on the biological evidence that was originally collected during the investigations of the crimes for which they were convicted. It mandates that the government has to preserve collected biological evidence so that it can be tested after the defendant is convicted. Finally, it provides funds to allow certain agencies to test evidence to identify perpetrators of unsolved crimes.

# CHAPTER 8
# PROBATION AND PAROLE

Most of the correctional population of the United States—those under the supervision of correctional authorities—are walking about freely. They are people on probation or parole. According to Lauren E. Glaze and Thomas P. Bonczar of the Bureau of Justice Statistics (BJS), in *Probation and Parole in the United States, 2005* (November 2006, http://www.ojp.usdoj.gov/bjs/pub/pdf/ppus05.pdf), 4.2 million people were on probation, 784,000 were on parole, and 2.2 million were in jail or prison in 2005. For every person behind bars, more than two people convicted of crimes were on the street. Probationers and parolees, however, were still under official supervision, and most had to satisfy requirements placed on them as a condition of freedom or of early release from correctional facilities.

A probationer is someone who has been convicted of a crime and sentenced—but the person's sentence has been suspended on condition that he or she behaves in the manner ordered by the court. Probation sometimes follows a brief period of incarceration; more often it is granted by the court immediately.

A parolee is an individual who has served a part of his or her sentence in jail and prison but, because of good behavior or legislative mandate, has been granted freedom before the sentence is fully served. The sentence remains in effect, however, and the parolee continues to be under the jurisdiction of a parole board. If the person fails to live up to the conditions of the release, the parolee may be confined again.

Glaze and Bonczar indicate that since 1995 the number of people on probation has grown by 35.2%, with an average annual increase of 2.5%. The increase from 2004 to 2005 was 0.5%, less than half the average growth rate. Between 1995 and 2005 the number of people on parole increased from 679,000 to 784,000; this is an increase of 15.4%, with an annual average increase of 1.4%.

## PROBATION
### Characteristics of Probationers

Glaze and Bonczar report that those released by the courts for probation are deemed to be the least dangerous among those arrested and the most likely to stay clear of the justice system in the future, even though only 59% of those on probation appeared to succeed in 2005. (See Table 8.1.) Whereas all people in prison serve sentences for felonies, only 50% of probationers were felons in 2005; 49% had been sentenced for misdemeanors and the remainder for other infractions. In 1995, 54% had felony sentences and 44% had misdemeanors.

According to Glaze and Bonczar, 76% of those entering probation in 2005 did so without any incarceration; 59% of those leaving probation had completed their probation successfully—a far higher percentage than those leaving parole (45%). Among those leaving probation in 2005, whether or not they completed probation successfully, 16% returned to incarceration or were incarcerated for the first time. In contrast, 38% of those leaving parole were put behind bars again for failure to live up to the rules or committing a new offense. The single largest category of serious offense committed by probationers was a drug violation (28%), followed by driving while intoxicated (15%).

In comparing Glaze and Bonczar's data to that in *Prisoners in 2005* (November 2006, http://www.ojp.usdoj.gov/bjs/pub/pdf/p05.pdf) by Paige M. Harrison and Allen J. Beck of the BJS, a larger proportion of probationers were female (23% versus 7% of state and federal prisoners) and white (55% versus 34.6% of those in prison) in 2005. A smaller proportion of probationers were African-American (30% of probationers versus 39.5% of prisoners) and Hispanic (13% of probationers versus 20.2% of prisoners).

### Geographical Distribution

Glaze and Bonczar note that, nationally, 1,858 per 100,000 adults were under probation in 2005, but rates

TABLE 8.1

## Characteristics of adults on probation, 1995, 2000, and 2005

| Characteristic | 1995 | 2000 | 2005 |
|---|---|---|---|
| Total | 100% | 100% | 100% |
| **Gender** | | | |
| Male | 79% | 78% | 77% |
| Female | 21 | 22 | 23 |
| **Race/Hispanic origin** | | | |
| White[a] | 53% | 54% | 55% |
| Black[a] | 31 | 31 | 30 |
| Hispanic | 14 | 13 | 13 |
| American Indian/Alaska Native[a] | 1 | 1 | 1 |
| Asian/Native Hawaiian/other Pacific Islander[a] | — | 1 | 1 |
| **Status of probation** | | | |
| Direct imposition | 48% | 56% | 57% |
| Split sentence | 15 | 11 | 10 |
| Sentence suspended | 26 | 25 | 22 |
| Imposition suspended | 6 | 7 | 9 |
| Other | 4 | 1 | 2 |
| **Status of supervision** | | | |
| Active | 79% | 76% | 70% |
| Inactive | 8 | 9 | 9 |
| Absconder | 9 | 9 | 10 |
| Supervised out of state | 2 | 3 | 2 |
| Residential/other treatment program | N/A | N/A | 1 |
| Warrant status | N/A | N/A | 6 |
| Other | 2 | 3 | 2 |
| **Type of offense** | | | |
| Felony | 54% | 52% | 50% |
| Misdemeanor | 44 | 46 | 49 |
| Other infractions | 2 | 2 | 1 |
| **Most serious offense[b]** | | | |
| Sexual assault | N/A | N/A | 3% |
| Domestic violence | N/A | N/A | 6 |
| Other assault | N/A | N/A | 10 |
| Burglary | N/A | N/A | 5 |
| Larceny/theft | N/A | N/A | 12 |
| Fraud | N/A | N/A | 6 |
| Drug law violations | N/A | 24 | 28 |
| Driving while intoxicated | 16 | 18 | 15 |
| Minor traffic offenses | N/A | 6 | 5 |
| **Adults entering probation** | | | |
| Without incarceration | 72% | 79% | 76% |
| With incarceration | 13 | 16 | 18 |
| Other types | 15 | 5 | 6 |

TABLE 8.1

## Characteristics of adults on probation, 1995, 2000, and 2005 [CONTINUED]

| Characteristic | 1995 | 2000 | 2005 |
|---|---|---|---|
| **Adults leaving probation** | | | |
| Successful completions | 62% | 60% | 59% |
| Incarceration | 21 | 15 | 16 |
|    With new sentence | 5 | 3 | 4 |
|    With the same sentence | 13 | 8 | 7 |
| Unknown | 3 | 4 | 5 |
| Absconder[c] | N/A | 3 | 3 |
| Discharge to custody, detainer, or warrant | N/A | 1 | 1 |
| Other unsuccessful[c] | N/A | 11 | 13 |
| Death | 1 | 1 | 1 |
| Other | 16 | 9 | 7 |

Note: For every characteristic there were persons of unknown type. Detail may not sum to total because of rounding.
—Less than 0.5%.
N/A Not available.
[a]Excludes persons of Hispanic origin.
[b]Does not include all offenses; therefore, will not add to 100%.
[c]In 1995 absconder and other unsuccessful statuses were reported among other.

SOURCE: Lauren E. Glaze and Thomas P. Bonczar, "Table 3. Characteristics of Adults on Probation, 2005," in *Probation and Parole in the United States, 2005*, U.S. Department of Justice, Office of Justice Programs, Bureau of Justice Statistics, November 2006, http://www.ojp.usdoj.gov/bjs/pub/pdf/ppus05.pdf (accessed January 24, 2007)

varied considerably from state to state and from region to region. In broad terms populations of probationers paralleled the general population with some differences. The South and Midwest had proportionally more probationers. In the South 2,067 per 100,000 adults were on probation, and in the Midwest the rate was 1,950 per 100,000. (See Table 8.2.) The West (1,546 per 100,000) and Northeast (1,658 per 100,000) had proportionately fewer probationers.

Table 8.2 shows these data for all fifty states and the District of Columbia in 2005. Texas had the highest number of probationers of any state at the end of 2005 (430,312), followed by Georgia (422,848), California (388,260), Florida (277,831), and Ohio (239,036). Mississippi (17.1%), West Virginia (9.6%), Wyoming (9.2%), and Kentucky (8%) had the greatest increases in probationers in 2005. Rhode Island

(3,091 per 100,000 population), Minnesota (2,988), Delaware (2,828), and Texas (2,580) had the highest rates of probationers to population. The states with the fewest probationers per 100,000 adult U.S. residents were New Hampshire (457), West Virginia (533), Utah (578), and Nevada (709).

### Federal Probation Violations

The BJS reports in the *Compendium of Federal Justice Statistics, 2004* (December 2006, http://www.ojp.usdoj.gov/bjs/pub/pdf/cfjs04.pdf) that probation can be a successful sentencing approach. In fiscal year (FY) 2004, 82.3% of federal probationers successfully completed the terms of their probation. (See Table 8.3.) Of the 15.9% who did violate probation, most had either committed a new crime (5.4% of all probationers) or used drugs (3.1%). Those convicted of violent, weapon, and immigration offenses were more likely to end probation by committing new crimes (8.8%, 8.5%, and 7.7%, respectively) than probationers convicted of property (4.6%) or drug (3.9%) offenses.

### Probation Officers

Community corrections has a cost to the community—although it is lower than the cost of housing and feeding prisoners and providing them with health care. A major part of that cost is the employment of skilled probation officers to supervise probationers.

According to Ann L. Pastore and Kathleen Maguire of the Utilization of Criminal Justice Statistics Project, in the *Sourcebook of Criminal Justice Statistics 2003* (2005, http://www.albany.edu/sourcebook/), in 1975 the U.S. government employed 1,377 probation officers to supervise 64,261 federal

**TABLE 8.2**

**Adults on probation, by region and jurisdiction, 2005**

| Region and jurisdiction | Probation population, 1/1/2005 | 2005 | | Probation population, 12/31/05 | Percent change, 2005 | Number on probation per 100,000 adult residents, 12/31/05 |
|---|---|---|---|---|---|---|
| | | Entries | Exits | | | |
| U.S. total | 4,143,466 | 2,228,300 | 2,209,700 | 4,162,536 | 0.5% | 1,858 |
| Federal | 28,602 | 12,135 | 14,402 | 26,719 | −6.6% | 12 |
| State | 4,114,864 | 2,216,200 | 2,195,300 | 4,135,817 | 0.5 | 1,846 |
| **Northeast** | 702,328 | 277,800 | 285,700 | 694,396 | −1.1% | 1,658 |
| Connecticut[a] | 54,067 | 28,250 | 26,245 | 56,072 | 3.7 | 2,092 |
| Maine | 8,907 | 4,890 | 5,677 | 8,120 | −8.8 | 776 |
| Massachusetts[a] | 163,719 | 84,343 | 82,697 | 165,365 | 1.0 | 3,350 |
| New Hampshire | 4,285 | 3,440 | 3,110 | 4,615 | * | 457 |
| New Jersey | 143,315 | 45,136 | 49,360 | 139,091 | −2.9 | 2,117 |
| New York | 124,853 | 34,644 | 40,472 | 119,025 | −4.7 | 810 |
| Pennsylvania[a, b] | 167,366 | 67,300 | 67,100 | 167,561 | 0.1 | 1,741 |
| Rhode Island[a] | 26,085 | 5,410 | 5,882 | 25,613 | −1.8 | 3,091 |
| Vermont[a] | 9,731 | 4,341 | 5,138 | 8,934 | −8.2 | 1,820 |
| **Midwest** | 958,730 | 609,500 | 594,300 | 973,807 | 1.6% | 1,950 |
| Illinois[a] | 143,871 | 60,951 | 61,686 | 143,136 | −0.5 | 1,500 |
| Indiana[a] | 121,675 | 98,681 | 99,342 | 121,014 | −0.5 | 2,583 |
| Iowa | 22,408 | 15,829 | 14,833 | 23,404 | 4.4 | 1,018 |
| Kansas | 14,439 | 19,755 | 19,184 | 15,010 | 4.0 | 723 |
| Michigan[a, b] | 176,630 | 130,200 | 128,300 | 178,609 | 1.1 | 2,350 |
| Minnesota | 113,121 | 70,752 | 66,800 | 117,073 | 3.5 | 2,988 |
| Missouri | 54,848 | 25,179 | 26,413 | 53,614 | −2.2 | 1,208 |
| Nebraska | 17,994 | 15,330 | 14,856 | 18,468 | 2.6 | 1,387 |
| North Dakota | 3,749 | 2,808 | 2,597 | 3,960 | 5.6 | 791 |
| Ohio[a, b] | 230,758 | 141,300 | 133,000 | 239,036 | 3.6 | 2,745 |
| South Dakota | 5,372 | 3,196 | 3,260 | 5,308 | −1.2 | 899 |
| Wisconsin | 53,865 | 25,505 | 24,195 | 55,175 | 2.4 | 1,298 |
| **South** | 1,667,198 | 908,800 | 894,600 | 1,681,455 | 0.9% | 2,067 |
| Alabama[a] | 36,799 | 14,039 | 11,843 | 38,995 | 6.0 | 1,121 |
| Arkansas | 28,771 | 8,435 | 6,958 | 30,248 | 5.1 | 1,431 |
| Delaware | 18,725 | 14,643 | 14,906 | 18,462 | −1.4 | 2,828 |
| District of Columbia[a] | 7,585 | 7,216 | 7,414 | 7,387 | −2.6 | 1,696 |
| Florida[a, b] | 278,606 | 240,000 | 240,800 | 277,831 | −0.3 | 2,002 |
| Georgia[a, b, c] | 423,547 | 215,500 | 216,200 | 422,848 | * | * |
| Kentucky | 32,619 | 20,800 | 18,300 | 35,230 | 8.0 | 1,100 |
| Louisiana | 38,231 | 13,772 | 13,695 | 38,308 | 0.2 | 1,133 |
| Maryland | 76,676 | 38,282 | 39,365 | 75,593 | −1.4 | 1,793 |
| Mississippi | 20,375 | 8,124 | 4,635 | 23,864 | 17.1 | 1,096 |
| North Carolina | 111,537 | 62,157 | 62,068 | 111,626 | 0.1 | 1,693 |
| Oklahoma[a, b] | 28,404 | 14,600 | 14,100 | 28,865 | 1.6 | 1,065 |
| South Carolina | 38,941 | 14,768 | 14,360 | 39,349 | 1.0 | 1,212 |
| Tennessee[a, b] | 47,099 | 24,800 | 22,600 | 49,302 | 4.7 | 1,072 |
| Texas | 428,836 | 181,333 | 179,857 | 430,312 | 0.3 | 2,580 |
| Virginia[a] | 43,470 | 27,078 | 24,959 | 45,589 | 4.9 | 788 |
| West Virginia[b] | 6,977 | 3,200 | 2,500 | 7,646 | 9.6 | 533 |
| **West** | 786,608 | 420,100 | 420,500 | 786,159 | −0.1% | 1,546 |
| Alaska | 5,547 | 1,022 | 878 | 5,680 | 2.4 | 1,182 |
| Arizona[a, b] | 70,532 | 39,700 | 39,100 | 71,138 | 0.9 | 1,606 |
| California[a] | 384,852 | 195,343 | 191,935 | 388,260 | 0.9 | 1,462 |
| Colorado[a, b] | 57,779 | 29,900 | 31,000 | 56,623 | −2.0 | 1,613 |
| Hawaii[d] | 16,113 | 6,236 | 5,524 | 16,825 | 4.4 | 1,693 |
| Idaho[a, e] | 44,579 | 35,717 | 36,584 | 43,712 | * | * |

probationers, a ratio of 1 officer per 47 probationers. (See Table 8.4.) By 2005, 4,585 officers supervised 112,931 probationers, yielding a ratio of almost 25 per officer. The federal government has been expending resources to lower the ratio of probationers to officers. Between 2000 and 2005 the number of probationers increased by 12%, whereas the number of officers increased by 15%.

## SUPERVISED RELEASE

The Sentencing Reform Act of 1984 created an alternative to parole and probation for federal offenders—supervised release—which occurs after an offender's term of imprisonment is completed. Following his or her release, an offender is sentenced to a period of supervision in the community. The act calls for supervised release to follow any term of imprisonment that exceeds one year or if required by a specific statute. The court may also order supervised release to follow imprisonment in any other case. Offenders on supervised release are supervised by probation officers. The BJS notes in the *Compendium of Federal Justice Statistics, 2004* that in FY 2004, 77,332 (or 70%) of federal offenders under

**TABLE 8.2**

**Adults on probation, by region and jurisdiction, 2005** [CONTINUED]

| Region and jurisdiction | Probation population, 1/1/2005 | 2005 | | Probation population, 12/31/05 | Percent change, 2005 | Number on probation per 100,000 adult residents, 12/31/05 |
|---|---|---|---|---|---|---|
| | | Entries | Exits | | | |
| Montana[a, b] | 7,634 | 4,500 | 3,900 | 8,233 | 7.8 | 1,121 |
| Nevada | 12,645 | 6,305 | 6,019 | 12,931 | 2.3 | 709 |
| New Mexico[a, b] | 17,725 | 8,500 | 7,500 | 18,706 | 5.5 | 1,287 |
| Oregon | 43,324 | 17,852 | 16,323 | 44,853 | 3.5 | 1,597 |
| Utah | 10,267 | 5,312 | 5,500 | 10,079 | -1.8 | 578 |
| Washington[a, b, d] | 111,193 | 66,900 | 73,800 | 104,293 | -6.2 | 2,155 |
| Wyoming | 4,418 | 2,828 | 2,420 | 4,826 | 9.2 | 1,216 |

Note: Because of nonresponse or incomplete data, the probation population for some jurisdictions on December 31, 2005, does not equal the population on January 1, plus entries, minus exits.

*Not calculated.

[a]Some oral data are estimated.

[b]Data for entries and exits were estimated for nonreporting agencies.

[c]Counts include private agency cases and may overstate the number under supervision.

[d]Due to a change in the state agency's record keeping procedures, data are not comparable to previous reports.

[e]Counts include estimates for misdemeanors based on admissions.

SOURCE: Lauren E. Glaze and Thomas P. Bonczar, "Table 2. Adults on Probation, 2005," in *Probation and Parole in the United States, 2005*, U.S. Department of Justice, Office of Justice Programs, Bureau of Justice Statistics, November 2006, http://www.ojp.usdoj.gov/bjs/pub/pdf/ppus05.pdf (accessed January 24, 2007)

community supervision were serving a term of supervised release. Most offenders sentenced to supervised release (41,681, or 54%) were convicted for drug offenses. Only 4,805 (or 6%) had been convicted of violent offenses.

Table 8.5 shows that in FY 2004, 32,930 offenders terminated their supervised release. Most (62.1%) had not violated the terms of their release and successfully completed their sentence. Some 13.7% had violated their supervised release by committing a new crime and 7.2% had used drugs.

In the *Compendium of Federal Justice Statistics, 2004*, the BJS reports that in FY 2004 men were more likely to violate the terms of their supervised release than women; only 60% of men successfully completed their supervised release, compared with 74% of women. Of those sentenced to supervised release, the youngest (nineteen- and twenty-year-olds) and the least educated (less than high school) were the most likely to violate the terms of their sentence.

## PAROLE

### Trends in Parole

Discretionary parole is administered by parole boards. Their members examine prisoners' criminal histories and prison records and decide whether to release prisoners from incarceration. Since the mid-1990s several states have abolished discretionary parole in favor of mandatory parole. Mandatory parole is legislatively imposed at the state level and, with some exceptions, takes away parole boards' discretion. Mandatory parole provisions ensure that sentences for the same crime require incarceration for the same length of time. The prisoner can shorten his or her sentence only by good behavior—but time off for good behavior is also prohibited in some states. In some jurisdictions parole can only begin after prisoners have served 100% of their mini-

mum sentences. Jeremy Travis and Sarah Lawrence of the Urban Institute report in *Beyond the Prison Gates: The State of Parole in America* (November 2002, http://www.urban.org/UploadedPDF/310583_Beyond_prison_gates.pdf) that the share of discretionary prison releases decreased from 65% in 1976 to 24% by 1999.

Travis and Lawrence indicate that even though states rely more and more on mandatory release dates to decide when to release prisoners, states have different prison release methods. Some states have cut back on parole supervision, releasing more prisoners directly to the community. Other states have aggressively enforced the conditions of parole, leading to the identification of more parole violations. In these states more parolees are being sent back to prison. States handle different types of offenses differently. Some allow victims or prosecutors to participate in release decisions; others do not. Many states still rely heavily on parole boards to make release decisions, whereas others no longer use parole boards and have mandatory release policies for all their prisoners.

According to Travis and Lawrence, most parole agencies now use drug testing to determine whether a parolee has kept his or her promise to remain drug free. In a number of states parole officers are being permitted to carry weapons. Furthermore, parolees in several jurisdictions are required to wear electronic bracelets so that officials can monitor their movement.

Glaze and Bonczar note that in 1995, 50% of adults who entered parole did so under discretionary parole; by 2005 discretionary paroles made up only 31% of the total. In 1995 mandatory parole accounted for 45% of all paroles; by 2005, 51% of those paroled were under a mandatory parole.

**TABLE 8.3**

**Outcomes of probation supervision, by offense, October 1, 2003–September 30, 2004**

| Most serious offense of conviction | Number of probation terminations | Percent of probation supervisions terminating with— | | | | | |
| | | | Technical violations[a] | | | New crime[b] | Administrative case closures |
| | | No violation | Drug use | Fugitive status | Other | | |
|---|---|---|---|---|---|---|---|
| **All offenses** | 15,721 | 82.3% | 3.1% | 2.2% | 5.2% | 5.4% | 1.8% |
| **Felonies** | 8,251 | 84.9% | 2.8% | 1.7% | 4.4% | 4.5% | 1.7% |
| Violent offenses | 171 | 69.6% | 1.8% | 5.8% | 11.7% | 8.8% | 2.3% |
| Murder[c] | 10 | — | — | — | — | — | — |
| Assault | 48 | 64.6 | 4.2 | 8.3 | 16.7 | 6.3 | 0.0 |
| Robbery | 63 | 79.4 | 0.0 | 1.6 | 3.2 | 11.1 | 4.8 |
| Sexual abuse[c] | 41 | 53.7 | 2.4 | 7.3 | 24.4 | 9.8 | 2.4 |
| Kidnapping | 4 | — | — | — | — | — | — |
| Threats against the President | 5 | — | — | — | — | — | — |
| Property offenses | 4,461 | 84.9% | 2.6% | 1.8% | 4.2% | 4.6% | 1.8% |
| Fraudulent | 3,634 | 86.3% | 2.1% | 1.8 % | 3.7% | 4.4% | 1.6% |
| Embezzlement | 346 | 93.4 | 0.9 | 0.9 | 2.9 | 1.7 | 0.3 |
| Fraud[c] | 2,759 | 87.6 | 1.8 | 1.3 | 3.2 | 4.2 | 1.8 |
| Forgery | 76 | 73.7 | 5.3 | 5.3 | 5.3 | 9.2 | 1.3 |
| Counterfeiting | 453 | 74.6 | 4.6 | 5.3 | 7.3 | 6.6 | 1.5 |
| Other | 827 | 79.1% | 4.8% | 1.8% | 6.2% | 5.3% | 2.8% |
| Burglary | 23 | 56.5 | 13.0 | 0.0 | 21.7 | 8.7 | 0.0 |
| Larceny[c] | 676 | 77.8 | 5.3 | 1.9 | 6.2 | 5.9 | 2.8 |
| Motor vehicle theft | 41 | 87.8 | 2.4 | 2.4 | 7.3 | 0.0 | 0.0 |
| Arson and explosives | 24 | 87.5 | 0.0 | 0.0 | 0.0 | 0.0 | 12.5 |
| Transportation of stolen property | 49 | 95.9 | 0.0 | 0.0 | 2.0 | 0.0 | 2.0 |
| Other property offenses[c] | 14 | 78.6 | 0.0 | 7.1 | 0.0 | 14.3 | 0.0 |
| Drug offenses | 1,418 | 85.0% | 3.9% | 1.5% | 4.7% | 3.9% | 0.9% |
| Trafficking | 1,284 | 85.3 | 3.4 | 1.6 | 4.8 | 4.1 | 0.8 |
| Possession and other drug offenses | 134 | 82.8 | 9.0 | 0.0 | 3.7 | 2.2 | 2.2 |
| Public-order offenses | 1,431 | 89.9% | 1.5% | 1.0% | 3.4% | 2.4% | 1.9% |
| Regulatory | 604 | 88.7% | 2.6% | 1.7% | 3.8% | 2.0% | 1.2% |
| Agriculture | 1 | — | — | — | — | — | — |
| Antitrust | 11 | 100.0 | 0.0 | 0.0 | 0.0 | 0.0 | 0.0 |
| Food and drug | 32 | 87.5 | 3.1 | 0.0 | 3.1 | 3.1 | 3.1 |
| Transportation | 26 | 88.5 | 3.8 | 3.8 | 0.0 | 3.8 | 0.0 |
| Civil rights | 8 | — | — | — | — | — | — |
| Communications | 37 | 97.3 | 0.0 | 0.0 | 2.7 | 0.0 | 0.0 |
| Custom laws | 27 | 81.5 | 0.0 | 3.7 | 14.8 | 0.0 | 0.0 |
| Postal laws | 46 | 82.6 | 4.3 | 2.2 | 4.3 | 2.2 | 4.3 |
| Other regulatory offenses | 416 | 88.7 | 2.9 | 1.7 | 3.6 | 2.2 | 1.0 |
| Other | 827 | 90.8% | 0.6% | 0.5% | 3.0% | 2.7% | 2.4% |
| Tax law violations[c] | 270 | 94.1 | 0.0 | 0.0 | 1.1 | 2.2 | 2.6 |
| Bribery | 79 | 97.5 | 0.0 | 0.0 | 1.3 | 0.0 | 1.3 |
| Perjury, contempt, and intimidation | 60 | 86.7 | 1.7 | 1.7 | 5.0 | 1.7 | 3.3 |
| National defense | 3 | — | — | — | — | — | — |
| Escape | 27 | 92.6 | 0.0 | 0.0 | 3.7 | 0.0 | 3.7 |
| Racketeering and extortion | 158 | 93.0 | 0.6 | 0.0 | 2.5 | 0.6 | 3.2 |
| Gambling | 35 | 97.1 | 0.0 | 0.0 | 0.0 | 2.9 | 0.0 |
| Nonviolent sex offenses | 60 | 81.7 | 1.7 | 0.0 | 1.7 | 10.0 | 5.0 |
| Obscene material[c] | 10 | — | — | — | — | — | — |
| Wildlife | 21 | 85.7 | 0.0 | 4.8 | 0.0 | 9.5 | 0.0 |
| Environmental | 12 | 91.7 | 0.0 | 0.0 | 0.0 | 0.0 | 8.3 |
| All other offenses | 92 | 78.3 | 2.2 | 2.2 | 13.0 | 4.3 | 0.0 |
| Weapon offenses | 390 | 76.2% | 5.4% | 1.0% | 6.7% | 8.5% | 2.3% |
| Immigration offenses | 323 | 84.8% | 2.2% | 2.2% | 1.9% | 7.7% | 1.2% |

## Characteristics of Parolees

According to Glaze and Bonczar, there were 784,408 federal and state parolees in the United States in 2005. (See Table 8.6.) Most (693,197) were paroled under state jurisdiction, whereas 91,211 had been paroled under federal jurisdiction. The number of state parolees grew by 1.6% from 2004 to 2005, which was higher than the average annual increase of 1.4% since 1995. The number of parolees has increased by 104,987, or 15.4%, since 1995.

In 2005, 12% of parolees were women; this percentage had not changed since 2000, but it had increased from 1995, when 10% of parolees were women. (See Table

8.7.) In 1995, 34% of parolees were white, 45% were African-American, and 21% were Hispanic. Ten years later the proportion of whites had grown substantially, and a higher proportion of parolees were white (41%) in 2005 than black (40%) or Hispanic (18%). Only 1% of parolees were Native American or Alaskan Native, and another 1% were Asian, Pacific Islander, or Native Hawaiian. In general, the gender and racial/ethnic distribution of parolees more closely matched that of the prison population than that of people on probation.

Table 8.7 also shows that 83% of parolees were under the active supervision of parole officers in 2005.

## TABLE 8.3

### Outcomes of probation supervision, by offense, October 1, 2003–September 30, 2004 [CONTINUED]

| Most serious offense of conviction | Number of probation terminations | Percent of probation supervisions terminating with— | | | | | |
|---|---|---|---|---|---|---|---|
| | | | Technical violations[a] | | | New crime[b] | Administrative case closures |
| | | No violation | Drug use | Fugitive status | Other | | |
| Misdemeanors[c] | 7,470 | 79.4% | 3.4% | 2.8% | 6.0% | 6.4% | 1.9% |
| Fraudulent property offense | 537 | 90.7 | 1.1 | 2.0 | 2.2 | 2.8 | 1.1 |
| Larceny | 717 | 79.5 | 3.1 | 3.3 | 6.4 | 6.8 | 0.8 |
| Drug possession[c] | 1,446 | 75.2 | 7.6 | 2.6 | 6.5 | 6.3 | 1.8 |
| Immigration misdemeanors | 949 | 73.8 | 3.0 | 4.0 | 4.7 | 14.2 | 0.3 |
| Traffic offenses | 2,039 | 81.4 | 2.3 | 2.5 | 6.0 | 5.0 | 2.9 |
| Other misdemeanors | 1,782 | 80.1 | 2.4 | 2.6 | 7.4 | 5.1 | 2.5 |

Note: Offenses for 57 felony offenders could not be classified.
—Too few cases to obtain statistically reliable data.
[a]Supervision terminated with incarceration or removal to inactive status for violation of supervision conditions other than charges for new offenses.
[b]Supervision terminated with incarceration or removal to inactive status after arrest for a "major" or "minor" offense.
[c]In this table "murder" includes nonnegligent manslaughter; "sexual abuse" includes only violent sex offenses; "fraud" excludes tax fraud; "larceny" excludes transportation of stolen property; "other property offenses" excludes fraudulent property offenses and includes destruction of property and trespassing; "tax law violations" includes tax fraud; "obscene material" denotes the mail or transport thereof; "misdemeanors" includes misdemeanors, petty offenses, and unknown offense levels; and "drug possession" also includes other drug misdemeanors.

SOURCE: "Table 7.3. Outcomes of Probation Supervision, by Offense, October 1, 2003–September 30, 2004," in *Compendium of Federal Justice Statistics, 2004*, U.S. Department of Justice, Office of Justice Programs, Bureau of Justice Statistics, December 2006, http://www.ojp.usdoj.gov/bjs/pub/pdf/cfjs0407.pdf (accessed January 24, 2007)

## TABLE 8.4

### Persons under the supervision of the federal probation system and number of authorized probation officers, 1975–2005

| | Number of persons under supervision | Number of probation officers |
|---|---|---|
| 1975 | 64,261 | 1,377 |
| 1976 | 64,246 | 1,452 |
| 1977 | 64,427 | 1,578 |
| 1978 | 66,681 | 1,604 |
| 1979 | 66,087 | 1,604 |
| 1980 | 64,450 | 1,604 |
| 1981 | 59,016 | 1,534 |
| 1982 | 58,373 | 1,637 |
| 1983 | 60,180 | 1,574 |
| 1984 | 63,092 | 1,690 |
| 1985 | 65,999 | 1,758 |
| 1986 | 69,656 | 1,847 |
| 1987 | 73,432 | 1,879 |
| 1988 | 76,366 | 2,046 |
| 1989 | 77,284 | 2,146 |
| 1990 | 80,592 | 2,361 |
| 1991 | 83,012 | 2,802 |
| 1992 | 85,920 | 3,316 |
| 1993 | 86,823 | 3,516* |
| 1994 | 89,103 | NA |
| 1995 | 85,822 | NA |
| 1996 | 88,966 | 3,473 |
| 1997 | 91,434 | 3,603 |
| 1998 | 93,737 | 3,842 |
| 1999 | 97,190 | 3,913 |
| 2000 | 100,395 | 3,981 |
| 2001 | 104,715 | 4,345 |
| 2002 | 108,792 | 4,476 |
| 2003 | 111,281 | 4,560 |
| 2004 | 112,643 | 4,490 |
| 2005 | 112,931 | 4,585 |

*Approximate.

SOURCE: Ann L. Pastore and Kathleen Maguire, editors, "Table 6.7.2005. Persons under Supervision of the Federal Probation System and Authorized Probation Officers," in *Sourcebook of Criminal Justice Statistics 2003*, 31st ed., U.S. Department of Justice, Office of Justice Programs, Bureau of Justice Statistics, 2005, http://www.albany.edu/sourcebook/pdf/t672005.pdf (accessed February 16, 2007)

Of parolees leaving parole, only 45% had successfully completed the terms of their parole. As a group, parolees are more serious offenders than probationers, given that 94% have been sentenced to one year or more of prison for felonies.

### Parole Geography

Glaze and Bonczar report that at the end of 2005 California had the largest number of parolees (111,743), and Maine had the smallest number (32). (See Table 8.6.) The District of Columbia had the highest number (1,214) of parolees per 100,000 adult residents, followed by Pennsylvania (787), Arkansas (782), and Oregon (766). The U.S. average was 350 per 100,000 population; this figure includes people on parole under federal jurisdiction. Besides California, Texas (101,916) and Pennsylvania (75,732) had the largest numbers of parolees. The number of parolees increased significantly in several states, including Arkansas (22.7%), North Dakota (16.7%), West Virginia (16.4%), and New Mexico (16.1%). The parole populations decreased in several states, including Nebraska (16.7%), Hawaii (7.7%), and Massachusetts (7.1%). Overall, the West had the greatest increase in parolees (3.2%) in 2005, whereas the Northeast had a decline of 1.4%.

### Parole Violation and Rearrest Trends

The overall success rate for parolees has remained fairly stable for several years. As shown in Table 8.7, 45% of individuals on parole completed their sentences successfully in both 1995 and 2005.

In the *Compendium of Federal Justice Statistics, 2004*, the BJS notes that the success rate for federal parolees was higher than the national average. In FY

TABLE 8.5

**Outcomes of supervised release, by offense, October 1, 2003–September 30, 2004**

| Most serious offense of conviction | Number of supervised release terminations | Percent of supervised releases terminating with— | | | | | |
|---|---|---|---|---|---|---|---|
| | | No violation | Technical violations[a] | | | New crime[b] | Administrative case closures |
| | | | Drug use | Fugitive status | Other | | |
| All offenses | 32,930 | 62.1% | 7.2% | 5.5% | 9.5% | 13.7% | 1.9% |
| Felonies | 32,284 | 62.0% | 7.2% | 5.5% | 9.5% | 13.8% | 1.9% |
| Violent offenses | 2,486 | 42.8% | 10.1% | 10.0% | 16.5% | 18.2% | 2.5% |
| Murder[c] | 121 | 46.3 | 4.1 | 10.7 | 25.6 | 10.7 | 2.5 |
| Negligent manslaughter | 4 | — | — | — | — | — | — |
| Assault | 319 | 43.9 | 5.3 | 11.0 | 21.0 | 17.9 | 0.9 |
| Robbery | 1,802 | 42.5 | 12.0 | 9.7 | 14.2 | 19.0 | 2.7 |
| Sexual abuse[c] | 189 | 40.2 | 5.3 | 13.2 | 24.9 | 14.3 | 2.1 |
| Kidnapping | 35 | 57.1 | 2.9 | 2.9 | 11.4 | 20.0 | 5.7 |
| Threats against the President | 16 | 25.0 | 0.0 | 0.0 | 18.8 | 37.5 | 18.8 |
| Property offenses | 7,462 | 67.7% | 4.9% | 5.2% | 9.5% | 11.0% | 1.7% |
| Fraudulent | 6,171 | 70.8% | 4.1% | 4.3% | 8.8% | 10.4% | 1.6% |
| Embezzlement | 667 | 85.2 | 1.3 | 2.1 | 5.1 | 5.4 | 0.9 |
| Fraud[c] | 4,669 | 72.5 | 3.3 | 3.7 | 8.6 | 10.1 | 1.8 |
| Forgery | 105 | 56.2 | 10.5 | 8.6 | 13.3 | 11.4 | 0.0 |
| Counterfeiting | 730 | 49.5 | 10.4 | 8.9 | 13.3 | 16.3 | 1.6 |
| Other | 1,291 | 52.9% | 8.8% | 9.9% | 12.6% | 13.8% | 2.0% |
| Burglary | 86 | 27.9 | 12.8 | 18.6 | 20.9 | 19.8 | 0.0 |
| Larceny[c] | 803 | 52.9 | 9.5 | 10.8 | 12.0 | 13.0 | 1.9 |
| Motor vehicle theft | 171 | 55.6 | 5.3 | 5.8 | 13.5 | 17.5 | 2.3 |
| Arson and explosives | 127 | 52.8 | 7.9 | 7.9 | 14.2 | 12.6 | 4.7 |
| Transportation of stolen property | 81 | 75.3 | 7.4 | 3.7 | 2.5 | 9.9 | 1.2 |
| Other property offenses[c] | 23 | 47.8 | 4.3 | 8.7 | 26.1 | 13.0 | 0.0 |
| Drug offenses | 15,408 | 65.2% | 8.0% | 4.8% | 8.2% | 12.0% | 1.8% |
| Trafficking | 13,970 | 64.8 | 8.2 | 5.0 | 8.0 | 12.2 | 1.8 |
| Possession and other drug offenses | 1,438 | 69.1 | 6.5 | 3.1 | 9.8 | 10.1 | 1.5 |
| Public-order offenses | 2,701 | 73.2% | 4.0% | 3.5% | 7.1% | 9.8% | 2.4% |
| Regulatory | 747 | 69.7% | 5.6% | 2.9% | 6.3% | 13.0% | 2.4% |
| Agriculture | 1 | — | — | — | — | — | — |
| Antitrust | 6 | — | — | — | — | — | — |
| Food and drug | 9 | — | — | — | — | — | —- |
| Transportation | 27 | 77.8 | 0.0 | 3.7 | 11.1 | 3.7 | 3.7 |
| Civil rights | 61 | 82.0 | 3.3 | 3.3 | 4.9 | 6.6 | 0.0 |
| Communications | 16 | 100.0 | 0.0 | 0.0 | 0.0 | 0.0 | 0.0 |
| Custom laws | 40 | 67.5 | 12.5 | 2.5 | 5.0 | 7.5 | 5.0 |
| Postal laws | 33 | 42.4 | 21.2 | 9.1 | 12.1 | 9.1 | 6.1 |
| Other regulatory offenses | 554 | 68.2 | 5.1 | 2.7 | 6.3 | 15.5 | 2.2 |
| Other | 1,954 | 74.6% | 3.3% | 3.7% | 7.4% | 8.6% | 2.4% |
| Tax law violations[c] | 316 | 90.8 | 0.0 | 0.9 | 2.8 | 4.4 | 0.9 |
| Bribery | 84 | 89.3 | 3.6 | 3.6 | 2.4 | 1.2 | 0.0 |
| Perjury, contempt, and intimidation | 76 | 75.0 | 2.6 | 3.9 | 1.3 | 11.8 | 5.3 |
| National defense | 7 | — | — | — | — | — | — |
| Escape | 153 | 37.9 | 11.8 | 12.4 | 16.3 | 20.3 | 1.3 |
| Racketeering and extortion | 690 | 78.4 | 2.9 | 2.6 | 6.4 | 6.7 | 3.0 |
| Gambling | 34 | 76.5 | 0.0 | 0.0 | 5.9 | 17.6 | 0.0 |
| Nonviolent sex offenses | 359 | 74.7 | 0.8 | 2.5 | 10.0 | 9.2 | 2.8 |
| Obscene material[c] | 24 | 66.7 | 4.2 | 4.2 | 8.3 | 12.5 | 4.2 |
| Wildlife | 19 | 94.7 | 0.0 | 5.3 | 0.0 | 0.0 | 0.0 |
| Environmental | 4 | — | — | — | — | — | — |
| All other offenses | 188 | 54.8 | 9.0 | 8.0 | 12.8 | 12.2 | 3.2 |
| Weapon offenses | 2,858 | 46.8% | 10.8% | 6.4% | 13.3% | 20.5% | 2.3% |
| Immigration offenses | 1,344 | 40.1% | 4.6% | 9.2% | 8.6% | 36.2% | 1.3% |

2004, 49.3% of federal parolees completed their sentences successfully. The success rate for those who had committed violent offenses was 36.6%, whereas for those who had committed property offenses it was 55.1%. More than half (60.4%) of drug offenders successfully completed their parole sentences.

Of those who violated federal parole in FY 2004, most had either violated their parole by committing a new crime (17.3%) or using drugs (10.8%). (See Table 8.8.) Male parolees were almost three times as likely to terminate parole by committing a new crime as female parolees, and they were almost twice as likely to use drugs than female parolees. (See Table 8.9.) The success rate was 61.9% for white parolees, 39.9% for African-Americans, and 36% for Native Americans or Alaskan Natives. The level of education seemed to make a difference in the success rates of parolees. Those with college degrees had a success rate of 82.5%, whereas only 47.8% of those with less than a high school education were successful. Drug use also had a slight effect. Those with no known drug abuse problem had a success rate of 62.5%, whereas those with a known history of drug abuse had a 58% success rate.

**TABLE 8.5**

**Outcomes of supervised release, by offense, October 1, 2003–September 30, 2004** [CONTINUED]

| Most serious offense of conviction | Number of supervised release terminations | Percent of supervised releases terminating with— | | | | | |
|---|---|---|---|---|---|---|---|
| | | No violation | Technical violations[a] | | | New crime[b] | Administrative case closures |
| | | | Drug use | Fugitive status | Other | | |
| **Misdemeanors**[c] | **646** | **66.4 %** | **7.9%** | **5.9%** | **8.5%** | **9.0%** | **2.3%** |
| Fraudulent property offense | 61 | 72.1 | 4.9 | 4.9 | 13.1 | 4.9 | 0.0 |
| Larceny | 100 | 57.0 | 12.0 | 11.0 | 10.0 | 10.0 | 0.0 |
| Drug possession[c] | 191 | 55.0 | 13.1 | 8.4 | 9.4 | 12.0 | 2.1 |
| Immigration misdemeanors | 17 | 64.7 | 0.0 | 0.0 | 23.5 | 0.0 | 11.8 |
| Traffic offenses | 79 | 77.2 | 6.3 | 0.0 | 6.3 | 6.3 | 3.8 |
| Other misdemeanors | 198 | 76.3 | 3.0 | 4.0 | 5.1 | 8.6 | 3.0 |

Note: Offenses for 25 felony offenders could not be determined.
— Too few cases to obtain statistically reliable data.
[a]Supervision terminated with incarceration or removal to inactive status for violation of supervision conditions other than charges for new offenses.
[b]Supervision terminated with incarceration or removal to inactive status after arrest for a "major" or "minor" offense.
[c]In this table "murder" includes nonnegligent manslaughter; "sexual abuse" includes only violent sex offenses; "fraud" excludes tax fraud; "larceny" excludes transportation of stolen property; "other property offenses" excludes fraudulent property offenses and includes destruction of property and trespassing; "tax law violations" includes tax fraud; "obscene material" denotes the mail or transport thereof; "misdemeanors" includes misdemeanors, petty offenses, and unknown offense levels; and "drug possession" also includes other drug misdemeanors.

SOURCE: "Table 7.5. Outcomes of Supervised Release, by Offense, October 1, 2003–September 30, 2004," in *Compendium of Federal Justice Statistics, 2004,* U.S. Department of Justice, Office of Justice Programs, Bureau of Justice Statistics, December 2006, http://www.ojp.usdoj.gov/bjs/pub/pdf/cfjs0407.pdf (accessed January 24, 2007)

**TABLE 8.6**

## Adults on parole by region and jurisdiction, 2005

| Region and jurisdiction | Parole population, 1/1/05 | 2005 Entries | 2005 Exits | Parole population 12/31/05 | Percent change, 2005 | Number on parole per 100,000 adult residents, 12/31/05 |
|---|---|---|---|---|---|---|
| **U.S. total** | 771,852 | 516,400 | 503,800 | 784,408 | 1.6% | 350 |
| Federal | 89,589 | 36,121 | 34,549 | 91,211 | 1.8% | 41 |
| State | 682,263 | 480,300 | 469,300 | 693,197 | 1.6 | 309 |
| **Northeast** | 154,309 | 70,200 | 72,400 | 152,120 | −1.4% | 363 |
| Connecticut | 2,552 | 2,813 | 2,794 | 2,571 | 0.7 | 96 |
| Maine | 32 | 1 | 1 | 32 | 0.0 | 3 |
| Massachusetts | 3,854 | 5,062 | 5,337 | 3,579 | −7.1 | 73 |
| New Hampshire | 1,212 | 861 | 671 | 1,402 | * | 139 |
| New Jersey | 13,880 | 10,818 | 10,824 | 13,874 | 0.0 | 211 |
| New York | 54,524 | 23,340 | 24,331 | 53,533 | −1.8 | 364 |
| Pennsylvania[a] | 76,989 | 26,300 | 27,500 | 75,732 | −1.6 | 787 |
| Rhode Island[b] | 344 | 381 | 389 | 338 | −1.7 | 41 |
| Vermont[b, c] | 922 | 657 | 520 | 1,059 | 14.9 | 216 |
| **Midwest** | 127,338 | 99,252 | 95,760 | 130,830 | 2.7% | 262 |
| Illinois | 34,277 | 35,636 | 35,337 | 34,576 | 0.9 | 362 |
| Indiana | 6,627 | 6,446 | 5,778 | 7,295 | 10.1 | 156 |
| Iowa[b] | 3,325 | 2,665 | 2,430 | 3,560 | 7.1 | 155 |
| Kansas[b] | 4,525 | 4,500 | 4,359 | 4,666 | 3.1 | 225 |
| Michigan | 20,924 | 10,429 | 11,375 | 19,978 | −4.5 | 263 |
| Minnesota | 3,676 | 5,035 | 4,745 | 3,966 | 7.9 | 101 |
| Missouri | 17,400 | 13,458 | 12,484 | 18,374 | 5.6 | 414 |
| Nebraska | 801 | 869 | 1,003 | 667 | −16.7 | 50 |
| North Dakota | 246 | 728 | 687 | 287 | 16.7 | 57 |
| Ohio | 18,882 | 9,956 | 9,326 | 19,512 | 3.3 | 224 |
| South Dakota | 2,217 | 1,848 | 1,621 | 2,444 | 10.2 | 414 |
| Wisconsin | 14,438 | 7,682 | 6,615 | 15,505 | 7.4 | 365 |
| **South** | 229,775 | 104,986 | 100,733 | 234,007 | 1.8% | 288 |
| Alabama | 7,745 | 3,030 | 3,523 | 7,252 | −6.4 | 208 |
| Arkansas | 13,476 | 8,130 | 5,075 | 16,531 | 22.7 | 782 |
| Delaware | 539 | 361 | 300 | 600 | 11.3 | 92 |
| District of Columbia[c] | 5,253 | 2,112 | 2,180 | 5,288 | 0.7 | 1,214 |
| Florida | 4,484 | 6,198 | 5,897 | 4,785 | 6.7 | 34 |
| Georgia | 23,344 | 11,366 | 11,859 | 22,851 | −2.1 | 338 |
| Kentucky | 8,255 | 5,727 | 4,420 | 9,562 | 15.8 | 298 |
| Louisiana | 24,219 | 13,330 | 13,477 | 24,072 | −0.6 | 712 |
| Maryland | 14,351 | 7,658 | 7,738 | 14,271 | −0.6 | 339 |
| Mississippi | 1,758 | 996 | 784 | 1,970 | 12.1 | 90 |
| North Carolina | 2,882 | 3,506 | 3,287 | 3,101 | 7.6 | 47 |
| Oklahoma[c] | 4,329 | 1,488 | 1,800 | 4,017 | −7.2 | 148 |
| South Carolina | 3,237 | 1,050 | 1,132 | 3,155 | −2.5 | 97 |
| Tennessee[b] | 8,223 | 3,748 | 3,126 | 8,721 | 6.1 | 190 |
| Texas | 102,072 | 32,701 | 32,857 | 101,916 | −0.2 | 611 |
| Virginia | 4,392 | 2,570 | 2,463 | 4,499 | 2.4 | 78 |
| West Virginia | 1,216 | 1,015 | 815 | 1,416 | 16.4 | 99 |
| **West** | 170,841 | 205,866 | 200,380 | 176,240 | 3.2% | 347 |
| Alaska[b] | 949 | 645 | 621 | 973 | 2.5 | 202 |
| Arizona | 5,728 | 11,782 | 11,402 | 6,108 | 6.6 | 138 |
| California[b] | 110,262 | 162,329 | 160,848 | 111,743 | 1.3 | 421 |
| Colorado | 7,383 | 6,880 | 6,067 | 8,196 | 11.0 | 234 |
| Hawaii | 2,296 | 632 | 722 | 2,119 | −7.7 | 213 |
| Idaho | 2,370 | 1,443 | 1,331 | 2,482 | 4.7 | 233 |
| Montana[b] | 810 | 570 | 545 | 835 | 3.1 | 114 |
| Nevada | 3,610 | 2,612 | 2,257 | 3,965 | 9.8 | 217 |

**TABLE 8.6**

**Adults on parole by region and jurisdiction, 2005** [CONTINUED]

| Region and jurisdiction | Parole population, 1/1/05 | 2005 | | Parole population 12/31/05 | Percent change, 2005 | Number on parole per 100,000 adult residents, 12/31/05 |
|---|---|---|---|---|---|---|
| | | Entries | Exits | | | |
| New Mexico | 2,469 | 1,439 | 1,042 | 2,866 | 16.1 | 197 |
| Oregon | 20,515 | 9,037 | 8,053 | 21,499 | 4.8 | 766 |
| Utah | 3,246 | 2,502 | 2,471 | 3,277 | 1.0 | 188 |
| Washington[d] | 10,640 | 5,668 | 4,740 | 11,568 | 8.7 | 239 |
| Wyoming | 563 | 327 | 281 | 609 | 8.2 | 153 |

Note: Because of nonresponse or incomplete data, the parole population for some jurisdictions on December 31, 2005, does not equal the population on January 1, plus entries, minus exits.

*Not calculated.

[a]Data for entries and exits were estimated for nonreporting county agencies.

[b]Excludes parolees in one of the following categories: absconder, out of state, or inactive.

[c]All data were estimated.

[d]Due to a change in recordkeeping procedures, data are not comparable to previous reports.

SOURCE: Lauren E. Glaze and Thomas P. Bonczar, "Table 4. Adults on Parole, 2005," in *Probation and Parole in the United States, 2005*, U.S. Department of Justice, Office of Justice Programs, Bureau of Justice Statistics, November 2006, http://www.ojp.usdoj.gov/bjs/pub/pdf/ppus05.pdf (accessed January 24, 2007)

**TABLE 8.7**

## Characteristics of adults on parole, 1995, 2000, and 2005

| Characteristic | 1995 | 2000 | 2005 |
|---|---|---|---|
| Total | 100% | 100% | 100% |
| **Gender** | | | |
| Male | 90% | 88% | 88% |
| Female | 10 | 12 | 12 |
| **Race/Hispanic origin** | | | |
| White[a] | 34% | 38% | 41% |
| Black[a] | 45 | 40 | 40 |
| Hispanic | 21 | 21 | 18 |
| American Indian/ Alaska Native[a] | 1 | 1 | 1 |
| Asian/Native Hawaiian/other Pacific Islander[a] | — | — | 1 |
| **Status of supervision** | | | |
| Active | 78% | 83% | 83% |
| Inactive | 11 | 4 | 4 |
| Absconder | 6 | 7 | 7 |
| Supervised out of state | 4 | 5 | 4 |
| Other | — | 1 | 1 |
| **Sentence length** | | | |
| Less than1 year | 6% | 3% | 6% |
| 1 year or more | 94 | 97 | 94 |
| **Type of offense** | | | |
| Violent | N/A | N/A | 25% |
| Property | N/A | N/A | 25 |
| Drug | N/A | N/A | 37 |
| Public order | N/A | N/A | 6 |
| Other | N/A | N/A | 7 |
| **Adults entering parole** | | | |
| Discretionary parole | 50% | 37% | 31% |
| Mandatory parole | 45 | 54 | 51 |
| Reinstatement | 4 | 6 | 8 |
| Other | 2 | 2 | 10 |
| **Adults leaving parole** | | | |
| Successful completion | 45% | 43% | 45% |
| Returned to incarceration | 41 | 42 | 38 |
|    With new sentence | 12 | 11 | 12 |
|    With revocation pending | 18 | 30 | 25 |
|    Unknown | 11 | 1 | 1 |
| Absconder[b] | N/A | 9 | 11 |
| Other unsuccessful[b] | N/A | 2 | 2 |
| Transferred | 2 | 1 | 1 |
| Death | 1 | 1 | 1 |
| Other | 10 | 2 | 2 |

Note: For every characteristic there were persons of unknown type. Detail may not sum to total because of rounding.
—Less than 0.5%.
—Not available.
[a]Excludes persons of Hispanic origin.
[b]In 1995 absconder and other unsuccessful statuses were reported among other.

SOURCE: Lauren E. Glaze and Thomas P. Bonczar, "Table 6. Characteristics of Adults on Parole, 1995, 2000, and 2005," in *Probation and Parole in the United States, 2005*, U.S. Department of Justice, Office of Justice Programs, Bureau of Justice Statistics, November 2006, http://www.ojp.usdoj.gov/bjs/pub/pdf/ppus05.pdf (accessed January 24, 2007)

**TABLE 8.8**

Outcomes of parole, by offense, October 1, 2003–September 30, 2004

| Most serious offense of conviction | Number of parole terminations | No violation | Technical violations[a] | | | New crime[b] | Administrative case closures |
|---|---|---|---|---|---|---|---|
| | | | Drug use | Fugitive status | Other | | |
| **All offenses** | 1,391 | 49.3% | 10.8% | 7.0% | 9.3% | 17.3% | 6.2% |
| **Felonies** | 1,385 | 49.2% | 10.8% | 7.1% | 9.3% | 17.4% | 6.1% |
| Violent offenses | 525 | 36.6% | 14.9% | 9.1% | 9.7% | 23.0% | 6.7% |
| Murder[c] | 59 | 28.8 | 15.3 | 3.4 | 8.5 | 35.6 | 8.5 |
| Assault | 39 | 38.5 | 10.3 | 5.1 | 20.5 | 12.8 | 12.8 |
| Robbery | 383 | 38.6 | 14.6 | 9.9 | 8.9 | 21.7 | 6.3 |
| Sexual abuse[c] | 14 | 28.6 | 42.9 | 7.1 | 14.3 | 7.1 | 0.0 |
| Kidnapping | 29 | 27.6 | 10.3 | 13.8 | 6.9 | 37.9 | 3.4 |
| Threats against the President | 1 | — | — | — | — | — | — |
| Property offenses | 127 | 55.1% | 4.7% | 5.5% | 8.7% | 18.1% | 7.9% |
| Fraudulent | 57 | 64.9% | 3.5% | 3.5% | 10.5% | 12.3% | 5.3% |
| Embezzlement | 3 | — | — | — | — | — | — |
| Fraud[c] | 45 | 66.7 | 2.2 | 2.2 | 11.1 | 13.3 | 4.4 |
| Forgery | 7 | — | — | — | — | — | — |
| Counterfeiting | 2 | — | — | — | — | — | — |
| Other | 70 | 47.1% | 5.7% | 7.1% | 7.1% | 22.9% | 10.0% |
| Burglary | 29 | 31.0 | 6.9 | 0.0 | 10.3 | 34.5 | 17.2 |
| Larceny[c] | 18 | 55.6 | 5.6 | 11.1 | 5.6 | 11.1 | 11.1 |
| Motor vehicle theft | 14 | 50.0 | 7.1 | 14.3 | 7.1 | 21.4 | 0.0 |
| Arson and explosives | 5 | — | — | — | — | — | — |
| Transportation of stolen property | 1 | — | — | — | — | — | — |
| Other property offenses[c] | 3 | — | — | — | — | — | — |
| Drug offenses | 560 | 60.4% | 8.0% | 5.2% | 8.4% | 12.5% | 5.5% |
| Trafficking | 484 | 62.6 | 7.4 | 4.8 | 7.6 | 12.6 | 5.0 |
| Possession and other drug offenses | 76 | 46.1 | 11.8 | 7.9 | 13.2 | 11.8 | 9.2 |
| Public-order offenses | 100 | 50.0% | 9.0% | 8.0% | 15.0% | 14.0% | 4.0% |
| Regulatory | 11 | 63.6% | 0.0% | 0.0% | 9.1% | 27.3% | 0.0% |
| Transportation | 2 | — | — | — | — | — | — |
| Custom laws | 1 | — | — | — | — | — | — |
| Other regulatory offenses | 8 | — | — | — | — | — | — |
| Other | 89 | 48.3% | 10.1% | 9.0% | 15.7% | 12.4% | 4.5% |
| Tax law violations[c] | 2 | — | — | — | — | — | — |
| Bribery | 2 | — | — | — | — | — | — |
| Perjury, contempt, and intimidation | 5 | — | — | — | — | — | — |
| Escape | 9 | — | — | — | — | — | — |
| Racketeering and extortion | 42 | 69.0 | 0.0 | 4.8 | 4.8 | 14.3 | 7.1 |
| Nonviolent sex offenses | 12 | 33.3 | 33.3 | 0.0 | 16.7 | 8.3 | 8.3 |
| All other offenses | 17 | 5.9 | 29.4 | 17.6 | 35.3 | 11.8 | 0.0 |
| Weapon offenses | 69 | 43.5% | 17.4% | 8.7% | 7.2% | 15.9% | 7.2% |
| Immigration offenses | 2 | — | — | — | — | — | — |
| **Misdemeanors[c]** | 6 | — | — | — | — | — | — |
| Drug possession[c] | 3 | — | — | — | — | — | — |
| Immigration misdemeanors | 1 | — | — | — | — | — | — |
| Other misdemeanors | 2 | — | — | — | — | — | — |

—Too few cases to obtain statistically reliable data.

[a]Supervision terminated with incarceration or removal to inactive status for violation of supervision conditions other than charges for new offenses.

[b]Supervision terminated with incarceration or removal to inactive status after arrest for a "major" or "minor" offense.

[c]In this table "murder" includes nonnegligent manslaughter; "sexual abuse" includes only violent sex offenses; "fraud" excludes tax fraud; "larceny" excludes transportation of stolen property; "tax law violations" includes tax fraud; "misdemeanors" includes misdemeanors, petty offenses, and unknown offense levels; and "drug possession" also includes other drug misdemeanors.

SOURCE: "Table 7.7. Outcomes of Parole, by Offense, October 1, 2003–September 30, 2004," in *Compendium of Federal Justice Statistics, 2004*, U.S. Department of Justice, Office of Justice Programs, Bureau of Justice Statistics, December 2006, http://www.ojp.usdoj.gov/bjs/pub/pdf/cfjs0407.pdf (accessed January 24, 2007)

**TABLE 8.9**

**Characteristics of offenders terminating parole, October 1, 2003–September 30, 2004**

| Offender characteristic | Number of parole terminations | No violation | Technical violations[a] | | | New crime[b] | Administrative case closures |
|---|---|---|---|---|---|---|---|
| | | | Drug use | Fugitive status | Other | | |
| **All offenders[c]** | 1,391 | 49.3% | 10.8% | 7.0% | 9.3% | 17.3% | 6.2% |
| **Male/female** | | | | | | | |
| Male | 1,343 | 48.9% | 10.9% | 6.9% | 9.3% | 17.7% | 6.3% |
| Female | 46 | 60.9 | 6.5 | 10.9 | 10.9 | 6.5 | 4.3 |
| **Race** | | | | | | | |
| White | 622 | 61.9% | 5.1% | 6.4% | 8.2% | 12.9% | 5.5% |
| Black or African American | 662 | 39.9 | 15.3 | 7.4 | 8.9 | 21.6 | 6.9 |
| American Indian or Alaska Native | 25 | 36.0 | 8.0 | 4.0 | 16.0 | 36.0 | 0.0 |
| Asian /Native Hawaiian or other Pacific Islander | 4 | — | — | — | — | — | — |
| **Ethnicity** | | | | | | | |
| Hispanic or Latino | 128 | 53.9% | 3.9% | 7.8% | 11.7% | 15.6% | 7.0% |
| Not Hispanic or Latino | 1,245 | 49.1 | 11.5 | 7.0 | 9.1 | 17.3 | 6.1 |
| **Age** | | | | | | | |
| 19–20 years | 1 | — | — | — | — | — | — |
| 21–30 years | 67 | 46.3% | 11.9% | 7.5% | 9.0% | 16.4% | 9.0% |
| 31–40 years | 203 | 34.5 | 15.8 | 7.4 | 12.8 | 23.6 | 5.9 |
| Over 40 years | 1,120 | 52.1 | 9.8 | 7.0 | 8.8 | 16.3 | 6.1 |
| **Education** | | | | | | | |
| Less than high school graduate | 575 | 47.8% | 9.7% | 8.2% | 8.9% | 17.7% | 7.7% |
| High school graduate | 478 | 48.1 | 13.2 | 6.3 | 10.3 | 17.6 | 4.6 |
| Some college | 171 | 63.7 | 9.4 | 2.9 | 8.8 | 11.1 | 4.1 |
| College graduate | 40 | 82.5 | 2.5 | 2.5 | 2.5 | 5.0 | 5.0 |
| **Drug abuse** | | | | | | | |
| No known abuse | 636 | 62.5% | 4.4% | 4.4% | 7.4% | 8.8% | 12.5% |
| Drug history | 719 | 58.0 | 5.0 | 5.9 | 5.0 | 14.3 | 11.8 |

— Too few cases to obtain statistically reliable data.

[a]Violation of supervision conditions other than charges for new offenses.

[b]Includes both "major" and "minor" offenses.

[c]Total includes offenders whose characteristics could not be determined.

SOURCE: "Table 7.8. Characteristics of Offenders Terminating Parole, October 1, 2003–September 30, 2004," in *Compendium of Federal Justice Statistics, 2004*, U.S. Department of Justice, Office of Justice Programs, Bureau of Justice Statistics, December 2006, http://www.ojp.usdoj.gov/bjs/pub/pdf/cfjs0407.pdf (accessed January 24, 2007)

# CHAPTER 9
# JUVENILE CRIME

## WHO IS A JUVENILE?

Howard N. Snyder and Melissa Sickmund of the National Center for Juvenile Justice, in *Juvenile Offenders and Victims: 2006 National Report* (2006, http://ojjdp .ncjrs.org/ojstatbb/nr2006/downloads/NR2006.pdf), observe that "in most states, the juvenile court has original jurisdiction over all youth charged with a law violation who were younger than age eighteen at the time of the offense, arrest, or referral to court."

As of 2004, thirty-seven states and the District of Columbia retained juvenile court jurisdiction over offenders aged seventeen; ten states had an upper age limit of sixteen for juveniles; and three states limited juvenile court jurisdiction to those aged fifteen and younger. (See Table 9.1.) Many states place certain young offenders in the jurisdiction of the criminal court rather than the juvenile court based on the youth's age, offense, or previous court history.

## JUVENILE ARRESTS

The Federal Bureau of Investigation (FBI) compiles the Uniform Crime Reports (UCR) annually. In *Crime in the United States, 2005* (September 2006, http://www.fbi .gov/ucr/05cius/index.html), the UCR notes that in 2005 juveniles accounted for 1.6 million arrests, or 15.3% of all arrests, in the United States. Juveniles under age eighteen accounted for 5,834 (48.6%) of all arson arrests, 76,817 (37.2%) of all vandalism arrests, and 148,795 (29.7%) of all disorderly conduct arrests. (See Table 1.5 in Chapter 1.)

According to the UCR, between 1996 and 2005 the number of juvenile arrests decreased by 24.9%. The number of juveniles arrested for motor vehicle theft dropped by 54% during this period, and 52.1% fewer juveniles were arrested for forgery and counterfeiting. Furthermore, arrests of juveniles for buying, receiving, and possessing stolen property were down 47.8%. How-

ever, the number of juveniles arrested for prostitution and commercialized vice increased by 20.3% between 1996 and 2005 and the number arrested for disorderly conduct grew by 3.3%.

The Office of Juvenile Justice and Delinquency Prevention (OJJDP) reports in the *OJJDP Statistical Briefing Book* (September 8, 2006, http://ojjdp.ncjrs.gov/ojstatbb/) that an estimated 2.2 million juveniles were arrested in 2004. This number represents a decrease of 22% from 1995 and a decrease of 2% from 2003. (See Table 9.2.) Most of the juveniles who were arrested were males and were age fifteen or older. The only categories of crime in which juveniles under fifteen accounted for the majority of juvenile arrests were arson (61%) and sex offenses other than forcible rape and prostitution (51%). Juveniles under age fifteen accounted for about four out of ten juvenile arrests for forcible rape, larceny-theft, vandalism, and disorderly conduct. Arrest rates for female juvenile offenders in 2004 were highest for prostitution and commercialized vice (72% of all juvenile arrests for these crimes), running away (59%), larceny-theft (42%), offenses against family and children (38%), and embezzlement (37%).

### Handling of Juvenile Arrests

Police have a variety of options when dealing with juvenile offenders. According to the UCR, 20.2% of all juvenile cases in 2005 were handled within the police department, and the offenders were released. (See Table 9.3.) Some 7.4% were referred to criminal or adult court, whereas 70.7% were referred to juvenile court. Rural counties were more likely than metropolitan and suburban counties to refer cases to criminal or adult court (14%), whereas metropolitan counties were more likely than suburban or rural counties to refer cases to juvenile court (73.8%). Cities with populations over 250,000 were more likely than smaller cities to handle cases within the police department (31.5%), whereas cities with populations of 100,000 to 249,000 were more likely to refer juveniles to juvenile courts (73.7%) than larger or smaller cities.

## TABLE 9.1

**Oldest age for original juvenile court jurisdiction in delinquency matters, 2004**

| Age | State |
|---|---|
| 15 | Connecticut, New York, North Carolina |
| 16 | Georgia, Illinois, Louisiana, Massachusetts, Michigan, Missouri, New Hampshire, South Carolina, Texas, Wisconsin |
| 17 | Alabama, Alaska, Arizona, Arkansas, California, Colorado, Delaware, District of Columbia, Florida, Hawaii, Idaho, Indiana, Iowa, Kansas, Kentucky, Maine, Maryland, Minnesota, Mississippi, Montana, Nebraska, Nevada, New Jersey, New Mexico, North Dakota, Ohio, Oklahoma, Oregon, Pennsylvania, Rhode Island, South Dakota, Tennessee, Utah, Vermont, Virginia, Washington, West Virginia, Wyoming |

SOURCE: Howard N. Snyder and Melissa Sickmund, "Oldest Age for Original Juvenile Court Jurisdiction in Delinquency Matters, 2004," in *Juvenile Offenders and Victims: 2006 National Report*, U.S. Department of Justice, Office of Justice Programs, Office of Justice and Juvenile Delinquency Prevention, 2006, http://ojjdp.ncjrs.gov/ojstatbb/nr2006/downloads/chapter4 .pdf (accessed January 25, 2007)

## Arrest Rates by Gender

Even though the majority of juveniles arrested are males, the number of female arrests has decreased less in recent years than the male arrests in most categories. According to Howard N. Snyder of the National Center for Juvenile Justice, in *Juvenile Arrests in 2004* (December 2006, http://www.ncjrs.gov/pdffiles1/ojjdp/214563.pdf), between 1980 and 2004 the number of females arrested for aggravated assault grew by 93%, compared to 11% for males. Similarly, the number of juveniles arrested for simple assault increased by 290% for females and 106% for males, and for weapons law violations by 160% for females and 22% for males.

The UCR reports that in 2005, 70% of arrested juveniles were male and 30% were female. The ratio of juvenile male to female arrests was even higher for violent crime: in 2005, 82% were male and 18% were female. Even though more male juveniles were arrested for most types of crimes than female juveniles, more female juveniles were arrested for prostitution and commercialized vice (668 females versus 202 males) and running away (39,809 females versus 28,987 males). About half as many females as males were arrested for

## TABLE 9.2

**Estimated number of juvenile arrests, 2004**

| Most serious offense | 2004 estimated number of juvenile arrests | Percent of total juvenile arrests | | Percent change | | |
|---|---|---|---|---|---|---|
| | | Female | Under age 15 | 1995–04 | 2000–04 | 2003–04 |
| Total | 2,202,000 | 30% | 32% | −22% | −9% | −2% |
| Violent crime index | 91,100 | 19% | 32% | −31% | −5% | −1% |
| Murder and nonnegligent manslaughter | 1,110 | 9% | 12% | −63% | −8% | 0% |
| Forcible rape | 4,210 | 3% | 38% | −22% | −10% | 0% |
| Robbery | 25,340 | 10% | 24% | −44% | −5% | 0% |
| Aggravated assault | 60,450 | 24% | 35% | −23% | −6% | −2% |
| Property crime index | 452,300 | 34% | 36% | −40% | −15% | −3% |
| Burglary | 81,600 | 12% | 35% | −39% | −15% | −4% |
| Larceny-theft | 323,500 | 42% | 37% | −38% | −14% | −2% |
| Motor vehicle theft | 39,300 | 17% | 25% | −53% | −21% | −9% |
| Arson | 7,800 | 14% | 61% | −34% | −10% | −3% |
| Nonindex | | | | | | |
| Other assaults | 249,900 | 33% | 43% | 8% | 7% | 1% |
| Forgery and counterfeiting | 4,900 | 34% | 15% | −47% | −31% | 5% |
| Fraud | 7,500 | 36% | 18% | −35% | −29% | −2% |
| Embezzlement | 1,000 | 37% | 5% | −21% | −46% | −12% |
| Stolen property (buying, receiving, possessing) | 23,300 | 17% | 27% | −49% | −18% | −4% |
| Vandalism | 103,400 | 14% | 44% | −32% | −11% | −4% |
| Weapons (carrying, possessing, etc.) | 40,500 | 11% | 35% | −30% | 11% | 6% |
| Prostitution and commercialized vice | 1,800 | 72% | 12% | 36% | 44% | 7% |
| Sex offenses (except forcible rape and prostitution) | 18,000 | 9% | 51% | 12% | −3% | 0% |
| Drug abuse violations | 193,900 | 17% | 17% | −4% | −6% | −2% |
| Gambling | 1,700 | 3% | 15% | −30% | 27% | −5% |
| Offenses against the family and children | 5,800 | 38% | 35% | −24% | −30% | −10% |
| Driving under the influence | 19,900 | 21% | 2% | 20% | −10% | −3% |
| Liquor law violations | 130,200 | 35% | 10% | −4% | −22% | −5% |
| Drunkenness | 16,900 | 23% | 12% | −30% | −23% | −4% |
| Disorderly conduct | 198,800 | 32% | 42% | −2% | 7% | 2% |
| Vagrancy | 4,800 | 28% | 31% | −45% | 105% | −12% |
| All other offenses (except traffic) | 379,000 | 28% | 28% | −13% | −11% | −2% |
| Suspicion | 600 | 25% | 28% | −72% | −50% | 18% |
| Curfew and loitering | 137,400 | 31% | 29% | −15% | −12% | −8% |
| Runaways | 119,300 | 59% | 35% | −46% | −18% | −1% |

SOURCE: "Juvenile Arrests: Estimated Number of Juvenile Arrests, 2004," in *OJJDP Statistical Briefing Book*, U.S. Department of Justice, Office of Justice Programs, Office of Juvenile Justice and Delinquency Prevention, September 8, 2006, http://ojjdp.ncjrs.org/ojstatbb/crime/qa05101.asp?qaDate=2004 (accessed January 24, 2007)

TABLE 9.3

## Police disposition of juvenile offenders taken into custody, 2005

[2005 estimated population]

| Population group | | Total^a | Handled within department and released | Referred to juvenile court jurisdiction | Referred to welfare agency | Referred to other police agency | Referred to criminal or adult court | Number of agencies | 2005 estimated population |
|---|---|---|---|---|---|---|---|---|---|
| Total agencies: | Number | 660,974 | 133,664 | 467,288 | 2,461 | 8,808 | 48,753 | 5,138 | 120,999,116 |
| | Percent^b | 100.0 | 20.2 | 70.7 | 0.4 | 1.3 | 7.4 | | |
| Total cities | Number | 553,741 | 116,983 | 389,513 | 1,903 | 6,330 | 39,012 | 3,926 | 85,869,567 |
| | Percent^b | 100.0 | 21.1 | 70.3 | 0.3 | 1.1 | 7.0 | | |
| Group I (250,000 and over) | Number | 133,474 | 42,044 | 90,205 | 143 | 453 | 629 | 30 | 22,983,307 |
| | Percent^b | 100.0 | 31.5 | 67.6 | 0.1 | 0.3 | 0.5 | | |
| Group II (100,000 to 249,999) | Number | 75,918 | 14,152 | 55,947 | 132 | 2,020 | 3,667 | 90 | 13,382,824 |
| | Percent^b | 100.0 | 18.6 | 73.7 | 0.2 | 2.7 | 4.8 | | |
| Group III (50,000 to 99,999) | Number | 101,901 | 20,675 | 72,643 | 656 | 1,477 | 6,450 | 227 | 15,306,602 |
| | Percent^b | 100.0 | 20.3 | 71.3 | 0.6 | 1.4 | 6.3 | | |
| Group IV (25,000 to 49,999) | Number | 77,522 | 13,613 | 56,157 | 347 | 1,282 | 6,123 | 356 | 12,452,163 |
| | Percent^b | 100.0 | 17.6 | 72.4 | 0.4 | 1.7 | 7.9 | | |
| Group V (10,000 to 24,999) | Number | 90,272 | 14,592 | 63,233 | 360 | 482 | 11,605 | 799 | 12,789,350 |
| | Percent^b | 100.0 | 16.2 | 70.0 | 0.4 | 0.5 | 12.9 | | |
| Group VI (under 10,000) | Number | 74,654 | 11,907 | 51,328 | 265 | 616 | 10,538 | 2,424 | 8,955,321 |
| | Percent^b | 100.0 | 15.9 | 68.8 | 0.4 | 0.8 | 14.1 | | |
| Metropolitan counties | Number | 83,412 | 12,923 | 61,531 | 369 | 2,187 | 6,402 | 566 | 26,400,332 |
| | Percent^b | 100.0 | 15.5 | 73.8 | 0.4 | 2.6 | 7.7 | | |
| Nonmetropolitan counties | Number | 23,821 | 3,758 | 16,244 | 189 | 291 | 3,339 | 646 | 8,729,217 |
| | Percent^b | 100.0 | 15.8 | 68.2 | 0.8 | 1.2 | 14.0 | | |
| Suburban area^c | Number | 286,787 | 50,915 | 200,494 | 1,499 | 3,737 | 30,142 | 3,136 | 59,655,663 |
| | Percent^b | 100.0 | 17.8 | 69.9 | 0.5 | 1.3 | 10.5 | | |

^aIncludes all offenses except traffic and neglect cases.
^bBecause of rounding, the percentages may not add to 100.0.
^cSuburban area includes law enforcement agencies in cities with less than 50,000 inhabitants and county law enforcement agencies that are within a metropolitan statistical area. Suburban area excludes all metropolitan agencies associated with a principal city. The agencies associated with suburban areas also appear in other groups within this table.

SOURCE: "Table 68. Police Disposition of Juvenile Offenders Taken into Custody, 2005," in *Crime in the United States 2005*, U.S. Department of Justice, Federal Bureau of Investigation, September 2006, http://www.fbi.gov/ucr/05cius/data/table_68.html (accessed January 24, 2007)

fraud (1,714 females versus 3,065 males), offenses against the family and children (1,173 females versus 1,894 males), and curfew and loitering law violations (26,589 females versus 61,069 males).

### Arrests by Race

As with adult arrest rates, minorities are disproportionately represented in juvenile arrests. The UCR reports that even though African-American youths comprise roughly 15% of the total juvenile population, of nearly 1.6 million juvenile arrests in 2005, 469,382 (29.9%) of those arrested were African-American and 1 million (67.5%) were white.

According to Snyder, a majority (78%) of all juveniles arrested in 2004 were white, 17% were African-American, 4% were Asian or Pacific Islander, and 1% were Native American (most Hispanics were classified as white). Of juveniles arrested for violent crimes in 2004, 52% were white and 46% were African-American, and for property crimes, 69% were white and 28% were African-American. Table 9.4 shows the African-American proportion of juveniles arrested in 2004 for a variety of both violent and property offenses. Of all juveniles arrested for murder, for example, half (50%) were African-American. African-Americans made up 63% of juveniles arrested for

TABLE 9.4

## Arrests of African-American youths as a percentage of all juvenile arrests, 2004

| Most serious offense | Black proportion of juvenile arrests in 2004 |
|---|---|
| Murder | 50% |
| Forcible rape | 34 |
| Robbery | 63 |
| Aggravated assault | 39 |
| Simple assault | 37 |
| Burglary | 27 |
| Larceny-theft | 27 |
| Motor vehicle theft | 40 |
| Weapons | 33 |
| Drug abuse violations | 27 |
| Runaways | 21 |
| Vandalism | 18 |
| Liquor laws | 5 |

SOURCE: Howard N. Snyder, "Juvenile Arrests Disproportionately Involved Minorities," in *Juvenile Arrests 2004*, U.S. Department of Justice, Office of Justice Programs, Office of Juvenile Justice and Delinquency Prevention, December 2006, http://www.ncjrs.gov/pdffiles1/ojjdp/214563.pdf (accessed February 19, 2007)

robbery, 40% for motor vehicle theft, 39% for aggravated assault, and 37% for simple assault.

Snyder reports that in 2004 the rate of arrests for African-American juveniles was 746 per 100,000 juveniles, whereas for white juveniles it was 182 per 100,000, for Native American juveniles, 173 per 100,000, and for Asian juveniles, 78 per 100,000. The rate of property crime arrests for African-American juveniles was 2,288 per 100,000, for Native American juveniles, 1,300 per 100,000, for white juveniles, 1,198 per 100,000, and for Asian juveniles, 557 per 100,000.

According to Snyder, between 1980 and 2004 the difference in arrest rates for African-American and white juveniles decreased. In 1980 the violent crime arrest rate for African-Americans was 6.3 times higher than the white rate; this difference had decreased to 4.1 by 2004. The decrease in the arrest rate differences was mostly due to the decline in differences in arrest rates for robbery from 11.5 in 1980 to 8.4 in 2004.

According to the *OJJDP Statistical Briefing Book*, the African-American juvenile arrest rate reached its highest point in 1995 and has since declined. For white, Asian, and Native American juveniles, "the arrest rates peaked in 1996. Between their peak years and 2005, the juvenile arrest rates declined for each racial group: the decline was 35% for black juveniles, 57% for Asians, 34% for whites, and 33% for American Indians."

## Disposition of Juveniles Arrested

A change in the disposition of juveniles arrested appeared in the 1970s. According to Ann L. Pastore and Kathleen Maguire of the Utilization of Criminal Justice Statistics Project, in the *Sourcebook of Criminal Justice Statistics 2003* (2005, http://www.albany.edu/sourcebook/), in 1972, 50.8% of those arrested were referred to juvenile courts and 45% were handled within police departments and released; only 1.3% were transferred by referral to criminal or adult courts. (See Table 9.5.) By 2004 cases handled internally (followed by release) had dropped to 20.8%. The majority of cases were referred to juvenile court (69.5%). The cases referred to adult jurisdictions had escalated to 7.9% of all cases.

**TABLE 9.5**

**Percent distribution of juveniles taken into police custody, 1972–2004**

[By method of disposition]

| | Referred to juvenile court jurisdiction | Handled within department and released | Referred to criminal or adult court | Referred to other police agency | Referred to welfare agency |
|---|---|---|---|---|---|
| 1972 | 50.8% | 45.0% | 1.3% | 1.6% | 1.3% |
| 1973 | 49.5 | 45.2 | 1.5 | 2.3 | 1.4 |
| 1974 | 47.0 | 44.4 | 3.7 | 2.4 | 2.5 |
| 1975 | 52.7 | 41.6 | 2.3 | 1.9 | 1.4 |
| 1976 | 53.4 | 39.0 | 4.4 | 1.7 | 1.6 |
| 1977 | 53.2 | 38.1 | 3.9 | 1.8 | 3.0 |
| 1978 | 55.9 | 36.6 | 3.8 | 1.8 | 1.9 |
| 1979 | 57.3 | 34.6 | 4.8 | 1.7 | 1.6 |
| 1980 | 58.1 | 33.8 | 4.8 | 1.7 | 1.6 |
| 1981 | 58.0 | 33.8 | 5.1 | 1.6 | 1.5 |
| 1982 | 58.9 | 32.5 | 5.4 | 1.5 | 1.6 |
| 1983 | 57.5 | 32.8 | 4.8 | 1.7 | 3.1 |
| 1984 | 60.0 | 31.5 | 5.2 | 1.3 | 2.0 |
| 1985 | 61.8 | 30.7 | 4.4 | 1.2 | 1.9 |
| 1986 | 61.7 | 29.9 | 5.5 | 1.1 | 1.8 |
| 1987 | 62.0 | 30.3 | 5.2 | 1.0 | 1.4 |
| 1988 | 63.1 | 29.1 | 4.7 | 1.1 | 1.9 |
| 1989 | 63.9 | 28.7 | 4.5 | 1.2 | 1.7 |
| 1990 | 64.5 | 28.3 | 4.5 | 1.1 | 1.6 |
| 1991 | 64.2 | 28.1 | 5.0 | 1.0 | 1.7 |
| 1992 | 62.5 | 30.1 | 4.7 | 1.1 | 1.7 |
| 1993 | 67.3 | 25.6 | 4.8 | 0.9 | 1.5 |
| 1994 | 63.2 | 29.5 | 4.7 | 1.0 | 1.7 |
| 1995 | 65.7 | 28.4 | 3.3 | 0.9 | 1.7 |
| 1996 | 68.6 | 23.3 | 6.2 | 0.9 | 0.9 |
| 1997 | 66.9 | 24.6 | 6.6 | 0.8 | 1.1 |
| 1998 | 69.2 | 22.2 | 6.8 | 0.9 | 1.0 |
| 1999 | 69.2 | 22.5 | 6.4 | 1.0 | 0.8 |
| 2000 | 70.8 | 20.3 | 7.0 | 1.1 | 0.8 |
| 2001 | 72.4 | 19.0 | 6.5 | 1.4 | 0.7 |
| 2002 | 72.8 | 18.1 | 7.0 | 1.4 | 0.7 |
| 2003 | 71.0 | 20.1 | 7.1 | 1.2 | 0.6 |
| 2004 | 69.5 | 20.8 | 7.9 | 1.3 | 0.5 |

Note: These data include all offenses except traffic and neglect cases. Because of rounding, percents may not add to 100.

SOURCE: Ann L. Pastore and Kathleen Maguire, editors, "Table 4.26.2004. Percent Distribution of Juveniles Taken into Police Custody, by Method of Disposition, United States, 1972–2004," in *Sourcebook of Criminal Justice Statistics 2003*, 31st ed., U.S. Department of Justice, Office of Justice Programs, Bureau of Justice Statistics, 2005, http://www.albany.edu/sourcebook/pdf/t4262004.pdf (accessed February 19, 2007)

**FIGURE 9.1**

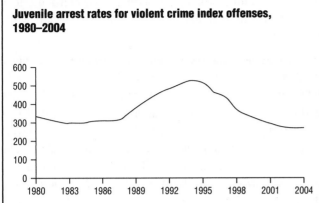

Juvenile arrest rates for violent crime index offenses, 1980–2004

Note: Rates are arrests of persons ages 10–17 per 100,000 persons ages 10–17 in the resident population. The violent crime index includes the offenses of murder and nonnegligent manslaughter, forcible rape, robbery, and aggravated assault.

SOURCE: "Juvenile Arrest Rate Trends: Juvenile Arrest Rates for Violent Crime Index Offenses, 1980–2004," in *OJJDP Statistical Briefing Book*, U.S. Department of Justice, Office of Justice Programs, Office of Juvenile Justice and Delinquency Prevention, September 8, 2006, http://ojjdp.ncjrs.org/ojstatbb/crime/JAR_Display.asp?ID=qa05201 (accessed February 19, 2007)

**FIGURE 9.2**

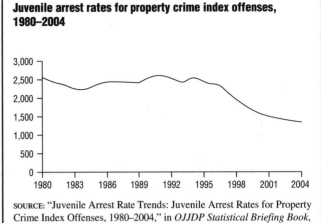

Juvenile arrest rates for property crime index offenses, 1980–2004

SOURCE: "Juvenile Arrest Rate Trends: Juvenile Arrest Rates for Property Crime Index Offenses, 1980–2004," in *OJJDP Statistical Briefing Book*, U.S. Department of Justice, Office of Justice Programs, Office of Juvenile Justice and Delinquency Prevention, September 8, 2006, http://ojjdp.ncjrs.org/ojstatbb/crime/JAR_Display.asp?ID=qa05206 (accessed January 24, 2007)

## Violent Crimes

The *OJJDP Statistical Briefing Book* reports that the rate of juvenile arrests for violent crimes increased dramatically in the late 1980s and early 1990s, peaking in 1994 at 525.4 per 100,000 youths aged ten to seventeen. Between 1994 and 2004 juvenile arrests for Violent Crime Index offenses (murder, nonnegligent manslaughter, forcible rape, robbery, and aggravated assault) declined by 49% to a rate of 269.5 arrests for every 100,000 people aged ten to seventeen. (See Figure 9.1.) For juveniles fifteen to seventeen years of age, the Violent Crime Index arrest rate declined by 43% between 1994 and 2001, compared to a 23% decline for adults eighteen to twenty-four years of age, a 27% drop for arrestees twenty-five to twenty-nine years old, and a 19% decline for adult arrestees thirty to thirty-nine years of age.

Since the 1990s the largest decline in juvenile violent crime arrests is in the murder rate. According to the *OJJDP Statistical Briefing Book*, arrests of juveniles for murder peaked in 1993. Between 1993 and 2004 this rate had dropped by 77% to 1,110 arrests.

The *OJJDP Statistical Briefing Book* notes that juvenile arrest rates for forcible rape, robbery, and aggravated assault also declined from their peak levels in the early to mid-1990s. Between 1980 and 1991 the juvenile arrest rate for forcible rape increased by 44%, from 15.9 to 23. By 2004 the rate had fallen to 12.4, a decrease of 22% from its 1980 level. Between 1995 and 2002 the juvenile arrest rate for robbery fell from 198.9 to 75, a decrease of 62%; however, since 2002 this rate has been slowly rising. The juvenile arrest rate for aggravated assault fell by 39% between 1994 and 2004,

from 293.2 to 178.1. Regardless, the 2004 rate was still 23% higher than it was in 1980 (144.3).

## Property Crimes

The *OJJDP Statistical Briefing Book* reports that from 1980 to 2004 the juvenile arrest rate for Property Crime Index offenses (burglary, larceny-theft, motor vehicle theft, and arson) declined by 47% to a twenty-five-year low, from 2,562.2 to 1,345.4. (See Figure 9.2.) Consistent with a twenty-year trend, in 2001 the Property Crime Index arrest rates were higher for sixteen-year-olds than for any other age group. Adults aged thirty to forty-nine comprised the only age group to register a higher arrest rate in 2001 than in 1980.

According to the *OJJDP Statistical Briefing Book*, between 1994 and 2004 the juvenile arrest rate for burglary declined from 479.6 to 239.9, a decrease of nearly 50%. Compared to 1980, when 230,500 juveniles were arrested for burglary, only 81,600 juveniles were arrested for this offense in 2004. After remaining relatively constant between 1980 and 1997, the juvenile arrest rate for larceny-theft had declined from 1,597.2 in 1997 to 967.4 in 2004, a decrease of 39%. In 2004 females accounted for 43% of all juvenile arrests for larceny-theft. Between 1983 and 1990 the juvenile arrest rate for motor vehicle theft rose by 137%, from 146.1 to 347. Between 1990 and 2004 this rate declined to 116.5. After rising by 55%, from 22 in 1987 to 34.1 in 1994, the number of juvenile arson arrests declined by 36% to 21.7 in 2004, its lowest point since 1983.

## Drug Abuse Violations

The *OJJDP Statistical Briefing Book* indicates that the juvenile arrest rate for drug abuse violations increased from 291.6 in 1983 to 745.7 in 1997, a rise of 155%. (See Figure 9.3.) By 2004 the arrest rate declined 23% to 576.

FIGURE 9.3

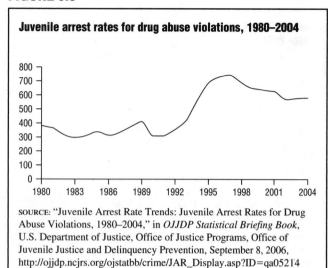

**Juvenile arrest rates for drug abuse violations, 1980–2004**

SOURCE: "Juvenile Arrest Rate Trends: Juvenile Arrest Rates for Drug Abuse Violations, 1980–2004," in *OJJDP Statistical Briefing Book*, U.S. Department of Justice, Office of Justice Programs, Office of Juvenile Justice and Delinquency Prevention, September 8, 2006, http://ojjdp.ncjrs.org/ojstatbb/crime/JAR_Display.asp?ID=qa05214 (accessed January 24, 2007)

However, the 2004 arrest rate was still almost twice the 1990 rate (304.1). The arrest rate for female juveniles increased much more rapidly than for males; between 1990 and 2004 the arrest rate for females increased 194%, from 69.4 to 204.3, compared to 76% for males, from 526.9 to 929.8.

## JUVENILES AND GUNS

Schools and neighborhoods can be dangerous places for many young Americans. Knives, revolvers, and even shotguns turn up in searches of school lockers. News reports describe incidents of children being shot on playgrounds or of youths firing rifles as they cruise the streets in cars. The use of deadly weapons in violent incidents has increased fear among citizens of all ages.

The OJJDP explains in *Juvenile Offenders and Victims: 2006 National Report* that murders committed by juveniles increased more than 200% from 1,010 in 1984 to 3,125 in 2002 (http://ojjdp.ncjrs.org/ojstatbb/nr2006/downloads/chapter3.pdf). Murders of nonrelatives by juveniles using firearms increased 345% from 566 in 1984 to 2,519 in 1994, accounting for 90% of the overall increase in murders by juveniles during that period. Murders by juveniles declined steadily after 1994 to 1,067 in 2002; 80% of this decrease was due to the drop in murders of nonfamily members by juvenile males with a firearm. In 2002, 698 victims of juvenile murders were killed with a firearm.

Of known juvenile offenders who committed murder between 1993 and 2002, 74% used a firearm. Males were twice as likely to use a firearm as females—77% compared with 35%. Those aged seventeen were more likely than younger juveniles to use a firearm when committing murder; 77% of seventeen-year-olds used a gun compared with 74% of sixteen-year-olds and 70% of those younger than age sixteen. African-American youth were more likely to use a gun (80%) than white youth (66%).

According to the *2005 Youth Risk Behavior Survey* (June 9, 2006, http://www.cdc.gov/mmwr/PDF/SS/SS5505.pdf), 6.5% of U.S. high school students said in 2005 that they had carried a weapon (such as a gun, knife, or club) on school property in the past thirty days. Males (10.2%) were more likely to say that they carried a weapon at school than females (2.6%). In addition, 18.5% of students said that they had carried a gun (anywhere) in the previous thirty days.

## SCHOOL CRIME

As reported by the National Center for Education Statistics (NCES) and the Bureau of Justice Statistics (BJS) in *Indicators of School Crime and Safety: 2006* (December 2006, http://nces.ed.gov/pubs2007/2007003.pdf), students 12 to 18 years of age were the victims of approximately 1.4 million nonfatal crimes at school during the 2004–05 school year. Of these crimes, most were thefts (863,000). Of the 583,000 violent crimes, 107,000 included rape, sexual assault, robbery, or aggravated assault.

Among young people aged five to eighteen, there were twenty-one homicides that occurred at school, on the way to or from school, or at a school-related event during the 2004–05 school year, a considerable increase from the eleven counted in 2000–01. However, the 2004–05 number is still lower than the number of homicides of school-aged youth for most years during the 1990s, when the numbers of school-related murders ranged from twenty-eight to thirty-four per year. There were also seven suicides of students at school in 2004–05. The rate of homicide or suicide of a school-aged youth at school was about one per two million students in 2004–05.

In 2005, 25% of students in grades 9–12 reported that drugs were readily available on school property, and 8% of students reported that they had been threatened or injured with a weapon while on school property during the previous 12 months. Some 14% of students in grades 9–12 reported that they had been in a fight on school property during the previous 12 months. In addition 4% of high school students had consumed at least one alcoholic drink, and 5% had used marijuana on school property during the past thirty days.

Approximately 6% of students aged twelve to eighteen reported in 2005 that they were afraid of being attacked or harmed at school, and 5% were afraid of being attacked or harmed elsewhere. The percentage of students who said that they were afraid of being attacked at school (including on the way to or from school) dropped from 12% to 6% between 1995 and 2001 and has remained steady since that time. African-American (9%) and Hispanic (10%) students were more likely than white (4%) students to be afraid of being attacked or harmed. Some 6% of students aged twelve to eighteen said fear of attack had led them to avoid a school activity or some part of their school during the previous six months; 2% avoided a school activity and 4% avoided certain places in school. Students in urban areas were more likely (6%) to avoid places in school than suburban (4%) and rural (4%) students.

## School Shootings

Despite the relative safety of schools, several school shootings have received national media attention in the past several years.

- April 16, 2007: Cho Seung-Hui, a twenty-three-year-old student at Virginia Tech, opened fire at the school and killed thirty-two people before shooting himself. Some of those killed were still in their teens. Considered the worst school shooting in U.S. history, the incident was followed by bomb threats and other threats of violence at various schools across the country, prompting school administrators, politicians, parents, and students to once again review safety procedures and new ways to keep the learning environment safe.

- October 3, 2006: Thirty-two-year-old Charles Roberts IV shot ten schoolgirls aged six to thirteen years old at the one-room West Nickel Mines Amish School in Nickel Mines, Pennsylvania, before shooting himself. Five of the girls and Roberts died.

- March 21, 2005: A sixteen-year-old killed his grandfather and companion. He then went to Red Lake High School in Red Lake, Minnesota, and killed five students, a security guard, a teacher, and finally himself.

- April 14, 2003: One fifteen-year-old student was killed and three were wounded at John McDonogh High School in New Orleans, Louisiana, by gunfire from four teenagers (none was a student at the school).

- March 5, 2001: Two were killed and thirteen wounded at Santee High School in Santana, California, when a student opened fire from a school bathroom.

- February 29, 2000: A six-year-old student was killed at Theo J. Buell Elementary School near Flint, Michigan, by a fellow student (also six years old) who brought a handgun to school.

- April 20, 1999: Twelve students and a teacher were fatally shot at Columbine High School in Littleton, Colorado, by students Eric Harris, eighteen, and Dylan Klebold, seventeen, who eventually killed themselves after an hour-long rampage.

## Nonfatal School Crimes

According to *Indicators of School Crime and Safety: 2006*, between 1992 and 2004 the victimization rates for students aged twelve to eighteen declined both at school and away from school. This decrease applied to total crime rates, as well as rates of theft, violent crime, and serious violent crime. The total crime and theft victimization rates for students at school were lower in 2004 than 2003. Specifically, the victimization rate for students aged twelve to eighteen at school decreased from 73 per 1,000 students in 2003 to 45 per 1,000 in 2004, and theft victimization rates declined from 45 per 1,000 students in 2003 to 33 per 1,000 in 2004.

Older students (aged fifteen to eighteen) were less likely to be victims of crime at school than younger students (aged twelve to fourteen). Female students were less likely to be crime victims or victims of serious violent crimes at school than male students. Also, in 2005, no measurable differences were detected in the percentages of white, African-American, or Hispanic students who reported being victims of any crime, or of theft or violent crime. However, students in urban schools were more likely (5%) to report being a crime victim or a victim of theft (4%) than students in rural schools (3% for crime victimization, 2% for theft victimization).

## Crimes against Teachers

Teachers are also subject to violence in the schools, either committed by students or by people from outside the school. *Indicators of School Crime and Safety: 2006* observes that a smaller percentage of teachers reported that they had been threatened with injury or physically attacked by a student during the previous twelve months in 2003–04 (7%) than in 1993–94 (12%) or 1999–2000 (9%).

Some 10% of teachers in central city schools were threatened with injury by students in 2003–04, compared with 6% of teachers in urban fringe schools and 5% in rural schools. In addition, 5% of teachers in central city schools were attacked by students, compared with 3% in urban fringe and 2% in rural schools. Female teachers were more likely (9%) than male teachers (6%) to have been threatened with injury by a student; they were also more likely than male teachers to have been physically attacked (4% versus 3%).

## YOUTH GANGS

Although gangs have been a part of American life since the early eighteenth century, modern street gangs pose a greater threat to public safety and order than ever before. Many gangs originated as social clubs. In the early twentieth century, most were small groups who engaged in delinquent acts or minor crimes, such as fighting with other gangs. By the late twentieth century, however, they were frequently involved in violence, intimidation, and the illegal trafficking of drugs and weapons. An increasing number supported themselves by the sale of crack cocaine, heroin, and other illegal drugs, and had easy access to high-powered guns and rifles.

In "Highlights of the 2004 National Youth Gang Survey" (April 2006, http://www.iir.com/nygc/publications/fs200601.pdf), Arlen Egley Jr. and Christina E. Ritz of the National Youth Gang Survey (NYGS) note that by 2004 there were an estimated 24,000 active gangs in the United States with approximately 760,000 participating gang members. Although this represented an overall decline of 2% from 2000 levels, a higher percentage of cities reported gang problems in the 2002–04 period than they did in the 1999–2001 period. Approximately 85% of the estimated gang members lived in larger cities and suburban counties in 2004. Almost four out of five (79.8%) larger cities (population 50,000 or more), 40% of suburban counties, 28.4% of smaller cities (population 2,500 to 49,999), and 12.3% of rural counties reported gang problems in the 2002–04 period.

According to data from the NYGS, an overwhelming majority of gang members are male. In the *National Youth Gang Survey, 1999–2001* (July 2006, http://www.ncjrs.gov/pdffiles1/ojjdp/209392.pdf), Egley, James C. Howell, and Aline K. Major estimate that only 10% of gang members are female. Law enforcement agencies reported in the 2001 NYGS that approximately half of all gang members were Hispanic, whereas about one-third were African-American and one out of ten gang members was non-Hispanic white. Another 5% were Asian. Minorities are overrepresented among gang members because gangs typically arise and persist in economically disadvantaged and socially disorganized areas, and minority populations are overrepresented in these communities.

## CURFEWS

Curfews for young people have existed off and on since the 1890s, when curfews were enacted to curb crime among immigrant youths. States and cities tend to pass curfew ordinances when citizens perceive a need to maintain more control over juveniles. Because of the rising juvenile crime rates in the late 1980s and early 1990s, more than 1,000 jurisdictions across the United States imposed youth curfews. Most curfew laws restrict juveniles to their homes or property between the hours of 11 P.M. and 6 A.M. weekdays, allowing them to stay out later on weekends. The laws allow exceptions for young people going to and from school, church events, or work and for those who have a family emergency or are accompanied by their parents.

Critics of curfew ordinances argue that they violate the constitutional rights of children and parents. First, Fourth, Ninth, and Fourteenth Amendment rights, they argue, are endangered by curfew laws—especially the rights of free speech and association, privacy, and equal protection. The critics also argue that no studies have proven the effectiveness of curfew laws.

### Are Curfews Successful in Reducing Crime?

To be successful, curfews need sustained enforcement and community support and involvement. Other factors for success include creating recreational, educational, and job opportunities for juveniles; building anti-drug and anti-gang programs; and providing hotlines for community questions or problems.

The National League of Cities surveyed officials from 436 cities about youth curfews in 2005 (http://www.nlc.org/Newsroom/press_room/7831.cfm). More than half of these cities had implemented a daytime or nighttime curfew at the time of the survey. Almost all (96%) of the officials regarded their curfew laws as very or somewhat effective in fighting juvenile crime in their communities, and 93% said that curfew enforcement is a good use of police officers' time. Nine out of ten surveyed officials (89%) thought that youth curfews were somewhat or very effective in limiting gang violence, and 95% reported no increase in police costs associated with curfews.

In 78% of communities police were trained to recognize signs of troubled youth and refer them as needed to such services as teen shelters, mental health institutions, recreation programs, and local nonprofit agencies.

## THE CRIMES—COURT STATISTICS

The OJJDP publishes statistics on juvenile court cases and on juvenile cases sent for trial in adult criminal court. The OJJDP uses two categories of juvenile crime:

- Delinquency offenses—acts that are illegal regardless of the age of the perpetrator

- Status offenses—acts that are illegal only for minors, such as truancy, running away, or curfew violations

Juvenile courts handled 1.6 million delinquency cases in 2003, 2% less than in 1999 but 42% more than in 1985. (See Table 9.6.) A case can include more than one charge. For example, a youth brought on three different robbery charges at the same time is counted as one case. According to the *OJJDP Statistical Briefing Book*, between 1985 and 1996 the total delinquency case rate increased by 43%, from 43.7 to 62.7. By 2003 this rate had declined to 52.2, a 17% decrease from 1996. Despite this recent decline, delinquency case rates were higher in 2003 than in 1985.

According to the *OJJDP Statistical Briefing Book*, juvenile courts take delinquency cases referred by law

**TABLE 9.6**

**Estimated number of delinquency cases, 2003**

| | | Percent change | | | |
|---|---|---|---|---|---|
| | Number of cases | 1985 to 2003 | 1994 to 2003 | 1999 to 2003 | 2002 to 2003 |
| Total delinquency | 1,628,800 | 42% | −2% | −2% | 0% |
| **Person offenses** | 396,200 | 118% | 10% | 5% | 2% |
| Criminal homicide | 2,000 | 68% | −32% | 2% | 12% |
| Forcible rape | 5,100 | 22% | −16% | 23% | 9% |
| Robbery | 23,200 | −7% | −39% | −7% | 9% |
| Aggravated assault | 44,200 | 24% | −42% | −9% | 5% |
| Simple assault | 280,300 | 184% | 37% | 9% | 2% |
| Other violent sex offenses | 16,300 | 144% | 44% | 41% | −1% |
| Other person offenses | 25,000 | 143% | 16% | −18% | −3% |
| **Property offenses** | 615,500 | −12% | −29% | −11% | −2% |
| Burglary | 102,700 | −27% | −30% | −9% | 0% |
| Larceny-theft | 278,000 | −15% | −29% | −11% | −3% |
| Motor vehicle theft | 37,100 | −4% | −40% | −4% | 0% |
| Arson | 7,800 | 12% | −20% | −8% | −7% |
| Vandalism | 94,900 | 11% | −26% | −8% | −1% |
| Trespassing | 49,900 | −8% | −27% | −14% | −3% |
| Stolen property offenses | 21,700 | −22% | −39% | −19% | 0% |
| Other property offenses | 23,500 | 31% | −17% | −10% | −10% |
| **Drug law violations** | 189,500 | 153% | 46% | 1% | −1% |
| **Public order offenses** | 427,600 | 121% | 40% | 6% | 2% |
| Obstruction of justice | 208,500 | 213% | 87% | 11% | 7% |
| Disorderly conduct | 102,700 | 133% | 25% | 13% | −4% |
| Weapons offenses | 37,800 | 94% | −26% | −1% | 8% |
| Liquor law violations | 27,100 | 47% | 72% | 15% | −3% |
| Nonviolent sex offenses | 15,000 | 10% | 43% | 14% | −2% |
| Other public order offenses | 36,400 | 17% | 8% | −26% | −7% |
| **Violent crime index**[a] | 74,500 | 13% | −39% | −7% | 6% |
| **Property crime index**[b] | 425,600 | −17% | −30% | −10% | −2% |

[a]Includes criminal homicide, forcible rape, robbery and aggravated assault.
[b]Includes burglary, larceny-theft, motor vehicle theft, and arson.
Note: Detail may not add to totals because of rounding. Percent-change calculations are based on unrounded numbers.

SOURCE: "Juvenile Court Cases: Estimated Number of Delinquency Cases, 2003," in *OJJDP Statistical Briefing Book*, U.S. Department of Justice, Office of Justice Programs, Office of Juvenile Justice and Delinquency Prevention, September 8, 2006, http://ojjdp.ncjrs.org/ojstatbb/court/qa06201.asp?qaDate=2003 (accessed January 24, 2007)

enforcement agencies, social service agencies, schools, parents, probation officers, or victims. In 2003 law enforcement agencies referred 81% of delinquency cases to juvenile court. Figure 9.4 shows juvenile court processing for a typical one thousand delinquency cases in 2003.

Out of 1.6 million cases in 2003, there were 615,500 (38%) property offense cases, with the most frequent charge being larceny-theft, which accounted for 278,000 (or 17%) delinquency cases. (See Table 9.6.) About 396,200 (24%) of delinquency cases involved an offense against people. Public order offenses, such as disorderly conduct, weapons offenses, and liquor law violations, amounted to 427,600 (26%) cases. Drug law violations made up 189,500 (or 12%) of total cases, a 46% increase since 1994.

The *OJJDP Statistical Briefing Book* reports that even though the number of delinquency cases rose by 42% from 1985 to 2003, the increases varied by offense. The number of cases involving obstruction of justice increased by 213%, followed by simple assault (184% increase), disorderly conduct (133%), and weapons offenses (94%). The

number of delinquency cases for some crimes decreased between 1985 and 2003; for example, the number of burglary cases decreased by 27%, stolen property offenses by 22%, and larceny-thefts by 15%.

**Age**

In 2003 delinquency case rates increased with age across all offense categories. (See Figure 9.5.) The steepest increase in case rates between ages thirteen and seventeen was for drug offenses. The case rate for all categories of crime (person, property, drugs, and public order) was higher at age seventeen than at younger ages.

**CASE PROCESSING**

No nationwide uniform procedure exists for processing juvenile cases, but cases do follow similar paths. An intake department first screens cases. The intake department can be the court itself, a state department of social services, or a prosecutor's office. The intake officer may decide that the case will be dismissed for lack of evidence, handled formally (petitioned), or resolved informally

## FIGURE 9.4

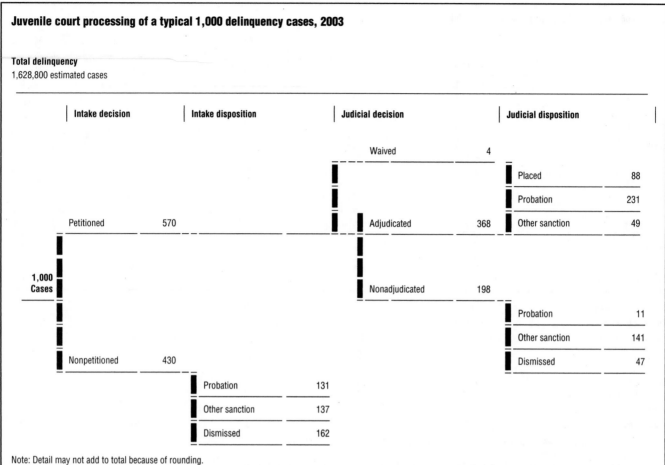

**Juvenile court processing of a typical 1,000 delinquency cases, 2003**

Total delinquency
1,628,800 estimated cases

| Intake decision | Intake disposition | Judicial decision | Judicial disposition |
|---|---|---|---|
| | | Waived 4 | Placed 88 |
| | | | Probation 231 |
| Petitioned 570 | | Adjudicated 368 | Other sanction 49 |
| 1,000 Cases | | Nonadjudicated 198 | |
| | | | Probation 11 |
| | | | Other sanction 141 |
| | | | Dismissed 47 |
| Nonpetitioned 430 | Probation 131 | | |
| | Other sanction 137 | | |
| | Dismissed 162 | | |

Note: Detail may not add to total because of rounding.

SOURCE: "Case Flow by Detailed Offense: Juvenile Court Processing for a Typical 1,000 Delinquency Cases, 2003," in *OJJDP Statistical Briefing Book*, U.S. Department of Justice, Office of Justice Programs, Office of Juvenile Justice and Delinquency Prevention, September 8, 2006, http://ojjdp.ncjrs.org/ojstatbb/court/JCSCF_Display.asp (accessed January 24, 2007).

## FIGURE 9.5

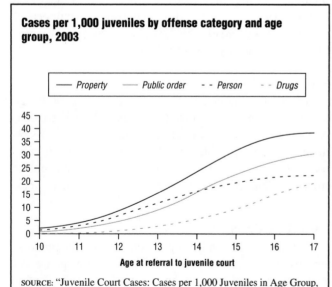

**Cases per 1,000 juveniles by offense category and age group, 2003**

— Property    — Public order    - - Person    - - Drugs

Age at referral to juvenile court

SOURCE: "Juvenile Court Cases: Cases per 1,000 Juveniles in Age Group, 2003," in *OJJDP Statistical Briefing Book*, U.S. Department of Justice, Office of Justice Programs, Office of Juvenile Justice and Delinquency Prevention, September 8, 2006, http://ojjdp.ncjrs.org/ojstatbb/court/qa06202.asp?qaDate=2003 (accessed February 19, 2007).

(nonpetitioned). Formal processing can include placement outside the home, probation, a trial in juvenile court, or transfer to an adult court. Informal processing may consist of referral to a social services agency, a fine, some form of restitution, or informal probation. Both formal and informal processing can result in dismissal of the charges and release of the juvenile.

According to the *OJJDP Statistical Briefing Book*, in 2003, 39% of delinquency cases were either adjudicated or waived to criminal court, up from 29% in 1985. During this period the number of adjudicated delinquency cases that resulted in formal probation doubled from 1985 to 2003. The number of adjudicated delinquency cases receiving other court-ordered sanctions (such as community service and restitution) increased by 124% between 1985 and 2003. (See Figure 9.6.)

## Detention

Juvenile courts may place youths in a detention facility during court processing. Detention may be needed to protect the community from the juvenile, to protect the juvenile, or

## FIGURE 9.6

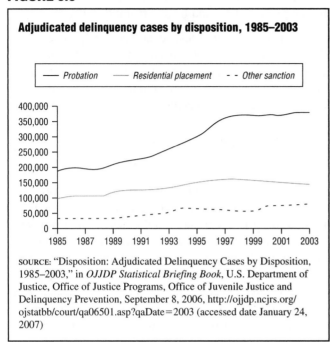

**Adjudicated delinquency cases by disposition, 1985–2003**

— Probation    — Residential placement    - - Other sanction

SOURCE: "Disposition: Adjudicated Delinquency Cases by Disposition, 1985–2003," in *OJJDP Statistical Briefing Book*, U.S. Department of Justice, Office of Justice Programs, Office of Juvenile Justice and Delinquency Prevention, September 8, 2006, http://ojjdp.ncjrs.org/ojstatbb/court/qa06501.asp?qaDate=2003 (accessed date January 24, 2007)

both. In addition, detention is sometimes necessary to ensure a youth's appearance at scheduled hearings or evaluations.

According to the *OJJDP Statistical Briefing Book*, youths were held in detention facilities at some point between referral to court intake and case disposition (final outcome of court processing) in 20% of all delinquency cases handled in 2003. A higher percentage of cases involving public order offenses (30%) included detention than people (29%), drug offenses (23%), or property offenses (19%).

There were 257,900 white youths detained in 2003, compared to 141,888 African-Americans, 6,300 Asians, and 5,100 Native Americans. The percent of juveniles who were detained at one point or another between referral to court and case disposition was 26% of delinquency cases involving Asians, 25% for African-Americans, 19% for Native Americans, and 18% for whites.

## CHANGING APPROACHES TO JUVENILE DELINQUENCY

Juvenile courts date to the late nineteenth century, when Cook County, Illinois, established the first juvenile court under the Juvenile Court Act of 1899. The underlying concept was that if parents failed to provide children with proper care and supervision, the state had the right to intervene benevolently. Other states followed Illinois's initiative. Juvenile courts were in operation in most states by 1925. Juvenile courts favored a rehabilitative rather than a punitive approach and evolved less formal approaches than those in place in adult courts. They had exclusive jurisdiction over juveniles. Adult courts could try a juvenile only if the juvenile court waived its jurisdiction.

This approach began to change in the 1950s and 1960s because rehabilitation techniques were judged to be ineffective. A growing number of juveniles were being institutionalized until they reached adulthood because "treatment" did not seem to modify their behavior. Under the impetus of a number of U.S. Supreme Court decisions, juvenile courts became more formal to protect juveniles' rights in waiver situations or if they were to be confined. Congress passed the Juvenile Delinquency Prevention and Control Act in 1968. The act suggested that so-called "status offenders" (noncriminal offenders such as runaways) no longer be handled inside the court system. The Juvenile Justice and Delinquency Prevention Act of 1974 mandated that juvenile offenders be separated from adult offenders. The act was amended in 1980; part of the amendment required that juveniles be removed from adult jails. In the 1970s the national policy became community-based management of juvenile delinquents.

### Prosecuting Juveniles as Adults

Public perception changed again during the 1980s. Juvenile crime was growing, and the systems in place were perceived as being too lenient in dealing with delinquents. According to the OJJDP in *Juvenile Offenders and Victims: 2006 National Report*, public opinion was based on a "substantial misperception regarding increases in juvenile crime." Nonetheless, state legislatures responded in various ways:

> Some laws removed certain classes of offenders from the juvenile justice system and handled them as adult criminals in criminal court. Others required the juvenile justice system to be more like the criminal justice system and to treat certain classes of juvenile offenders as criminals but in juvenile court....

> As a result, offenders charged with certain offenses now are excluded from juvenile court jurisdiction or face mandatory or automatic waiver to criminal court. In several states, concurrent jurisdiction provisions give prosecutors the discretion to file certain juvenile cases directly in criminal court rather than juvenile court. In some states, certain adjudicated juvenile offenders face mandatory sentences.

> —*Juvenile Offenders and Victims: 2006 National Report*, Chapter 4, p. 96

The National Center for Juvenile Justice reports that as of 2006, all states allow juveniles to be tried in criminal court under some circumstances (http://www.ncjj.org/stateprofiles/overviews/transfer_state_overview.asp). These circumstances include the use of firearms or other weapons and a history of criminality, indicating that the individual has not benefited from previous participation in juvenile justice programs. Forty-five states allow juvenile court judges to determine whether individual suspects are prosecuted in juvenile or adult criminal court. States without discretionary waiver provisions are Massachusetts, Montana, Nebraska, New Mexico, and New York. Fifteen states allow prosecutors to determine whether to file cases in juvenile or adult criminal court. Twenty-nine states have laws that determine which court holds jurisdiction over cases, depending on the age of the suspect and the crime committed.

Cases can also be transferred from criminal court to juvenile court under certain circumstances. States that allow prosecutors to file charges directly in criminal court often have provisions for a judicial review hearing once the case is underway in adult court. In some cases the laws require certain types of cases to be waived to criminal court, but juveniles are given an opportunity to appeal the transfer if they can show extraordinary circumstances. According to the National Juvenile Justice Network (2005, http://www.njjn.org/fastfacts.html), thirty-four states have laws requiring that once a youthful offender has been tried as an adult for any offense, he or she must be prosecuted in criminal court for any future offenses.

Discretionary judicial waiver was the most common mechanism for transferring juvenile offenders from juvenile court to criminal court until the 1960s. Beginning in the 1970s, however, states began amending their laws to establish standards for juvenile transfers based on the age of the offender and the seriousness of the offense rather than on the opinion of a juvenile court judge. The OJJDP reports in *Juvenile Offenders and Victims: 2006 National Report* that since 1992 all states except Nebraska have changed their transfer statutes to make it easier for juveniles to be tried in criminal court.

According to the OJJDP, the number of delinquency cases waived to criminal courts increased by 83% between 1985 and 1994, from 7,200 to 13,200 (http://ojjdp.ncjrs.org/ojstatbb/nr2006/downloads/chapter6.pdf). However, the number of waived cases began to decrease in 1994 and was 6,300 in 2001. In most years between 1993 and 2002, the number of person offense cases waived to criminal courts was higher than the number of property offense cases. The number of waived person offense cases increased 130% between 1985 and 1994. It then declined by 47% to 2002; the overall increase between 1985 and 2002 was therefore 23%. During this period, the number of waived property offense cases decreased by 33% and public order offenses by 2%.

## STATUS OFFENSE CASES

Status offenses are acts that are against the law only because the people who commit them are juveniles. The four major status offense categories used by the OJJDP are running away, truancy, alcohol possession, and ungovernability (also known as incorrigibility or being beyond parental control). Between 1985 and 2002, according to the OJJDP publication *Juvenile Court Statistics 2001–2002* (December 2005, http://www.ncjrs.gov/pdffiles1/ojjdp/216251.pdf), liquor law violations accounted for

42% of status offense cases for 17-year-olds, followed by running away (9%), and ungovernability (8%).

In many communities, social service agencies rather than juvenile courts are responsible for accused status offenders. National estimates of informally handled status offense cases are not calculated because of differences in screening procedures. The statistics presented here, therefore, report only on status offense cases handled through the juvenile justice system.

### Age, Sex, and Race

*Juvenile Court Statistics 2001–2002* reports that youths aged sixteen and seventeen accounted for three-fourths of all liquor law violations among juveniles between 1985 and 2002. Children aged fifteen and younger made up two-thirds of all the runaway cases during the same period. Truancy was most common among fifteen-year-olds (30% of juvenile cases). Running away (29% of all juvenile cases) and ungovernability (26%) were also more common among fifteen-year-old juveniles than those who were younger or older.

Between 1985 and 2002 females accounted for a larger proportion of petitioned status offense cases than delinquency cases. The offense profiles of male and female status offense cases show the relatively high male involvement in liquor law violations (70%) and the higher female involvement in runaway cases (61%). Males accounted for 54% of all ungovernability cases and 54% of all truancy cases.

Between 1985 and 2002 white youths were held in 73% of runaway, 73% of truancy, 71% of ungovernability, and 90% of all status liquor law violation cases. Compared with their representation in the general population, white youths were overrepresented in liquor law violation cases and underrepresented in the other three categories. African-Americans accounted for 24% of runaway, 24% of truancy, and 27% of ungovernability cases. (Nearly all Hispanic youth are included in the white racial category.)

### Detention and Case Processing

The handling of status crimes has changed considerably since the mid-1980s. The Juvenile Justice and Delinquency Prevention Act of 1974 (P.L. 93-415) offered substantial federal funds to states that tried to reduce the detention of status offenders. The primary responsibility for status offenders was often transferred from the juvenile courts to child welfare agencies. As a result, the character of the juvenile courts' activities changed.

Prior to this change many juvenile detention centers held a substantial number of young people whose only offense was that their parents could no longer control them. By not routinely institutionalizing these adolescents, the courts demonstrated that children deserved the same rights as adults. A logical extension of this has been that juveniles accused of violent crimes are also now being treated legally as if they were adults.

Those involved in petitioned status offense cases are rarely held in detention. From 1985 to 2002, according to *Juvenile Court Statistics 2001–2002*, only 16% of runaway cases, 4% of truancy cases, 10% of ungovernability cases, and 8% of liquor law cases were detained. Males accounted for a majority of detentions for liquor violation (77%), truancy (56%), and ungovernability (54%) cases. However, 58% of juveniles detained for running away were female.

According to OJJDP, except for runaway cases, most petitioned status offense cases from 1985 to 2002 resulted in adjudication (ruling in a court). For whites 46% of runaway, 63% of truancy, 64% of ungovernability, and 63% of liquor law cases were adjudicated. For African-Americans the numbers were slightly lower: 44% of runaway, 63% of truancy, 57% of ungovernability, and 52% of liquor law cases. In general, males and females were equally likely to have their cases adjudicated. Of the cases that were adjudicated, 61% of runaway cases, 78% of truancy cases, 66% of ungovernability cases, and 57% of liquor law cases received probation. Other dispositions include placement outside of the home, such as in a detention home or boot camp, and other sanctions, such as restitution or community service.

## HOLDING PARENTS RESPONSIBLE

For many decades, civil liability laws held parents at least partly responsible for damages caused by their children. Also, child welfare law included actions against those who contributed to the delinquency of a minor. Most researchers recognize that parental involvement is key to juvenile rehabilitation, yet that involvement has been problematic because many parents are seen as contributing to their children's problems rather than helping to resolve them. In addition, some parents assumed an adversarial role with the juvenile justice system, hoping to protect their children from prosecution. By the 1990s, in response to rising juvenile crime rates, communities and states passed stronger laws about parental responsibility. Several states enacted laws making parents criminally responsible for their children's crimes.

In "From Columbine to Kazaa: Parental Liability in a New World" (*University of Illinois Law Review*, 2005), Amy L. Tomaszewski reports that advocates of parental liability believe that the laws motivate adults to become better parents to avoid serious penalties, including jail terms. According to Tomaszewski, although parental liability laws are not new, states have established a broader range of civil and criminal penalties for parents who do not control their children. However, research shows that juvenile crime rates started declining before most parental

liability laws were enacted. For example, between 1994 and 2001, the arrest rates for juvenile murder, rape, robbery, and aggravated assault dropped 44%.

Furthermore, legislators find it very difficult to determine the age when parents are no longer responsible for their children's actions. Parents might be legitimately responsible for a small child's behavior but teenagers are more independent, so it is more difficult to decide whether teenage crimes are really the result of poor parenting.

Although some research has shown a relationship between lax parenting and juvenile crime, the research also shows that punishing parents is not an effective way to prevent juvenile crime. In many cases, the parents need support and assistance, not punishment, to handle their children's behavior problems. For example, many of these parents do not know how to discipline their children effectively.

## JUVENILES IN RESIDENTIAL PLACEMENT

Children who are found guilty of crimes in courts belonging to the juvenile justice system may be sentenced to a residential placement facility. These institutions may be under the administration of the state or operated by private nonprofit or for-profit corporations or organizations and staffed by employees of the corporation or organization. Private facilities are usually smaller than public facilities. As a result although there are more private facilities than public facilities in the country, most juvenile offenders are held in public facilities. According to OJJDP in *Juvenile Offenders and Victims: 2006 National Report*, the United States had 2,861 juvenile residential placement facilities in 2003. Of these, 1,170 were public (501 state and 669 local), 1,682 were private, and 9 were tribal.

The *Sourcebook of Criminal Justice Statistics* reports that 96,655 juveniles aged ten and up were held in public and private residential custody facilities in 2003 (http://www.albany.edu/sourcebook/pdf/t692003.pdf). In 2003, 66,210 juveniles in residential placement were in public facilities, and 30,321 were in private facilities. These totals translate to a rate of 307 juveniles in placement per 100,000 in the population. Both the number and rate of juveniles in residential placement have declined since 1997, when 105,055 juveniles were in residential facilities and the rate was 356 per 100,000.

California (16,782) and Florida (8,208) had the highest number of children in residential placement in 2003, but rates were highest in the District of Columbia (625 per 100,000 youths), Wyoming (606 per 100,000), and South Dakota (564 per 100,000). Vermont and Hawaii experienced both the lowest numbers and the lowest rates of juveniles in residential placement in 2003. Vermont held 51 juvenile offenders for a rate of 72 per 100,000, and Hawaii held 129 juvenile offenders for a rate of 97 per 100,000.

Of juveniles in public facilities, 98% were held for delinquency offenses, and only 2% were held for status offenses such as running away or truancy, according to *Juvenile Offenders and Victims: 2006 National Report*. A higher proportion of private facility inmates (11%) were held for status offenses. The largest percentage of youths in residential placement in 2003 were held for crimes against persons (34%), followed by property crimes (28%), public order offenses (10%), drug offenses (8%), and status offenses (5%). The number of juveniles in residential placement for sexual assault increased by 68% between 1997 and 2003. Other large increases were for public order offenses other than weapons violations (29%), drug offenses other than trafficking (28%), and simple assault (25%). During this period, the number of juveniles in residential facilities for running away decreased by 43%. Other major decreases were for truancy (32%), drug trafficking (24%), weapons violations (24%), and robbery (22%).

## JUVENILE BOOT CAMPS

Boot camps are specialized residential facilities for "midrange" offenders—those who have failed with lesser sanctions like probation but are not yet considered hardened criminals. First proposed in the 1980s, juvenile boot camps typically share the 90–120-day duration of military boot camps. They employ military customs and have correctional officers acting as uniformed drill instructors who use intense verbal tactics designed to break down inmates' resistance. Boot camps emphasize vigorous physical activity, drill and ceremony, and manual labor. The offenders have little free time and strictly enforced rules govern all aspects of conduct and appearance. Because of state-mandated education rules, programs spend a minimum of three hours daily on academic education. Most programs also include some vocational education, work-skills training, or job preparation. As of 2003, according to the OJJDP, 7% of juvenile offenders who were in a residential placement facility were in a boot camp.

The first boot camp for juvenile offenders in the United States was established in Orleans Parish, Louisiana, in 1985. Within a decade similar facilities were operated in about thirty states. Juvenile boot camp programs typically exclude some types of offenders, such as sex offenders, armed robbers, and youths with a record of serious violence. Definitions of terms like "nonviolent" vary from program to program. Boot camps operate under the assumption that making a marked, positive change in the life of young offenders can benefit society in the long run by reducing recidivism, reducing prison populations, and reducing costs.

### Are Juvenile Boot Camps Effective?

Several factors seem to have a direct bearing on the success or failure rates for boot camp participants, including the length of the sessions and the amount of post-release supervision. In a study of many boot camps across the country (*Correctional Boot Camps: Lessons from a Decade of Research*, U.S. Department of Justice, Office of Justice Programs, June 2003), it was reported that:

> [P]articipants reported positive short-term changes in attitudes and behaviors and had better problem solving and coping skills. With few exceptions, however, these positive changes did not lead to reduced recidivism. The boot camps that did produce lower recidivism rates offered more treatment services, had longer sessions, and included more intensive post-release supervision. However, not all programs with these features had successful results. Results suggest that under a narrow set of conditions, boot camps can lead to small relative reductions in prison population and correctional costs.

According to the National Mental Health Association in *Mental Health Treatment for Youth in the Juvenile Justice System: A Compendium of Promising Practices* (2004, http://www1.nmha.org/children/JJCompendiumof BestPractices.pdf), juvenile boot camps do not prevent offenders from committing new offenses. Several studies of adult and juvenile boot camps show that graduates of these programs are just as likely to commit new offenses as offenders who were placed in prison or jail and, in some cases, as those sentenced to regular probation supervision.

However, the National Mental Health Association states that many juveniles sentenced to boot camps say that these programs helped them and that they feel more positive about their futures. What is not clear is whether these attitudes last once the youths leave the boot camp. It is also not clear if changes in attitude translate into behavioral changes once the juveniles return to their communities.

### JUVENILES IN ADULT PRISONS AND JAILS

In 2005, 9,025 juveniles were in adult jails or prisons, according to the BJS in *Prison and Jail Inmates at Mid-year 2005* (May 2006, http://www.ojp.usdoj.gov/bjs/pub/pdf/pjim05.pdf). These youths had been transferred to the jurisdiction of adult courts, usually by waiver or under statutorily mandated rules. Of these juveniles, 6,759 were in jail (5,900 held as adults) and 2,266 were in state prisons. (See Table 9.5 and Table 9.7.) Juvenile males (2,175) far outnumbered females (91) in state prisons.

According to the BJS, the number of juveniles in jail increased steadily between 1990, when 2,301 juveniles were in local jails, and 1999, when there were 9,458

**TABLE 9.7**

**Number of inmates under age 18 held in state prisons, by gender, selected years 1995–2005**

| Year | Inmates under age 18 | | |
| | Total | Male | Female |
|------|-------|------|--------|
| 2005 | 2,266 | 2,175 | 91 |
| 2004 | 2,485 | 2,375 | 110 |
| 2003 | 2,741 | 2,627 | 114 |
| 2002 | 3,038 | 2,927 | 111 |
| 2001 | 3,147 | 3,010 | 137 |
| 2000 | 3,896 | 3,721 | 175 |
| 1995 | 5,309 | — | — |

—Not available.

SOURCE: Paige M. Harrison and Allen J. Beck, "Table 5. Number of Inmates under Age 18 Held in State Prisons, by Gender, June 30, 1995, and 2000–05," in *Prison and Jail Inmates at Midyear 2005*, U.S. Department of Justice, Office of Justice Programs, Bureau of Justice Statistics, May 2006, http://www.ojp.usdoj.gov/bjs/pub/pdf/pjim05.pdf (accessed January 17, 2007)

juvenile jail inmates. Since then, the number of juvenile jail inmates has dropped steadily.

According to the OJJDP in *Juvenile Offenders and Victims: 2006 National Report*, juveniles accounted for 4.3% of all new prisoners sentenced to state prisons for robbery in 2002. They accounted for a smaller proportion of new prisoners in other offense categories: 2.5% of new homicide inmates, 1.6% of those committed for assault, and 1% of new inmates serving time for weapons offenses. Juveniles committed to state prison in 2002 were more likely than young adults aged eighteen to twenty-four to have committed violent offenses (primarily robbery and assault) and less likely to have committed drug offenses (especially drug trafficking). Most juveniles admitted to prison in 2002 were seventeen years old. Most new admissions were African-American (59%), followed by whites (28%), Hispanics (11%), and youth of other races or ethnicities (2%).

## JUVENILES AND THE DEATH PENALTY

In *Roper v. Simmons* (543 U.S. 551, 2005), the U.S. Supreme Court struck down the death penalty for juveniles. The Court found that state laws authorizing capital punishment for those under age eighteen who commit murder violate the Eighth Amendment's provision against cruel and unusual punishment and are therefore unconstitutional. Since that decision, juveniles who commit serious crimes can be sentenced to a maximum of life in prison. The ruling changed the law in twenty-one states that had authorized the death penalty for juvenile offenders and took seventy-three prisoners off of death row.

Historically, it was rare for a juvenile to be sentenced to death. According to the BJS, in sixteen states allowing the death penalty in 2003, the minimum age authorized for capital punishment was eighteen years. Those states included California, Colorado, Connecticut, Illinois, Indiana, Kansas, Maryland, Missouri, Nebraska, New Jersey, New Mexico, New York, Ohio, Oregon, Tennessee, and Washington. The federal system observed eighteen years as well. However, five states—Florida, Georgia, New Hampshire, North Carolina, and Texas—had authorized the death penalty at seventeen years. The minimum age for capital punishment was sixteen years or less in thirteen other states. Alabama, Delaware, Kentucky, Mississippi, Nevada, Oklahoma, and Wyoming set sixteen years as the minimum, whereas Arkansas, Utah, and Virginia used fourteen years. States without specific age limits were Arizona, Idaho, Louisiana, Montana, Pennsylvania, South Carolina, and South Dakota. Twelve states do not authorize capital punishment at any age: Alaska, Hawaii, Iowa, Maine, Massachusetts, Michigan, Minnesota, North Dakota, Rhode Island, Vermont, West Virginia, Wisconsin.

# IMPORTANT NAMES AND ADDRESSES

**American Bar Association**
321 N. Clark St.
Chicago, IL 60610
1-800-285-2221
E-mail: askaba@abanet.org
URL: http://www.abanet.org/

**American Civil Liberties Union (ACLU)**
**National Prison Project**
915 15th St. NW, 7th Floor
Washington, DC 20005
(202) 393-4930
FAX: (202) 393-4931
URL: http://www.aclu.org/prison/index.html

**American Correctional Association**
206 N. Washington St., Suite 200
Alexandria, VA 22314
1-800-ACA-JOIN
(703) 224-0000
E-mail: jeffw@aca.org
URL: http://www.aca.org/

**American Jail Association**
1135 Professional Ct.
Hagerstown, MD 21740-5853
(301) 790-3930
E-mail: dorothyd@aja.org
URL: http://www.corrections.com/aja/index.shtml

**Anti-Defamation League**
823 United Nations Plaza
New York, NY 10017
(212) 885-7700
FAX: (212) 867-0779
E-mail: webmaster@adl.org
URL: http://www.adl.org/

**Bureau of Alcohol, Tobacco, Firearms, and Explosives**
**U.S. Department of Justice**
650 Massachusetts Ave. NW, Room 8290
Washington, DC 20226
(202) 927-8500
FAX: (202) 927-1083
E-mail: atfmail@atf.gov
URL: http://www.atf.treas.gov/

**Bureau of Engraving and Printing**
**U.S. Department of the Treasury**
14th and C Streets SW
Washington, DC 20228
1-877-874-4114
(202) 874-3019
URL: http://www.bep.treas.gov/

**Bureau of Justice Statistics**
**U.S. Department of Justice**
810 7th St. NW
Washington, DC 20531
(202) 307-0765
E-mail: askbjs@usdoj.gov
URL: http://www.ojp.usdoj.gov/bjs

**Coalition for Juvenile Justice**
710 Rhode Island Ave. NW, 10th Floor
Washington, DC 20036
(202) 467-0864
FAX: (202) 887-0738
E-mail: info@juvjustice.org
URL: http://www.juvjustice.org/

**Federal Bureau of Investigation**
J. Edgar Hoover Bldg.
935 Pennsylvania Ave. NW
Washington, DC 20535-0001
(202) 324-3000
URL: http://www.fbi.gov/

**Federal Bureau of Prisons**
320 1st St. NW
Washington, DC 20534
(202) 307-3198
E-mail: info@bop.gov
URL: http://www.bop.gov/

**Federal Judicial Center**
Thurgood Marshall Federal
Judiciary Bldg.
1 Columbus Circle NE
Washington, DC 20002-8003
(202) 502-4000
FAX: (202)502-4099
URL: http://www.fjc.gov/

**Federal Trade Commission**
600 Pennsylvania Ave. NW
Washington, DC 20580
(202) 326-2222
URL: http://www.ftc.gov/

**Internal Revenue Service Criminal**
**Investigation Division**
1111 Constitution Ave. NW, Room 2501
Washington, DC 20224
1-800-829-0433
(202) 283-9665
URL: http://www.irs.gov/irs/article/
0,,id=98398,00.html

**Justice Research and Statistics**
**Association**
777 N. Capitol St. NE, Suite 801
Washington, DC 20002
(202) 842-9330
FAX: (202) 842-9329
E-mail: cjinfo@jrsa.org
URL: http://www.jrsa.org/

**National Center for Victims of Crime**
2000 M St. NW, Suite 480
Washington, DC 20036
(202) 467-8700
FAX: (202) 467-8701
E-mail: webmaster@ncvc.org
URL: http://www.ncvc.org/

**National Center on Institutions and**
**Alternatives**
7222 Ambassador Rd.
Baltimore, MD 21244
(410) 265-1490
E-mail: aboring@ncianet.org
URL: http://www.ncianet.org/

**National Conference of State Legislatures**
7700 E. First Pl.
Denver, CO 80230
(303) 364-7700
FAX: (303) 364-7800
E-mail: ncslnet-admin@ncsl.org
URL: http://www.ncsl.org/

**National Consumers League**
1701 K St. NW, Suite 1200
Washington, DC 20006
(202) 835-3323
FAX: (202) 835-0747
E-mail: info@nclnet.org
URL: http://www.nclnet.org/

**National Correctional Industries
Association**
1202 N. Charles St.
Baltimore, MD 21201
(410) 230-3972
FAX: (410) 230-3981
E-mail: info@nationalcia.org
URL: http://www.nationalcia.org/
index2.html

**National Council on Crime and
Delinquency**
1970 Broadway, Suite 500
Oakland, CA 94612
(510) 208-0500
FAX: (510) 208-0511
URL: http://www.nccd-crc.org/

**National Crime Prevention Council**
1000 Connecticut Ave. NW, 13th Floor
Washington, DC 20036
(202) 466-6272
FAX: (202) 296-1356
URL: http://www.ncpc.org/

**National Criminal Justice Association**
720 7th St., 3rd Floor
Washington, DC 20001-3716
(202) 628-8550
FAX: (202) 628-0080
E-mail: info@ncja.org
URL: http://www.ncja.org/

**National Criminal Justice Reference
Service**
P.O. Box 6000
Rockville, MD 20849-6000
1-800-851-3420
(301) 519-5500
FAX: (301) 519-5212
URL: http://www.ncjrs.gov/

**National Institute of Corrections**
320 First St. NW
Washington, DC 20534
1-800-995-6423
(202) 307-3106
URL: http://www.nicic.org/

**National Institute of Justice**
810 7th St. NW
Washington, DC 20531

(202) 307-2942
URL: http://www.ojp.usdoj.gov/nij/

**National Legal Aid and Defender
Association**
1140 Connecticut Ave. NW, Suite 900
Washington, DC 20036
(202) 452-0620
FAX: (202) 872-1031
E-mail: info@nlada.org
URL: http://www.nlada.org/

**National Organization for Victim
Assistance**
510 King St., Suite 424
Alexandria, VA 22314
1-800-879-6682 (information hotline)
(703) 535-6682
FAX: (703) 535-5500
URL: http://www.try-nova.org/

**National White Collar Crime Center**
10900 Nuckols Rd., Suite 325
Glen Allen, VA 23060
1-800-221-4424
URL: http://www.nw3c.org/

**Office for Victims of Crime
U.S. Department of Justice**
810 7th St. NW, 8th Floor
Washington, DC 20531
(202) 307-5983
FAX: (202) 514-6383
URL: http://www.ojp.usdoj.gov/ovc/

**Office of Juvenile Justice and
Delinquency Prevention
U.S. Department of Justice**
810 7th St. NW
Washington, DC 20531
(202) 307-5911
URL: http://www.ojjdp.ncjrs.org/

**The Sentencing Project**
514 10th St. NW
Washington, DC 20004
(202) 628-0871
FAX: (202) 628-1091
E-mail: staff@sentencingproject.org
URL: http://www.sentencingproject.org/

**Southern Poverty Law Center**
400 Washington Ave.
Montgomery, AL 36104
(334) 956-8200
URL: http://www.splcenter.org/

**Supreme Court of the United States**
One 1st St. NE
Washington, DC 20543

(202) 479-3211
URL: http://www.supremecourtus.gov/

**U.S. Census Bureau**
4600 Silver Hill Rd.
Washington, DC 20233
(301) 763-2495
E-mail: webmaster@census.gov
URL: http://www.census.gov/

**U.S. Department of Justice**
950 Pennsylvania Ave. NW
Washington, DC 20530-0001
(202) 514-2000
E-mail: askdoj@usdoj.gov
URL: http://www.usdoj.gov/

**U.S. Parole Commission**
5550 Friendship Blvd., Suite 420
Chevy Chase, MD 20815-7286
(301) 492-5990
FAX: (301) 492-6694
URL: http://www.usdoj.gov/uspc/

**U.S. Postal Service
Office of the Inspector General**
1735 N. Lynn St., 10th Floor
Arlington, VA 22209-2020
1-888-877-7644
E-mail: hotline@uspsoig.gov
URL: http://www.uspsoig.gov/

**U.S. Securities and Exchange
Commission**
100 F St. NE
Washington, DC 20549
(202) 551-6551
E-mail: help@sec.gov
URL: http://www.sec.gov/

**U.S. Sentencing Commission**
Office of Public Affairs
1 Columbus Circle NE
Washington, DC 20002-8002
(202) 502-4500
E-mail: pubaffairs@ussc.gov
URL: http://www.ussc.gov/

**Urban Institute**
2100 M St. NW
Washington, DC 20037
(202) 833-7200
URL: http://www.urban.org/

**Violence Policy Center**
1730 Rhode Island Ave. NW, Suite 1014
Washington, DC 20036
(202) 822-8200
E-mail: info@vpc.org
URL: http://www.vpc.org/

# RESOURCES

The various agencies of the U.S. Department of Justice are the major sources of crime and justice data in America. The Bureau of Justice Statistics (BJS) compiles statistics on virtually every area of crime and reports that data in a number of publications. The annual BJS *Sourcebook of Criminal Justice Statistics*, prepared by the Hindelang Criminal Justice Research Center, State University of New York at Albany, is a comprehensive compilation of criminal justice statistics. The annual BJS *National Crime Victimization Survey* provides data for several studies, the most important of which is *Criminal Victimization in the United States*. Other valuable BJS publications include *Compendium of Federal Justice Statistics, 2004* (2006), *Drug Use and Dependence, State and Federal Prisoners, 2004* (2006), *Federal Law Enforcement Officers, 2004* (2006), *Felony Sentences in State Courts, 2002* (2004), *Hate Crime Reported by Victims and Police* (2005), *HIV in Prisons* (2006), *Identity Theft, 2004* (2006), *Justice Expenditure and Employment in the United States, 2003* (2006), *Mental Health Problems of Prison and Jail Inmates* (2006), *Prison and Jail Inmates at Midyear 2005* (2006), *Prisoners in 2005* (2006), *Probation and Parole in the United States, 2005* (2006), and *Sexual Violence Reported by Correctional Authorities, 2005* (2006). The Bureau of Justice Statistics and the National Center for Education Statistics jointly published *Indicators of School Crime and Safety: 2006* (2006).

The Federal Bureau of Investigation (FBI) collects crime data from state law enforcement agencies through its Uniform Crime Reports program. The FBI annual *Crime in the United States* is the most important source of information on crime reported to law enforcement agencies. Information on white-collar crime came from the FBI in *Financial Institution Fraud and Failure Report, Fiscal Year 2005* (2005) and the National White Collar Crime Center in *IC3 2005 Internet Crime Report* (2006). The National White Collar Crime Center also published the results of a national survey on white-collar crime in *The 2005 National Public Survey on White Collar Crime* by John Kane and April Wall (January 2006).

The Office of Juvenile Justice and Delinquency Prevention (OJJDP) published several helpful resources on juvenile crime and justice issues, including *Juvenile Arrests in 2004* (2006), *Juvenile Court Statistics, 2001–2002,* (2005), *Juvenile Offenders and Victims: 2006 National Report* (2006), and *Statistical Briefing Book* (2006).

The Department of the Treasury published *The Use and Counterfeiting of United States Currency Abroad* (2006) and *SAR Activity Review: Trends, Tips, and Issues* (2006). The Federal Trade Commission, through its Identify Theft Clearinghouse, published *Identity Theft Victim Complaint Data, January–December, 2006* (2007). The National Counterterrorism Center published descriptions of terrorism incidents around the world in its *Report on Incidents of Terrorism, 2005* (2006) and *Worldwide Incidents Tracking System* (2006). The U.S. Sentencing Commission published *2006 Federal Sentencing Guidelines Manual* (2006).

Several sources provide data on hate crimes in the United States. The Anti-Defamation League produces *Map of State Statutes for Hate Crimes* as a reference guide on the nation's hate crime legislation. The Southern Poverty Law Center of Montgomery, Alabama, publishes data on hate crimes in its periodical *Intelligence Report*. *Hate Crimes* by Jack Levin and Jack McDevitt (Northeastern University, 2005) defines different categories of hate crimes.

The Sentencing Project conducts research on criminal justice issues and promotes sentencing reform. They published *U.S. Prison Populations—Trends and Implications* (December 2004). Key information was also acquired from polling results reported by the Gallup Organization.

Other publications that provide useful information include *Monitoring the Future Study National Results on Adolescent Drug Use: Overview of Key Findings 2001* (2002), completed by the Survey Research Center of the Institute for Social Research at the University of Michigan. The *National Law Journal* provided valuable survey data on Americans' opinions of the death penalty. The Violence Policy Center reported on the use of guns in high-profile shootings in its report *Where'd They Get Their Guns? An Analysis of the Firearms Used in High-Profile Shootings, 1963 to 2001* (2002).

The Urban Institute is a nonpartisan economic and social policy research organization that publishes several reports on crime victims, corrections and prisoners, courts and policing, and juvenile justice. The many valuable Urban Institute reports include *Baltimore Prisoners' Experiences Returning Home* (2004), *Evaluating the Effectiveness of Supermax Prisons* by Daniel Mears (2006), *Families Left Behind: The Hidden Costs of Incarceration and Reentry* by Jeremy Travis, Elizabeth Cincotta McBride, and Amy L. Solomon (2005), and *Returning Home: Understanding the Challenges of Prisoner Reentry* by Christy Visher et al. (2004).

Other publications used in this book include the *2002 National Retail Security Survey* by Richard Hollinger et al. (University of Florida, 2006). Cornerstone Research published *Securities Class Action Case Filings, 2006: A Year in Review* (2007). The Institute of Public Policy described different alternative sentencing strategies in *Alternative Sentencing & Strategies for Successful Prisoner Reentry* (Truman School of Public Affairs, University of Missouri, 2006).

The Highway Loss Data Institute provided valuable information on trends in motor vehicle thefts. The Computer Security Institute published the *2003 Computer Crime and Security Survey* (2003). The Educational Testing Service published *Locked Up and Locked Out: An Educational Perspective on the U.S. Prison Population* by Richard Coley and Paul Barton (2006).

# INDEX

*Page references in italics refer to photographs. References with the letter* t *following them indicate the presence of a table. The letter* f *indicates a figure. If more than one table or figure appears on a particular page, the exact item number for the table or figure being referenced is provided.*

## A

Abramoff, Jack, 69
Abuse of public office, 69
Advertising misrepresentation, 58
African-Americans
    hate crime victimization, 4
    juvenile arrests, 143(*t*9.4)
Age
    arrests, 6, 9*t*
    delinquency cases, 149, 150(*f*9.5)
    family violence victimization rates, 33*t*–34*t*
    inmates, 109, 110*t*
    juvenile court jurisdiction, 142(*t*9.1)
    juvenile offenders, 141
    murder offenders, 13(*t*1.11)
    status offense cases, 152
    victims, 26–27
    violent crime victims, 27*f*
Aggravated assault, 17, 17*t*
Aguila, Barbara Del, 60
Air Transportation Safety and System Stabilization Act, 41
Airlines, 41
*Albers, Whitney v.*, 124
Alternative sentencing, 81–85
Andrade, Leandro, 81
Animal Liberation Front, 53–54
Animal rights groups, 53–54
Anthrax incidents, 52
Anti-Muslim hate crime, 45–46
Anti-spyware legislation, 63
Antitrust violations, 64, 64*f*

Arabs, 45–46
Arar, Maher, 52
Arrests
    African-American juveniles, 143(*t*9.4)
    age, 9*t*
    aggravated assault, 17
    arson, 19
    burglary, 18
    by crime, 8*t*
    demographic aspects, 6, 8
    gender, 10*t*
    inmate population growth, as factor in, 102
    juvenile case disposition, 143(*t*9.3), 144, 144*t*
    juvenile drug abuse violations arrest rates, 145–146, 146*f*
    juvenile property crimes arrest rates, 145, 145(*f*9.2)
    juvenile violent crimes arrest rates, 145, 145(*f*9.1)
    juveniles, 142(*t*9.2)
    larceny and theft, 18
    motor vehicle theft, 19
    murder, 12
    percent of offenses cleared by arrest, 15*t*
    race/ethnicity, 11*t*
    rape, 14
    robbery, 16–17
    white-collar crime, 56
Arson, 19, 19*t*
Arthur Andersen, 59, 60
Atlanta, Georgia, 52
Auctions, Internet, 62
Automobile theft, 18–19
Avila, Porfirio, 47

## B

Background checks for firearm sales, 21
Bank fraud, 60
*Bell v. Wolfish*, 121, 125

*Blakely v. Washington*, 77
*Booker, United States v.*, 77–79
Boot camps, 83, 154
BOP (Bureau of Prisons), 92
Brabandt, David, 60
Brady Handgun Violence Prevention Act, 21
*Brandenburg v. Ohio*, 44
Brewer, Lawrence Russell, 47
Bribes, 69
Brokaw, Tom, 52
Budget issues. *See* Funding
Budgeting. *See* Funding
Buell Elementary School shooting, 147
Burglary, 17–18
Bush, George H. W., 40
Bush, George W., 40, 119, 121
Byrd, James, Jr., 47

## C

California, 74, 80, 81
*California, Ewing v.*, 124
CAN-SPAM Act, 63
Canada, 52
Capital punishment. *See* Death penalty
*Caruso, Hadix v.*, 124
Cazares, Fernando, 47
Censorship, 120
Chaney, James, 47
*Chapman, Rhodes v.*, 124
*City of St. Paul, R.A.V. v.*, 44
Civil rights of prisoners
    due process, 125–126
    Eighth Amendment cases, 121–125
    First Amendment cases, 120–121
    Fourth Amendment cases, 121
    overview, 117–119
Civil suits, 39
Clinton, Bill, 121
Columbine High School shootings, 147
*Commonwealth, Ruffin v.*, 117–118

Community service programs, 83
Community-based sanctions. *See* Alternative sentencing
Compensation, victim, 38–39
Comprehensive Crime Control Act, 40–41
Computer crime, 62–64
Computer Fraud and Abuse Act, 62
Confinement status of prisoners, 117
*Conner, Sandin v.*, 125
Consumer Protection against Computer Spyware Act (California), 63
Controlling the Assault of Non-Solicited Pornography and Marketing (CAN-SPAM) Act, 63
*Cooper v. Pate*, 118–119
Corporate crime, 58–62
Corrections
    costs, 103–106, 104*f*, 104*t*, 105*f*, 105*t*, 106*f*
    drug offenses, 102–103, 103*t*
    employment and payroll, 106*t*
    federal, 92–93, 93(*t*6.1)
    goals, 71, 73
    history, 91–92
    incarceration rates, 97, 99, 99(*t*6.7)
    jail capacity, 99, 102*t*
    juveniles, 153–155, 154–155
    prison capacities, 101*t*
    prison crowding, 99
    prison effectiveness, 73–74
    prison work programs, 106–107
    prisons compared to jails, 92
    private correctional facilities, 98*t*
    private facilities, 94, 96–97
    state, 93–94
    *See also* Inmates; Parole; Probation
Costs
    corrections, 103–106, 104*f*, 104*t*, 105*f*, 105*t*, 106*f*, 106*t*
    victimization, 34, 37
Counterfeiting, 65, 66*t*
Court cases
    *Bell v. Wolfish*, 121, 125
    *Blakely v. Washington*, 77
    *Brandenburg v. Ohio*, 44
    *Cooper v. Pate*, 118–119
    *Cutter v. Wilkinson*, 121
    *Ewing v. California*, 124
    *Furman v. Georgia*, 123
    *Hadix v. Caruso*, 124
    *Holt v. Sarver*, 122
    *Hudson v. McMillian*, 125
    *Hudson v. Palmer*, 121
    *Lynce v. Mathis*, 125
    *Mitchell v. Wisconsin*, 44
    *Nolan v. Fitzpatrick*, 120
    *Pell v. Procunier*, 120
    *Procunier v. Martinez*, 120
    *R.A.V. v. City of St. Paul*, 44
    *Rhodes v. Chapman*, 124

    *Roper v. Simmons*, 124, 155
    *Ruffin v. Commonwealth*, 117–118
    *Sandin v. Conner*, 125
    *Stroud v. Swope*, 118
    *Turner v. Safley*, 120
    *United States v. Booker*, 77–79
    *Whitney v. Albers*, 124
    *Wolff v. McDonnell*, 125
    *Woodson v. North Carolina*, 123
    *Zablocki v. Redhail*, 120
Crime clock, 8–9, 12(*t*1.9)
Crime control
    alternative sentencing, 81–85
    corrections system goals, 71, 73
    federal criminal justice budget authorities, 12*t*–13*t*
    federal government programs, 8
    federal sentencing guidelines, 76–79, 77*f*, 78*t*
    law enforcement, 71, 72*t*, 74*t*
    law enforcement officers killed, 73*t*
    prison effectiveness, 73–74
    public confidence, 86–87
    public opinion, 87(*t*5.13), 88*t*–89*t*
    rearrest rates, 73, 75*t*
    state sentences, 79–81
    state sentencing, 80*t*
    truth-in-sentencing, 75–76
Crime rates
    aggravated assault, 17
    arson, 19, 19*t*
    burglary, 17
    changes in, 3*t*
    by community type, 5*t*
    crime clock, 8–9, 12(*t*1.9)
    decline, 1–2
    factors, 1
    incarceration rates, compared with, 97, 99
    larceny and theft, 18*f*
    murder, 9, 11
    by offense, 16(*t*1.15)
    by offense and region, 13(*t*1.10)
    by population group and region, 4*t*
    property crimes, 6
    rape, 12–14, 16(*t*1.14)
    by region, 7*f*
    robbery, 14, 16
    Uniform Crime Reports, 2, 6
    white-collar crime, 55
Crime Victims' Rights Act, 40
Crowding, prison, 99, 101*t*
Cruel and unusual punishment, 121–125
Curfews, 148
Currency counterfeiting, 65, 66*t*
*Cutter v. Wilkinson*, 121

**D**

Daschle, Tom, 52
Day fines, 83–84

Day reporting centers, 84
Death penalty
    as cruel and unusual punishment, 123–124
    juveniles, 155
    public opinion, 86, 87(*t*5.14)
    victims' families, witnessing by, 40
Deaths, firearm-related, 20
Delinquency offenses. *See* Juvenile crime
Detention
    juveniles, 150–151, 152–153
    terrorism suspects, 51–52, 119–120
Determinate sentencing, 76
Diversionary treatment programs, 85
DNA evidence, 126
Domestic terrorism, 52–54, 53*t*
Domestic violence, 33*t*–34*t*, 37
Drug offenses
    federal prisoners, 103*t*
    juvenile arrest rates, 145–146, 146*f*
    prison population growth, impact on, 102–103
    War on Drugs, 75
Drug use by inmates, 115–116, 118*t*
Due process rights, 125–126

**E**

Early release, 125
Earth Liberation Front (ELF), 54
Eco-terrorism, 53–54
Economic issues
    burglary losses, 17
    corrections costs, 103–106, 104*f*, 104*t*, 105*f*, 105*t*, 106*f*, 106*t*
    larceny-theft losses, 18
    motor vehicle theft, 18
    property stolen and recovered, by type and value, 37*t*
    victimization costs, 34, 37
Education programs, 112–114
Eighth Amendment rights, 121–122
Elderly, scams against the, 69–70
Electronic monitoring programs (EMPs), 84–85
ELF (Earth Liberation Front), 54
Employment
    inmates, status of, 116*t*
    justice system, 106*t*
    prison work programs, 106–107
    work-release programs, 82–83
EMPs (electronic monitoring programs), 84–85
Enemy combatants, 119–120
Enron Corporation, 59–60
Enslen, Richard, 124
Environmental crime, 70
*Ewing v. California*, 124
Extremist environmental and animal rights groups, 53–54

**F**

Falsification of corporate data, 59–60
Family Justice Center Initiative, 8
Family violence. *See* Domestic violence
Fathers, 114
Faur, Victor, 64
FBI, 2, 6, 60
Fear of crime, 23, 85–86, 86(*t*5.12)
Federal Bureau of Investigation (FBI), 2, 6, 60
Federal corrections
  costs, 104–105
  drug offenses, 103*t*
  inmate demographics, 110(*t*7.2)
  inmates, 93(*t*6.2)
  jails, 96
  offense types, 109–110, 111(*t*7.5)
  overview, 92–93
  prison capacities, 101*t*
  prison work programs, 107
  prisoners, 93(*t*6.1)
  probation system and officers, 132(*t*8.4)
  probation violations, 128
Federal government
  computer crime legislation, 62
  computer hacking, 64
  crime control functions, 8
  criminal justice budget authorities, 12*t*–13*t*
  hate crime legislation, 43
  law enforcement, 71, 74*t*
  sentencing guidelines, 76–79, 77*f*, 78*t*, 79*t*
  victim assistance programs, 38–39
  victims' rights, 39–40
Federal Trade Commission (FTC), 56
Federal Victim and Witness Protection Act, 40
Ferrer, Danny, 64
Fifth Amendment, 125
Firearms
  background checks, 21
  crimes committed with, 19–20, 20*t*
  deaths, 20
  juveniles, 146
First Amendment cases, 120–121
*Fitzpatrick, Nolan v.*, 120
Force, use of, 124–125
Forgery, 65
Foster care, 115
Fourth Amendment rights, 121
Fraud, 60–63, 69–70
FTC (Federal Trade Commission), 56
Funding
  federal crime control programs, 8, 12*t*–13*t*
  justice expenditures, 37
  September 11th Victim Compensation Fund, 41
  victim assistance programs, 38–39
  victims of terrorism assistance, 41
*Furman v. Georgia*, 123

**G**

Gecko Communications Inc., 62
Gender
  arrests, 6, 10*t*
  family violence victimization rates, 33*t*–34*t*
  federal law enforcement officers, 74(*t*5.4)
  inmate education levels, 112
  inmates, 99(*t*6.8), 109, 110*t*
  inmates with mental health problems, 115
  jail inmates, 111(*t*7.3), 111(*t*7.4)
  juvenile arrests, 142–143
  juvenile inmates in state prisons, 155*t*
  murder offenders, 13(*t*1.11)
  murder rates, 9, 11
  parole termination, characteristics of offenders, 139
  parolees, 137*t*
  probationers, 128*t*
  reporting, 28*t*
  status offense cases, 152
  victimization rates, 29(*t*2.4), 31*t*
  victims, 25–26
Geneva Conventions guidelines, 51
*Georgia, Furman v.*, 123
Glisan, Ben, Jr., 59
Gonzales, Alberto, 52, 64
Goodin, Jeffrey Brett, 63
Goodman, Andrew, 47
Guantanamo Bay detainees, 51, 119–120

**H**

Habeas Act, 119
Hacking, computer, 63–64
*Hadix v. Caruso*, 124
Haq, Naveed Afzal, 47
Harris, Eric, 147
Hate Crime Statistics Act, 43
Hate crimes
  federal legislation, 43
  hate groups, 43
  incidents, by bias motivation and location, 48*t*
  incidents, offenses, and known offenders, by type of offense, 46(*t*3.4)
  incidents, offenses, victims, and known offenders, by bias motivation, 45(*t*3.2)
  incidents, by victim type and bias motivation, 46(*t*3.3)
  motivation, as perceived by victims, 45(*t*3.1)
  murder, 47
  offenses, 44
  offenses, by offender's race and bias motivation, 49*t*
  state laws, 44
Helder, Luke J., 52
History
  corrections, 91–92
  restitution, 37
HIV/AIDS, 115, 117*t*
HLS (Huntingdon Life Sciences), 53–54
*Holt v. Sarver*, 122
Homelessness, 115, 116*t*
Homosexuality, 44
House arrest, 84–85
*Hudson v. McMillian*, 125
*Hudson v. Palmer*, 121
Huntingdon Life Sciences (HLS), 53–54

**I**

IC3 (Internet Crime Complaint Center), 62
Identity theft, 56–58, 56*f*, 57*f*, 58*f*, 59*f*, 59*t*
Incarceration rates, 99(*t*6.7)
Income
  crime victimization, 28
  family violence victimization rates, 33*t*–34*t*
  victimization rates, 30*t*
Indeterminate sentencing, 75
Inmates
  censorship, 120
  confinement status, 117
  conviction status, 117
  cruel and unusual punishment, 121–125
  demographics, 109, 110*t*, 111(*t*7.3), 111(*t*7.4), 114*t*
  drug use, 115–116, 118*t*
  due process rights, 125–126
  early release, 125
  education levels, 112
  federal prison populations, 92–93
  First Amendment cases, 120–121
  gender, 99(*t*6.8)
  habeas corpus rights, 119–120
  HIV/AIDS, 115, 117*t*
  incarceration rates, 97, 99, 99(*t*6.7)
  jails, 94
  juveniles, 154–155
  medical issues, 116–117
  mental health issues, 115, 116*t*
  numbers, by state, 100*t*
  offense types, 109–111, 109–112, 111(*t*7.5), 112*f*, 113*t*
  parents, 114
  population growth factors, 102–103
  prison education programs, 112–114
  privately run prisons, 94
  reentry into the community, 75
  religious rights, 120–121
  rights, 117–119
  search and seizure rights, 121

sexual misconduct against, 121, 122*f*, 122*t*

state and federal prisoners in private facilities, 98*t*

state facilities, 93–94, 93(*t*6.2)

total numbers, 93(*t*6.2)

*See also* Parole; Probation

Innocence Protection Act, 126

Intellectual property crime, 64

Intensive Probation Supervision (IPS), 84

Internal Revenue Service, 65*t*

International money laundering, 66

Internet Crime Complaint Center (IC3), 62

Internet fraud, 62–63

Intimate partner violence. *See* Domestic violence

Inventory shrinkage, 67–68, 67*f*, 68*f*, 69*f*

IPS (Intensive Probation Supervision), 84

Isolation, prisoner, 122–123


**J**

Jails

capacity, 99, 102*t*

costs, 105–106

inmate demographics, 109, 114*t*

inmate drug use, 118(*t*7.12)

inmates, 111(*t*7.3), 111(*t*7.4)

juveniles, 154–155

medical problems in inmates, 116–117

offense types, 111–112, 113*t*, 114*t*

overview, 94–96

prisons, comparison with, 92

James Byrd Jr. Hate Crimes Act (Texas), 47

Judiciary Act, 119

Justice Department, Office on Violence Against Women, 8

Justice for All Act, 39–40, 126

Justice for Victims of Terrorism Act, 41

Juvenile crime

adults, prosecution as, 151–152

African-Americans, arrests of, 143(*t*9.4)

arrests, 6, 141–146, 142(*t*9.2)

boot camps, 154

case processing, 149–151, 150(*f*9.4)

cases, by offense category and age group, 150(*f*9.5)

curfews, 148

death penalty, 124, 155

defining juvenile, 141

delinquency cases, 148–149, 149*t*

delinquency cases, by disposition, 151*f*

detention, 150–151

disposition of arrests, 144, 144*t*

disposition of custody cases, 143(*t*9.3)

drug abuse violations arrest rates, 145–146, 146*f*

firearms, 146

oldest age for original juvenile court jurisdiction, 142(*t*9.1)

parental responsibility, 153

property crimes arrest rates, 145, 145(*f*9.2)

residential placement, 153–154

school crime, 146–147

status offense cases, 151, 152–153

violent crime arrest rates, 145, 145(*f*9.1)

youth gangs, 147–148

Juvenile Delinquency Prevention and Control Act, 151


**K**

Kaczynski, Theodore, 52

Kean, Thomas, 50

Keeping Children and Families Safe Act, 39

Kennedy, Anthony M., 124

Kessler, Gladys, 58, 61

Kickbacks, 69

Killen, Edgar Ray, 47

King, John William, 47

Klebold, Dylan, 147

Ku Klux Klan, 43, 47


**L**

Larceny and theft

inventory shrinkage rates, 67*f*, 68*f*, 69*f*

overview, 18–19

property stolen and recovered, by type and value, 36*t*

retail store theft, 67–68

types, 18*f*

Law enforcement

employees, 72*t*

officers, 73*t*, 74*t*

overview, 71

public confidence, 86–87

public opinion, 87(*t*5.13), 88(*t*5.15)–89*t*

Law Enforcement Assistance Administration, 23

Lawsuits, 39

Lay, Kenneth L., 59–60

Legislation

Air Transportation Safety and System Stabilization Act, 41

Brady Handgun Violence Prevention Act, 21

CAN-SPAM Act, 63

Comprehensive Crime Control Act, 40–41

Computer Fraud and Abuse Act, 62

Consumer Protection against Computer Spyware Act (California), 63

Crime Victims' Rights Act, 40

Federal Victim and Witness Protection Act, 40

Habeas Act, 119

Hate Crime Statistics Act, 43

Innocence Protection Act, 126

Judiciary Act, 119

Justice for All Act, 39–40, 126

Justice for Victims of Terrorism Act, 41

Juvenile Delinquency Prevention and Control Act, 151

Keeping Children and Families Safe Act, 39

Military Commissions Act, 119–120

Prison Rape Elimination Act, 121

Religious Land Use and Institutionalized Persons Act, 121

Sarbanes-Oxley Act, 60

Sentencing Reform Act, 75, 76, 129

USA Patriot Act, 62, 66

Victims of Crime Act, 38

Victim's Rights and Restitution Act, 40–41

Violence Against Women Act, 40

Violent Crime Control and Law Enforcement Act, 8, 43, 76

Liberty interests, 125–126

*Lynce v. Mathis*, 125


**M**

Mail censorship, 120

Mail crime, 62

Mandatory parole, 130

Mandatory treatment programs, 85

Marital status, 28, 31*t*, 33*t*–34*t*

Marriage, prisoners' right to, 120

Martinez, Alejandro, 47

*Martinez, Procunier v.*, 120

Mass violence victims, 41

Massachusetts Bay Colony, 91

*Mathis, Lynce v.*, 125

Maximum-security prisons, 73–74

*McDonnell, Wolff v.*, 125

McDonogh High School shootings, 147

*McMillian, Hudson v.*, 125

McRaith, Michael T., 61

McVeigh, Timothy, 52

Mediation, 82

Medical issues, 124

Mental health issues, 115, 116*t*, 154

Metropolitan statistical areas (MSAs), 2, 5*t*

Military Commissions Act, 119–120

Misrepresentation in advertising, 58

*Mitchell v. Wisconsin*, 44

Money counterfeiting, 65, 66*t*

Money laundering, 65–66, 67(*t*4.4)

Mothers, 114

Motor vehicle theft, 18–19

MSAs (metropolitan statistical areas), 2, 5*t*

Murder

arrests, 12

circumstances, 14*t*

hate-motivated, 47

by juveniles, 146

offenders, by age, sex, and race, 13(*t*1.11)

rates, 9, 11
school shootings, 147
Muslims, 45–46

## N

National Commission on Terrorist Attacks
Upon the United States, 50–51
National Consumers League (NCL), 61–62
National Counterterrorism Center (NCTC),
48–49
National Crime Victimization Survey,
23–24
National Mental Health Association, 154
NCL (National Consumers League), 61–62
NCTC (National Counterterrorism Center),
48–49
NCVS (National Crime Victimization
Survey), 23–24
Neo-Nazi groups, 43
Ney, Robert W., 69
Nichols, Terry, 52
Nickels, Greg, 47
9/11 Commission, 50–51
Nix, Erik K., 46
Nixon, Richard, 75
*Nolan v. Fitzpatrick*, 120
Non-reporting of crimes, 25
Noncitizen federal inmates, 92, 93(*t*6.1)
*North Carolina, Woodson v.*, 123

## O

O'Connor, Dennis, 52
Odysseus Marketing, Inc., 63
Offenders
family violence victimization rates, 34*t*
hate crimes, 45(*t*3.2), 46(*t*3.4), 47–48,
49*t*
restitution, 37, 39
victim/offender relationship, 28–29
violent crimes by victim-offender
relationship, type of crime, and weapon
used, 35*t*–36*t*
white-collar crime, 56
Office on Violence Against Women, U.S.
Department of Justice, 8
*Ohio, Brandenburg v.*, 44
Oil and gas investment fraud, 61
Oklahoma City bombing, 52
Olympic Games bombing, 52
Oregon, 82

## P

*Palmer, Hudson v.*, 121
Parental liability, 153
Parents, 114
Parole
characteristics of parolees, 131–132,
137*t*
geographic distribution, 132

outcomes, 138*t*
region and jurisdiction of parolees,
135*t*–136*t*
trends, 130
violations, 103, 139*t*
violations and rearrest, 132–133
*Pate, Cooper v.*, 118–119
Pearl, Daniel, 50
*Pell v. Procunier*, 120
Penn, William, 91
Pennsylvania, 91
Perry, Rick, 47
Personal crimes, 26*t*
Petitioned status offense cases, 152–153
PIECP (Prison Industry Enhancement
Certification Program), 107
Pollution, 70
President's Family Justice Center
Initiative, 8
Prison Industry Enhancement Certification
Program (PIECP), 107
Prison Rape Elimination Act, 121
Prisoners. *See* Inmates
Prisons. *See* Corrections
Private correctional facilities, 94, 96–97, 98*t*
Private industry work programs, 107
Probation
characteristics of probationers, 127, 128*t*
federal probation system and officers,
132(*t*8.4)
federal violations, 128
geographical distribution, 127–128
officers, 128–129
outcomes of probation supervision, by
offense, 131*t*–132*t*
region and jurisdiction of probationers,
129*t*–130*t*
supervised release, 129–130, 133*t*–134*t*
*Procunier, Pell v.*, 120
*Procunier v. Martinez*, 120
Property crimes
cost of victimization, 37
federal sentencing guidelines, 77
juvenile arrest rates, 145, 145(*f*9.2)
property stolen and recovered, by type
and value, 37*t*
types, 26*t*
urban areas, 6
victimization rates, 24–25
victimization rates, by type of crime,
region, and residence locality, 32*t*
by victim's activity at time of incident,
36(*t*2.11)
Public corruption, 68–69, 70*t*
Public institutions, 88(*t*5.14)
Public opinion
confidence in public institutions,
88(*t*5.14)
crime control, 87(*t*5.13)
crime levels, 85*t*, 86(*t*5.11)

criminal justice system, 86
death penalty, 86, 87(*t*5.14)
fear of crime, 23, 85–86, 86(*t*5.12)
law enforcement, 86–87, 88(*t*5.15)–89*t*
white-collar crime, 55
Puritans, 91

## Q

Quakers, 91

## R

Race/ethnicity
arrests, 6, 8, 11*t*
family violence victimization rates,
33*t*–34*t*
federal law enforcement officers,
74(*t*5.4)
hate crimes, 43–48, 49*t*
inmate education levels, 112
inmates, 109, 110*t*, 111(*t*7.3), 111(*t*7.4)
juvenile arrests, 143–144, 143(*t*9.4)
juvenile detainees, 151
murder offenders, 13(*t*1.11)
murder rates, 9, 11
parole termination, characteristics of
offenders, 139
parolees, 137*t*
probationers, 128*t*
reporting, 28*t*
status offense cases, 152
victimization rates, 29(*t*2.4), 29(*t*2.5)
victims, 27–28
Racketeering, 69
Rape, 12–14, 16(*t*1.14)
*R.A.V. v. City of St. Paul*, 44
Rearrest, 132–133
Recidivism, 73, 75*t*, 82, 132–133
Red Lake High School shootings, 147
*Redhail, Zablocki v.*, 120
Reform Movement, 91–92
Regional issues
crime rates, 4*t*, 6, 7*f*, 13(*t*1.10)
crime victimization, 28
murder rates, 9
parolees, 132
probationers, 127–128, 129*t*–130*t*
victimization rates, 32*t*
weapons used in aggravated assaults, 17*t*
Religious Land Use and Institutionalized
Persons Act, 121
Religious rights, 120–121
Reporting of crime, 25, 28*t*, 44
Residential community corrections, 85
Residential placement for juveniles,
153–155
Restitution, 37, 39, 40–41, 82
Retail store theft, 67–68, 67*f*, 68*f*
*Rhodes v. Chapman*, 124
Rich, Fred, 60

Rights of prisoners
  due process, 125–126
  Eighth Amendment cases, 121–125
  First Amendment cases, 120–121
  Fourth Amendment cases, 121
  habeas corpus, 119–120
  overview, 117–119
Robbery, 14, 16–17
Roberts, Charles, 147
*Roper v. Simmons*, 124, 155
Rudolph, Eric Robert, 52
Ruemmler, Kathryn, 59
*Ruffin v. Commonwealth*, 117–118
Rural areas, 2, 5t

# S

Safe Auto Insurance Company, 61
*Safley, Turner v.*, 120
Saldana, Gilbert, 47
*Sandin v. Conner*, 125
Santee High School shootings, 147
Sarbanes-Oxley Act, 60
SARs (Suspicious Activity Reports), 66, 67(t4.4)
*Sarver, Holt v.*, 122
Scams, 69–70
Scanlon, Michael, 69
School crime, 146–147
Schwerner, Michael, 47
Search and seizure, 121
Securities fraud, 61
Senior citizens, scams against, 69–70
Sentencing
  alternative, 81–85
  federal sentencing guidelines, 76–79, 77f, 78t, 79t
  inmate population growth, as factor in, 102
  states, 79–81, 80t
  truth-in-sentencing, 75–76, 103
  victims' participation, 40
Sentencing Reform Act, 75, 76, 129
September 11th attacks, 41, 49–51
Seung-Hui, Cho, 147
Sexual misconduct, 121, 122f, 123t
Sexual orientation, 44
Shock incarceration, 83
Shoplifting, 67–68, 67f, 68f, 69f
*Simmons, Roper v.*, 124, 155
Skilling, Jeffrey, 59–60
Souders, Timothy, 124
SOX (Sarbanes-Oxley) Act, 60
Spam, 62–63
Spyware, 63
Staffing, corrections, 93, 94, 95–96
State prisons
  AIDS-related deaths, 117(t7.10)
  costs, 105
  inmate drug use, 118(t7.11)

inmate numbers, 93(t6.2)
juvenile inmates, 155t
offense types, 110–111, 112f
overview, 93–94
work programs, 107
States
  anti-spyware legislation, 63
  computer hacking, 63–64
  death penalty for juveniles, 155
  hate crime legislation, 44
  inmates, 100t
  parolees, by region and jurisdiction, 135t–136t
  prison capacities, 101t
  sentencing, 79–81, 80t
  sexual misconduct against prisoners laws, 122f
  state and federal prisoners in private facilities, 98t
  victim services and assistance, 38, 39
  victims' rights, 39
Statistical information
  AIDS-related deaths in state prisons, 117(t7.10)
  antitrust suit fines, 64f
  arrests, by age, 9t
  arrests, by crime, 8t
  arrests, by gender, 10t
  arrests, by race/ethnicity, 11t
  arrests of African-American juveniles, 143(t9.4)
  arson rates, 19t
  counterfeiting, 66t
  crime, by volume and rate, and percent change in, 3t
  crime clock, 12(t1.9)
  crime rate changes, by population group and region, 4t
  crime rates, by offense and region, 13(t1.10)
  crime rates, by region, 7f
  crime rates by community type, 5t
  crimes, by victim's activity at time of incident, 36(t2.11)
  delinquency cases, 149t
  disposition of juvenile arrests, 144t
  disposition of juvenile custody cases, 143(t9.3)
  domestic terrorism incidents, 53t
  family violence victimization rates, 33t–34t
  federal criminal justice budget authorities, 12t–13t
  federal law enforcement officers, 74t
  federal prisoners, by type of offense, 111(t7.5)
  federal prisoners sentenced for drug offenses, 103t
  federal probation system and officers, 132(t8.4)
  firearms, crimes committed with, 20t

hate crime incidents, by bias motivation and location, 48t
hate crime incidents, by victim type and bias motivation, 46(t3.3)
hate crime incidents, offenses, and known offenders, by type of offense, 46(t3.4)
hate crime incidents, offenses, victims, and known offenders, by bias motivation, 45(t3.2)
hate crime motivation, as perceived by victims, 45(t3.1)
hate crimes, by offender's race and bias motivation, 49t
HIV-positive prison inmates, 117(t7.9)
identity theft awareness methods, 59t
identity theft complaints, 58(f4.3)
identity theft information use, 57f
identity theft reports, 56f
identity theft resolution time span, 59f
identity theft time intervals, 58(f4.4)
incarceration rates, 99(t6.7)
inmate drug use, 118t
inmate homelessness, employment status, and family background, by mental health status, 116t
inmate numbers, 93(t6.2)
inmate numbers, by state, 100t
inmates, by gender, 99(t6.8)
inventory shrinkage, 67f, 68f, 69f
jail capacity, 102t
jail inmate demographics, 111(t7.3), 111(t7.4), 114t
jail inmates, by type of offense, 113t, 114t
justice expenditures, 104f, 104t, 105f, 105t, 106f
justice system employment and payroll, 106t
juvenile arrests, 142(t9.2)
juvenile case processing, 150(f9.4)
juvenile cases, by offense category and age group, 150(f9.5)
juvenile drug abuse violations arrest rates, 146f
juvenile inmates in state prisons, 155t
juvenile property crimes arrest rates, 145(f9.2)
juvenile violent crimes arrest rates, 145(f9.1)
larceny and theft rates, 18f
law enforcement employees, 72t
law enforcement officers feloniously killed, 73t
money laundering, 67t
murder circumstances, 14t
murder offenders, by age, sex, and race, 13(t1.11)
noncitizen federal inmates, 93(t6.1)
offenses, by type, 16(t1.15)
offenses cleared by arrest, 15t

parole outcomes, 138*t*

parole termination, characteristics of offenders, 139

parolees, by region and jurisdiction, 135*t*–136*t*

parolees, characteristics of, 137*t*

personal and property crimes, 26*t*

prisoners, by gender, race/ethnicity, and age, 110*t*

probation supervision outcomes, by offense, 131*t*–132*t*

probationers, by region and jurisdiction, 129*t*–130*t*

probationers, characteristics of, 128*t*

property stolen and recovered, by type and value, 36*t*

public confidence in public institutions, 88(*t*5.14)

public corruption, 70*t*

public opinion on crime control, 87(*t*5.13)

public opinion on crime levels, 85*t*, 86(*t*5.11)

public opinion on fear of walking alone at night, 86(*t*5.12)

public opinion on law enforcement, 88(*t*5.15)–89*t*

public opinion on the death penalty, 87(*t*5.14)

rape, 16(*t*1.14)

reporting, 28*t*

reporting, by type of crime, gender, and race/ethnicity of victims, 28*t*

sentencing guidelines, 79*t*

sexual violence allegations in prisons and jails, 123*t*

state and federal prisoners in private facilities, 98*t*

state prisoners, by type of offense, 112*f*

state sentences, 80*t*

supervised release outcomes, 133*t*–134*t*

tax fraud investigations, 65*t*

U.S. citizen terrorism-related fatalities, by country, 50*f*

U.S. citizen terrorism-related injuries and kidnappings, by country, 51*f*

victimization rates, by type of crime, gender, and marital status, 31*t*

victimization rates, by type of crime, gender, and race of victims, 29(*t*2.4)

victimization rates, by type of crime, region, and residence locality, 32*t*

victimization rates, by type of crime and annual family income of victims, 30*t*

victimization rates, by type of crime and race of head of household, 29(*t*2.5)

victimization rates and percent change, 25*t*

violent crime rates, by age of victim, 27*f*

violent crimes by victim-offender relationship, type of crime, and weapon used, 35*t*–36*t*

weapons used in aggravated assaults, 17*t*

Status offense cases, 151, 152–153

*Stroud v. Swope*, 118

Supermax prisons, 73–74

Supervised release, 129–130, 133*t*–134*t*

Suspicious Activity Reports (SARs), 66, 67(*t*4.4)

*Swope, Stroud v.*, 118

## T

Tax fraud, 65*t*

Taylor, Ronald, 47

Teachers, 147

Telemarketing fraud, 61–62

Terrorism

    domestic incidents, 52–54, 53*t*

    eco-terrorism, 53–54

    money laundering, 66

    National Counterterrorism Center, 48–49

    September 11th attacks, 49–50

    suspects' treatment, 51–52

    U.S. citizen fatalities, by country, 50*f*

    U.S. citizen injuries and kidnappings, by country, 51*f*

    victims' assistance services, 41

Texas, 47

Theft. *See* Larceny and theft

Threat condition advisories, 51

Three strikes laws, 80–81, 124

Time served, 103

Time Warner Inc., 61

Tobacco industry, 58

Torture, 51–52

Trends in victimization, 34

Truth-in-sentencing, 75–76, 103

*Turner v. Safley*, 120

## U

"Unabomber," 52

UNICOR, 107

Uniform Crime Reports

    hate crimes, 44

    National Crime Victimization Survey, creation of the, 23–24

    overview, 2, 6

*United States v. Booker*, 77–79

Uniting and Strengthening America Act by Providing Appropriate Tools Required to Intercept and Obstruct Terrorism. *See* USA Patriot Act

Urban areas

    arson rates, 19*t*

    crime rates, 2, 5*t*

    property crimes, 6

U.S. Bureau of Prisons (BOP), 92

U.S. Postal Inspection Service, 62

U.S. Sentencing Commission (USSC), 75–76

USA Patriot Act, 62, 66

USSC (U.S. Sentencing Commission), 75–76

## V

Victims

    age, 26–27, 27*f*

    cost of victimization, 34, 37

    crimes, by victim's activity at time of incident, 36(*t*2.11)

    family violence victimization rates, 33*t*–34*t*

    federal legislation, 40–41

    gender, 25–26

    hate crime, 45(*t*3.2), 46(*t*3.3), 46(*t*3.4)

    hate crime motivation, as perceived by victims, 45(*t*3.1)

    income, marital status, and regions, 28

    National Crime Victimization Survey, 23–24

    offender/victim relationship, 28, 29

    public opinion on fear of becoming a victim, 23

    race/ethnicity, 27–28

    reporting, 25, 28*t*

    sentencing, participation in, 40

    services and assistance, 37–39

    victimization rates, 25*t*

    victimization rates, by crime type, gender, and race of victims, 29(*t*2.4)

    victimization rates, by gender and marital status, 31*t*

    victimization rates, by type of crime, and annual family income of victims, 30*t*

    victimization rates, by type of crime, region, and residence locality, 32*t*

    victimization rates, by type of crime and race of head of household, 29(*t*2.5)

    victimization trends, 34

    violent crime, 27*f*

    violent crime time and place, 30, 33–34

    violent crimes by victim-offender relationship, type of crime, and weapon used, 35*t*–36*t*

    white-collar crime, 56

    witnessing executions, 40

Victims of Crime Act, 38

Victims' Rights and Restitution Act, 40–41

Violence against women, 8

Violence Against Women Act, 40

Violent crime

    age of victims, 27*f*

    cost of victimization, 34, 37

    crimes, by victim's activity at time of incident, 36(*t*2.11)

    family violence victimization rates, 33*t*–34*t*

    juvenile arrest rates, 145, 145(*f*9.1)

    time and place, 30, 33–34

    Uniform Crime Reports, 2, 6

    by victim-offender relationship, type of crime, and weapon used, 35*t*–36*t*

    victimization rates, 24

    Violence Against Women Act, 40

Violent Crime Control and Law
   Enforcement Act, 8, 43, 76
Virginia Tech shootings, 147

## W

"War on drugs," 75
*Washington, Blakely v.*, 77
Weapons
   aggravated assault, 17*t*
   background checks for firearms, 21
   firearm-related deaths, 20
   firearms, crimes committed with, 19–20,
      20*t*
   juveniles, 146
   violent crime, 35*t*–36*t*
Weekend sentencing, 82–83
West Nickel Mines Amish School
   shootings, 147

White-collar crime
   antitrust violations, 64, 64*f*
   corporate crime, 58–62
   environmental crime, 70
   forgery and counterfeiting, 65, 66*t*
   identity theft, 56–58, 56*f*, 58*f*, 59*f*,
      59*t*
   intellectual property crime, 64
   money laundering, 65–66, 67*t*
   overview, 55–56
   public corruption, 68–69, 70*t*
   retail store theft, 67–68, 67*f*, 68*f*, 69*f*
   tax fraud, 65, 65*t*
Whitelaw, William, 83
*Whitney v. Albers*, 124
*Wilkinson, Cutter v.*, 121
*Wisconsin, Mitchell v.*, 44

*Wolff v. McDonnell*, 125
*Wolfish, Bell v.*, 121, 125
Women
   Office on Violence Against
      Women, U.S. Department of
      Justice, 8
   prisoners, 99
   Violence Against Women Act, 40
*Woodson v. North Carolina*, 123
Work programs, prison, 106–107
Work-release programs, 82–83

## Y

Youth gangs, 147–148

## Z

*Zablocki v. Redhail*, 120